ŚWIATOWIT Supplement Series E: Egyptology, vol. III

ed. Kazimierz Lewartowski

WARSAW EGYPTOLOGICAL STUDIES, vol. IV

eds. Karol Myśliwiec, Andrzej Niwiński,
Zbigniew E. Szafrański, Jan K. Winnicki

ŚWIATOWIT Supplement Series E: Egyptology, vol. III

ed. Kazimierz Lewartowski

WARSAW EGYPTOLOGICAL STUDIES, vol. IV

eds. Karol Myśliwiec, Andrzej Niwiński,
Zbigniew E. Szafrański, Jan K. Winnicki

PROCEEDINGS OF THE SECOND CENTRAL EUROPEAN CONFERENCE OF YOUNG EGYPTOLOGISTS.

EGYPT 2001: PERSPECTIVES OF RESEARCH
WARSAW 5-7 MARCH 2001

EDITED BY
JOANNA POPIELSKA-GRZYBOWSKA

INSTITUTE OF ARCHAEOLOGY
WARSAW UNIVERSITY 2003

Proceedings of the Second Central European Conference of Young Egyptologists.

Egypt 2001: Perspectives of Research

Warsaw 5-7 March 2001

EDITED BY

Joanna Popielska-Grzybowska

Warsaw 2003

Scientific Editor: Joanna Popielska-Grzybowska
Proof-reading in English by Joe Harper & Joanna Popielska-Grzybowska
Proof-reading in French by Frédéric Constant & Joanna Popielska-Grzybowska
DTP by Jadwiga Iwaszczuk assisted by Mikołaj C. Grzybowski
Graphics by Vinh Nguyen & Mikołaj C. Grzybowski
Cover photo by Zbigniew Kość: West Saqqara, Polish-Egyptian Archaeological Mission under the direction of Professor Karol Myśliwiec

ISBN 83-87496-76-6

Wydawnictwo ARTE
arte@arte.biz.pl www.arte.biz.pl
tel./faks (22) 756-12-42

Contents

Preface

Following the great success of our first Conference, we decided to convene the *Second Central European Conference of Young Egyptologists. Egypt 2001: Perspectives of Research* which was held from the 5th to the 7th of March 2001 in Warsaw.

This volume consists of the articles delivered during the Conference within four subject groups: Archaic Period and Old Kingdom Studies, New Kingdom Studies, Language and Literature and Varia. There are also included some articles by those who were unable to participate in the assemblage.

We wish to express our sincere appreciation for the presence of the guests and all participants.

The Organising Committee wishes to acknowledge and thank most sincerely the Board of Directors of the Institute of Archaeology at Warsaw University and the Directors of our Institute, Professor Tomasz MIKOCKI and Professor Kazimierz LEWARTOWSKI, for their warm-hearted encouragement.

We would like to express our deepest gratitude to Professor Jadwiga LIPIŃSKA and Professor Karol MYŚLIWIEC for their participation in the Conference and in the *Proceedings*, as well as for their inestimable encouragement, support and friendship.

We should also like to thank most sincerely the Director of the National Museum in Warsaw, Mr Ferdynand B. RUSZCZYC, for making available gratuitously the cinema hall for the Conference.

No less cordially, we acknowledge our debt to Ms Mirosława LATOSKA-IWASZCZUK, Ms Ewa DULNA-RAK (the owner of the "Arte" publishing house) and Mr Dariusz GÓRSKI for providing us with a clear-sighted assistance. We are very grateful to Ms Dagmara BIAŁEK and Ms Małgorzata RADOMSKA who helped us with the organisation of the Conference.

We are especially indebted to Prorector Magnificus, Professor Wojciech MACIEJEWSKI; UNIVERSITATIS VARSOVIENSIS – Fundacja Samorządu Studentów Warsaw University and to Mr Jan WALASZEK, the owner of the "Mardom" firm in Pułtusk, for covering some of the costs of the Conference.

This book owes a great deal especially to Ms Jadwiga IWASZCZUK and Mr Mikołaj C. GRZYBOWSKI who participated in the completion of the book's DTP process gratis, as well as to Mr Vinh NGUYEN and Mr Mikołaj C. GRZYBOWSKI who advanced extensively our work on the graphics free of charge. We also extend our grateful thanks to Mr Joe HARPER and Mr Frédéric CONSTANT who proofread the articles and to Ms Karen HAUFF who helped us with the German text free of cost.

This book would not have been possible without the generosity of Ms Barbara STĘPIEŃ, the owner of the "Drzewo Babel" publishing house in Warsaw.

On behalf of the Organising Committee
Joanna Popielska-Grzybowska
Piotr Laskowski

A Few Words of Introduction

Young Egyptologists from Central Europe met in Warsaw for the second time in 2001. The list of participants shows that the notion of the "Centre" is progressively widening westwards. If we had a scholar from Holland among our distinguished guests this year, it is not because "Bolandi" and "Holandi" are almost the same, at least phonetically, from a modern Egyptian perspective, and the two words would possibly have been subject to graphic jokes of ancient Egyptian scribes, if they could live in our times. We would like to welcome colleagues from all over the world, including the more and more numerous students of Egyptology in the east, those in the south who are naturally closer to Mediterranean civilisations, not to forget the north, with an already glorious tradition in this field as well.

Our second meeting coincided with an anniversary that is particularly full of meaning to Polish Egyptologists. A hundred years ago, on December 14th 1901, Professor Kazimierz MICHAŁOWSKI, the creator of the Polish Center for Mediterranean Archaeology of the Warsaw University in Cairo, was born. He passed away twenty years ago, in 1981. But his birthday is definitely the more important of the two dates, because the work of the late Professor is not only being continued, but also enlarged. The number of his scholarly "grandchildren", among whom are the organisers of this very Symposium, proves that MICHAŁOWSKI's *Ka* does not sleep, and that we, ourselves, being his "children", may optimistically look to the future, far beyond the "mirror of Hathor" that our Master had the honour to receive posthumously from the Egyptian Government during the 8th International Congress of Egyptologists in Cairo in 2000.

We do not stop thinking about future "centrifugal" Egyptological meetings in Central Europe.

Karol Myśliwiec

100 Years' Anniversary of the Birth of Professor Kazimierz Michałowski

(An Opening Lecture Delivered on the 5th of March 2001 in the National Museum in Warsaw)

This year we are commemorating the 100th anniversary of the birth and 20th anniversary of the death of the great Polish archaeologist – Professor Kazimierz MICHAŁOWSKI. He taught at Warsaw University for almost half a century, and for over forty years served here, in this very building, as the vice-director of the National Museum and founder of the Gallery of Ancient Art. We owe it to him, to open this conference with some words of recollection.

As many colleagues of his generation, he received a classical education, also studying the history of art, and took a degree at Lvov University. After working three years as an assistant at Lvov University, he took post-graduate studies at the universities and in the Archaeological Institutes of Berlin, Heidelberg, Münster, Paris, Rome and Athens. The names of his tutors read like a list of the most prominent scholars of the time, and he gained from them a deep knowledge of classical archaeology, deepened during field practice on the Greek islands of Delos, Tasos and Crete. His "habilitation" thesis was concerned with the Greco-Roman portraits from Delos, and was awarded the prestigious George Parrot prize from the Académie des Inscriptions et Belles Lettres.

After receiving his *veniam legendi* in 1929 he was appointed to Warsaw University (in 1930) where he organised the first Chair of Classical Archaeology, becoming its head. But already in 1934 he left for Egypt as *attaché étranger* to the French Institute in Cairo to enlarge his already broad knowledge by adding a new discipline – Egyptian Art and Archaeology. Before planning this trip he already had in mind organising Polish-French excavations in Egypt and obtaining, and then offering part of the finds for Warsaw University. He admitted frankly in his memoirs, that the decision to excavate in Egypt was caused by the pretty liberal antiquities law, allowing antiquities to be taken abroad. At that time there was only a small number of ancient Egyptian objects in Poland, and almost none at the Museum. He admitted that the main reason behind his decision to shift his interest to Egypt was the impossibility of obtaining exhibits from the "classical" countries: Greece, Italy and Turkey.

In Cairo MICHAŁOWSKI became acquainted with and a friend of colleagues at the French Institute, who later became the most prominent Egyptologists: Jacques VANDIER, Alexandre VARILLE, Clement ROBICHON, Georges POSENER, Michel MALININE, and life-long friend Jaroslav ČERNÝ. He spent several weeks at Deir el-Medina, working under Bernard BRUYÈRE together with another Polish scholar, historian Tadeusz WAŁEK-CZERNECKI.

He succeeded in his tasks, both in Egypt and in Poland: in Egypt he received the promise for a joint Polish-French mission to excavate at Tell Edfu, the site already partly explored by French scholars, and in Poland – the official agreement from Warsaw University for covering part of the expenditures, and from the National Museum in Warsaw – to take the finds and create a Gallery of Ancient Egyptian Art. The excavations started in 1936 and lasted until the outbreak of the Second World War, that is, for three seasons. During the first season BRUYÈRE headed the mission, but MICHAŁOWSKI was an able scholar and soon took the position of field director. Young Madam Christiane DESROCHES-NOBLECOURT was then a member of the staff. Two volumes of the excavations reports were published soon after the seasons ended, the third had to wait until the end of the war, and the finds were not even unpacked in Warsaw when the war started.

Generously, the French side resigned their share in the finds, offering everything discovered to the Polish. Moreover, the French Institute offered a fine gift of its own objects from Deir el-Medina and Meir. Objects from the first two campaigns at Edfu and the French donation were exhibited in 1938 on the special occasion of the inauguration of the newly built museum. MICHAŁOWSKI was appointed curator of the new Gallery.

Unfortunately the outbreak of war prevented activity, that had started so well. MICHAŁOWSKI took part in the war as an officer and was taken prisoner. He spent next five years in a camp, where he organised lectures and seminars for his fellow POWs, even working with the eminent architect Professor Jerzy HRYNIEWIECKI on original hieroglyphic fonts.

After his return to Warsaw he began to work on restoring the faculty at the university first as dean, then vice-president, at the same time serving as vice-director of the badly damaged National Museum and General Secretary of the Warsaw Scientific Society. He distinguished himself as an outstanding teacher and administrator. In no time he succeeded in reconstructing the staff at the university and at the museum, and educated a solid group of specialists in classical, Near Eastern and Egyptian art and archaeology. In 1948 a new Gallery of Ancient Art was opened in modernised halls with newly designed showcases and lighting. It was at the time considered one of the best presentations of objects of art in Europe.

MICHAŁOWSKI was not originally a museum man – his interests being much wider. But through him the Gallery of Ancient Art became a centre, where research and the care for and presentation of collections received equal attention.

In 1956 he organised his first excavations in the classical world – together with Russian colleagues he started to dig at the Greek colony of Mirmekeion on the Black Sea coast. One year later he returned to Egypt, but, because of the political situation, any resumption of the Polish-French excavations at Tell Edfu was impossible. So he took to excavating at Tell Atrib, a site some 50 km north of Cairo. The regular seasons there lasted until recently, with some of the finds enriching the museum. In 1959 Professor MICHAŁOWSKI began excavations at Palmyra in Syria, in 1960 in the centre of Alexandria. The great progress of the field work was made possible by his creation of the Polish Centre of Mediterranean Archaeology in Cairo, an institution providing shelter for itinerant archaeologists, help with logistics and coordination of various projects. And that task was most important, as at the same time the Centre was involved in the Campaign to Save Nubian Monuments, in the reconstruction work at the Hatshepsut temple at Deir el-Bahari, in excavating the Thutmosis III temple and in the above-mentioned field work in Alexandria and Palmyra. MICHAŁOWSKI was also appointed chairman to the Abu Simbel Executive Committee of the UNESCO Nubian Rescue campaign.

One of the greatest achievements of Kazimierz MICHAŁOWSKI was the discovery of the early Christian Cathedral at Faras, near the Egyptian-Sudanese border, where ca 120 mural paintings were removed from the walls and saved from the oncoming high water level in the Lake of Naser. Half of these are on display in a special "Faras Gallery" in this Museum, the other half is preserved in the National Museum in Khartoum.

It is impossible to enumerate here all the important discoveries made by MICHAŁOWSKI – they are described in series of thick volumes. Also thick are his studies on Egyptian, classical and early Christian art and archaeology.

The catalogue of his multi-faceted achievements in themselves convey little of the charm of the man's character and personality, his dignity and sense of humour. His combination of inexhaustible energy, intellectual distinction and diplomatic finesse brought him international prestige and friends among wide circles of the world's mighty and humble, and enabled him to operate and achieve success in such difficult times as post-war communist Poland. Thanks to his activity we are able to welcome you today in Warsaw, where he built a strong, active and progressive Egyptological centre.

Jadwiga Lipińska

Grażyna Bąkowska
Cracow

Ouroboros on Magical Gems. Some Remarks*

(Plate 1)

Ouroboros – the snake devouring its own tail – is found frequently in various cultures. It appears in Egyptian art, and is found in Elam. It was spread in the Greco-Roman Period, and was used by Gnostics in their theories. The motif also found its place in alchemy, and can be traced in modern art. A snake shedding its skin was considered a symbol of renewing life, and a snake biting its own tail as a symbol of eternity – everything ends and begins in its jaws, symbolising constant periodicity. As with the Egyptians, also for the later Gnosis, Ouroburos formed the border of the ordered world – encircling it and thus separating it from chaos. Ouroboros appears not only in cosmic symbolism. It also had protective functions, e.g. encircling the symbol of the nome of Hermopolis or as the fetish of Abydos. A snake devouring its own tail is also a metaphor for human life. The ring-shape of Ouroboros signified completeness – mandala. Its shape refers to the *šn* hieroglyph, a symbol for the eternity of the universe. All things encompassed by it were protected. An elongated form of *šn* is the cartouche encircling pharaohs' names.

A snake holding its tail in its jaws is depicted frequently in ancient Egyptian art.[1] As a symbol of eternity, it is depicted in the Book of Amduat. It also appears in the Book of Gates and the Book of Caverns. A snake in a circular form was already depicted in the art of the Predynastic Period.[2] The first typical depiction of Ouroboros dates from the New Kingdom period in a chapel of Tutankhamun's tomb – a mummy figure whose head and feet are surrounded by snakes catching their own tails.[3] Ouroboros in the form of a cartouche is depicted on the lid of pharaoh Merenptah's sarcophagus (1213-1203 BC).[4] This snake was identified with the *Mḥn* hieroglyph signifying "The Encircling Serpent".[5] A snake holding its tail in its jaws might constitute a symbol of separation and the imprisonment of an enemy. The Stele of Piye refers to this, describing the siege of Hierakonpolis Magna.[6] A snake devouring its own tail may also have a negative, self-destructive, aspect – the animal does not always symbolise positive powers. Occurring in the form of a snake are Kematef, Wadjit, Thermutis, and Apophis – the symbol of evil powers and the eternal enemy of the Sun, as well as the god Seth.

The motif of Ouroboros known from the art of ancient Egypt was also popular in the first centuries after Christ. It was depicted on gems, but is also well known from magical papyri that display connections with Gnosis. The depictions on magical gems show a continuation of traditions from the times of the pharaohs while displaying new trends in the civilisations of the Mediterranean world. The period the magical gems were produced is characterised by not yet fully recognised cultural and religious changes. The main production centre of these objects was Alexandria – a metropolis with mixed cultural influences from all

* I would like to heartily thank the members of the board of the Foundation Supporting Independent Polish Science and Culture for granting me a scholarship, which enabled me to carry out the research works on magical gems; and Mr J. SZYMKIEWICZ, the curator of the Department of Ancient Art of the National Museum in Poznań, for permission to publish the described in the paper gem.

[1] L. KÁKOSY, Uroboros, *LÄ* VI, cols. 886-894; E. CIAMPINI, *Precedenti faraonici di un'iconografia magica* and M.G. LANCELLOTTI, Il simbolismo del serpente nelle gemme magiche: osservazioni storico-religiose. *The Symposium in Verona, Gemme gnostiche e cultura ellenistica*, the materials in the press.

[2] W.C. HAYES, *The Scepter of Egypt* I, Cambridge 1953, p. 29, fig. 22.

[3] A. PIANKOFF, *The Shrines of Tut-Ankh-Amon*, New York 1955, pl. 48, fig. 41.

[4] J. ASSMANN, Die Inschrift auf dem äusseren Sarkophagdeckel des Merenptah, *MDAIK* 28 (1972), pp. 47-73.

[5] R.K. RITNER, Uterine Amulet in the Oriental Institute Collection, *JNES* 43 (1984), pp. 219-220.

[6] N.C. GRIMAL, *La Stèle triomphale de Pi('ankh)y au Musée du Caire*, Cairo 1981, pp. 14-15.

over the then world. On the gems, there appear Roman motifs together with Greek, Jewish, Persian, and above all, Egyptian ones. Ouroboros is not the simple completion of a depicted scene as has been suggested before[7] – rather it reaches back to deep-rooted ancient traditions.

One of the frequently repeated motifs is Ouroboros expressing the idea of time – the constant travel of the Sun, tying it to solar symbolism. On the Heryt-uben papyrus from the XXIst dynasty, Ouroboros circles the solar disc held by Aker – depicted as two lions joined together at the back – so that one faces east and the other west. Inside the disc is depicted a youthful god of the Sun with a lock of hair on his head. The god holds a flail and sceptre in his right hand. His left hand finger is held close to his mouth.

Solar symbols were also placed on magical gems. On one is depicted a solar barge with a lotus flower on which sits Harpocrates – he holds a flail in his left hand while his right hand touches his mouth.[8] Above his head is placed Ouroboros surrounding inscriptions and characteres signs. In other scenes, the snake surrounds either the whole depiction of Harpocrates on a barge,[9] or a barge on which there are seven deities.[10] Ouroboros also encircles a scene divided into four parts in each of which is depicted a different figure connected with the sun: Harpocrates on a lotus flower, cynocephalus, a scarab, and a falcon.[11] Harpocrates sitting on a lotus flower – a symbol of the sun and of revival, appears very often on magical gems.[12] Sometimes, the god is depicted standing holding a cornucopia in one hand and bringing the other hand to his mouth – a gesture which in the Greco-Roman Period has been interpreted as a sign for silence.[13]

Also connected with solar symbolism are gems showing a scarab surrounded by Ouroboros. The scene refers to Egyptian conceptions. In the Book of Amduat from the tomb of Sethy I, in the eighth hour a snake with five heads encircles the god of the Sun (with a scarab on his head). On some magical gems there is a scarab on Serapis'es head. One of the scenes depicts the god trampling a crocodile.[14] In this case on Serapis'es kalathos a scarab is visible. The whole scene is encircled by Ouroboros. The crocodile has been considered a symbol of evil, an incarnation of Seth (defeated by Horus). Sometimes it happens that a scarab was shown with the head of Helios surrounded by sunrays.[15] The gems with a scarab have solar symbols,[16] the characteres, and sometimes visible is the name of the Jewish god – Iao.[17] Ouroboros also protects the phoenix, which in Egypt was a symbol of the sun. The phoenix was also linked with the idea of immortality – it was believed to be a bird that continually dies then resurrects from itself.[18]

In the pharaohs' country, Osiris is mainly associated with resurrection. There is a gem that refers to both solar and Osirian concepts. On the obverse was shown the mummy of Osiris while the reverse depicts

[7] C. BONNER, *Studies in Magical Amulets, chiefly Graeco-Egyptian*, Ann Arbor 1950 (hereinafter referred to as: *SMA*), p. 250.

[8] E. ZWIERLEIN-DIEHL, *Die antiken Gemmen des Kunsthistorischen Museums in Wien* III, München 1991 (hereinafter referred to as: *Antiken Gemmen*), pp. 158-159, No 2194.

[9] A. DELATTE, Ph. DERCHAIN, *Les intailles magiques gréco-egyptiennes*, Bibliothéque Nationale. Cabinet des Médailles et Antiques, Paris 1964 (hereinafter referred to as: *Intailles magiques*), pp. 215-217, No 294.

[10] DELATTE, DERCHAIN, *Intailles magiques*, pp. 215-216, No 294.

[11] M. HENIG, *The Lewis Collection of Engraved Gemstones in Corpus Christi College*, BAR Supplementary Series I, Cambridge 1975, p. 58, No 24; DELATTE, La Clef de la matrice, *Musée Belge* 18 (1914), pp. 48-50 (concerning the connection between baboons and solar religion).

[12] A.M. el-KHACHAB, Some Gem-Amulets depicting Harpocrates seated on a lotus Flower, *JEA* 57 (1971), pp. 132-145.

[13] S.H. MIDDLETON, *Engraved Gems from Dalmatia. From the Collections of Sir John Gordiner Wilkinson and Sir Arthur Evans in Harrow School, at Oxford and elsewhere,* Oxford 1991, p. 84, No 128; concerning the gesture of Harpocrates see el-KHACHAB, *JEA* 57 (1971), pp. 133-134.

[14] DELATTE, DERCHAIN, *Intailles magiques*, p. 159, No 206.

[15] H. PHILIPP, *Mira et Magica*, Mainz am Rhein 1986 (hereinafter referred to as: *MM*), pp. 84-85, No 118.

[16] PHILIPP, *MM*, p. 84, No 117.

[17] DELATTE, DERCHAIN, *Intailles magiques*, p. 54, No 50; on Iao see A.R. MANDRIOLI, *La collezione di gemma del Museo CivicoArcheologico di Bologna,* Bologna 1987 and ZWIERLEIN-DIEHL, *Antiken Gemmen*, pp. 170-171 with literature.

[18] DERCHAIN, Intailles magiques du Musée de Numismatique d'Athene, *CdE* 39 (1964), p.186, No 14.

a scarab encircled by Ouroboros.[19] Perhaps the joining of the two guaranteed the owner of the amulet eternal life. A papyrus of the priestess Henuttaui from the XXIst dynasty shows Ouroboros circling both the solar disc and the fetish of Abydos representing Osiris – and thus the Underground Land of *Dwat*. A dead person in the form of a mummy standing on Ouroboros 'was becoming the resurrected' Osiris.[20] The mummy of Osiris on Ouroboros is visible in a scene carved on a gem[21]. The god is standing in front of a Nilometer or an obelisk, and a snake under his feet circles the word Iao. On Ouroboros there also stands another Egyptian god – Anubis,[22] and Anguipede[23] – a Gnostic creature. At other times, the snake encircles either Abraxas[24] or Solomon.[25]

Motifs referring to ancient Egyptian culture are visible on a gem depicting a lion holding a mummy on its back.[26] Above the corpse is depicted a crocodile and above the crocodile is Serapis. The whole scene is surrounded by Ouroboros. Sometimes, depictions show a mummy accompanied by Isis and Nepthys.[27] A scene with these two goddesses standing beside the mummified body of Osiris often appears in Egyptian art. A frequently appearing motif on the walls of tombs and sarcophagi is the udjat eye – a popular amulet.[28] It symbolised offering, victory over an enemy, and guaranteed health. These amulets were made of green faience. There is one gem depicting the udjat eye encircled by the protecting Ouroboros.[29] It was made of green jasper, which in Egypt meant good health.

The snake devouring its own tail is depicted most frequently on gems showing an uterus.[30] This type of amulet was once in the hands of Dominic Radziwiłł.[31] It was one of the earliest published magical gems.[32] On the uterus, which is locked by a key, stands Chnoubis with Isis and Anubis at his sides. When C. du MOLINET published the object in 1692, he described Ouroboros as a figure representing time. The inscription on the reverse of the amulet indicates that it was supposed to free the woman owning it from suffering caused by the displacement of her uterus. Ouroboros encircles the depicted uterus, protecting it from the external enemy, and along with the depicted key, it is the second symbol of closing.

The motif of closing or imprisonment often appears on gems with Pantheos.[33] The deity stands on a cartouche – usually formed by Ouroboros. Typically, the snake encircles various types of dangerous animals. On one amulet were depicted five animals – among them a scarab, a scorpion, and

[19] BONNER, *SMA*, p. 255, No 12.

[20] NIWIŃSKI, *Mity i symbole starożytnego Egiptu*, Warszawa 1995, pp. 97-100.

[21] PHILIPP, *MM*, p. 82, No 112.

[22] BONNER, *SMA*, p. 259, No 39. Anubis appears very frequently in Greco-Roman art, see: J.C. GRÉNIER, *Anubis alexandrin et romain*, EPRO 57 (1977), passim.

[23] BONNER, *SMA*, pp. 281-282, No 173; on Anguipede see: DELATTE, DERCHAIN, *Intailles magiques*, pp. 23-42.

[24] BONNER, *SMA*, p. 172, No 152, signification and motif: pp. 123-139 and J. ŚLIWA, *Egyptian scarabs and magical gems from the collection of Constantine Schmidt-Ciążyński*, Cracow 1989 (hereinafter referred to as: *Egyptian scarabs*), pp. 73-74 with literature, see also footnote 17.

[25] DELATTE, DERCHAIN, *Intailles magiques*, pp. 261-264, No 376; B. BAGATTI, Altre medaglie di Solomone cavaliere e loro origini, *Rivista di archeologia cristiana* XLVII (1971), pp. 331-342, writes about the depictions of Salomon, see also: M. HENIG, *Classical Gems Ancient and Modern Intaglios and Cameos in the Fitzwilliam Museum Cambridge*, Cambridge 1994 (hereinafter referred to as: *Classical Gems*), pp. 233-234, No 511 with literature.

[26] BONNER, *SMA*, pp. 235-237, Nos 354-357; P.J. SIPESTEJN, Magical Gems in the Allard Pierson Museum at Amsterdam, *BABesch* 45 (1970), pp. 175-176, No 1.

[27] BONNER, *SMA*, pp. 253, 254, Nos 2, 8.

[28] H. BONNET, *Reallexikon der ägyptischer Religionsgeschichte*, Berlin 1952, p. 854 and L. KÁKOSY, *La magia in Egitto ai tempi dei faraoni*, Mantova 1991, pp. 82-86.

[29] PHILIPP, *MM*, p. 32, No 7.

[30] Gems with a uterus belong to the category of medical gems. The subject is widely discussed by BONNER, *SMA*, pp. 79-94, A.A. BARB, *Diva Matrix*, *JWCI* 16 (1953), pp. 193-231 and G. BĄKOWSKA, Gemmy medyczne, *Meander* 6 (2000), pp. 557-570.

[31] BĄKOWSKA, Gemma magiczna z kolekcji Dominika Radziwiłła. Z dziejów jednego zabytku, in: E. PAPUCI-WŁADYKA, J. ŚLIWA *Studia Archeologica. Prace dedykowane Profesorowi Januszowi A. Ostrowskiemu w sześćdziesięciolecie urodzin*, Kraków 2001, pp. 17-23, figs. 1-2.

[32] C. du MOLINET, *Le Cabinet de bibliothèque de Sainte Geneviève*, Paris 1692, p. 126, pl. 29 I-II.

[33] BONNER, *SMA*, pp. 156-160, DELATTE, DERCHAIN, *Intailles magiques*, pp. 126-141, and BĄKOWSKA, Bes Pantheos. Some Remarks Concerning his Representation on Magical Gems, in: J. POPIELSKA-GRZYBOWSKA (ed.), *Proceedings of the First Central European Conference of Young Egyptologists. Egypt 1999: Perspectives of Research. Warsaw 7-9 June 1999*, Światowit Supplement Series E: Egyptology, vol. I, WES, vol. III, Warsaw 2001, pp. 11-14.

a snake.[34] On another gem, within Ouroboros there is only a scarab.[35] Sometimes there are carved inscriptions and signs inside cartouches.

There are a large number of gems on which decoration is limited to the Ouroboros circling either an inscription or characteres. The majority of this type are made of carnelian, although there are also amulets made of jasper and of greyish-white chalcedony. White chalcedony was used to produce a yet unpublished gem located in the National Museum in Poznań.[36] Only its obverse bears decoration. It depicts Ouroboros circling two pairs of signs. One pair consists of two crossed out Z-signs. This appears very frequently on magical gems. Such a sign was carved on gems with Chnoubis,[37] amongst others. Usually it repeats three times and refers perhaps to the name of Zeus.[38] The second sign is mysterious – its meaning is unknown. No identical sign was found on any other gem. The signs characteress are not yet recognised. Some hypotheses tie them with seals described in the *Books of Jeû* – due to these signs a soul could pass through the eons.[39] In the lower part of the described depiction, a snake with a grooved surface catches its tail in its jaws. On other gems, the snake's head is depicted in the upper part of a scene. Sometimes sunrays are visible on Ouroboros' head[40] – resembling rays around the head of Chnoubis,[41] or as is a marked 'beard'.[42] The described gem is slightly destroyed but one can trace delicate lines that perhaps mark a 'beard'. On the gem from Poznań, the snake's jaws faces left and its body has more or less the same thickness throughout its length. Similarly, a snake is shown on another gem where Ouroboros encircles two Z-signs, a rosette, and Greek letters. However, the body of this snake is thicker in the middle.[43] Comparing the two amulets, the one from Poznań seems to be made more cautiously. On the second gem, the jaws of Ouroboros also point to the left, encircling characteres and the word Abraxas.[44] The jaws are reminiscent of the head of a lion. There is also a beard marked. Such composition refer to pictures of either Chnoubis or Kronos-Sabaoth.[45]

The magical gem from Poznań is one more example of an ancient object bearing the motif of a snake devouring its own tail. Its description was the pretext for some remarks, which trace the manner of engraving and the functions of Ouroboros. Further research may lead to interesting new conclusions and observations concerning the motif.

---

[34] Z. KISS, Amulettes magiques gréco-égyptiennes au Musée National de Varsavie, in: K.M. CIAŁOWICZ, J.A. OSTROWSKI (eds.), *Les Civilisations du Bassin Méditerranéen. Hommages à Joachim Sliwa*, Cracovie 2000, pp. 375-382, figs. 3, 4.

[35] ŚLIWA, *Egyptian scarabs*, pp. 74-75, fig. 97 and IDEM, Gemma z przedstawieniem "Pantheosa" z kolekcji Konstantego Schmidta-Ciążyńskiego, *EOS* LXXVIII (1990), pp. 163-167.

[36] Inv. No V 188; 23 x 16.5 x 5 mm.

[37] BONNER, *SMA*, pp. 51-60.

[38] ŚLIWA, *Egyptian scarab*, pp. 75-76, fig. 98.

[39] HENIG, *Classical Gems*, pp. 227-228, No 501; C. SCHMIDT, *The Books of Jeû and the Untitled Text in the Bruce Codex*, Leiden 1978; E.A.W. BUDGE, *Amulets and Superstitions*, New York 1978 presents the subject of characteres and ancient magic, see also A. WYPUSTEK, *Magia antyczna*, Warszawa 2001.

[40] DELATTE, DERCHAIN, *Intailles magiques*, pp. 333-334, No 510.

[41] PHILIPP, *MM*, p. 118, No 190.

[42] M. SCHLÜTER, G. PLATZ-HORSTER, P. ZAZOFF, *Hannover, Kestner-Museum, Hamburg, Museum für Kunst und Gewerbe, Antike Gemmen in Deutschen Sammlungen* IV, Wiesbaden 1975, p. 312, No 1719.

[43] P. GERCKE, V. SCHERF, P. ZAZOFF, *Herzog-Anton-Ulrich-Museum Braunschweig, Sammlung im Archäologischen Institut der Universität Göttingen, Staatliche Kunstsammlungen Kassel, Antiken Gemmen in Deutschen Sammlungen* III, Wiesbaden 1970 (hereinafter referred to as: *Herzog-Anton-Ulrich-Museum*), No 205.

[44] E. BRAND, *Staatlich Münzsammlunng München, Antike Gemmen in Deutschen Sammlungen* I.3, München 1972, p. 279, No 2894.

[45] A. MASTROCINQUE, Metamorfosi di Kronos su una gemma di Bologna. The Symposium in Verona, *Gemme gnostiche – cultura ellenistica* (materials in the press). Sabaoth was the most powerful of the archonts – the rulers of heaven's spheres. According to MASTROCINQUE, three Hebrew names – Iao, Sabaoth, and Adonai – correspond to three animal forms. In his considerations, he writes about a snake, a lion, and a pig. The last animal is also mentioned on one magical gem – uoedh(z), where Ouroboros is depicted on the obverse encircling characteres, GERCKE, SCHERF, ZAZOFF, *Herzog-Anton-Ulrich-Museum*, p. 59, No 195.

Mikołaj Budzanowski
Cracow

The Sitting Statues of Hatshepsut in their Architectural Setting in the Temple *Djeser-Djeseru* at Deir el-Bahari*

(Plates 2-3)

The architectonic complex located in the Upper Terrace of Hatshepsut's temple in Deir el-Bahari is notable for the large number of chapels and cult niches decorated with reliefs depicting offerings made in front of a sitting statue of a monarch or her family.[1] This number has been recently increased to the total of 21, after several unknown fragments of chapels in the Solar Cult Complex and in the Sanctuary were discovered by the Polish Archaeological Mission[2] (**fig. 1**). Within each of these chapels the central function belonged to the sitting statues, as indicative of the sacral direction (this aspect of their positioning can be inferred from the relief decorations). The statues, carved in stone or cast in precious metal, were actual recipients of the cult and, save for the divine images, belonged to the most important objects located in the temple.[3] Two statues' dumped-places, unearthed by H. WINLOCK in the 1920s give us a clear idea of the statuary outfit inside the Upper Terrace.[4] But, the group of major import for our interest is that of five sitting statues, whose stylistics were comprehensively analysed by R. TEFNIN.[5] However, ever since their discovery in the Senenmut's Quarry almost no attention has been paid to the positioning of the statues on the temple's terraces or to their actual function.[6] Nevertheless, as these extensive studies furthered our knowledge of the architectural design of the Upper Terrace, we may undertake a discussion of this particular problem and attempt to locate the statues within the architectonic scheme.

This tentative reconstruction rests upon one crucial premise: the existence of a link connecting the relief decorations with the object displayed in a given place.[7] The chapel of Sethi I in Memphis may serve as a good example of such a link, as the sitting statues of the king and divinities we find there correspond to the chambers' reliefs.[8] An additional reference point is provided by another chapel belonging to the same king inside his famous temple in Abydos.[9] SOUROUZIAN convincingly attributes to the chapel the famous statue of the pharaoh in the Vienna

* I am deeply thankful to Dr Zbigniew E. SZAFRAŃSKI for his valuable support, commenting on this paper, encouragement and for permission to publish the material from Deir el-Bahari. My sincere appreciation goes to Professor Hourig SOUROUZIAN for her remarks and comments on the first draft of this paper.

[1] Eight of them are placed on the western wall of the Festival Courtyard; seven within the main sanctuary (six in the Bark-Hall room and one as the last, third room), four in the Solar Cult Complex and two in the southern part of the terrace.

[2] According to the concept of A. KWAŚNICA. Cf. F. PAWLICKI, Deir el-Bahari, The Temple of Queen Hatshepsut, 1997/1998, *PAM* X (1999), pp. 127-128, fig. 5.

[3] "...les sculptures de Pharaon assis ne font pas reference a une action du monarque, mais elles sont plutot passives, receptrice de l'action..." in: D. LABOURY, *La statuaire de Thoutmosis III. Essai d'interprétation d'un portait royal dans son contexte historique*, Ægyptiaca Leodiensia 5, Liège 1998 (hereinafter referred to as: *Statuaire de Thoutmosis III*), p. 436.

[4] The so-called Hatshepsut Hole and Senenmut Quarry, cf. P.F. DORMAN, *The Tombs of Senenmut. The Architecture and Decoration of Tombs 71 and 353*, New York, 1991, p. 21, fig. 1.

[5] R. TEFNIN, *La statuaire d'Hatshepsout. Portrait royal et politique sous la 18ᵉ Dynastie*, MonAeg 4, Bruxelles 1979 (hereinafter referred to as: *Statuaire d'Hatshepsout*), pp. 1-36, pl. I-VII.

[6] H. WINLOCK, *Excavations at Deir el-Bahari 1911-1931*, New York 1942 (hereinafter referred to as: *Excavations*), pp. 88 and 186. The author suggested, that the statues MMA 30.3.3 and MMA 29.3.3 were placed in Hathor chapel, while the famous alabaster (MMA 29.3.2) was located in the mortuary chapel of Hatshepsut.

[7] H. SOUROUZIAN, Statues et représentations de statues royales sous Sethi I, *MDAIK* 49 (1993), pp. 239-257, table 45-51.

[8] *Ibidem*, pp. 247-249, pls. 47, 48.

[9] A.M. CALVERLEY, M.F. BROOME, A.H. GARDINER, *The Temple of King Sethos I at Abydos* II, London-Chicago 1935, pls. 32, 35.

Museum.[10] The two images displayed several common iconographic details: clothes, head-cover and the presence of the Horus' falcon in the back part of the statue. In the case of statues from Deir el-Bahari, it seems that each of them had its own architectural context, while the divergence of style and dimensions exclude any possibility that all the five were originally located in one chamber or portico (in the latter case we would have to account for the possibility that they were placed in between the columns or at some entrance).[11] The statues seem to have been produced at some intervals so as to fit the needs of precise cult-chambers. Obviously, the destruction of the original floor impedes a solution of this problem – had it survived, we would be able to trace usual scratches or cavities marking a statue's position.[12]

Owing to this, we are forced to rely on the following criteria:

– iconography of the person portrayed and the throne,

– dimensions of each statue, particularly its total height;

The first criterion accounts for the clothes the portrayed person wears and the way her throne was decorated with the *sm3-t3wy* motif. As to the former, one should not forget that the relief decorations display a variety of the Queen's portrayals that are identical with that emerging in full statues and ranging between her representations as a female, in a female half-nude, or, finally, as a male. The positioning of the heraldic plants in the *sm3-t3wy* image, on the other hand, denotes the location of the sculpture with respect to the Nile.[13] If the lily is located in the back of a statue, the figure must have faced the river, standing on the east-west axis (**fig. 2b**). The lily in the front means, by contrast, that the sculpture faced southwards (**fig. 2a**). Meanwhile, the second criterion, accounting for the dimensions of a given object, will enable us to fit a given sculpture into the corresponding architectural context.

The starting point of our analysis is furnished by the representation of Hatshepsut, found in the Deir el-Bahari[14] (**fig. 3**). The decoration on a surviving fragment of a block was made in high relief, but the paintings beneath are unfortunately missing. The Queen is depicted in a female form, sitting on a block-throne, face to the right. The position of her arms is typical of the niche-representations, the right one lying flat on the thigh, while the left, bent at the elbow, is raised to the chest as the Queen holds a piece of cloth in this hand. The figure is clothed in the fashion befitting the Great Royal Wife: a long, closely fitting dress supported by two straps, and a vulture-hat over a tripartite wig. Additionally, an outline of a necklace is still visible on her chest. Erasures are limited to some parts of the figure: the head together with its cover, arms to the elbows, right palm together with the knee and partly the thigh.[15] Additionally the *šn*-ring and the stem of the sign *šwt* have been erased from the fans in the back of the throne. All of these attest to the purposeful nature of the erasures.

Carving of the four signs *s3*, *ḏd*, *ʿnḫ* and *w3s* was completed, while the *s* and the feminine form of the pronomen *s* are left unfinished. The so-called chequer-frieze that closes the whole composition disappears at the height of the last sign. Yet, the erasures and the attributes of the royal power that are located at the back of the throne (the fans, destined respectively

[10] Vienna, ÄS 5910, Kunsthistorisches Museum, SOUROUZIAN, *MDAIK* 49 (1993), pp. 255-256, pl. 51.

[11] This idea was suggested by J. KARKOWSKI, Der Tempel der Hatschepsut in Deir el-Bahari, in: *Geheimnisvolle Königin Hatschepsut. Ägyptische Kunst des 15. Jahrhunderts v. Chr.*, Warschau 1997, p. 43; IDEM, The Decoration of the Temple of Hatshepsut at Deir el-Bahari, in: Z.E. SZAFRAŃSKI (ed.), *Queen Hatshepsut and her Temple 3500 Years Later*, Warsaw 2001 (hereinafter referred to as: Decoration of Temple of Hatshepsut), p. 151.

[12] Cavities for the 23 sitting statues are well preserved in the Valley Temple of Khafre at Giza, cf. M. SEIDEL, *Die königlichen Statuengruppen.* I. *Die Denkmäler vom Alten reich bis zum Ende der 18. Dynastie*, HÄB 42, Hildesheim 1996, p. 21, pl. 4a. Another well known parallel is provided by the statuary group of Horemheb kneeling before Atum from Luxor-cachette, M. el-SAGHIR, *Das Statuenversteck im Luxortempel*, Mainz am Rhein 1992, pp. 35-40, figs. 82-84. Scratches on the pavement are preserved together with sitting statues of Tuthmosis I dedicated by his daughter Hatshepsut in the newly discovered niches inside the 4th pylon in Karnak, cf. F. LARCHÉ, New Statues at Karnak, *Egyptian Archaeology* 16 (2000), p. 31.

[13] LABOURY, *Statuaire de Thoutmosis III*, p. 82.

[14] Fragment of block 48 cm high and 66.5 cm wide. The relief has been known of for a very long time, probably discovered during the excavations of E. NAVILLE. Interestingly enough the block was prepared to be robbed from the place, as its heavy backside was carefully cut off by a saw.

[15] This unique example proofs that the erasures were made according to certain rules. The body of the Queen has been cut

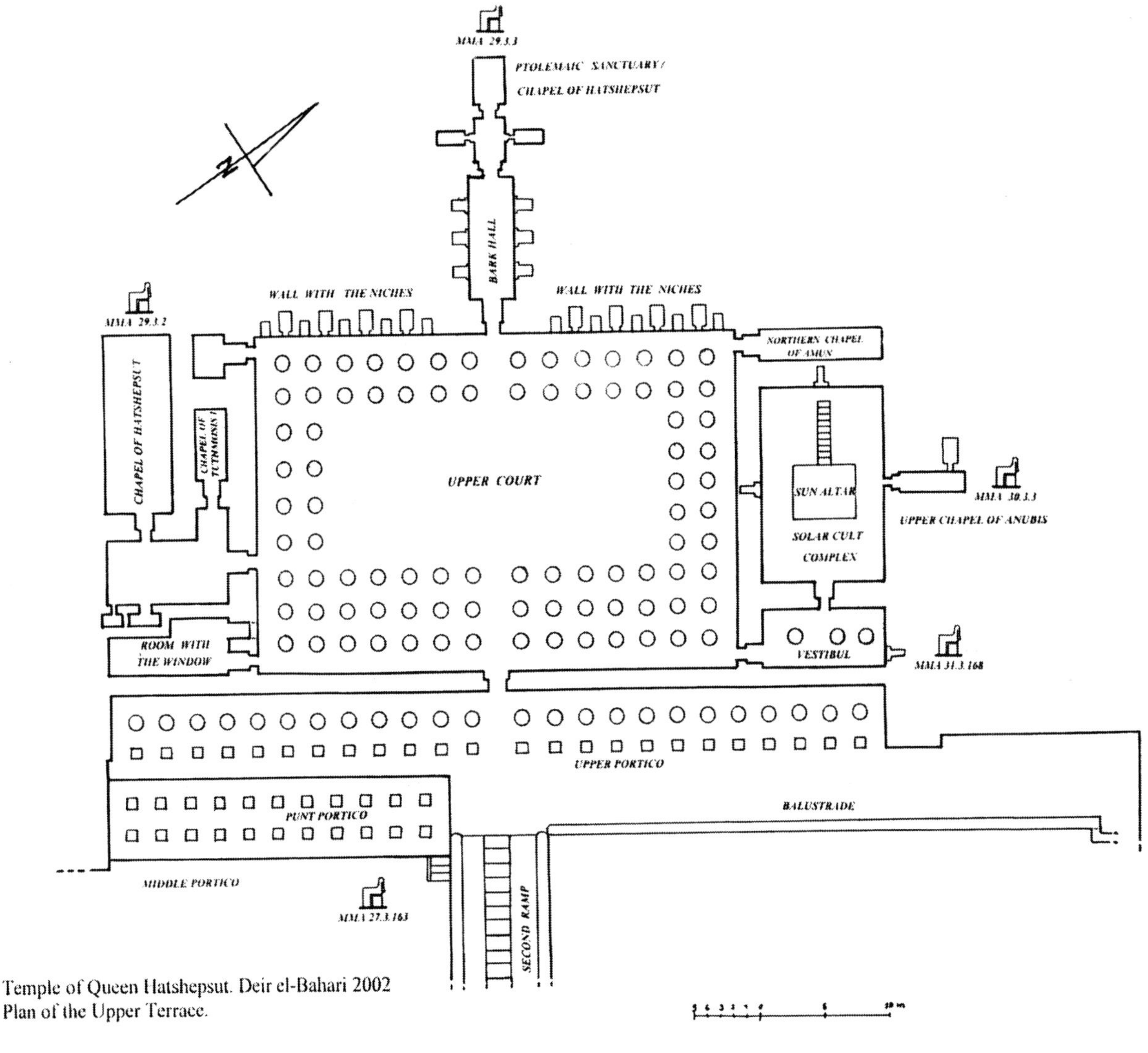

Fig. 1. Plan of the Upper Terrace after latest architectural studies of A. KWAŚNICA (drawn by M. BUDZANOWSKI)

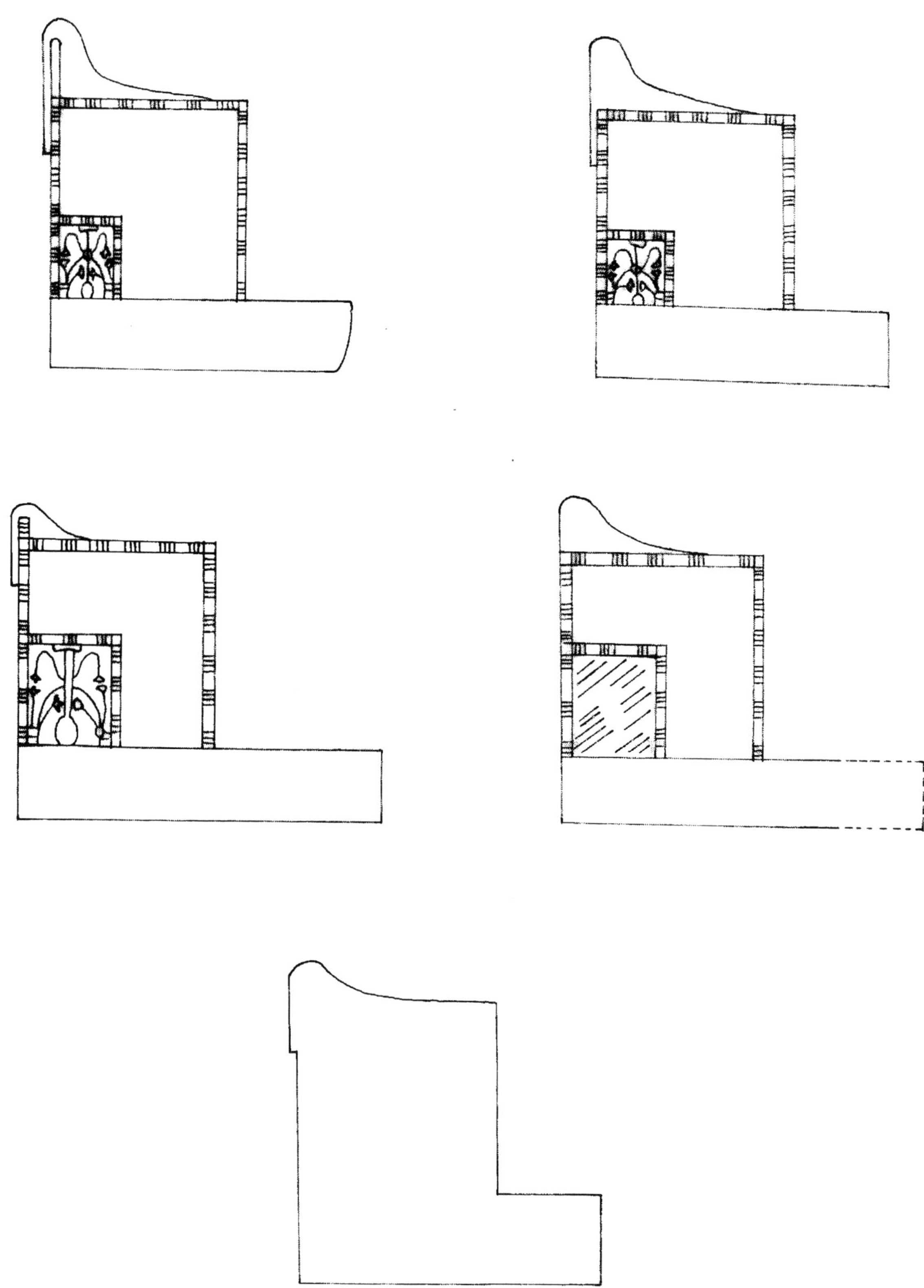

Fig. 2. Thrones of the sitting statues of Hatshepsut; side-walls (drawn by M. BUDZANOWSKI, after TEFNIN, *Statuaire d'Hatshepsout*, fig.1 – the drawings of the *smꜣ-tꜣwy* motif underwent slight modifications after comparing with the original photographs of the statues)

for the Queen and for her *ka*) leave no doubt that the person depicted on our relief is Hatshepsut. Consequently, the piece constitutes the oldest portrayal of the Queen as the Great Royal Consort, in the female attire and vulture-hat. Yet, Hatshepsut is simultaneously depicted as the recipient of offered gifts and is the object of an everyday cult. At the height of her arms we note the natron sign *bd* – this forms a part of a well-known formula, recurrent throughout the niche-images: *bd nsw*.[16] On the edge of our piece, at the height of the Queen's right palm, a dot of natron is still visible, as are closely above it fragments of *bd* and *t͟3*. Thus, the likely form of the legend may have been:[17] *bd nsw t͟3 5 bd mḥ t͟3 5* dots of the royal natron. This certainly points at the possible function of the chamber as a place of sacrifice and ritual treatment of the cult statue of the Queen. Hence, the only likely location for this relief would be in the third, last, chamber of the Sanctuary, northern wall.[18] The erasures were made during Tuthmosis III's reign, which means that the chapel was not dismantled until after Hatshepsut's death. The only chamber fitting the dimensions of the scene of the sacrifice made before the Queen as reconstructed by A. KWAŚNICA and possibly existent in Tuthmosis' times was later used for the construction of the Ptolemaic Sanctuary, where the oracle of Imhotep and Amenhotep, son of Hapu was installed[19] (**pl. 3, fig. 2**).

Additionally, it may be worth remembering at this point that another sitting image of a female figure survives in the temple. The image of Ahmes in the northwest niche of the Bark Hall is characterised by a similar formal arrangement.[20] Nevertheless, it is the lotus flower, not a piece of cloth, that firms an attribute of the deceased woman. Next, there is the arrangement of light-openings that bears witness to the assumption that the Sanctuary was in use during Hatshepsut's reign. The openings are located in the two preceding chambers, the Bark Hall and the chapel, where the cult-statue of Amun was housed (**fig. 1**).[21] Coming through these skylights and passing the middle room, the daylight would focus on the third chamber, the present Ptolemaic Sanctuary. Thus, they were actually designed to light the last chamber and the statue housed there.

Two sitting statues of Hatshepsut display a close resemblance with the discussed relief decoration. Carved respectively in black diorite[22] (MMA 30.3.3) and red granite-stone[23] (MMA 29.3.3) show the Queen in her female form, wearing a long, tightly fitting dress. The difference is limited to the arrangement of hands, in the statuary form lying flat on the Queen's knees, and to the head-cover (*khat*-wig in the diorite statue, *nemes* in the granite one). The dimensions are slightly diverse as far as the statues' height is concerned: 150 cm diorite, 165 cm granite, respectively. Concerning the throne-decorations a significant difference may be observed in the arrangement of the *sm3-t3wy* motif. On the granite statue the lily is placed in the rear part of the throne (**fig. 2b**), while the diorite one displays a unique reverse composition (**fig. 2a**). Such placing of the heraldic plants would mean that the diorite sculpture faced southwards (we may exclude the possibility that the sculpture faced westwards – it would mean that it was turned away from the temple's

into several pieces. The torso, together with breast, forearm, left hand holding a tissue, thigh and the top of the nose with lips were left intact.

[16] NAVILLE, *The Temple of Deir el Bahari* (hereinafter referred to as: *Deir el Bahari*) V, London 1897-1908, pls. CXLVI-CXLVII.

[17] NAVILLE, *Deir el Bahari* IV, pl. CX.

[18] PAWLICKI, *PAM* X (1999), pp. 127-128; IDEM, Deir el-Bahari. The Temple of Queen Hatshepsut, 1998/1999, *PAM* XI (2000), p. 164, IDEM, *Królewskie świątynie w Deir el-Bahari* (Royal temples in Deir el-Bahari), Warsaw 2000 (hereinafter referred to as: Świątynie królewskie), pp. 114-117. The author erroneously identifies the image of the female Hatshepsut with her representation as the Great Royal Wife, p. 115.

[19] E. LASKOWSKA-KUSZTAL, *Le sanctuaire Ptolémaïque de Deir el-Bahari*, Deir el-Bahari III, Warszawa 1984; PAWLICKI, *PAM* X (1999), pp. 127-128.

[20] NAVILLE, *Deir el Bahari* V, pl. CXLVI; KARKOWSKI, Hatshepsut Temple. The Epigraphic Mission 1996, *PAM* VIII (1997), p. 52, fig. 3.

[21] SZAFRAŃSKI, Exceptional Queen, Unique Temple: Polish Activity in the Temple of Hatshepsut, in: Z.E. SZAFRAŃSKI (ed.), *Queen Hatshepsut and her Temple 3500 Years Later*, Warsaw 2001, pp. 66-67, pls. 8-9; KARKOWSKI, Decoration of Temple of Hatshepsut, pp. 140-141, pls. 20-21.

[22] W.C. HAYES, *The Scepter of Egypt* II, London 1959 (hereinafter referred to as: *Scepter*), p. 100; TEFNIN, *Statuaire*, pp. 2-6, pl. Ia; J.-F. PECOIL, Les visages du pouvoir, *Les Dossiers d'Archéologie* 187 (1993), p. 19 (plate).

[23] HAYES, *Scepter* II, p. 89 and p. 100, fig. 55; TEFNIN, *Statuaire*, pp. 6-11, pls. Ib-c, II, IIIa; C. ROEHRIG, Hatshepsut and the Metropolitan Museum of Art *KMT* 1 (1990), p. 33.

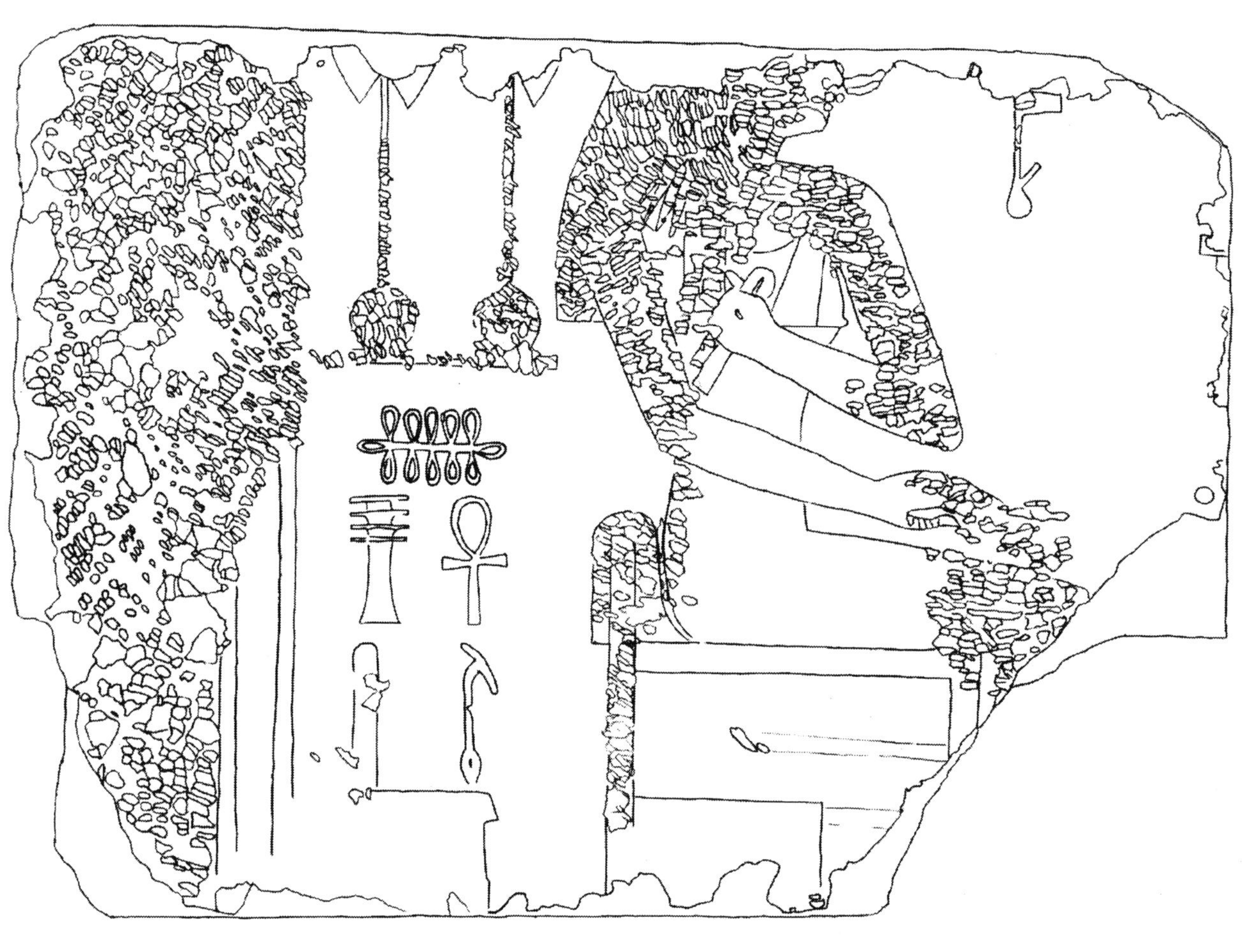

Fig. 3. Fragment of a decorated block with female representation of Hatshepsut (drawn by M. BUDZANOWSKI)

facade). The granite statue, by contrast, could face the Nile (eastern direction) or it could face northwards. The latter possibility can also be eliminated, as we know that almost no cult chapel on the Upper Terrace opened to the north. The only possible exception is a cult-niche found in the southern wall in the courtyard belonging to the Solar Cult Complex,[24] yet the place is much to small for the sculpture to fit in there. Moreover, as the two sculptures belong to the oldest in the temple, they have to be belong to the period when the Upper Terrace was first constructed and decorated. This narrows our possibilities to the deeper interior of the Sanctuary and the courtyard laid out in the northern part of the Terrace, where the sun-altar was originally located.[25]

The farthest, third, chapel of the Sanctuary was positioned on the east-west axis, opening to the east. Thus, a sculpture displayed in this room had to share in several important characteristics. First, the heraldic plants had to be placed in the right order, including a lily in the back. Second, the Queen had to be portrayed in the female form, and last, the total height of the statue could not exceed 170-180 cm.[26] The red granite statue MMA 29.3.3 fits all these requirements (**fig. 2b**). Moreover, if the statue, with a height of 165 cm, was located in the center of the chapel, it would be lit by daylight coming through the previously mentioned openings. The important thing is that the focal point of this in-flowing light would be precisely the face of our statue.

There was another chapel existent on the Upper Terrace, even if it has not survived until today in its original form (**fig. 4**).[27] Inferring from the preserved pieces of the decorated stone walls we may conclude that the missing chapel was built in the form typical of a cult niche destined for a royal statue, as they are found in the Solar Cult Complex and on the western wall of the Main Courtyard. The architectonic research of KWAŚNICA locates the niche-chapel in the place corresponding to that of the surviving Anubis' Sanctuary.[28] As the figures of Amun and Inmutef were not erased from the decorations during the Amarna Period, we are entitled to think that the chapel was dismantled during a rebuilding of the Upper Terrace. Nevertheless, this very chapel fits two major requirements that allow us to locate the black diorite statue MMA 30.3.3 there. The first – and most important – is that it would allow the sculpture to stand facing southwards. Secondly, the relevant dimensions seem compatible enough, the niche being 160 cm high (for the 150 cm of the sculpture). Unfortunately, lack of the whole decoration on the back wall of the niche impedes any tentative guess concerning the representation of the Queen as it could appear there. Yet, considering the relatively early date of the chapel, one may suspect she would have been portrayed in the female form.[29]

A notable change occurs in the course of the temple's building as far as royal representations are concerned. The southern wall of the chapel of the cult-statue inside the Sanctuary portrays Hatshepsut twice performing a daily ritual in front of a standing image of Amun.[30] Interestingly, the Queen is wearing the traditional male attire, the apron and kilt, but the body is unmistakably of a woman, as breasts are outlined. The female sex of the personage is moreover emphasised by the yellow-

[24] Measurements: H. 158 cm; D. 129.5 cm; W. 70 cm. KARKOWSKI, Decoration of Temple of Hatshepsut, pp. 151-152, pl. 29.

[25] Building of the upper terrace went through several changes, cf. Z. WYSOCKI, The Temple of Queen Hatshepsut at Deir el-Bahari: The Raising of the Structure in view of Architectural Studies, *MDAIK* 48 (1992), pp. 233-254.

[26] This is determined by the height of the chapel. The room had a vaulted roof of some 2.5 m high?

[27] 11 decorated fragments are preserved from this niche. Interestingly the representations of divine persons – Amun and Inmutef are preserved intact and have been never chiseled out by iconoclasts during Amarna Period. The reason of this phenomena is obvious: the niche was dismantled before the death of the Queen and reused in the construction of Anubis Chapel.

[28] Cf. M.G. WITKOWSKI, Deir el-Bahari et l'enigme des chapelles redoublees, *Les Dossiers d'Archéologie* 187 (1993), pp. 80-83; PAWLICKI, The Worship of Queen Hatshepsut in the temple at Deir el-Bahari, in: A. NIWIŃSKI (ed.), *Essays in Honour of Prof. Dr. Jadwiga Lipińska*, WES I, Warsaw 1997, pp. 45-52; KARKOWSKI, Decoration of Temple of Hatshepsut, p. 153, pl. 30. The study of the niche will be the subject of an article by the author and KWAŚNICA, entitled – *An unknown cult-niche in the temple of Hatshepsut in Deir el-Bahari*, in: Z.E. SZAFRAŃSKI (ed.), *Deir el-Bahari. Time of Hatshepsut. Recent Researches*, in: WES II, Warsaw 2002 (in the press).

[29] After the dismantling of the niche, the statue could have been reused in other niches of the complex or transferred to the Mortuary Chapel of Hatshepsut.

[30] P. GILBERT, Le sens des portraits intacts d'Hatshepsout à Deir el-Bahari, *CdE* 56 (1953), pp. 219-222, fig. 17 (=PECOIL, *Les Dossiers d'Archéologie* 187, p. 18).

ish shade of the skin, contrasting with the traditional red of Tuthmosis III's representations that appear on the opposite, northern wall.[31] The Bark Hall displays similar stylistic design – the side walls of the niches show Hatshepsut seated on a throne as a recipient of Inmutef's offers.[32] One of the niche representations, erasures notwithstanding, shows an outline of womanly breasts and a short apron. In some places the original yellow hue used to paint the body survives.

The pattern originated from the relief decoration was later employed by the statuary portrayals. The sitting alabaster statue (MMA 29.3.2) shows Hatshepsut wearing a short apron, her head dressed with *nemes*.[33] Still, the emphasized breasts do not leave much doubt where the sex of the person portrayed is concerned. However, this is hardly the only interesting feature that needs to be noted in this particular sculpture: with a total height of 195 cm it is significantly larger than the two previously discussed. Consequently, it had to be housed in a room larger than the Sanctuary's chambers or any of the niches. The *smꜣ-tꜣwy* informs us that the sculpture originally faced eastwards (**fig. 2c**). Only one location in the Upper Terrace would offer a similar placing of such a large object: this is a funerary chapel on the Terrace's southern part[34] (**fig. 1**). The architectonic studies confirm that this chapel, though originally built according to the traditional style of funerary chapels as prevalent in the Old Kingdom, was built later. P. JÁNOSI has distinguished seven constituent features of this chamber, the center of which was the royal statue.[35] Thus, in our case the northern and the southern walls showed rituals related to the daily cult of the royal statue. The Queen is portrayed sitting in a male attire and wearing a *nemes* headdress. Unfortunately, erasures are considerable and we are in no position to discuss whether the outline of breast was originally present or not. Nevertheless on some figures from the day-and-night ritual on the vaulted roof one can still recognize on the male body the outline of a female breast. It is very probable that the Queen was represented in the scene below according to the second type, as woman in a male guise. The alabaster statue was located in this precise chamber by H. WINLOCK, though the criteria employed were mainly aesthetic.[36] Today, the *smꜣ-tꜣwy* motif and the architecture of the whole complex may be viewed as a confirmation of his theory, though, we cannot ascertain the exact position of the sculpture within the chapel. As no inscriptions appear on its pillar, one may be inclined to think that it was placed with its back to the western wall or that it stood in front of the false door, on the other side of the offering table. Should we look for parallels, the nearby temple of Mentuhotep II Nebhepetre would support the latter solution.[37]

The monumentalising tendency becomes even clearer in the red granite statue (MMA 27.3.163). The sculpture, 2.28 m high,[38] portrays the Queen wearing the *nemes* and the apron with kilt. Any traces of the female sex disappear both in the sculpture itself and in the surviving inscriptions: pronouns are not female, while Hatshepsut is spoken of as a son, not a daughter of

[31] The scenes representing ritual purification of the Amun's statue were cleaned off the layer of soot by conservators Dr Maria LULKIEWICZ-PODKOWIŃSKA and Katarzyna RACHUTA during the season 1998/1999, cf. PAWLICKI, *PAM* X (1999), p. 127.

[32] On the rear-walls of the niches Hatshepsut performs a daily ritual before the standing statue of Amun from *Djeser-Djeseru*. The yellow colour of skin on the queens' body is also preserved in the decoration around the Festival Courtyard (tympanums of the niches) and inside the niches of the western wall.

[33] HAYES, *Scepter* II, p. 98, fig. 54; TEFNIN, *Statuaire d'Hatshepsout*, pp. 11-16, pls. IIIb-c, IV, V; J. YOYOTTE, Le cas Hatshepsout, *Les Dossiers d'Archéologie* 187 (1993), p. 2 (plate); E. RUSSMANN, in: *Egyptian Art* (catalogue of the exhibition), BMMA Winter 1983/84, p. 25, No 24; A. GRIMM, S. SCHOSKE, *Hatschepsut. KönigIN Ägyptens*, München 1999, figs. 34, 37; ROEHRIG, *KMT* 1 (1990), p. 32.

[34] NAVILLE, *Deir el Bahari* IV, pp. 6-11; PAWLICKI, *Świątynie królewskie*, pp. 128-131; KARKOWSKI, Decoration of Temple of Hatshepsut, pp. 146-151, pl. 27, p. 224 (plate).

[35] P. JÁNOSI, Die Entwicklung und Deutung des Totenopferraumes in den Pyramidentemplen des Alten Reiches, in: R. GUNDLACH, M. ROCHHOLZ (eds.), *Ägyptische Tempel – Struktur, Funktion und Programm*, HÄB 37, Hildesheim 1994, pp. 143-173.

[36] H. WINLOCK, *Excavations*, p. 186: "...since it is by far the most beautifully carved of the temple statues, it is obvious that it must have been designed for a very important place – perhaps the center of the actual mortuary chapel of the queen herself".

[37] Di. ARNOLD, *Der Tempel des Königs Mentuhotep von Deir el-Bahari*, Mainz am Rhein 1974, I, pp. 40-42, pls. 32-33, II, fig. 6-7.

[38] HAYES, *Scepter* II, p. 97; TEFNIN, *Statuaire d'Hatshepsout*, pp. 16-18, pl. VI.

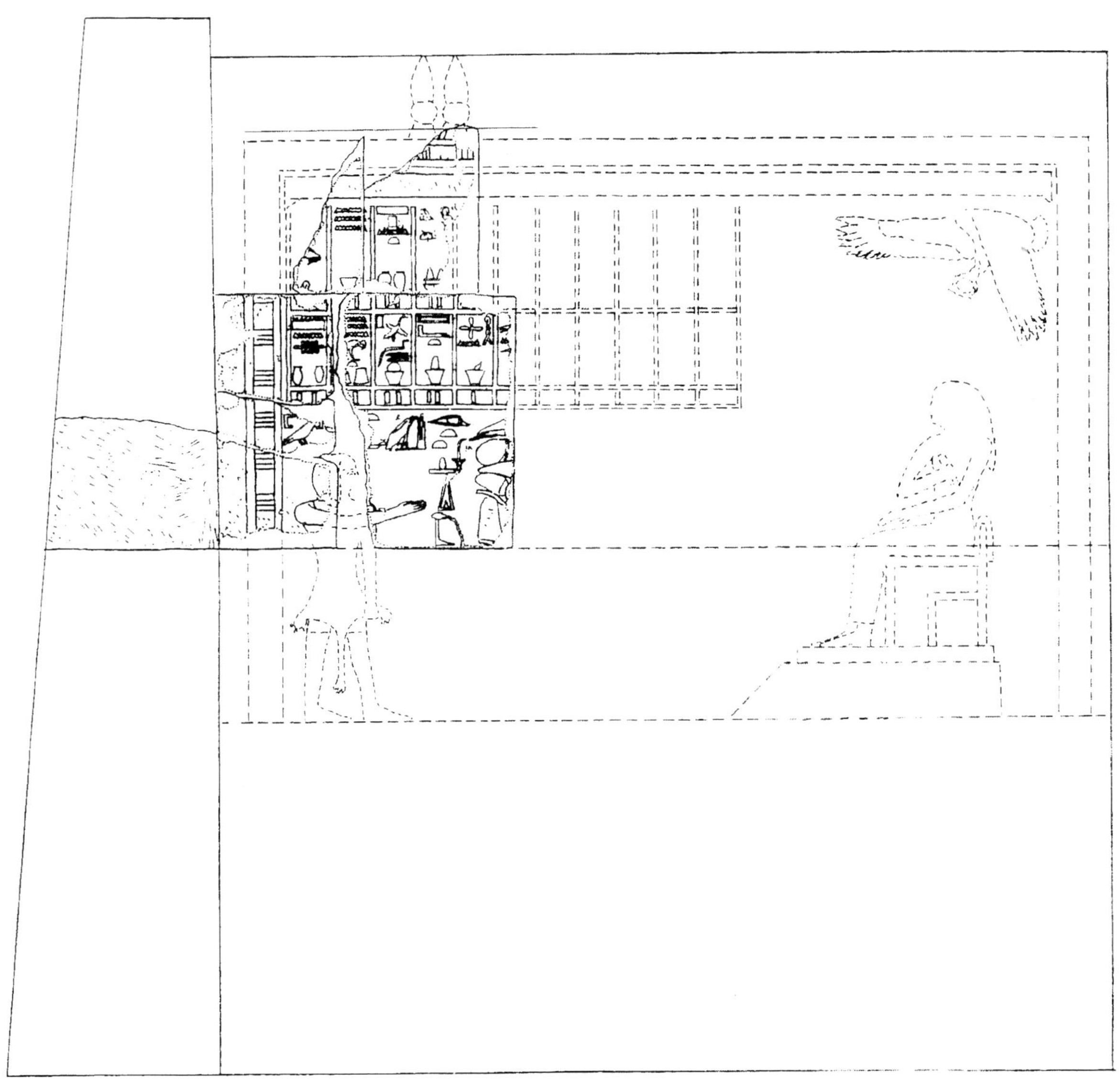

Fig. 4. Northern niche of the Solar Cult Courtyard; western wall
(after reconstruction by A. KWAŚNICA)

Amun. All these suggest that the statue was carved in the later period and, moreover, that it was well suited for public display. The *smꜣ-tꜣwy* motif indicates that it faced the Nile – thus, it would probably have been positioned with its back to the western wall (**fig. 2d**). Unfortunately, the present architecture of the Terrace leaves no chamber where the statue could have been displayed.[39]

At this point we are aided by the monumental scene depicted on the northern wall of the Punt Portico[40] (**pl. 3, fig. 1**). The ornately decorated chapel portrays Hatshepsut sitting on a throne, a composite crown on her head, and accompanied by a personification of royal *ka*. The Queen receives a delegation of three high court officials (Nehesi, Senenmut, Hapuseneb?) – the accompanying inscription is actually a decree foretelling the Punt expedition (undertaken in the 9th year of Hatshepsut's reign). Naos, containing a sitting statue of the Queen, is positioned on a high pedestal, equipped with stairs and decorated with an image of twin lions together with *rekhyt* figures. The image seems to be mirrored in the design of the northern part of the portico. The floor level rises by 75 cm, while stairs leading to the structure were built along the ramp-wall. The scene described in the chapel would possibly confirm the existence of a similar chapel built on a more durable pedestal. We know that a similarly shaped naos once existed in the Amun temple in Karnak, a structure built by Sesostris I.[41] The temple shows no traces of the possible existence of any additional podium – thus, one may suspect that the raised floor in the northern part of the Punt Portico could have served as a basis for the relatively light chapel. The red granite statue could have been placed in the very place, parallel to the relief representation of the Queen (the images are linked by similar proportions).

The fragmentarily surviving sitting statue (MMA 31.3.168) is the last object to be analysed here.[42] With the today missing upper part of the corpus, the sculpture would originally measure 160 cm in height. The Queen was portrayed wearing the apron with kilt, her hands lying flat on her knees. Since the statue lacks the *smꜣ-tꜣwy* motif, it is impossible to ascertain its exact position with respect to the north-south or east-west axes, yet the highly polished surface confirms that it was actually finished and prepared to be exhibited somewhere in the temple complex (**fig. 2e**). Yet, the unimpressive dimensions and lack of inscriptions suggest that the statue could have been housed in one of the niches dedicated to Hatshepsut and found in the Solar Cult Complex. There is a possibility that the building of four niches went through three phases. The first was established by the northern niche, which was described above (SC1). The second comprised two chapels on the western and the southern walls of the courtyard (SC2, 3). During the last phase the niche in the vestibul was erected.[43] It stands out by a rather poor stylistic of the relief decoration and the fact that the representations on the side walls were not erased, except the cartouches. The Queen is depicted in her male-incarnation without any female features. According to the stylistic study of R. TEFNIN, the above mentioned sitting statue was the youngest in the group, thus making it chronologically close to the last niche in the vestibul of the Solar Cult Complex (SC 4, **fig. 1**).

To conclude: the chapels and cult-niches dominate in the architectonic design of the Upper Terrace, attesting to the importance of the royal cult within this complex. At the same time, both relief and statuary representations confirm the evolutionary character of this cult. The similarities observed between these two kinds of sculptures and the architecture of the Terrace, allow us to place four of five surviving statues within the general frame of the temple complex. At the same moment they enable us to draw some chronological conclusions: the third, inner chamber of the Sanctuary, built after an idea known from Mentuhotep II Nebhepetre's temple, was probably the original seat of the royal cult: false doors still survive on the western wall of the chapel, marking the possible location of the red granite statue (MMA

[39] Sanctuary, Sun and Royal Cult Complexes together with two chapels adjacent to the courtyard should be excluded because of lack of free space. The south chamber with the window according to a new theory was used as a slaughterhouse, not as "royal palace" (personal communication with Dr Z.E. SZAFRAŃSKI and Mr A. KWAŚNICA).

[40] NAVILLE, *Deir el Bahari* III, pls. LXXXV-VI.

[41] L. GABOLDE, Karnak sous le règne de Sésostris Ier, *Égypte, Afrique & Orient* 16 (Janvier-Février 2000), p. 18, fig. 5.

[42] TEFNIN, *Statuaire d'Hatshepsout*, pp. 18-19, pl. VIIa.

[43] NAVILLE, *Deir el Bahari* I, p. 6, pls. III-IV; A. GRIMM, Zu einer getilgten Darstellung der Hatschepsut im Tempel von Deir el-Bahari, *GM* 68 (1983), p. 93, pl. 1.

29.3.3). The female representation of the Queen in diorite stone (MMA 30.3.3) would be placed in the more recent niche within the Solar Cult Complex, though the niche would be later pulled down. Then, the royal cult was transferred to the six niches of the Bark Hall, involving not only Hatshepsut, but also other members of the Tuthmoside dynasty. Thus, the eight niches of the western wall were dedicated to the Queen and her co-ruler Tuthmosis III. We do not know the exact form of statues that were originally located there, yet it seems plausible to think of dyads. Finally, the individual cult of Hatshepsut will be transferred to the royal complex: the largest chamber, the funerary chapel, was dedicated to the Queen. It is in that chamber that one would plausibly locate the alabaster statue (MMA 29.3.2). In the light of new studies it seems plausible to locate the second diorite statue (MMA 31.3.168) within the niche of the vestibul of the Solar Cult Complex. On the other hand, lack of any appropriate indications and traces make difficulties in locating the third granite statue, (MMA 27.3.163) – certainly, there is no more suitable place for such a statue elsewhere on the Upper Terrace. It seems most probable that the place for it should be the northern part of the Punt Portico.

Krzysztof M. Ciałowicz, Mariusz Jucha
Cracow

Tell el-Farkha 1998-2000. Stratigraphy and Chronology of the Western Kom
(Plates 4-12)

The site of Tell el-Farkha is situated in the Nile Delta about 120 km northeast of Cairo. Both the older – Italian excavation[1] – and the present – Polish research[2] – have brought data that allow us to date this site from the Predynastic – Lower Egyptian Culture through Naqada II and Naqada III (Protodynastic and Early Dynastic) phases to the Old Kingdom.

The preserved part of the site consists of three Koms: Western, Central and Eastern. At the present state of research we can distinguish seven main occupation phases – five of them (phases 1 to 5) were attested on the Western Kom. In the following report we concentrate on the stratigraphy and chronology of that Kom.

Phase 1

The oldest phase 1 is associated with Lower Egyptian Culture. The pottery consist mostly of rough ware but a few brown or reddish-brown coated potsherds as well as potsherds with temper which look like hairlines are also present. Very characteristic are potsherds with impressed or incised zigzag patterns (**pl. 4, figs. 1-2**). This decoration is absent in subsequent phases. Moreover, a few small bag shaped rough ware vessels with slightly pointed bottom (**pl. 4, fig. 3**) and oval vessels with pointed base, straight or concave neck (**pl. 4, fig. 4**) as well as hole-mouth jars (**pl. 4, fig. 5**) and different small bowls (**pl. 4, figs. 6-8**) were also found. At the end of phase 1 also occur a few fine ware potsherds with painted decoration (**pl. 4, figs. 9-10**) – which are connected with the Naqada Culture.

At the present state of research our phase 1 belonging to Lower Egyptian Culture seems to be contemporary of the second half of the Naqada Culture of Upper Egypt – probably Naqada (IIb?) IIc-d1.

The attribution of this phase to Lower Egyptian Culture is evidenced not only by pottery finds but also by the characteristic settlement features. Already present in the lowermost strata are numerous round and oval pits, often intersecting each other. These are probably the remnants of storage pits. Adjacent to them is a concentration of small, round pits. A series of furrows forming rectangular ground plans have been recorded next to the pits. These most probably represent the remains of structures built of organic materials. Higher up the stratigraphical sequence, in layers still dating from phase 1, the features denoted by furrows are still present and the number of pits decreases. In the higher strata of phase 1 the structure extending over practically the entire area excavated in the season of 2000 was discovered. The building was oriented to the NE and must have had walls of organic substances. All the remains of the structure are relatively narrow furrows.

[1] M. CHŁODNICKI, Some Remarks about Late Predynastic, Early Dynastic and Old Kingdom Bread Moulds, *ET* XVII (1995), pp. 23-27; CHŁODNICKI, R. FATTOVICH, S. SALVATORI, Italian Excavations in the Nile Delta and New Hypotheses on the 4th Millennium Cultural Development of Egyptian Prehistory, *Rivista di Archeologia* 15 (1991), pp. 5-33; IIDEM, The Nile Delta in Transition: A View from Tell el-Farkha, in: E.C.M. van den BRINK (ed.), *The Nile Delta in Transition: 4th-3rd Millenium BC*, Tel Aviv 1992, (hereinafter referred to as: Nile Delta), pp. 171-190; IIDEM, The Italian Archaeological Mission of the C.S.R.L-Venice to the Eastern Nile Delta: A preliminary report of the 1987-1988 field seasons, *CRIPEL* 14 (1992), pp. 45-62.

[2] CHŁODNICKI, K.M. CIAŁOWICZ, Tell el-Farkha. Explorations, 1998, *PAM* X (1999), pp. 63-70; IIDEM, Tell el-Farkha (Ghazala). Explorations, 1999, *PAM* XI (2000), pp. 59-76; M. JUCHA, Cylindrical Jars from Tell el-Farkha, in: CIAŁOWICZ, J.A. OSTROWSKI (eds.), *Les Civilisations du Bassin Méditerranéen. Hommages à Joachim Śliwa*, Cracovie 2000, pp. 105-111; IDEM, Initial Results of Research on Predynastic and Early Dynastic Pottery from Tell el-Farkha (1998-1999), in: J. POPIELSKA-GRZYBOWSKA (ed.), *Proceedings of the First Central European Conference of Young Egyptologists. Egypt 1999: Perspectives of Research. Warsaw 7-9 June 1999*, Światowit Supplement Series E: Egyptology, vol. I, WES, vol. III, Warsaw 2001, pp. 39-45, pl. 7-15.

Explorations revealed two or even three phases of rebuilding. The older construction measures ca 8 m in length and 3.20 m in width. The structure is denoted by a series of furrows. Moreover, few small mud-lined pits as well as storage pits were discovered. The principal part of the youngest structure (**pl. 5**) was at least 11 m long and 4.50 m wide. The interior division into many small compartments is noteworthy as well as many pits lined with mud. Some of them (especially the ones within the outline of the furrows) must have been of structural importance, serving to mount the post that had once supported the walls and roof. The biggest of these pits, sometimes bearing obvious evidence of burning through and yielding D-shaped bricks, could have been used as fireplaces. The complex interior division may be due to the fact that parts of the house, clearly of a domestic character, could have been separated from the other areas by low walls made of organic substances or silt.

Phase 2

At the present state of research our phase 2 seems to be characteristic of the beginning of the transition between the Lower and Upper Egyptian traditions. While some kinds of the pottery known from the previous, phase 1, still occur, pottery which can be connected with the Upper Egyptian tradition also appear.

The presence of the Upper Egyptian tradition is also manifested by a few examples of fine ware pottery with painted decoration (**pl. 4, figs. 11-14**): *ss* – birds,[3] aloe (?) or wavy lines, as well as fragments belonging to the pots with wavy handles (**pl. 4, fig. 15**). All these kinds of decoration fit well into the second half of Naqada II.

The majority of the pottery is the rough ware. The shapes include different roll-rimmed jars (**pl. 4, figs. 16-21**) sometimes with high shoulders as well as narrower forms with thickened external rims. Those jars seem to be similar to Upper Egyptian forms dated to the second half of Naqada II and beginning of Naqada III.[4] The shapes of the associated bases include flat (**pl. 4, figs. 22-23**) or pointed forms (**pl. 4, figs. 24-25**). Roll-rimed jars – especially forms probably with flat bases are more numerous in the subsequent phase 3. Other jars, probably with pointed bases seem to be mostly connected with our phase 2. Different rough ware bowls – which are still present in phase 3 as well as these known from phase 1 (**pl. 4, figs. 26-27**) also occur. Moreover, fragments of different small jars and potsherds belonging to large very deep basins were also found. The local tradition may be manifested by the presence of a few examples of hair-tempered pottery – characteristic especially of the Lower Egyptian phase 1. Probably belonging to local tradition (?) are also potsherds of hole mouth jars[5] – which were found both in phase 1 and even in subsequent phases.

Some kinds of the pottery seem to be similar to the forms known from phase 1, but in our phase 2 there were no attested (until now) potsherds with zig-zag decorations. Apart from this, among the pottery of our transitional phase, are forms which were not known in phase 1 and which are still present in subsequent phases.

At the present state of research we can tentatively suggest that our transitional phase 2 – where both Upper and Lower Egyptian tradition are present – should be placed at the end of Naqada II (probably Naqada IId2 or beginning of IID2).

The transition is echoed also by the architecture of the period: mud-brick constructions, which are considered to be typical of societies in the south of the country, begin to appear alongside buildings that

[3] S. HENDRICKX, *The relative chronology of the Naqada culture: problems and possibilities* (Paper delivered at the British Museum colloquium on "Early Egypt", London, 22nd July 1993), (hereinafter referred to as: *Relative Chronology*), p. 72; J.C. PAYNE, *Catalogue of the Predynastic Egyptian Collection in the Ashmolean Museum*, Oxford 1993, p. 106, No 849, fig. 39, p. 106, No 856, fig. 40; p. 107, Nos 858-860, fig. 40; p. 108, No 869, fig. 43, p. 114, No 932 and No 935, fig. 51; W.M.F. PETRIE, *Corpus of Prehistoric Pottery and Palettes*, London 1921 (hereinafter referred to as: *Prehistoric Pottery*), tabs. XXXIII-XXXIV.

[4] HENDRICKX, *Relative Chronology*, p. 82; W. KAISER, Zur inneren Chronologie der Naqadakultur, *Archaeologia Geographica* 6 (1957), tab. 23; Ch. KÖHLER, *Tell el-Fara 'în – Buto* III, Mainz 1998 (hereinafter referred to as: *Buto* III), pp. 17-18, 112-113, tab. 8; PETRIE, *Prehistoric Pottery*, tabs. XLI-XLIII.

[5] B. ADAMS, R. FRIEDMAN, Imports and Influences in the Predynastic and Protodynastic settlement and Funerary Assemblages at Hierakonpolis, in: E.C.M. van den BRINK (ed.), *The Nile Delta in Transition: 4th-3rd Millenium BC,* Tel Aviv 1992 (hereinafter referred to as: Imports), pp. 324-326, fig. 7; R. FRIEDMAN, The Early Dynastic and Transitional Pottery of Mendes: the 1990 season, in: E.C.M. van den BRINK (ed.), *The Nile Delta in*

can be attributed to northern cultures. Among architectural remnants, a 9.5 m long mud-brick wall situated on the NE-SW axis was discovered. Its northern extent links up with a semicircular construction bordered by a broad band of compacted silt. Another, independent, construction was revealed in strata of phase 2 – immediately beyond the southern end of the previously mentioned wall. Noteworthy are bricks of a characteristic shape, different from the common sort in this that they were flat on one side and convex on the other, resembling the letter "D", in the section. The 4 x 4 m structure is comprised (as it turned out in the lower layers) of three adjacent circles (**pl. 6, fig. 1**). Stacked D-shaped bricks burned through inconsistently, from mud-coloured examples to ones that are red and even entirely black surrounded the edges. It is noteworthy that mud-bricks constitute a significant majority in the lowermost layer, suggesting apparently that the firing was quite accidental. Outside the circles three post-holes were recorded, the posts presumably supporting the roof. Numerous flat pieces of clay, thin and backed with impressions of plants and human fingers coming from the layer of ashes and burnt earth inside the structure, are suggestive of a roof that had been made of organic substances and coated with mud.

Below the burnt earth – in the higher levels of the construction – a layer of D-shaped bricks following different arrangements was uncovered. Finally the next, lower, level yielded conclusive evidence of circles made of the D-shaped bricks and formed the circular elements of the whole structure. A flat brick lay in the centre of each circle. Around these there were a number of brick set into the ground at an angle, intended as a support for the big, relatively narrow-bottomed vats. The difference in brick shapes should also be emphasised. Some are simple (of different lengths) with sections ranging from practically semicircular to trapezoid and even almost triangular. Others, which are also of different length, are flatter and evidently concave at one of the ends, the depression having been made carelessly with finger impressions clearly visible on the sidewalls. The two kinds of bricks can be put together so that the convexities of one fit the concavities of the other. The flat bricks presumably either lay on the ground or were dug into it, and convex ones lying in the depressions stuck out upwards supporting the vat or vessel. Fire was used inside these structures to heat whatever was inside the vats. It was presumably a place for brewing beer. If the conclusion is correct, then what we have here is the oldest known brewery from the Delta of the Nile, the only older one being a brewery found at Hierakonpolis.[6]

Probably some time at the end of this phase starts the earliest stage of the great construction which existed until the beginning of phase 3 and after rebuilding was inhabited until the end of phase 3 (described below).

Phase 3

Phase 3 is characterised by the occurrence of large quantity of Naqada pottery, indicating that the tradition of the south of the country had been adopted at the site. The majority of the pottery found in this phase still belongs to rough ware (R2). Most of the shapes are characteristic of the Upper Egyptian tradition. The shapes include different kinds of roll-rimmed jars[7] which occurred in phase 2 but are now more numerous (**pl. 7, figs. 1-9**). Among the different forms, roll-rimed jars with or without necks or with reinforced rims occur. The associated bases are mostly flat, (**pl. 7, figs. 10-13**) though a few pointed forms were also found. Most of these jars seem to be similar to Upper Egyptian rough ware forms. Some of them may belong to jars with pointed bases – but, though they may occur in phase 3, this form seems to be mostly connected with phase 2. Other forms may be similar to roll-rimmed jars with different flat bases showing affinity to R84 and related groups.[8] These

Transition: 4th-3rd Millenium BC, Tel Aviv 1992 (hereinafter referred to as: Mendes), pp. 200-204, fig. 2:d; fig. 4:d.

[6] J. GELLER, From Prehistory to History: Beer in Egypt, in: R. FRIEDMAN, B. ADAMS (eds.), *The Followers of Horus. Studies Dedicated to M.A. Hoffman,* Oxford 1992, pp. 19-26.

[7] PETRIE, *Prehistoric Pottery*, tabs. XLI-XLIII.

[8] ADAMS, FRIEDMAN, Imports, pp. 324-326, fig. 7; FRIEDMAN, Mendes, pp. 200-204, figs. 2:a-b, 4:a; HENDRICKX, *Relative Chronology*, pp. 34-36, 38, 83-84; KAISER, *Archaeologia Geographica* 6 (1957), pls. 23 and 24; KÖHLER, *Buto* III, pp. 17-18; pp. 112-113; pls. 8-9; PETRIE, *Prehistoric Pottery,* tabs. XLII-XLIII; S. SEIDLMAYER, Keramikgefässe, in: *Statuetten, Gefässe und Geräte, Ägyptische Bildwerke* II. *Liebieghaus-Museum Alter Plastik,* Melsungen 1991, pp. 369, 375, Cat. No 244; pp. 370, 375, Cat. No 245; pp. 370-371, 375, Cat. No 246.

are rather more numerous in phase 3 then in phase 2 or phase 4. Two almost complete examples of large storage oval jars with rounded bottoms and two smaller jars with broken bottoms were also found. In one case the bottom (of one of the smaller jars) was situated inside a small bowl. Among other forms occur: two complete, small pointed jars (**pl. 7, fig. 14**), fragments and complete examples of rough ware small bag-shaped jars similar to R65 and related groups (**pl. 7, fig. 15**), hole mouth jars (**pl. 7, fig. 16**), different kinds of small bowls (**pl. 7, figs. 17-19**) and miniature vessels (**pl. 7, figs. 20-23**) – one of them (with two handles (**pl. 7, fig. 23**)) – is especially interesting and unknown from other archaeological sites of this period. A few potsherds with handles were also found. Among them one example of a ledge handle of Canaanite origin (**pl. 7, fig. 24**) – belonging to fully developed handles which occur at Early Bronze sites in Canaan as well as examples of local wavy handles (**pl. 7, figs. 25-26**) – which seem to belong to earlier forms of this class with protruding two wavy handles. Only a few examples belong to pottery with painted decoration though of unclear decoration pattern.

At the present state of research we can tentatively suggest that phase 3 should be dated to the end of Naqada II and beginning of Naqada III – probably Naqada IId2/IIIa1 – beginning of Naqada IIIa2 (?) or the end of IID2 – beginning of IIIA1 (?).

The most important structure of this phase – though explored only partially – was discovered in 2000. The mud-brick building had at last two occupational phases. To judge by the preserved ceramic evidence, the older stage starts sometime in the end of phase 2 (?) and lasts into phase 3. The later stage is dated to phase 3.

Though the older stage (**pl. 6, fig. 2**) seems to begin at the end of phase 2, due to the subsequent rebuilding of this construction in phase 3 it will be described here. The main wall belonging to the structure of this older stage follows the NE-SW direction. On the south it forms a rectangular corner. The width of the wall here is 1.6 m. During the subsequent stages the main wall became increasingly wide. Moreover, we can see a clear division into smaller compartments. Since the uncovered part obviously constitutes the foundation, a casamate construction may be assumed: relatively thin walls (0.30-0.60 m) forming spaces that were later filled with earth. Within the wall of the subsequent structure of younger date (**pl. 8, fig. 1**), at the junction of the inner and outer part, three round pits were distinguished (1 m in diameter), spaced regularly next to each other. This construction was discovered under two layers, of which the bottom one was undoubtedly a layer of burning with black, occasionally red, burnt-through soil and lighter ashes. On top of this was a layer of steel grey clay. The layer is indubitable proof of the structure having been burnt at some point and then flooded by the waters of the Nile. The wall of this younger structure at the southern extreme ends in a large rounded corner. This structure of younger date and the size that may be termed almost monumental, comprises a wall 2.5 m thick following the NE-SW direction. Since sections of the same wall have been identified in one of the new pits abutting the explored trench on the north-east, it may be said that the structure measured at least 17 m in length and 12 m in width. The wall was actually made of two differently constructed sections. The inside part was erected of yellowish brick with an obviously considerable amount of sand, set in a dark grey mud mortar. The outside face is definitely mud-brick bonded in a light yellowish mortar tempered with sand. Moreover, inside the building there was a much damaged floor of bricks. The interpretation of this complex cannot be fully undertaken at the present level of research. The size of the structure and the thickness of the main wall are noteworthy – apparently the largest Naqadian structure discovered in Egypt so far. As the greater part of this structure is unknown (it will be explored in the following seasons) – it should be considered a preliminary to the present dating – especially of the older stage of this construction. The younger stage of the previously described construction should be considered in connection with another structure discovered further to the east (**pl. 9**). This structure, discovered in 1999, comprises the relict remains of a large rectangular room which was almost 7 m long (identified in the subsequent season in 2000) and had a 50 cm thick wall. Inside this room – among the numerous potsherds – two complete vessels standing in pits lined with thick coatings of mud, small jars (two of them with fish bones) and miniature vessels were found. A structure with rounded corners (1.2 x 1.5 m) abutted the room on the south – it was surrounded with a low brick wall equal in width to the thickness of one length of brick (ca 30 cm). A similar wall surrounded a semicircular space (ca 4.6 x 4 m) adjoining the main wall on the southeast. The continuation of this structure was discovered during the excavation in 2000 to the north of it. It is almost a square space (ca 4.5 x 5 m) with two storage vessels standing inside it (**pl. 8, fig. 2**). Neither had a bottom and they stood, one in a lump of pure clay and the other in a bowl. Different whole vessels were also found. Evidence clearly points to a rather sudden abandonment of the complex.

Phases 4 and 5

The last two phases – 4 and 5 – attested on the Western Kom should be linked with the period of state formation in Egypt. In the pottery material we can observe a continuation from phases 4 to 5 both in fabric as well as in most of the pottery shapes. The majority of the pottery found in our phase 4 to 5 were made of Nile silt. Among the wares we can distinguish rough pottery tempered with medium to coarse sand grains and fine to medium chaff or coarse straw (R1). The number of this ware increases through the strata and it is more numerous in phase 5 then in phase 4. Most of the potsherds of this kind of ware found in phases 4 and 5 belong to thick walled breadmoulds of shallow spherical forms with rounded bases and rounded rim tops (**pls. 10, fig. 1; 11, fig. 1**). Shallow forms, sometimes with flattened base are also present but they occur in less quantity. There are also known examples with flattened rim tops. Rarely occuring are also forms with slightly concave rim tops. Both forms with flat or concave rim tops are less in number then those with rounded tops. Potmarks have been recorded also on the walls of some bread-moulds. They occur mostly inside the vessels (but there are also known examples with potmarks situated outside). Those potmarks consist of vertical, diagonal or crossing lines. Impressed dots also occur. A few specimens are decorated with impressed dots situated at the top of the rims (**pl. 11, fig. 2**).

The second group of rough ware pottery tempered with fine to medium sand and fine to medium straw (R2) (which occurred in previous phases) are still abundant, though less so in phase 5 than in phase 4. Dated mostly to phase 4 are tall tapering vessels without bottoms (**pl. 10, fig. 2**), which were probably narrow and flattened. These vessels were found abandoned in different fireplaces/stoves. Pots were placed on a kind of a saucer. These vessels differ in height. Moreover, fragments of narrow jars with external rims and almost straight or slightly convex sides were found. They were collected mostly in phase 4. The majority of these pottery may be jars with very narrow flattened or irregular bases, as may suggest associated bases types (**pl. 10, figs. 3-5**) found among others in the same strata.[9] Hole mouth jars (**pls. 10, fig. 6; 11, fig. 3**) known from previous phases are still present especially in phase 4. Among bowls are small forms known from previous phases (**pl. 10, figs. 7-8**) as well as new forms – found both in phases 4 and 5 with concave walls and simple rim (**pls. 10, fig. 9; 11, fig. 4**) or slightly thickened external extensions (**pl. 11, fig. 5**)[10] and cups with straight (divergent) sides and simple rims.[11]

Moreover, small rounded jars of pale brown polished pottery with narrow and high neck were found in phase 4.

Strata of phases 4 and 5 also contain different types of fine and mostly red-coated bowls generally made of Nile silt with fine to medium sand and sporadically very fine organic material. Sometimes also coarser inclusions are present. Most of the bowls are red to reddish-brown coated and burnished. Very characteristic are vertically burnished bowls. They are sometimes horizontally burnished outside and vertically inside. Sometimes the upper part of the inner surface just below the rim is also horizontally burnished but the lower part is still vertically burnished. Shapes include mostly simple shallow to medium or deep forms with more or less convex (**pls. 10, fig. 10; 11, fig. 6**) or straight walls and simple rims. Sometimes bowls with a breakdown of the walls in their upper parts (**pls. 10, fig. 11; 11, fig. 7**) occur. Forms with thickened external rim are also present (**pls. 11, fig. 12; 11, fig. 8**).

---

[9] S. HENDRICKX, *Elkab* V. *The Naqada III Cemetery*, Brussel 1994 (hereinafter referred to as: *Elkab* V), p. 211, tab. XXI; IDEM, *Chronology*, p. 75; PETRIE, *Prehistoric Pottery*, tab. XLVI: W.M.F. PETRIE, *Corpus of Proto-Dynastic Pottery*, BSEA LXVI (B), London 1953 (hereinafter referred to as: *Proto-Dynastic Pottery*), tab. X.

[10] W.B. EMERY, *Archaic Egypt*, Harmondsworth 1961, p. 213, fig. 122:26; R. GOPHNA, The Egyptian Pottery of 'En Besor, in: IDEM, *Excavations at 'En Besor*, Tel Aviv 1995 (hereinafter referred to as: Egyptian Pottery), pp. 73-74, fig.1; KÖHLER, *Buto* III, p. 25, pl. 33.

[11] KÖHLER, *Buto* III, p.25, pl. 32.

Fragments of very hard, fine ware pottery made of Nile silt untempered or, with very fine sand inclusions or, in a few examples, made also of marl clay occur in both phases 4 and 5. The surface of this kind of pottery is very well smoothed. In most cases these fragments are connected with different kinds of necked jars (**pls. 10, figs. 13-15; 11, figs. 9-11**).[12] Sometimes fragments of these jars have marks of a turning device on the necks. Potmarks also occur on a few potsherds of this class. These potmarks consist of lines: straight, parallel, perpendicular and/or crossing each other. Sometimes squares, or in one example, a triangle situated inside the square occur. Fragments and a few complete examples of fine ware small drop-shaped vessels were also found among the material of phases 4 and 5.

Among different kinds of decorated potsherds, examples with punctuated decoration occur – both in phases 4 and 5 (**pls. 10, fig. 16; 11, fig. 12**).[13] Examples belonging to jars and bowls, decorated in this way, as well as flat bases were found. Moreover, a few fragments are decorated with impressed (punctated) dots and incised pictures.

Potsherds with painted decoration – belonging to phases 4 and 5 – in most cases have decoration patterns composed of wavy lines and wavy parallel lines in short groups (**pls. 10, fig. 17; 11, fig. 13**).[14]

Moreover a few examples of protruding well-modelled wavy handles probably of Canaanite origin as well as fine ware examples made locally in Egypt were found. Another kind of decoration – found in phases 4 and 5 – is composed of modelled wavy design (band) (**pls. 10, fig. 18; 11, fig. 14**).[15]

In the collected material there are also present several potsherds with cut, lightly impressed or smoothed row of arches/bows on the shoulders (**pls. 10, fig. 19; 11, fig. 15**).[16] Among the potsherds a few examples with thinner walls and modelled, probably double wavy pattern, as well as with probably continuous wavy band were found mostly in strata of phase 4 (**pl. 10, fig. 20**). Other examples with thinner walls from phases 4 and 5 were decorated with slightly impressed patterns (**pls. 10, fig. 21; 11, fig. 16**). Moreover, three – almost complete and well preserved (in the state allowing the reconstruction of the form) – cylindrical jars were found in the layers, which belong to phase 4. More fragments of cylindrical jars, with different impressed or incised decoration patterns were also found both in our phases 4 and 5 (**pls. 10, fig. 22; 11, fig. 17**).

The pottery of phases 4 and 5 found on the Western Kom seems to be characteristic of the period of state formation in Egypt. Tentatively, on the basis of present research, we can suggest that our phase 4 should be dated to Naqada IIIa2 with the end of this phase somewhere during the Naqada IIIb (or IIIA1-IIIB), while our phase 5 should be dated to Naqada IIIb/c1 (or end of IIIB-C1) and it seems that the end of our phase 5 should be placed somewhere during the Ist dynasty – most probably at its beginning or slightly later.

In the strata of phase 4 we discovered two sections of wall running parallel to each other. Both are built of dried mud-brick (yellow in colour). The walls run along the NW-SE axis (1.5 brick thick, 2.5 m long). Moreover, the part of a large house belonging to phase 4 was discovered (**pl. 12**). The main mud-brick wall, about 90 cm thick, stands on the NE-SW axis. A narrower wall (ca 45 cm thick) stands 3.30 m to the east of this wall, running parallel to it. A partition wall stands between them. Stoves were discovered inside the construction as well as to the west of the thick exterior wall. Inside stoves, vessels similar to each other – without bottoms – were positioned, standing on a "saucer" made of pure silt.

Evidence of the youngest, fifth, settlement phase is extremely scant. There is no distinct gap between phase 5 and phase 4. The remnants of dried mud-brick and compacted silt walls were revealed in phase 5. Among the walls that survived in best condition, are those constituting a house with at least two rooms. The longer walls, running NW-SW, are ca 45 cm thick. The thick-

[12] FRIEDMAN, Mendes, fig. 3a; GOPHNA, Egyptian Pottery, pp. 82-85; fig. 8:5, 7; HENDRICKX, *Elkab* V, tabs. XII-XIV; KÖHLER, *Buto* III, pls. 52:12, 53:2-3.

[13] ADAMS, FRIEDMAN, Imports, pp. 323-324; fig. 4:a-d; KÖHLER, *Buto* III, p. 138, pl. 57:3, 4, 6.

[14] HENDRICKX, *Relative Chronology*, pp. 37-38, 71; KAISER, *Archaeologia Geographica* 6 (1957), pl. 24; KÖHLER, *Buto* III, p. 35; pl. 64:1-8; PETRIE, *Prehistoric Pottery*, tab. XXXII:D20, D21; IDEM, *Proto-Dynastic Pottery*, tabs. IX:53f; XXVI:87k, XXVII:91D7, XXIX:94k.

[15] KÖHLER, *Buto* III, pls. 60 and 61; T. von der WAY, Tell el-Fara'in – Buto. 3.Bericht, *MDAIK* 44 (1988), pp. 295-296, fig. 7:1-3.

[16] KÖHLER, *Buto* III, p. 34; pls. 59:6-11, 71:6.

ness of the transverse wall is approximately 50 cm. The uppermost strata yield not only rectangular structural features but also round ones (ca 2.50 m in diameter) in the form of a silt floor surface surrounded by a thin layer of compacted mud (ca 10 cm).

To date only a few potsherds from Western Kom found on the surface or in the surface strata may belong to the later pottery and most of the potsherds of phase 5 seems to be connected rather with the end of the Protodynastic and beginning of the Early Dynastic Period we can tentatively suggest that this phase is the last phase attested on this Kom. But the site Tell el-Farkha was not abandoned. A later habitation area was concentrated on the Central Kom. So the subsequent phases – Early Dynastic – phase 6 and Old Kingdom – phase 7 – were attested in the uppermost strata of the Central Kom, which was also inhabited from the Lower Egyptian phase 1 though, in contrast to the Western Kom, occupation lasted longer.

Dorota Czerwik
Warsaw

Some Aspects of the Civil Law in the Light of the Old Kingdom Tomb Inscriptions

All societies must be regulated by certain principles which obligate every person and every part of the society to behave in a specified way. The activities of a person as an individual or as a member of a community are influenced by the principles obliging that person to make a decision to act or not to act in a certain way. One is able to separate these principles as follows: moral, ethical, cultural, religious, professional, economic.[1] The spontaneous and permanent observance of these principles creates customs which may become Customary laws when accepted by a society as necessary (*opinio necessitatis*) and used invariably for a long time.[2] The evolution of such law is gradual and runs parallel to the development of a society. Usually government sanction is conferred on the principles already existing in a society. Establishing legal rules by a monarch appeared only during later periods. They were coexisting with the Customary law for a long time.[3]

There are three branches of the law: Civil, Administrative, and Criminal. Civil law, which is the topic of the present paper, regulates personal relations and property transactions.[4] The characteristic feature of this law is the autonomy of subjects and absence of the immediate control of government.[5]

Usually, each society at some stage of its political and economic development tends to unify its legal system and create a written base. The legal system in the Old Kingdom of Egypt had no codes defining the Civil law's rules and orders.[6] Although there was no statute law the Egyptians regulated their civil matters by the principles of the Customary law.[7] Civil matters concerned purchases – disposal deed, hire or inheritance.

This raises a vital question. Did Civil law contracts take written or verbal form?[8]

To answer this question in the light of the ancient egyptian law in the Old Kingdom one should take note of the characteristic environment in which the law was created. Ancient Egyptian civilisation differed from other early civilisations. According to DIODOR SICULUS, the Egyptian tradition says that the first ruler and legislator of Egypt – Menes – received the law in his hands from the God Thot.[9] In this case the rules have a divine origin and there was no need to create their written base. Each pharaon was the depositary in the matter of truth and justice by virtue of his divine heritage.[10] Central to the Egyptians' views of kingship was the concept of Maat – referred to as the ideal state of the universe and society – "der Wille des Königs".[11] The king introduced

[1] W. ROZWADOWSKI, *Prawo rzymskie*, Poznań 1992 (hereinafter referred to as: *Prawo rzymskie*), p. 15.

[2] *Ibidem*, p. 34, A. STELMACHOWSKI, *Zarys teorii prawa cywilnego*, Warszawa 1998 (hereinafter referred to as: *Zarys*), p. 311.

[3] *Ibidem*, p. 16.

[4] ROZWADOWSKI, *Prawo rzymskie*, p. 57.

[5] STELMACHOWSKI, *Zarys*, p. 26.

[6] A.I. HARRARI, *Contribution a l'étude de la procedure judiciaire dans l'Ancien Empire égyptien*, Le Caire 1950 (hereinafter referred to as: *Contribution*), pp. 41, 44-45; A. THÉODORIDÈS, A propos de la loi dans l'Egypte pharaonique, in: *Vivre de Maât*, Louven 1995, subsidia I, pp. 45-47, 54-56.

[7] THÉODORIDÈS, Le probleme du droit egyptien ancien, in: *Le droit égyptien ancien. Colloque organisé par l'Institut des Hautes Etudes de Belqique les 18 et 19 mars 1974*, Bruxelles 1974, p. 14.

[8] Even in ancient Rome – a society with a Statute law – the verbal form of contracts in the Civil Law was of the same value as the written one. One can analyse the *emptio-venditio* contracts, *stipulatio* or last wills as verbal contracts. ROZWADOWSKI, *Prawo rzymskie*, pp. 141-142, 148-175, 212-215.

[9] B. MENU, *Recherches sur l'histoire juridique, économique et sociale de l'ancienne Égypte*, Le Caire 1998 (hereinafter referred to as: *Recherches*), p. 272.

[10] D. O'CONNOR, D.P. SILVERMAN, *Ancient Egyptian Kingship*, Leiden, New York, Köln 1995, pp. XIX-XXV; HARRARI, *Contribution*, p. 34.

[11] J. ASSMANN, *Ma'at. Gerechtigkeit und Unsterblichkeit im Alten Ägypten*, München 2001, pp. 53-55.

orders in the world of man in the form of "natural" morality.

In such a society all private initiative must be restricted. The individual has his own place in the state, in a society established to maintain the harmony of the world. All were under controll of the king and his administration system.[12] The pharaoh was the owner of all land but was also able to bestow privilages – land for bilding a house, a place for a tomb, the profits coming from the tomb fundation, or other, mobile things.[13] Moreover, the abillity to freely dispose private property was restricted and the real state of possessions, as N. KANAWATI argues, could be questioned.[14]

Regarding Civil Law in the Old Kingdom great importance is given to the texts concerning the dispositions of private property – during a person's life – the purchase-sale acts,[15] and after their death – their last wills.[16] The present paper focuses on the last of these. For our purposes here these texts should be regulated by some juridical orders, but there exists no written command according to the Succession law in the Old Kingdom. All known texts relating to the inheritance of private persons in those times were located in the tombs. However, their presence in this place, near the autobiography inscriptions, the appeal to the living as well as the prayers underlining their religious, commemorative but not neccesary juridical character. There is also no evidence for the existance of the last wills written on papyrus from the Old Kingdom contrary to the Middle and New Kingdom.[17] In the texts from the Old Kingdom one can find no words which could provide to such supposal. The act of the succession and division of the obligations of heirs was introduced in the tomb inscription by the words *wḏt-mdw*[18] – "a command", "das an Worten Befohlene (zu Befehlende)", "das was Worte befehlen",[19] which evidently refers to the oral disposition. It is used in the sentence:

a) *ir.f wḏt-mdw* – "he made a command" (Nikaure,[20] Wpemneferet,[21] Nikaankh I,[22] Nebkauhor[23])

b) *wḏt-mdw irt n* – "a command made by" (Nikaankh II,[24] Kaemneferet[25])

c) *imy wḏt* – "contents of a command" (Meten[26]).

The word understood as a last will, *imyt-pr*,[27] cannot be perceived as a document. Many scholars define *imyt-pr* differently, namely as a testament,[28] not as a document, but rather as a donation, as

[12] J. BAINES, *Kingship, Definition of Culture and Legitimation*, in: O'CONNOR, SILVERMAN, *Ancient Egyptian Kingship*, Leiden, New York, Köln 1995, p. 6.

[13] H.K. JACQUET-GORDON, *Les noms des domaines funéraires sous l'Ancien Empire égyptien*, Le Caire 1962, pp. 7-9, 14; HARARI, La fondation cultuelle de N.k. wi. ankh à Tehneh, *ASAE* 54 (1957), pp. 317-318.

[14] N. KANAWATI, *The Egyptian Administration in the Old Kingdom*, Westminster 1977, p. 72.

[15] P. POSENER-KRIÉGER, Le prix des étoffes, in: *Festschrift E. Edel*, Bamberg 1979, pp. 318-331; T. MRSICH, *Untersuchungen zur Hausurkunde des Alten Reiches. Ein Beitrag zum altägyptischen Stiftungsrecht*, MÄS 13, Berlin 1968 (hereinafter referred to as: *Untersuchungen*); THÉODORIDÈS, L'Acte (?) de vente d'Ancien Empire (26e s. av. J.-C.), in: *Vivre de Maât*, Louven 1995, pp. 717-771; MENU, *Recherches*, pp. 271-287.

[16] H. GOEDICKE, *Die privaten Rechtsinschriften aus dem Alten Reich*, Wien 1970 (hereinafter referred to as: *Privaten Rechtsinschriften*); THÉODORIDÈS, Le testament dans l'Égypte ancienne, in: *Vivre de Maât*, subsidia II, Louven 1995 (hereinafter referred to as: Testament), pp. 409-506; IDEM, Du rapport entre un contrat et un acte disposition appelé "imyt-pr" en égyptien, in: *Vivre de Maât*, subsidia I, Louven 1995 (hereinafter referred to as: Rapport), pp. 369-400; K. GOEDECKEN, *Eine Betrachtung der Inschriften des Meten in Rahmen der sozialen und rechtlichen Stellung von privatleuten in ägyptischen Alten Reich*, ÄA 19, Wiesbaden 1976; MENU, *Recherches*, pp. 271-294.

[17] In the later time such documents were collected in the archives, see THÉODORIDÈS, Rapport, pp. 386-394; IDEM, Testament, pp. 483-496.

[18] *Wb* I, p. 396, 9-10.

[19] MRSICH, *Untersuchungen*, p. 71, footnote 507.

[20] *Urk.* I, p. 16, 15.

[21] GOEDICKE, *Privaten Rechtsinschriften*, p. 31, pl. III.

[22] *Urk.* I, p. 24, 15.

[23] GOEDICKE, *Privaten Rechtsinschriften*, p. 83, pl. IX.

[24] *Urk.* I, p. 162, 2.

[25] *Ibidem*, p. 11, 5.

[26] *Ibidem*, p. 4, 3.

[27] *Wb* I, p. 73; literally "das was im Haus ist", "das worin das Haus ist", "das was dem Haus gleichkommt" – see: MRSICH, *Untersuchungen*, p. 31-35; E. EDEL, *Altägyptische Grammatik*, Ann Or 34, Roma 1955 (hereinafter referred to as: *AäG*), §§ 369, 370.

[28] J. PIRENNE, *Histoire des institutions et du droit privé de l'Ancienne Égypte* II, Bruxelles 1935 (hereinafter referred to as: *Histoire des institutions*), pp. 301-304; GOEDICKE,

G.P.F. van den BOORN states: "integral transfer of an office and its assets".[29]

In the Old Kingdom inscriptions it is used in the sentence:

a) *m rdit irt.n(.i) n.f m imyt-pr* – "in order to give that what was done for him by me as[30] *imyt-pr*" (Nikaankh II[31])

b) *m rdit m imyt pr* – "in order to give as *imyt-pr*" (Kaemneferet,[32] Senenuankh,[33] an inscription from Lisht[34])

c) *rdiw.n(.i) n.sn (...) m imyt-pr* – "I gave them (...) as *imyt-pr* (Nikaankh I[35])

d) *rdiw n(.i) in it.i pn m imyt-pr* – "were given me by my father as *imyt-pr*" (Pepi[36])

e) *ir.s imyt-pr im n* – "she makes there (of that?) *imyt-pr* for" (Meten[37])

There is no doubts that those words define a command of the deceased reffering to the administration of his property. I think that the meaning of *imyt-pr* is close to *wḏt-mdw*, but limited to the legacy cases. In the inscription of Nebkauhor these two sentences are given in the same line, paralelly, introduced by the verb *iry*.[38]

We have some texts which may allow us to think that the command of succession was the oral disposition. There are two letters to the dead dated to the end of the Old Kingdom in which are found the appellations to the last wills of the deceased. In both texts the last will is perceived as an oral disposition. It is in the text on linen from Cairo[39] where a widow reminds the deceased of the moment when he made an oral disposition that was not executed. Seankhenptah – the addressee of the letter made the succession command laying in bed – probably beceause of illness. The oral disposition was made in the presence of a witness, who – in efect – was not acquitted of this. In this case the widow asks him for help to fulfil his own will.[40]

In the other letter to the dead written on a bowl from Kaw el-Kebir[41] one can also find direct oral commands of succession. In the seventh line of the text there is a quotation from the deceased: *sk ḏd.n.k n s3.k im mn išt nb m s3 špsi* – "you said to this thy son:[42] all my property is vested in my son Shepsi".[43]

If there were a written document, an act regulating inheritance, people should mention this, should refer to it. There is no indications which allow us to suppose that such a document existed. These letters allow one to conclude that the last will could have been ordered as an oral disposition.

The entire inscription from the Old Kingdom concerning the last will or the disposal deed was introduced by the words *imyt-pr* or (and) *wḏt-mdw*. They both refer to the verbal disposition. There is no papyrus document with such a decree. The texts where the testament was mentioned perceived it as an oral act.[44] There is nothing which could point to its written form. The word *sš* – "a writing", "a docu-

---

Privaten Rechtsinschriften, p. 204; MRSICH, *Untersuchungen*, pp. 137-142; B. GRDSELOFF, Deux inscriptions juridiques de l'ancien empire, *ASAE* 42 (1943), p. 33; A. SCHARFF, E. SEIDL, *Einführung in die Ägyptische Rechtsgeschichte bis zum Ende des Neuen Reiches.* I. Juristischer Teil, ÄF 10, München 1939, p. 58; Translation *imyt-pr* as a testament is common relating to documents coming from the later time than the Old Kingdom, see: THÉODORIDÈS, Testament, pp. 413-416.

[29] THÉODORIDÈS, Rapport, p. 395.

[30] On the issue of "*m* of predication" see: EDEL, *AäG*, § 758; A.H. GARDINER, *Egyptian Grammar*, Oxford 1994, § 116-117; § 162,2; § 200.

[31] *Urk.* I, p. 162, 8.

[32] *Ibidem*, p. 12, 9.

[33] *Ibidem*, p. 36, 9.

[34] GOEDICKE, *Privaten Rechtsinschriften*, pp. 113-118, pl. IX.

[35] *Urk.* I, p. 31.

[36] *Ibidem*, p. 35, 11-12; EDEL, *AäG*, § 646.

[37] *Urk.* I, p. 2, 10.

[38] GOEDICKE, *Privaten Rechtsinschriften*, p. 98, pl. VIb.

[39] GARDINER, K. SETHE, *Letters to the Dead*, London 1928 (hereinafter referred to as: *Letters*), pp. 1-3, 13-16.

[40] PIRENNE, *Histoire des institutions* III, pp. 366-368.

[41] GARDINER, SETHE, *Letters*, pp. 3-5, 17-18;

[42] Compare: P.C. SMITHER, An Old Kingdom Letter concerning the Crimes of Count Sabni, *JEA* 28 (1942), p. 18.

[43] The author's unpublished MA thesis written with the scientific help of Professor Karol MYŚLIWIEC: D. CZERWIK, *Listy do zmarłych jako efekt przemian społeczno-gospodarczych i religijnych okresu końca Starego Państwa i I Okresu Przejściowego*, Warszawa 1999, pp. 43-45.

[44] THÉODORIDÈS, *Rapport*, p. 374; However we know from the Old Kingdom some papyrus document of the Civil

ment"[45] or the verb *sš* – "to write"[46] were not used by the authors of these texts.[47]

In the light of the fact that there is evidence of the papyrus documents from later times,[48] one can consider the way in which Customary law evolved. The first level of development of the Customary law is always the custom itself. The custom is a spontaneous, standardised permanent process – accepted by a society as necessary and used invariably over a long period.[49] There was no need to codify such a law as its rules grew from the principles accepted by society. There was also no need to write the orders of the testaments since the verbal dispositions had a legal force. The oral command was executed when the inheritance conformed to the Customary law. It is probable that the written form was used in the case of a threat not to fulfil the command (?).[50] Nevertheless, it is interesting why in the Old Kingdom people located them among the tomb inscriptions instead on papyrus. Did they have legal or only commemorative character?

It should be believed that the Egyptians wanted to guarantee the execution of their last wills and inserting them in the tomb was the best solution. A place near the autobiography inscriptions, the appeal to the living as well as prayers underline their religious, commemorative character. The tomb was a place where the sphere of *profanum* was connected with the sphere of *sacrum*. It was a place of conntact with the deceased, with an Afterlifes and also with the gods who could secure the execution of the testament and the obligations of the inheritors.[51]

In terms of legislation, there remains the question of whether the Egyptians themselves were conscious of the Civil law or acted in conformity with the principles they perceived on a religious level – as living in accordance with Maat?

law character: the contracts related to purchase of the house, cf. footnote 15 above.

45 *Wb* III, pp. 476-477.

46 *Ibidem*, p. 475.

47 The word *sš* is used in the spell 305 of The Pyramid Texts was understood by S.A.B. MERCER as a testament, see: S.A.B. MERCER, *The Pyramid Texts in Translation and Commentary* II, New York 1952, p. 223. However, it concerns the heritage of a king.

48 THÉODORIDÈS, Rapport, pp. 386-394; IDEM, Testament, pp. 483-496.

49 STELMACHOWSKI, *Zarys*, p. 311.

50 In a situation when the deceased wanted to disinherit a child or distinguish him or a wife, to create a donation with a trustee, to establish a division of his ancestors – without an act of transfer, to create a foundation. Compare evidence from later times: THÉODORIDÈS, Rapport, pp. 469-471.

51 Later it was the royal administration which assured the execution of the last wills, cf. footnote 48 above.

Eva-Maria Engel
Münster

Tombs of the Ist Dynasty at Abydos and Saqqara: Different Types or Variations on a Theme?*

1. Introduction

In 1937 Walter B. EMERY excavated tomb S 3357 at Saqqara-North. He identified it as the tomb of the first ruler of the Ist dynasty, King Aha, and proposed that all kings of that dynasty had been buried at this site. Since the tombs of these rulers had only 40 years previously been located at Umm el-Qa'ab / Abydos by PETRIE, EMERY's publication triggered a debate on the burial place of the first pharaohs of Egypt which has not ended yet.

At Umm el-Qa'ab, Émile AMÉLINEAU and William M.F. PETRIE had, at the turn of the century, excavated ten mud-brick structures. Inscribed stelae and other finds helped to attribute the buildings to the seven kings and one queen of the Ist dynasty and two to kings of the IInd dynasty. Nothing was preserved of the superstructures, while the substructures which were built from mud-brick in huge pits sunk in the sandy desert ground remained more or less intact.

At Saqqara, EMERY uncovered over the years more than 20 impressive mud-brick mastabas with elaborate niches on all sides. The superstructures were not always well preserved but could be determined in one case (S 3507) as being at least 2.5 m high.[1] The substructures, on the other hand, were sunk into the local limestone. They are composed of parts cut out of the limestone and additions in mud-brick. The tombs were attributed to different owners again with the aid of inscribed material, in these cases mostly seal impressions and inscribed stone vessels. But EMERY had to face the problem that on one hand he had far too many burials for the kings of the Ist dynasty and on the other hand that no burial could be attributed to King Semerkhet. Therefore, he explained that the largest tombs had to be those of the kings, while the smaller ones were those of queens and other members of the royal family or important members of the court and that the missing tomb had not been discovered yet.

Other Egyptologists followed in giving explanations for the archaeological findings at both sites. The main hypotheses were the following:

1. Pro Abydos, contra Saqqara
The kings were buried at Umm el-Qa'ab, officials and members of the royal family at Saqqara and other places.[2]

2. Pro Saqqara and Abydos
The kings were buried at Saqqara, the buildings at Umm el-Qa'ab are cenotaphs.[3] The additional mastabas at Saqqara are the second and the third tombs of the kings or belong to the queens.[4]

3. Pro Abydos and Saqqara
The kings were buried at Umm el-Qa'ab, the mastabas at Saqqara are cenotaphs.[5]

* I would like to thank Günter DREYER and Jochem KAHL for many helpful discussions in preparing this paper and Jana JONES for correcting my English.

[1] W.B. EMERY, *Great Tombs of the First Dynasty* III, *Excavations at Saqqara*, London 1958 (hereinafter referred to as: *Great Tombs* III), p. 76.

[2] E.g. EMERY, *Great Tombs of the First Dynasty* II, *Excavations at Saqqara*, Oxford 1954 (hereinafter referred to as: *Great Tombs* II), pp. 1-4; B.J. KEMP, The Egyptian 1st Dynasty Royal Cemetery, *Antiquity* 41 (1967), p. 23.

[3] H. RICKE, *Bemerkungen zur ägyptischen Baukunst des Alten Reichs* II, BeiträgeBf 5, Kairo 1950 (hereinafter referred to as: *Bemerkungen* II), p. 13.

[4] E.g. EMERY, *Great Tombs* II, pp. 1-4.

[5] H.W. MÜLLER, *Gedanken zur Entstehung, Interpretation und Rekonstruktion ältester ägyptischer Monumentalarchitektur*, in: *Ägypten – Dauer und Wandel*, SDAIK 18, Mainz 1985, pp. 7ff.; D. ARNOLD, *Lexikon der ägyptischen Baukunst*, Düsseldorf, Zürich [2]1997 (hereinafter referred to as: *Lexikon*), p. 220 (s.f. Saqqara): "Wohl eher Gräber hoher Beamter, einige bestenfalls königliche Kenotaphe."; R. GUNDLACH, *Der Pharao und sein Staat. Die Grundlegung der ägyptischen Königsideologie im 4. und 3. Jahrtausend*, Darmstadt 1998 (hereinafter referred to as: *Pharao und sein Staat*), p. 121: "Ich vermute nun, daß die Zweiteilung des Grabbezirks in Körpergrab und Statuengrab,

4. Abydos and Saqqara
The Kings were buried at Umm el-Qa'ab or Saqqara depending on the place they died.[6]

Each of the mentioned hypotheses found its proponents and opponents. There are contrasting statements on the relation between both sites as, for instance, the following by Walter B. EMERY, who, in his later publications, modified his view of the two types to a certain extent: "In the south at Abydos, the superstructures of the royal tombs or cenotaphs were certainly entirely different in design from their counterparts in the north.... However, the substructures of the Abydos monuments in general conform to the same line of evolution as at Sakkara."[7] While he hints at similarities between both sites concerning the substructures, other authors emphasise the differences, for instance, Dieter ARNOLD: "Die Entwicklung der Abydos-Gräber verläuft anders als die der Saqqara-Gräber; sie beginnt und endet früher als dort."[8] or Rainer STADELMANN: "Dieser offensichtliche Mangel einer Entwicklung [of the Abydos tombs] und einer Entfaltung über fast zwei Jahrhunderte in einer an sich so dynamischen Zeit wirkt in der Tat erstaunlich und deutet doch vielleicht schon auf ein provinzielles Stagnieren und auf eine spürbare Distanz von dem Zentrum künstlerischer und geistiger Aktivität hin."[9] or Toby A.H. WILKINSON: "Unlike the contemporary mastabas at North Saqqara which emphasised the superstructure, the Ist dynasty royal tombs at Abydos seem to have concentrated on the subterranean element. During the early Ist dynasty the burial chamber was dug progressively deeper, culminating with the tomb of Den in which the burial chamber is 6 metres below ground level."[10]

Although they disagreed on many details, most participants in the debate agreed on two basic principles:

– the attempt to relate the size of the tomb to the proposed status of the owner. This argument was first used to suggest that Saqqara was the burial place since the tombs at that site are larger than those at Abydos. Later, after KAISER[11] and KEMP[12] had independently shown that the 'Talbezirke' at Kom el-Sultan belong to the royal burials at Umm el-Qa'ab and that, therefore, the labour input to construct those tombs was much larger than at Saqqara, the same argument was used in favour of Abydos.

– the assumption of two different types of tombs connected with the two parts of Egypt and/or two different population groups.[13] The criteria by which the two types were differentiated are summarised in **table 1**. They consist of quantitative (i.e. the depth of the burial chamber) as well as of qualitative criteria (i.e. the presence/absence of certain features). Surprisingly, even scholars who noticed similarities between tombs at both sites never questioned the validity of this principle.[14]

wie sie im Djoserbezirk gegeben ist, auch bei der Doppelung Abydos – Saqqara in der 1. Dynastie vorliegt. Das würde bedeuten, daß wir in den königlichen Gräbern in Saqqara von der Existenz von Königsstatuen ausgehen müssen, die dort die königliche Präsenz bewirkten."

[6] J.-P. LAUER, Sur le dualisme de la monarchie égyptienne et son expression architecturale sous les première dynasties, *BIFAO* LV (1955), p. 159; ARNOLD, E. HORNUNG, Königsgräber, *LÄ* III, p. 512, footnote 5; R. STADELMANN, *Die ägyptischen Pyramiden*, Mainz ³1997 (hereinafter referred to as: *Pyramiden*), p. 11.

[7] EMERY, *Archaic Egypt*, Harmondsworth 1961 (hereinafter referred to as: *Archaic Egypt*), p. 130.

[8] ARNOLD, *Lexikon*, p. 12 (s.f. Abydos).

[9] STADELMANN, *Pyramiden*, p. 12.

[10] T.A.H. WILKINSON, *Early Dynastic Egypt*, London, New York 1999 (hereinafter referred to as: *Early Dynastic Egypt*), p. 233. In this, he followed W. KAISER, Zur Entwicklung des abydenischen Königsgrabes, in: KAISER, G. DREYER, Umm el-Qaab. Nachuntersuchungen im frühzeitlichen Königsfriedhof, 2. Vorbericht, *MDAIK* 38 (1982), p. 256.

[11] KAISER, Zu den königlichen Talbezirken der 1. und 2. Dynastie in Abydos und zur Baugeschichte des Djoser-Grabmals, *MDAIK* 25 (1969) (*Gedenkschrift Stock*), pp. 1ff.

[12] KEMP, Abydos and the Royal Tombs of the First Dynasty, *JEA* 52 (1966), pp. 13-22.

[13] RICKE, *Bemerkungen zur ägyptischen Baukunst des Alten Reichs* I, BeiträgeBf 4, Zürich 1944, p. 40; IDEM, *Bemerkungen* II, pp. 18-19.

[14] EMERY, *Great Tombs of the First Dynasty* I, Cairo 1949 (hereinafter referred to as: *Great Tombs* I), p. 12, IDEM, *Great Tombs* III, p. 5 and KAISER, in: KAISER, DREYER, *MDAIK* 38 (1982), p. 251 on the similarities between S X and S 3338 on one hand with the tomb of Qa'a at Umm el-Qa'ab on the other; W. WOOD, The Archaic Stone Tombs at Helwan, *JEA* 73 (1987), pp. 59ff. compares the tombs at Umm el-Qa'ab with private burials at Helwan; G.A. REISNER, *The Development of the Egyptian Tomb*

2. The Tomb of Qa'a[15]

In 1991/92 the German Institute of Archaeology in Cairo re-examined the tomb of King Qa'a at Umm el-Qa'ab. In contrast to PETRIE's excavation, who, due to his excavation technique, had seen only parts of the tomb at one time, the structure as a whole was cleared. This proved that it had been built in several phases. The original layout consisted only of the burial chamber with a staircase descending from the north and two chambers, one on each side of the stair which were accessible from the staircase. 14 smaller chambers surrounded the burial chamber on its eastern, southern and western sides. In several subsequal phases, the building was expanded until, in the last phase, there were six magazines along the stair, five large magazines and 26 smaller chambers which were used for burials or also as magazines.[16]

The first phase, therefore, resembles the subterranean part of a certain "type" of tomb which can be found at Saqqara and other sites (e.g. Helwan). It is composed of burial chamber, staircase and two chambers accessible from the staircase (S 3505,[17] 3500,[18] 3338,[19] X[20]).

On the other hand, by expanding the tomb of Qa'a during the later building phases, its central part resembled more and more the tombs of the IInd dynasty at Saqqara and Umm el-Qa'ab. Their main characteristic is the presence of long corridors from which several chambers branch off. But if there are similarities in the subterranean part between the proposed different tomb types at both sites during the reign of one king, there might be similarities during the other reigns as well. By comparing the ground plans of the tombs, several resemblances can indeed be identified.

3. Comparison of Groundplan of the Subterranean Parts

The first buildings at both sites, for instance, consist of several large chambers built in a row: The tomb of King Aha at Abydos in Cemetery B[21] and the tombs S 3357,[22] 3503[23] and 3471[24] follow this scheme.

The next stage consists of tombs with a central burial chamber with smaller magazines first on three, later on four sides. Examples are the tombs of Djer,[25] Wadj and Meretneith[26] at Umm el-Qa'ab as well as S 3504[27] and 3111[28] at Saqqara.

During the next stage, a staircase gives direct access to the burial chamber at one of its smaller sides. Examples are the tomb of Den[29] at Abydos and tomb S 3036,[30] which, on the other hand, still resembles the tomb of Meretneith at Umm el-Qa'ab in the arrangement of its burial chamber and surrounding magazines.

Later, the staircase ends next to one corner at one of the longer sides of the burial chamber. The magazines are placed at the smaller sides. Examples are the tombs of Adjib[31] and Semerkhet[32] at Umm el-Qa'ab and S 3038[33] at Saqqara. The earlier tombs S 3035,[34] 3507[35] and 3506[36] might be intermediary stages between the last and this type.

Down to the Accession of Cheops, Cambridge 1936 (hereinafter referred to as: *Development of Egyptian Tomb*), pp. 336-337 considers the tombs of Semerkhet and Qa'a at Umm el-Qa'ab to be the forerunners of private tombs of the IInd dynasty; on the similarities between tombs of the IInd dynasty at both sites: STADELMANN, *Die Oberbauten der Königsgräber der 2. Dynastie in Sakkara*, in: *Mélanges Gamal Eddin Mokhtar*, BdÉ XCVII/2, Le Caire 1985, pp. 298-299.

[15] In order to identify this – and the other tombs at Umm el-Qa'ab – as the royal burial place see below 5.

[16] E.-M. ENGEL, Grabkomplex des Qa'a, in: DREYER, ENGEL, U. HARTUNG, T. HIKADE, E.Ch. KÖHLER, F. PUMPENMEIER, Umm el-Qaab. Nachuntersuchungen im frühzeitlichen Königsfriedhof. 7./8. Vorbericht, *MDAIK* 52 (1996), pp. 57ff.

[17] EMERY, *Great Tombs* III, pl. 4.

[18] *Ibidem*, pl. 114.

[19] EMERY, *Great Tombs* I, pl. 55.

[20] *Ibidem*, pl. 43.

[21] W.M.F. PETRIE, *Royal Tombs of the Earliest Dynasties* II, *MEEF* 21, London 1901 (hereinafter referred to as: *Royal Tombs* II), pl. LIX.

[22] EMERY, *Hor-Aha, Excavations at Saqqara*, Cairo 1939 (hereinafter referred to as: *Hor-Aha*), pl. 1.

[23] IDEM, *Great Tombs* II, pl. XXXVIII.

[24] IDEM, *Great Tombs* I, pl. 2.

[25] PETRIE, *Royal Tombs* II, pl. LX.

[26] IDEM, *Royal Tombs of the First Dynasty* I, *MEEF* 18, London 1900 (hereinafter referred to as: *Royal Tombs* I), pl. LXI.

[27] EMERY, *Great Tombs* II, pl. II.

[28] IDEM, *Great Tombs* I, pl. 36.

[29] PETRIE, *Royal Tombs* II, pl. LXII.

[30] IDEM, *Great Tombs* I, pl. 14.

[31] PETRIE, *Royal Tombs* I, pl. LXI.

[32] *Ibidem*, pl. LX.

[33] EMERY, *Great Tombs* I, pl. 25.

[34] IDEM, *The Tomb of Hemaka, Excavations at Saqqara*, Cairo 1938 (hereinafter referred to as: *Hemaka*), pl. 1.

[35] IDEM, *Great Tombs* III, pl. 85.

[36] *Ibidem*, pl. 40.

S 3506 especially resembles the layout of tomb T at Abydos: Although the stair ends on the smaller side of the burial chamber in the tomb of Den and on a longer one in S 3506, in both cases the burial chambers are surrounded by smaller rooms on a higher level, which are set further away in the case of Den, but close to the burial chamber in case of S 3506. The row of magazines continues over the main stair, a rather unique feature. Both tombs also have a second stair on the wall opposite the main staircase. For the tomb of Den, this was interpreted as leading to an annex that contained a statue of the king, of which a limestone base was found.[37]

Finally, as seen in the tomb of Qa'a and others at Saqqara, the staircase again ends at one of the small sides of the burial chamber.

Most of the architectural differences can be explained by the different types of underground at each site. The local limestone at Saqqara which is covered by a layer of gravel[38] requires different treatment than the sandy desert floor at Umm el-Qa'ab. While at Saqqara many architectural features were cut out of the rock with only additional partitioning walls and the superstructure built of mud-brick, at Abydos every part of the tomb had to be built of mud-brick since the sandy ground did not, for instance, support the weight of large wooden beams with which the roofs were constructed.

The previous sorting of Ist dynasty tombs depended solely on architectural criteria. But as the example of the tomb of Qa'a has shown, where only the re-excavation proved the modification of the layout, probably some more tombs were built in different stages. A similar change took place in the tombs of King Aha[39] and King Khasekhemui[40] at Umm el-Qa'ab which were also recently re-examined. Nothing can be said at present about the others. In Saqqara, on the other hand, Emery observed different building phases only for the tombs S 3506[41] and S 3038,[42] but it seems likely that others were also subjected to changes during the building process.

The preceeding points to two different problems:

1. While the sequence of burials at Umm el-Qa'ab is established, not all of the tombs at Saqqara can securely be dated to the reign of one king, and, unfortunately, the state of publications does not permit one to order the tombs from a reign of a single king in a single sequence.[43] Additionally, the finds only give a terminus *ante quem*: the sequence they are sorted according to their funerary equipment might not be the same as the sequence they were built, since some of the structures might have begun decades before the burial took place. In some cases, however, the time span between the introduction of a variant in which a tomb was built and the burial seems to be too large so that one can assume that once a tomb variant was developed it was in use for a longer period.

2. An "ideal" burial layout probably did not exist.[44] Each tomb consists of different elements (burial chamber, magazines, superstructure, sometimes subsidiary graves, etc) which could be combined in different ways. Different factors determined the actual choice of arrangement, including technical possibilities, finances and status reasons of the tomb owner's, as well as the preference of a certain variant at different periods.

4. The Size of the Tombs

The tomb types were also differentiated by several quantitative criteria. On one hand, the size of the

[37] DREYER, Umm el-Qaab. Nachuntersuchungen im frühzeitlichen Königsfriedhof. 3./4. Vorbericht, *MDAIK* 46 (1990), pp. 76-78.

[38] REISNER, *Development of Egyptian Tomb*, p. 122.

[39] DREYER, *MDAIK* 46 (1990), p. 63.

[40] IDEM, Grab des Chasechemui, in: DREYER, A. von den DRIESCH, ENGEL, R. HARTMANN, HARTUNG, HIKADE, V. MÜLLER, J. PETERS, Umm el-Qaab. Nachuntersuchungen im frühzeitlichen Königsfriedhof. 11./12. Vorbericht, *MDAIK* 56 (2000), p. 124.

[41] EMERY, *Great Tombs* III, pp. 39-40.

[42] IDEM, *Great Tombs* I, pp. 82-83.

[43] In some cases, the sealings seem to indicate a sequence of the burials, as suggested by P. KAPLONY, *Die Inschriften der ägyptischen Frühzeit* I, ÄA 8, Wiesbaden 1963, p. 107 for the reign of King Den: "Aus den Mustern und Belegzahlen der zwei- und einzeiligen Domänensiegel lässt sich die Reihenfolge der vier grossen Gräber der Dwn-Zeit: Sakkara 3504, Mrjt-Nt-Grab in Abydos, Sakkara 3506 und Königsgrab in Abydos, welches naturgemäss das letzte der Regierung ist, mit Sicherheit bestimmen."

[44] The variation in tomb equipment points to the same conclusion.

tombs themselves: it was generally stated that the tombs at Saqqara were much larger than those at Umm el-Qa'ab, and, therefore, the probable place of the royal burial as illustrated by the following quote from WILKINSON: "The impressive size and architecture of the North Saqqara tombs led scholars to question the identification of the smaller tombs on the Umm el-Qaab."[45]

But is there really a measurable difference between the tombs at both sites?

Table 2 shows the size of the burial chamber in square metres. The burial chamber of the tomb of Aha at Umm el-Qa'ab, for instance, is, with more than 40 m², much larger than those of the contemporary tomb at Saqqara, with about 10 m², or the slightly later ones with 8.8-25 m². The same can be said for the reign of Den with the exception of S 3506, which nearly reaches the size of the royal burial chamber. It also shows that during the reign of that king burial chambers are larger than during other periods. In general, the burial chambers at Umm el-Qa'ab seem to be larger than those at Saqqara.

How, then, did the generally accepted image of large tombs at Saqqara and their smaller counterparts at Abydos occur? This idea is probably the result of the differential preservation: While only the subterranean parts are preserved at Umm el-Qa'ab, at Saqqara the extensions of the superstructure were measured. Therefore, the underground parts of the tombs without adding the subsidiary graves at Umm el-Qa'ab were compared to the above ground parts at Saqqara.[46]

The other differentiation was the depth of the tombs. Those at Umm el-Qa'ab were considered to be deep, while those at Saqqara were taken to be rather shallow. This seemed to fit into the assumed origin of the Lower Egyptian type from the Delta, since the geological conditions in the Delta did not seem to permit the building of deep graves to prevent the flooding of the burials during inundation.[47]

But the mapping of the relevant data – the floor level of the burial chamber under the surrounding surface – shows a different picture: The equation *Abydos = deep* versus *Saqqara = shallow* only works for the time of King Aha. During all the other reigns, there seems to be no tendency for the Saqqara tombs to remain shallow. On the contrary, the tomb S 3035 of Hemaka, at 8.4 m, and S 3036, at 6.5 m, both built during the reign of Den, are rather deep.

Two tendencies can be observed: During certain reigns, e.g. that of Den, deep burials were built at both sites. **Table 3** maps the depth of the burial chamber and the thickness of gravel at Saqqara. It indicates that there is a relation between both data: Rather deep tombs were built in areas in which the layer of gravel covering the limestone was rather thick so that less limestone had to be chiseled away to reach the intended depth. This correlation is rather clear until the reign of Den. After his reign, burials at Saqqara shifted to the second row behind the older ones – the favourable locations overlooking the Nile Valley had already been taken.

5. Conclusion

As we have seen, there are more similarities or at least less discrepancies between the tombs at both sites than suggested by the prevailing scheme of two different tomb types. Is it, then, justified to talk about two different types when dealing with the graves from both sites?

Unfortunately, not many archaeologists define what they consider to be a type and why. One of the few is Dorothea ARNOLD who differentiated types of pottery when the vessels were distinguished by at least three attributes[48].

According to W.Y. ADAMS and E.W. ADAMS, "types are differentiated from each other by the possession of unique attribute clusters. The attribute cluster which serves to define any type must have three characteristics: statistical significance, variability of association, and meaningfulness for the purposes of the typology."[49] They also state that "typologies are developed with reference to a specific purpose or purposes, and it is these purposes that give meaning to the individual types in the system. Archaeological typologies can legitimately serve many different pur-

[45] WILKINSON, *Early Dynastic Egypt*, p. 259.

[46] E.g. the representation by KAISER, in: KAISER, DREYER, *MDAIK* 38 (1982), fig. 13.

[47] But see, for instance, the burials at Minshat Abu Omar: K. KROEPER, D. WILDUNG, *Minshat Abu Omar* I, *Gräber 1-114*, Mainz 1994.

[48] Do. ARNOLD, Keramikbearbeitung in Dahschur 1976-1981, *MDAIK* 38 (1982), pp. 44, 47-48.

[49] W.Y. ADAMS, E.W. ADAMS, *Archaeological typology and practical reality. A dialectical approach to artifact classification and sorting*, Cambridge 1991, p. 241.

poses, and these will affect the way in which types are formulated and used."[50]

But what, then, was the purpose of the typology in case of the burials of the Ist dynasty? The only context in which this typology was ever used was the search for the burial place of the kings of that dynasty. This question also determined the choice of attributes as, for instance, the interpretation of the meaning of the accompanying boat burials which were taken to be a royal attribute by some, while others pointed to contemporary burials at other cemeteries which also featured boat burials and were never seen as being royal.

But the layout of the substructures of both "types" resembles each other very closely, as do the sizes and depths of the tombs. These attributes, therefore, can hardly be used to differentiate two types. As **table 1** has shown, there were other criteria used by one or the other author to support his view regarding the location of the royal tombs:

– The mound underneath one of the Saqqara mastabas (S 3038), once taken to be an architectural forerunner of the later pyramids, equals subterranean tumuli in several of the Abydos tombs.[51] It seems to be an element of many tombs of the Ist dynasty and cannot be taken as a distinction between the two types.

– A wooden shrine or lining of the burial chamber was a feature not only of the tombs at Umm el-Qa'ab, but also of many Saqqara mastabas.

– Another argument used to prove that the kings were buried at Saqqara was the presence of a temple to the north of S 3505 that is seen as the "Prototyp der späteren Pyramidenbezirke".[52] But Peter JÁNOSI points out that it is a vicious circle to identify S 3505 as a royal tomb only because of the presence of the temple.[53]

– The same holds true for the presence of boats which were first only seen in connection with the Saqqara mastabas. Other boats were found close to private tombs at Helwan and Abusir, and in 1991 also at the so-called Shuna el-Zebib, the 'Talbezirk' of King Khasekhemui at Kom el-Sultan/Abydos. Boats are, therefore, neither an exclusively royal nor private element and can also not be used to differentiate between the two types.

– Subsidiary burials occur at both sites. Therefore, it was not the simple presence of a royal tomb that was taken to be an attribute, but the number of burials.[54] Even with the undoubtedly royal structures at Umm el-Qa'ab, however, the number of these burials varies quite a lot during the Ist dynasty. It is therefore doubtful whether the sheer quantity can be a criteria to distinguish between the two different tomb types.

From the above-mentioned criteria, the shape and appearance of the superstructure, therefore, remains the only difference between tombs at both sites: the sandy tumulus at Umm el-Qa'ab opposed to the niched mudbrick mastaba at Saqqara. While the mastaba covers the complete substructure of the tomb, the tumulus was probably only erected above the burial chamber. But there is another niched feature that belongs to the tombs at Umm el-Qa'ab: the royal funerary enclosures, the so-called 'Talbezirke', that stand close to the ancient settlement at Kom el-Sultan. There are at least two formal similarities between these buildings and the superstructures of the Saqqara mastabas: Both are rectangular and oriented more or less north-south, and both are niched. The royal funerary enclosures seem to have fulfilled cultic purposes of still unknown character.[55] The development of the mastaba architecture shows that the niches that surround the mastaba during the Ist dynasty are soon reduced to two niches on its eastern side which were then used for offerings. I, therefore, assume that

[50] *Ibidem*, p. 240.

[51] DREYER, Zur Rekonstruktion der Oberbauten der Königsgräber der 1. Dynastie in Abydos, *MDAIK* 47 (1991) (*Festschrift Werner Kaiser*), pp. 93-104.

[52] STADELMANN, *Pyramiden*, p. 26.

[53] P. JÁNOSI, Bemerkungen zu den Nordkapellen des Alten Reiches, *SAK* 22 (1995), pp. 145-168: especially pp. 154ff.: The building north of S 3505 was identified as a temple only because of its similarities to the North-temple in the Zoser complex, and then taken to be the forerunner of royal mortuary temples.

[54] But see GUNDLACH, *Pharao und sein Staat*, p. 120: "Ich möchte nun die These aufstellen, daß die Gräber mit Nebengräbern königlichen Charakter hatten."

[55] See the debate between Barry KEMP, *Ancient Egypt: Anatomy of a Civilization*, New York ²1991, pp. 64ff. and

there are – apart from formal similarities between the royal funerary enclosures and the superstructures of the Saqqara mastabas – also some functional similarities, in that both structures marked the place of cultic procedures.

The question of the location of the royal burial place can, therefore, not be solved by using the above-mentioned quantitative criteria nor by insisting on different tomb types that seem to be only variations of a single type. Instead, contextual arguments should be considered: While the tombs at Saqqara seem to appear at that site only with the reign of King Aha, the tombs at Umm el-Qa'ab develop in their layout and distribution pattern without any interruption from the tombs of predynastic rulers on cemetery U at the same site and, therefore, show a certain continuity.[56] Another argument might be the distance of the tombs at Umm el-Qa'ab from other contemporary burials except the subsidiary tombs. The same pattern can later be observed for royal necropoleis during all periods of Egyptian history. The tombs at Saqqara, on the other hand, are not only part of a larger cemetery, but were also – at least partially – built over already during the IInd and IIIrd dynasties,[57] which should not have been the case had they been the place of the royal burials.

Finally, the presence of royal stelae, two of which accompanied every tomb at Umm el-Qa'ab, should point to Abydos as the site of the royal burials during the Ist dynasty.

attributes/tomb type	Lower Egyptian Tomb	Upper Egyptian Tomb
superstructure	mud-brick mastaba with niches	not preserved (reconstructed mound of sand or mud-bricks)
substructure[58]	shallow	deep
subterranean tumulus[59]	stepped	none
size of tomb[60]	large	small
burial chamber[61]	no wooden chamber	wooden chamber
temple[62]	one next to S 3505	none
boats[63]	with some tombs	no boats associated with tombs
subsidiary tombs[64]	with some mastabas less burials	with all tombs more burials

Table 1: Supposed Characteristics of Different Tomb Types of the Ist Dynasty

David O'CONNOR, The Status of Early Egyptian Temples: An Alternative Theory, in: B. ADAMS, R. FRIEDMAN (eds.), *The Followers of Horus. Studies dedicated to Michael Allen Hoffman 1944-1990*, Egyptian Studies Association Publication 2/Oxbow Monograph 20, Oxford 1992, pp. 83ff.

[56] KAISER, in: KAISER, DREYER, *MDAIK* 38 (1982), pp. 241-242.

[57] EMERY, *Hor-Aha*, p. 18, fig. 9.

[58] KAISER, in: KAISER, DREYER, *MDAIK* 38 (1982), pp. 256ff.; STADELMANN, *Pyramiden*, p. 11.

[59] STADELMANN, *Pyramiden*, p. 69.

[60] EMERY, *Hemaka*, p. 2; IDEM, *Hor-Aha*, pp. 1-2; IDEM, *Great Tombs* II, p. 3; IDEM, *Archaic Egypt*, pp. 47 (tomb of Narmer at Abydos and the so-called royal tomb at Naqada), 63 (tomb O and S 3471), 66 (tomb Y and S 3503), 70-71 (tomb Z and S 3504), 76 (tomb T and S 3035), 81-82 (tomb X and S 3038), 86ff. (tomb Q and S 3505); STADELMANN, *Die großen Pyramiden von Giza*, Graz 1990, p. 48.

[61] KAISER, Zu den Königsgräbern der 1. Dynastie in Umm el-Qaab, *MDAIK* 37 (1981), p. 252 interprets this (reconstructed) structure as "Vorstellung des Wohnens im Grab"; STADELMANN, *Pyramiden*, p. 12.

[62] STADELMANN, *Pyramiden*, p. 27; LAUER, Le premier temple de culte funéraire en Égypte, *BIFAO* 80 (1980), pp. 45ff.; KAISER, in: KAISER, DREYER, *MDAIK* 38 (1982), p. 259; KEMP, *Antiquity* 41 (1967), pp. 28ff.

[63] STADELMANN, *Pyramiden*, pp. 15-16, 29.

[64] EMERY, *Great Tombs* II, pp. 1-2; STADELMANN, *Pyramiden*, p. 20; GUNDLACH, *Pharao und sein Staat*, p. 120.

Table 2: Size of burial chambers

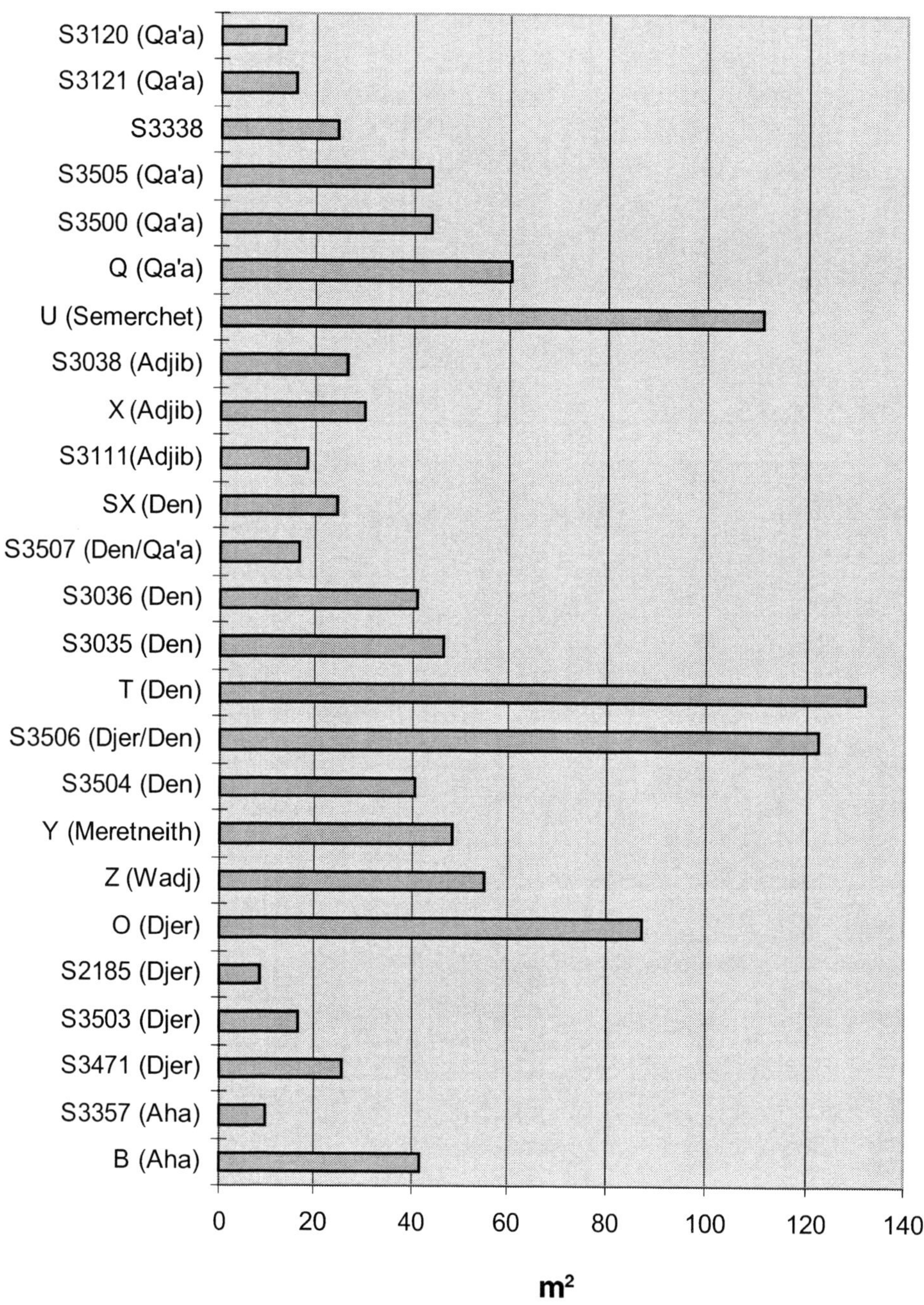

Table 3: Depth of burial chambers

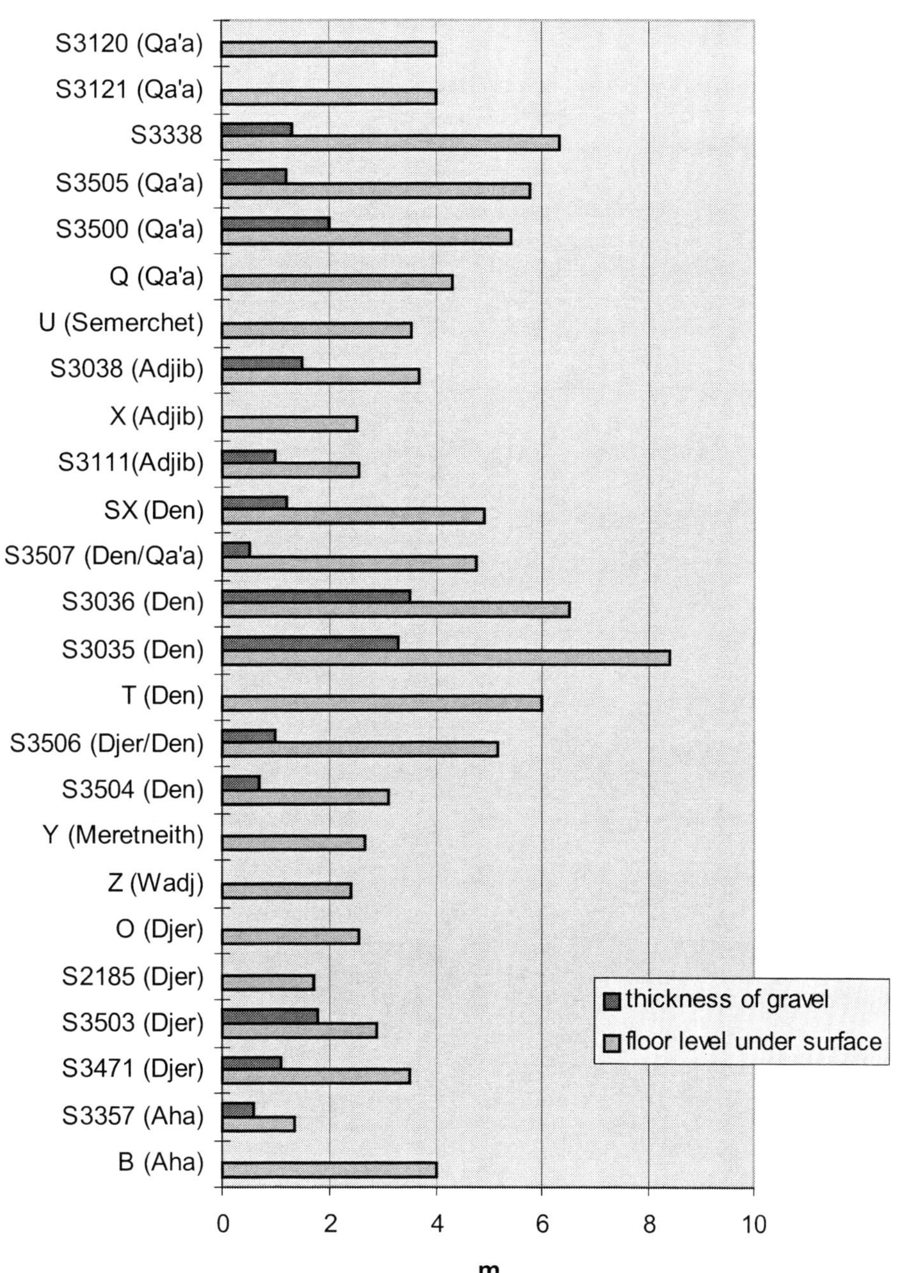

Renata Gryz
Varsovie

«Rê s'est séparé des hommes» – les conséquences de la «deuxième création» d'après le Livre de la Vache du Ciel
(Planches 13-14)

L'idée que les hommes et les dieux vivaient autrefois les uns à côté des autres sur la terre, constitue un sujet fréquent dans les mythes antiques. Le plus connu d'entre eux, est le récit biblique du Jardin d'Eden, où habitait le premier couple humain, et où Dieu se promenait de temps en temps. Cette proximité primordiale est considérée comme le Paradis ou l'Âge d'Or. Cependant, cette idylle s'est terminée dans des circonstances dramatiques où les hommes jouaient les rôles principaux. C'est pourquoi la question de la genèse du mal et de l'imperfection dans un monde créé et organisé par un Dieu bon constitue un problème capital, posé plus ou moins explicitement dans des narrations mythiques.

Une composition égyptienne, appelée le Livre de la Vache du Ciel, dont la version la plus ancienne provient du tombeau de Toutankhamon, donne un exemple des recherches très profondes sur la situation du monde á cette époque. La première partie du Livre – le mythe de la destruction de l'humanité – raconte comment l'unité primordiale des dieux et des hommes s'est terminée et dépeint les conséquences de cet événement. On peut dire que ces dernières sont de nature cosmique et sociale. La réalité primaire, établie et gouvernée par Rê, a subi une réorganisation fondamentale à un tel point qu'on peut la désigner comme une «deuxième création».[1] Cette phase de l'évolution de l'univers montre une division permanente. Contrairement à la «première fois», où le créateur est venu à l'existence lui-même et où il a séparé le ciel et la terre, ce qui avait un sens positif,[2] le second morcellement symbolise une opposition irrévocable des deux sphères ainsi que de leurs habitants. Cette différentiation entraîne alors d'autres antagonismes: celui de la vie et de la mort, du jour et de la nuit, du bien et du mal, du temps mythique et du temps historique. Étudié sous cet angle, le Livre de la Vache explique les origines de la condition humaine, misérable, et de l'état actuel du monde. Le caractère explicatif permet de définir ce mythe comme un mythe d'origine. Selon M. ELIADE «l'«essentiel» n'a pas été décidé à la Création du Monde, mais après, à un certain moment de l'époque mythique. Il s'agit toujours d'un Temps mythique, mais ce n'est plus le «premier», celui qu'on peut appeler le Temps «cosmogonique». L'«essentiel» n'est plus solidaire d'une ontologie (comment le Monde – le réel – est venu à l'être), mais d'une Histoire.»[3]

Sur le plan cosmologique, l'unité primordiale des dieux et des hommes est exprimée par l'expression *m iḫt wꜥtt* "comme une chose" = unité (v. 3: als Menschen und Götter noch vereint waren[4]) opposée à *iḫtj sntj* "deux choses" = dualité, différence (*CT* III 383).[5] Après la rébellion des hommes, Rê, las de l'ingratitude et de la méchanceté de ses créatures, décide de quitter la terre sur le dos de Nout, transformée en vache (v. 104-132). Une description détaillée de l'exécution de l'illustration de la vache est placée au milieu du texte (v. 166-201), de même que la seule illustration se trouve au milieu de la composition (**pl. 13, fig. 1**). Le ventre de la vache, semé d'étoiles, symbolise le ciel, à travers lequel la barque solaire voyage sans cesse. Au-dessous du firmament céleste se trouve le dieu Chou et les huit dieux Heh

[1] Cf. une «deuxième fois» de N. GUILHOU, Réflexions sur la conception du mal à travers quelques grands mythes antiques, dans: *Hommages à F. Daumas*, Montpellier (cité par la suite: Conception du mal), 1986, p. 363.

[2] H. Te VELDE, *The Theme of the Separation of Heaven and Earth in Egyptian Mythology*, Stud. Aeg. III, Budapest, 1977, p. 161: «... the cosmos exists because it is differentiated into heaven and earth.»

[3] M. ELIADE, *Aspects du mythe*, Paris, 1963, p. 138.

[4] Traduction d'E. HORNUNG, *Der ägyptische Mythos von der Himmelskuh. Eine Ätiologie des Unvollkommenen*, OBO 46, Fribourg (cité par la suite: *Himmelskuh*), 1982.

[5] E. OTTO, Das «Goldene Zeitalter» in einem ägyptischen Text, dans: *Religions en Égypte hellénistique et romaine*, Paris (cité par la suite: Goldene Zeitalter), 1969, note 1, p. 100.

qui représentent tous des supports du ciel. Toute la composition préfigure des cosmographies religieuses très élargies, comme celles connues par les tombeaux des rois de la XIXe et XXe dynasties, et qui décrivent le périple quotidien du soleil.[6]

Le second élément d'ordre nouveau – la terre – est évoqué dans le contexte de la fuite au désert de l'humanité révoltée (v. 42). Cette région figure le chaos, le désordre complet d'où le dieu est absent, où les forces du mal triomphent. Le désert, c'est encore le pays de Seth, habité par des serpents. Dans les livres de l'au-delà, le grand ennemi du soleil apparaît sous forme d'un serpent, Apophis, qui attend la barque solaire sur une île de sable pour boire toute de l'eau de la rivière et arrêter son cours.[7] Dans le Livre de la Vache, des serpents sont evoqués à l'occasion des avertissements énoncés par Rê à Geb. La magie est un moyen efficace pour les apaiser. De plus, Rê s'adresse à des serpents de l'au-delà (v. 215-219) qui jouent un rôle positif, par exemple défensif et protecteur, pour leur assurer un approvisionnement constant, indispensable à l'éternité. Rê en a confié le patronage à Osiris (v. 222), afin qu'il transmette leur force magique à tout le monde (v. 224-225). Ce passage fait allusion au célèbre fragment de l'Enseignement pour Mérikare (P. 136-137) dans lequel le Créateur donne la magie aux hommes comme une arme contre le mal.[8]

L'apparition d'Osiris et la fonction qu'il vient d'obtenir sont liées à la troisième sphère créée pendant la «deuxième fois». On retrouve des allusions à l'au-delà directement après les mentions du soulèvement du ciel. Dans les verses 150-154, Rê fait venir à l'existence les Champs d'Offrandes et ceux de Roseaux qui sont localisés dans le ciel parmi des étoiles infatigables. Une autre région est signalée pendant le discours de Rê à Thoth (v. 229-250). Il s'agit d'un voyage nocturne du dieu, au cours duquel sa lumière pénètre l'Ile des Deux Âmes, où le ba de Rê s'unit à celui d'Osiris.[9] Dans ce fragment, on parle encore de «créatures révoltées», à savoir les Akeru, contre lesquelles le défunt doit se protéger.[10] Le monde souterrain, visité chaque nuit par le dieu dans sa barque, est à la fois le royaume des morts, créé après le départ de Rê, parce que la chute des hommes, immortels au temps de l'Âge d'Or,[11] avait pour conséquence la guerre et la mort.

La nouvelle structure de l'univers, considéré comme le résultat du seconde acte créateur, présente trois régions différentes: le ciel – habité par les dieux –, la terre – pays des hommes –, le monde souterrain – destination des défunts et des forces du mal. La réalité primordiale caractérisait l'ordre, le jour constant et la vie en harmonie avec les dieux, garantie par la présence du créateur. La dissonance suscitée par le «péché originel» a causé une opposition inévitable entre le ciel et la terre, le jour et la nuit, la naissance et la mort. Le monde est devenu complexe et compliqué à l'inverse de l'unité et de la simplicité des origines. La séparation du ciel et de la terre n'est plus alors regardée comme un événement positif, mais comme une sorte de peine.[12] Aussi peut-on reconnaître dans les ténèbres suivant le départ de Rê une métaphore de son absence absolue. Néanmoins, il ne les a pas laissés sans soins; il a chargé Thoth de le remplacer dans le ciel nocturne.

La succession constante du jour et de la nuit, qui appartient à la «deuxième création», détermine la dimension temporelle. Les deux termes Neheh et Djet sont mentionnés dans les parties finales du livre (v. 313-330). Le défunt qui connaît leurs noms, renaîtra dans l'autre monde comme dieu et sera intégré au cours solaire. Les deux notions sont à nouveau personnifiées sur une illustration jointe au livre **(pl. 13, fig. 2)** sous la forme d'un homme et d'une femme tenant des sceptres *w3s*, symboles de stabi-

[6] Cf. A. PIANKOFF, *Le Livre du Jour et de la Nuit*, Le Caire, 1942; G. ROULIN, *Le Livre de la Nuit*, OBO 147(1-2), Fribourg, 1996.

[7] E. HORNUNG, *Die Nachtfahrt der Sonne*, Zürich, 1991, pp. 112-113.

[8] E. BLUMENTHAL, Die Lehre für König Merikare, *ZÄS* 107 (1980), p. 20; D. LORTON, God's Beneficent Creation: Coffin Texts Spell 1130, The Instructions for Merikare, and the Great Hymn to the Aton, *SAK* 20 (1993), p. 134.

[9] HORNUNG, *Himmelskuh*, note 155, p. 60.

[10] Cf. E. BLUMENTHAL et al. (éd.), *Mythen und Epen* III. *Texte aus der Umwelts des Alten Testament*, Gütersloh, 1995, note II.2.4.6 a, p. 1033.

[11] L'idée de l'immortalité originale est proposée par L. KÁKOSY, Ideas about the Fallen State of the World in Egyptian Religion: Decline of the Golden Age, dans: IDEM, *Selected Papers (1956-1973)*, Studia Aegyptiaca VII, Budapest (cité par la suite: Ideas), 1981, p. 87.

[12] S. BICKEL, *La cosmogonie égyptienne avant le Nouvel Empire*, OBO 134, Fribourg (cité par la suite: *Cosmogonie*), 1994, p. 198.

lité, et apparaissant comme des supports du ciel. Au-dessous d'eux, se trouve un texte dit par le mort: «Je connais les noms de ces deux grands dieux: Neheh et Djet». Ce sont les plus anciennes représentations des dieux.[13] On retrouve Neheh et Djet encore une fois dans le verse 276 où le dieu dit de lui-même: «Ich bin mit ihnen [les *bas* des dieux – *R.G.*] bis an das Ende der Zeit, die von den Jahren erzeugt wird».[14] Selon Erik HORNUNG, Neheh et Djet évoquent la dimension temporelle du voyage du soleil.[15] La fonction de support du ciel correspond à celle de Chou et Tefnout des Textes des Sarcophages: «Vois, Chou est la pérennité, Tefnout est l'éternité» (*CT* 80 II 28d).[16]

L'espace entre le ciel et la terre, l'au-delà, de même que le temps, organisent la nouvelle création.[17] Tous les éléments délimitent la vie humaine, sa durée et son déroulement, ainsi que la destinée extra-terrestre. La description de cette réalité occupe plus de place que celle de la rébellion. Celle-ci est mentionnée en passant; on ne cherche pas à expliquer ses motifs ou sa forme. En punition de ses péchés, l'humanité est massacrée par la déesse Hathor transformée en lionne dangereuse (v. 49). Il semble que cette révolte comprenne une série de faits, connus des textes égyptiens, où l'ordre universel est mis en danger. Par exemple, dans le Livre des Morts, on cite les «enfants de Nout» révoltés (*BD* ch. 175; L.b. col 2) et les «enfants de la Déchéance» (*BD* ch. 17; La col. 5), ou, plus généralement, les «rebelles». Le Naos d'Ismailia parle des «enfants d'Apopis», qui se dressent contre Chou.[18] Dans le Livre de la Vache, il est intéressant de voir que tout près de la mention de la révolte se trouve quelques lignes concernant l'état de Rê. Le dieu a vieilli alors que ses os étaient en argent, ses membres en or et ses cheveux en lapis lazuli (v. 5-7). Pour la première fois il a perdu ses forces physiques et psychiques (v. 105). De la même manière, la vieillesse du créateur est présenté dans le mythe «Ruse d'Isis», où on dit que la salive goutte de la bouche de dieu.[19] Absence de forces, grande faiblesse et épuisement du dieu indiquent un moment crucial pour l'existence du monde. Le fait que le dieu soit affaibli permet de supposer que la structure de l'univers contient un germe de dégénérescence, ce qui expliquerait cet état des choses. Tout ce qui existe est continuellement exposé à l'affaiblissement et, en conséquence, au vieillissement et à la mort. C'est pourquoi HORNUNG définit le texte du Livre de la Vache comme «étiologie de l'imparfait». La révolte des hommes est donc une réaction à la faiblesse du Créateur. Par conséquent, le mal incarné dans les images des ténèbres, de la guerre (v. 133-139) et de la mort, constitue une partie intégrale de la nature du monde créé.[20] Cette interprétation de la genèse du mal enlève toute la responsabilité directe aux hommes. La faute se trouve de part et d'autre, elle a ses raisons dans la nature de la création, soumise à la destruction, ainsi que dans la violation de l'ordre divin.[21] Malgré tout, Rê ne veut pas exterminer l'humanité; mais le prix du salut se trouve dans la rupture de la communauté des hommes et des dieux. Le dieu quitte la terre parce qu'il ne supporterait pas plus longtemps le mal.[22] Le retour à l'état antérieur qu'est la proximité avec le dieu n'est possible qu'après la mort. D'où des instructions concernant la récitation du livre, lesquelles permettent d'interpréter celui-ci comme un texte funéraire. Sa connaissance garantit la régénération dans le royaume des morts et la vie parmi des dieux.[23] Il semble que

---

[13] HORNUNG, *Himmelskuh*, p. 102.

[14] Trad. de HORNUNG, *Himmelskuh*, p. 46.

[15] *Ibidem*, p. 103.

[16] BICKEL, *Cosmogonie*, p. 134.

[17] J. ASSMANN dans son article: Das Doppelgesicht der Zeit im altägyptischen Denken, dans: A. PEISL, A. MOHLER (éds.), *Die Zeit, Dauer und Augenblick*, Heidelberg, 1983, pp. 189-223, fait une remarque que les hiéroglyphes utilisés dans ce deux noms contiennent le signe de soleil et celui de la terre ce qu'on peut probablement interprér comme allusion au cycle solaire et à la stabilité de la terre (p. 202).

[18] GUILHOU, Conception du mal, p. 362; G. GOYON, Les travaux de Chou et les tribulations de Geb d'après le naos d'Ismailia, *Kêmi* VI (1936), p. 27.

[19] E. BRUNNER-TRAUT, *Altägyptische Märchen*, Düsseldorf, 1976, p. 115.

[20] Cf. OTTO, Goldene Zeitalter, note 4, p. 95: «Unordnung zum Wesen der Welt gehört». Le désordre est alors l'absence de Mâat, et l'absence de Mâat le mal.

[21] Le célèbre fragment des Textes des Sarcophages Spell 1130 dit: «je n'ai pas ordonné qu'ils commettent le mal; c'est leurs cœurs qui ont désobéi à ce que j'avais dit.» Trad. de BICKEL, *Cosmogonie*, p. 212.

[22] ASSMANN, Königsdogma und Heilserwartung. Politische und Kultische Chaosbeschreibungen, dans: D. HELLHOLM (éd.), *Apocalypticism in the Mediterranean World and the Near East*, Tübingen (cité par la suite: Königsdogma), 1983, note 63, p. 272.

[23] ASSMANN, *Ägypten – Theologie und Frömmigkeit*

l'au-delà soit alors devenu un pays de bonheur, d'abondance et de prospérité, où les hommes et les dieux vivent ensemble.[24]

En dehors du caractère funéraire, il faut mettre aussi l'accent sur le contenu rituel de ce livre. Cela concerne les étiologies qui prennent la forme de jeux de mots pour expliquer la genèse de certains manifestations divines, par exemple Sakhmet sous un aspect dangereux, celui d'Hathor (v. 57-58) et des animaux saints de Thoth (v. 39-40, 48). On cherche encore à éclairer justification la provenance d'un lieu de culte d'Hathor à Imau (v. 93-94) et d'une fête de la bière liée au retour de la déesse (v. 96-100). Le double sens de la fête s'applique d'une part à une fonction de la «sainte ivresse» comme moyen de sauver l'humanité du massacre, et d'autre part aux célébrations annuelles de retour d'Hathor, fille de Rê,[25] qui répètent le mythe et le reproduisent sur le plan existentiel de l'expérience humaine. A l'aide de la fête, la réalité mythique acquiert une actualité, et le précédent mythique a déjà une place stable dans le temps cyclique. Pendant la fête du retour de déesse,[26] on honorait celle-ci sons un aspect dangereux de Sekhmet et en tant que Bastet, la chatte douce, en dansant et en buvant de la bière. L'apaisement grâce à la bière de Sakhmet, avide de sang, symbolise dans le langage du mythe l'écartement du moment critique.[27] Cette fonction est perpétuée dans l'image du pharaon qui offre à Hathor un pichet du vin.[28]

Dans le Livre de la Vache, le roi apparaît, dans une scène conservée chez Séti Ier, Ramses II et Ramses III (**pl. 2, fig. 1**), comme supporteur du ciel.[29] Sa présence est liée à la mission qu'il a à accomplir. Rê, s'éloignant vers le ciel, nomme le dieu Thoth comme son représentant pendant la nuit. Par contre, Chou, fils du Créateur et successeur au thrône selon le schéma mytho-cratogonique,[30] est placé entre le ciel et la terre par rapport à un intermédiaire (**pl. 2, fig. 2**). Le pharaon s'identifie avec lui par son attitude et par les mots: «Du sollst nicht müde werden, mein Sohn», «Dein Zustand ist wie der von einem, der immer lebt», «Dein Sohn bin ich, und Leben, Heil, Gesundheit mögen an jener deiner Nase sein!».[31] La théologie amarnienne exprimait littéralement cette identification:[32] Aton était le souverain véritable, et son fils – le pharaon – incarnait Chou en tant que médium de la lumière.[33]

L'activité d'un roi doit conduire à faire revenir l'Égypte à ce qu'elle était «au temps de Rê».[34] Cet aspect de la tâche du pharaon, qui consiste à anéantir le mal et à établir Mâat dans toutes les sphères de l'existence (cosmique, rituelle, sociale), est développé dans des prophéties politiques, comme par exemple celle de Neferti de la XVIIIe dynastie.[35] Dès que le dieu a quitté la terre, l'État qui compense l'absence des dieux pour les hommes[36] et le rois en tant que Grand Prêtre sert d'intermédiaire entre les hommes et les dieux.

Le Livre de la Vache du Ciel raconte des événements mythiques, ayant lieu dans un passé indeterminé, et en vue d'expliquer le présent. Le monde tel qu'il est en soi est illustré par la figure de la vache céleste avec les huit Heh au dessous du ventre, le dieu Chou au centre et la barque solaire en train de voyager. Cependant, cet état des cho-

einer frühen Hochkultur, Berlin, 1984, p. 140; GUILHOU, Temps de récit et temps du mythe des conceptions égyptiennes du temps à travers le Livre de la Vache Céleste, dans: *Mélanges à A. Gutbub*, Montpellier, 1984, p. 87.

[24] KÁKOSY, Ideas, p. 83.

[25] Le mythe de la destruction de l'humanité appartient à un cycle de récits sur l'œil de Rê et la Chatte nubienne.

[26] D'après le calendrier de l'époque gréco-romaine, on distinguait plusieurs célébrations liées avec des aspects différents d'Hathor. Cf. H. STERNBERG el-HOTABI, *Ein Hymnus an die Göttin Hathor und das Ritual «Hathor das Trankopfer Darbringen» nach den Tempeltexten der griechisch-römischen Zeit*, Rites Égyptiens VII, Bruxelles, 1992, pp. 101–109

[27] H. BRUNNER, Die theologische Bedeutung der Trunkenheit, *ZÄS* 79 (1954), pp. 81-83.

[28] HORNUNG, Pharao ludens, *Eranos* 51 (1982), pl. 1.

[29] Ch. MAYSTRE, Le Livre de la Vache du Ciel dans les tombeaux de la Vallée des Rois, *BIFAO* 40 (1941), pp. 54-55; F. ABITZ, *Pharao als Gott in den Unterweltsbüchern des Neuen Reiches*, OBO 146, Fribourg (cité par la suite: *Pharao*), 1995, p. 94.

[30] ASSMANN, *Ägypten. Eine Sinngeschichte*, München (cité par la suite: *Sinngeschichte*), 1996, p. 384.

[31] ABITZ, *Pharao*, pp. 98-99.

[32] C'est un argument en faveur de la datation du livre à l'époque post-amarnienne. Cf. HORNUNG, *Himmelskuh*, p. 80.

[33] Cf. Ph. DERCHAIN, Sur le nom de Chou et sa fonction, *RdE* 27 (1975), pp. 115-116.

[34] U. LUFT, *Beiträge zur Historisierung der Götterwelt und der Mythenschreibung*, Studia Aegyptiaca IV, Budapest, 1978, p. 215.

[35] ASSMANN, Königsdogma, pp. 271-278.

[36] IDEM, *Sinngeschichte*, p. 215.

ses est extrêmement fragile, et exposé à un danger constant de la part des forces du mal. Il est donc aussi supporté par Neheh et Djet qui assurent son existence pendant des millions d'années. La succession ininterrompue du jour et de la nuit garantit le renouvellement du monde. Dans cette perspective, la mort n'est qu'une sorte de «rite de passage», qui ouvre la porte de l'éternité. Bien que les dieux soient absents, les pratiques du culte, les fêtes et rituels funéraires donnent la possibilité d'accéder à la réalité divine. L'état terrestre, fixé à la place de la présence indirecte des dieux, et le pharaon, représentant de la divinité, suppriment tous deux en partie la séparation. La rencontre des deux sphères s'accomplit dans l'au-delà. La fonction «explicative» du mythe de la destruction de l'humanité consiste à présenter, à l'aide de mots et d'images, la genèse de la condition humaine et l'imperfection de la réalité.

András Gulyás
Budapest

The Gods of the Type «Amun of Ramesses» and their Meaning in the Context of Religious Developments of the Ramesside Period

(Plate 15)

A novelty of the Ramesside Period are the gods composed from the name of the ruler and a god. For the first time such gods appear during the reign of Ramesses II. In this practice he is followed by his successors, Merenptah or Ramesses III, where we find again and again statues of this form of god. In this paper I would like to discuss the gods such as Amon-of-Ramesses and Ptah-of-Ramesses and to contribute to a better understanding of their meaning by defining their context.

The comprehension of these forms of god is not easy because they usually stay alone, just the names are given, without any further explication. Let us mention some examples:

ḏd mdw jn Jmn-n-(Rˁ-msj-sw mrj-Jmn) m pr Jmn
To be recited by Amun-of-Ramesses II, in the house of Amun[1]

pꜣ Rˁ-n-(Rˁ-msj-sw mrj-Jmn) ntj rsj jnbw Mn-nfr
The Re-of-Ramesses II, south of Memphis[2]

As we can see, this form of god is not limited to the Nubian temples and they can be composed with various deities:

Ḏḥwtj n (Rˁ-msj-sw mrj-Jmn)
Thot-of-Ramesses II[3]

They occur after the rule of Ramesses II as well. So for example from the time of Merenptah:

Jmn-n-(Mrj.n-Ptḥ ḥtp-ḥr-mꜣˁt)
Amun-of-Merenptah[4]

Because of the examples where we find similar gods with the name of Merenptah[5] I cannot accept the intepretation of MONTET, according to which the addition of the name of Ramesses would be an abbreviation of "Per-Ramesses".[6]

We can find a similar god in the small temple of Ramesses III in the Karnak temple as well. Here the pharaoh makes an offering before such a god (**pl. 15, fig. 1**):

Jmn n (Rˁ-msj-sw ḥkꜣ Jwnw)
Amun-of-Ramesses III[7]

At first sight, we could think, as NAVILLE did, that the *n* in the names of these gods expresses the idea that the gods belong to the ruler, 'a kind of right of property or possession.'[8] Even if this idea is usually not so clearly formulated one has the impression that other researchers accept it as well. I can understand only, as the reflection of such an implicit, assumption that in the *Lexikon der Ägyptologie* the god of the temple of Gerf Hussein is simply said to be Ptah even if in reality he is Ptah-of-Ramesses.[9] The *n Rˁ-msj-sw* is treated as an addition that has nothing to do with the god himself.

In view of the Egyptian sculptures it would be rather unusual that the owner or the producer of

---

[1] *KRI* II, p. 737.

[2] *KRI* III, p. 435.

[3] *KRI* IV, p. 27.

[4] *Ibidem*, p. 27.

[5] We have also a god composed with Menes, from the Ramesside period. See WILDUNG, *Die Rolle ägyptischer Könige im Bewußtsein ihrer Nachwelt*, MÄS 17, Berlin 1969, pp. 12-15. I would like to express my thanks to Professor László KÁKOSY for this observation and for other critical remarks.

[6] P. MONTET, Les Dieux de Ramsès-aimé-d'Amon à Tanis, in: *Studies presented to F. Ll. Griffith*, London 1932, p. 406. Several theories concerning these god-forms are collected by EATON-KRAUSS, Ramesses-Re who creates the gods, in: *Fragments of a shattered visage, International Symposium of Ramesses the Great*, Memphis 1987.

[7] *Reliefs and Inscriptions at Karnak* I*: Ramesses III's temple within the great inclosure of Amun,* Part I. *by Epigraphic Survey*, OIP XXV, Chicago 1936, pl. 107.

[8] E. NAVILLE, *Bubastis (1887-1889)*, EEF Memoir 8, London 1981, p. 42.

[9] D. WILDUNG, Gerf Hussein, *LÄ* II, cols. 534-535.

a statue is indicated in this way. On the other hand, if this should be the primary meaning of the *n*, then we should have the same indication on other statues as well.

The groups of statues offer a clear evidence to consider the god form Ptah-of-Ramesses as a separate being clearly distinguished from Ptah and Ramesses as a god and to reject the opinion according to which the *n* indicates the owner or the producer.

In a group of four gods in Wadi es Sebua, although it is clear that all the statues of the sanctuary belong to the same ruler, Ramesses II, we have a composite name just in the case of one of them. Ptah-Tatonen and Ptah-of-Ramesses are taken to be two separate gods, meaning the *n Rᶜ-msj-sw* expresses a theological difference.

Ptḥ-n-(Rᶜ-msj-sw mrj-Jmn) m pr Jmn
Ptḥ tꜣ-ṯnn kꜣ šwtj spd ᶜbwy
(Rᶜ-msj-sw mrj-Jmn) m pr Jmn
Ḥwt- Ḥr nbt nht rst
Ptah-of-Ramesses II in the House of Amun
Ptah-Tatonen with tall plumes, with pointed horns
Ramesses II in the house of Amun
Hathor, the Lady of the Southern sycomore [10]

In a group of four gods in Gerf Hussein, the deified Ramesses had a separate statue between god forms composed with the *n Rᶜ-msj-sw* addition. This means that these composite gods cannot be simply identified with the deified Ramesses:

Ptḥ-n-(Rᶜ-msj-sw mrj-Jmn) m pr Ptḥ
nb ḫᶜw (Rᶜ-msj-sw mrj-Jmn) m pr Ptḥ
Ptḥ-tꜣ-ṯnn-n-(Rᶜ-msj-sw mrj-Jmn) m pr Ptḥ
Ḥwt- Ḥr n...
Ptah-of-Ramesses II in the House of Ptah
The Lord of the crowns, Ramesses II in the house of Ptah
Ptah-Tatonen-of-Ramesses II in the house of Ptah
Hathor of... [11]

A similar group of gods can be found in Abu Simbel. Here we have a triad of gods with the following names:

Jmn-n-Wsr-mꜣᶜt-Rᶜ stp.n-Rᶜ
Rᶜ-msj.sw
(Wsr-mꜣᶜt-Rᶜ stp.n-Rᶜ) dj ᶜnḫ
Amun of Ramesses II
Ramesses
Ramesses II given life[12]

In this interesting group of gods we can see two forms of the deified Ramesses II sitting one beside the other.

As a conclusion of this short survey we can observe that the addition *n* + Name of the ruler has a theological importance. These composite gods appear in the reign of Ramesses II but we find them with later rulers of the Ramesside Period as well. They occur from the Delta to the Nubian temples and they can be composed with various deities.

It is important to stress the fact that although this kind of god expresses a more or less strong unity between the ruler and the god in question, it is also clear that this kind of syncretism is not the same as for example in the case of Amun-Re or Re-Harachti. With these gods, the unity is more explicit, while the Ramesside rulers seem to have just wanted to express an essential and very strong relationship. The religious meaning of these gods can be best described by the inscriptions of the Osiris-columns of Gerf-Hussein. These inscriptions render probably the names of the statues:

(Rᶜ-msj-sw mrj-Jmn) ḫᶜ.(w) m nṯrw
Ramesses appeared as/in the gods[13]

The translation is not necessary simply «between» but may be «as» or «in» the gods, as well. The translation seems to be ambiguous not just because of our lack of knowledge, it is necessarily so because of the theological meaning the Egyptians wanted to express. These ambiguities of meaning make it possible in theology or philosophy to express conceptual nuances and to avoid clear cut distinctions.

There are several theories concerning the role and meaning of these gods. Some of them can be definitely excluded from acceptable solutions. Others are hypothetical, meaning we do not have evidence to

[10] *KRI* II, p. 734.
[11] *Ibidem*, p. 725.
[12] *Ibidem*, p. 763.
[13] *Ibidem*, p. 719.

accept or reject them.[14] Even if these gods express that they belong to a given pharaoh, they also mean something more, the *n* has some kind of theological meaning as well. As they appear for the first time in the Ramesside dynasties, it is appropriate to try to find their place in the contemporary religious developments. In this way we can at least get a better view of the "spirit" which led to such religious novelties as the god Amun-of-Ramesses.

If we try to grasp the meaning of these peculiar gods in the light of the religious developments of the Ramesside Period, we have to face the problem that in the famous hymns of this period, such as the Amun Hymn of Leiden or the Tura Hymn these gods do not play any significant role.[15] It is all the more surprising because in these hymns there is the first explicit theological explanation of the relationship of Amun to the other gods. It would be natural to see the characteristic gods like Amun-of-Ramesses in these hymns, but this is not the case. The reason for this peculiarity is probably that the temple-statues, reliefs and narrative hymns belong to two more or less different theological discourses.[16] As both the temple-theology and the hymns of this period have several new elements, characteristic concepts and thoughts never seen before, it is proper to talk about discourses and not simply about tradition or repetition of old ideas.

The different religious discourses can have several common elements or gods, but nevertheless they always have characteristic and distinctive ways of expression, texts, representations and gods as well. Let us mention just one example: even if Amun-Re played the most important role in the religious and funerary cults of the Theban area, in the religious program of the royal tombs he does not play any significant role.[17] It is for this difference of religious fields or discourses that the tombs of the Valley of the Kings have texts that usually cannot be found in the private tombs or temples of the Theban area.

For this reason, it is not appropriate to say that with the gods Amun-of-Ramesses, the god is a *ḫprw* or "Erscheinungsform" of the pharaoh. KOCH follows the arguments of WILDUNG in his excellent book about Egyptian religion when he says that "Statuen mit Namen wie "Ptah" oder "Atum des Königs NN" stellen weniger den Gott als den Pharao dar. "*Der König erwählt einen Gott als seine Erscheinungsform*".[18] The phrase comes from an article of WILDUNG which was the basis for the arguments of KOCH. But WILDUNG does not quote any texts where this kind of relationship would be clearly stated.[19] The assumption of WILDUNG seems to be quite plausible in the light of the theology of contemporary hymns. In the already mentioned Amun Hymn of Leiden, the relationship of Amun to the gods is described by these words:

"The Eight gods were thy first form, until thou didst complete them, being one."[20]

In the magical Harris papyrus Amun-Re is greeted with the following words:

"Hail, one who makes himself into millions..."[21]

But in these hymns the relationship of pharaoh and god is never described by the theological teaching of *ḫprw*. In the same way, on the statues one can never find any descriptions of such a relationship between god and ruler. Quite the opposite is true: ruler and god are represented as equal partners. In this case we have a clear example of the difference of expressions and concepts between the religious discourses of the Ramesside Period.

Instead, it is more appropriate to say that the pharaoh participates in the divine and magical forces of the gods. This participation can be expressed in several ways. In the Turin Museum we can see

[14] See for example the theory of Uphill in the above-mentioned article of EATON-KRAUSS.

[15] A.H. GARDINER, Hymns to Amon from a Leiden Papyrus, *ZÄS* 42 (1905), pp. 12-42; see also J. ASSMANN, *Egyptian Solar Religion in the New Kingdom: Re, Amun and the Crisis of Polytheism*, transl. by A. ALCOCK, London 1995 (hereinafter referred to as: *Egyptian Solar Religion*).

[16] ASSMANN analyses the Sun-hymns of the Theban private tombs as a discourse. See the *Einleitung* in: ASSMANN, *Sonnenhymnen in thebanischen Gräbern*, Theben 1, Mainz am Rhein 1983.

[17] See for example the monography of E. HORNUNG, *Tal der Könige – die Ruhestätte der Pharaonen*, Zürich 1999.

[18] K. KOCH, *Geschichte der ägyptischen Religion – von den Pyramiden bis zu den Mysterien der Isis*, Stuttgart 1993, p. 371.

[19] D. WILDUNG, Göttlichkeitsstufen des Pharao, *OLZ* LXVIII (1973), p. 559.

[20] pLeiden I. 350, Translated by GARDINER, *ZÄS 42* (1905), p. 30 (chapter 80).

[21] Section G. of the Harris Magical Papyrus from ASSMANN, *Egyptian Solar Religion*.

a group of statues of Ramesses II (**pl. 15, fig. 2**). Ramesses II sits together with three other deities and they are embracing one another. In Egyptian iconography such a representation does not express a kind of friendship or good relationship, it means something more. One has to consider the fact that the statues of gods were understood by the Egyptians themselves as sources of vital forces, but could be dangerous as well.[22]

Embracing such a statue was also to participate in its magical forces. This gesture was also something more than a simple expression of friendship, but was no unification, as is sometimes believed in the literature.[23] In a unification, the separate gods completely lose their distinct identities like in the god Amun-Re. Sometimes we observe something similar in the group of statues or the above-mentioned composite gods as well, but it is also true that there never exist gods like Ramesses-Amun.

The best expression to describe the relationship of the gods to one another in the Turin group of statues would be participation in the forces of the deity. This kind of contact with the god was a magical-ritual transmission of power, not simply the expression of emotions.[24]

This idea is implicit in all groups of statues where the ruler is seen in the company of other gods. Especially in the case of the groups of statues of the sanctuaries we can grasp this meaning. The temple was the house of god, why should he or she have to share it with some other deity? They do have some kind of hidden unity in common, even if this unity cannot be described by "unification". If the builder of the temple wanted simply to praise all these gods, he could have made separate chapels for all of them – as in the case of the Abydos temple of Sethos I. Or, he could have at least made separate thrones for the several deities. This was not the case, they sat on the same throne, one beside the other and the hidden unity they wanted to express is to be seen sometimes from the gestures, as in the Turin statue, sometimes from the names the gods had.

In several cases the names of these statues express clearly the rejection of discernable identities. In the above-mentioned statues of the sanctuaries of Nubian temples two different forms of Ptah sit one beside the other, as if neither were an appropriate expression of the god Ptah. In the same manner, Ramesses II participates in the divinity of Ptah in the god form Ptah-of-Ramesses, but he has a separate statue as well, in the same group. The example of the triad in Abu Simbel is a similar expression of this interconnection.

This participation of the ruler in the powers of a given god is expressed in the Amun-of-Ramesses god. Probably this is the meaning of these forms of god in light of contemporary religious developments. It is not a unity – then we should find Amun-Ramesses, without *n* – it is also not simply an additional remark concerning the commissioner or holder of the statue, as it could be seen earlier.

At this point we note a clear correspondence between statuary and theological literature of the Ramesside Period. It is no wonder that from this period comes an immense quantity of groups of statues, much more than from earlier times, where god and ruler are represented together, exactly at the time, when in the theological literature the concept of the hidden supreme god appears.[25]

The different religious discourses of a given period, as all discourses in the life of a culture or society, always have a common level as well.[26] In our case, the most important common level is that both the hymns of the Ramesside Period and the statue

[22] See for example the daily ritual, where the ceremoniating priest recites the following text when he arrives to the statue of Amun-Re: "Ich habe mich auf meinen Bauch gelegt aus Ehrfurcht vor dir, nachdem ich in Furcht geraten war vor deiner Majestät." (pBerlin 3055, IV,9-V,2; XI,8-10) translated as Spruch 13 in: W. GUGLIELMI, K. BUROH, Die Eingangssprüche des Täglichen Tempelrituals nach Papyrus Berlin 3055 (I,1-VI,3), in: J. van DIJK (ed.), *Essays on Ancient Egypt in Honour of H. te Velde*, Groningen 1997, p. 127.

[23] On this issue see: J.G. GRIFFITHS, Triune concepts of deity, *ZÄS* 100 (1973), pp. 28-32.

[24] For the meaning of embracing as a contact taking and a transmission of power see: ASSMANN, *Tod und Jenseits im alten Ägypten*, München 2001, pp. 62-63; H. ROEDER, *Mit dem Auge sehen – Studien zur Semantik der Herrschaft in den Toten- und Kulttexten*, SAGA 16, Heidelberg 1996, p. 227.

[25] See the relevant Chapter of ASSMANN, *Egyptian Solar Religion*.

[26] FOUCAULT in his monography, *Les mots et les choses – une archéologie des sciences humaines*, Paris 1966 investigated exactly this common level of discourses across several periods of European history.

groups where one of the gods is called Amun-of-Ramesses or Ptah-of-Ramesses, express the idea of the relativity of the god forms one can see on earth.

But it is also true, as was written earlier, that the common level ends at this point. In the theological literature Amun-Re is hidden, the other gods are just *ḫprw*, while in the statuary they are sitting beside each other, in the sanctuary of the temple of Abu Simbel for example, Ramesses II beside Amun-Re, Ptah and Re-Harachti, all equal to one another.

The growing transcendence of the Ramesside Period led to a relative rejection of the separate, observable god statues.[27] In the hymns, the result of this development was the *ḫprw* teaching. In the statuary, the preference of statue groups to one god. In the sanctuaries of several temples of this period, there was not just one, but several more deities as if they could only express the true god together.

This proliferation of gods and their growing interdependence at the same time is a clear consequence of the increasing transcendence of this time. In the temple theology the supremacy of one of the gods is not so clearly stated as in the famous contemporary hymns. It seems that the Ramesside rulers, even if they felt the religious and spiritual necessity of the transcendent god-concept, did not want to be clearly subordinated to a hidden god and lose their own right to be the *nṯr* on earth.

[27] For the paradigma of the transcendent god-concept see: S. MORENZ, *Gott und Mensch im alten Ägypten*, Leipzig 1984 and IDEM, *Die Heraufkunft des transzendenten Gottes in Ägypten*, Berlin 1964.

Zoltán Horváth
Budapest

Sahurē and his Cult-Complex in the Light of Tradition

(Plates 16-18)

As we can formulate, the term "tradition" should be seen as a metacultural phenomenon, or to be more exact, a process that gains its meaning as a link between subsequent generations. In case of ancient Egypt, as opposed to classical antiquity, one should confine oneself to discuss a specialised mode of operation labelled "the flow of tradition" with central (invariable) and peripheral/marginal (variable) values to act.[1] For an archaeologist it is crucial to find the place and evaluate the role that a monument (a tomb, a temple, a commemorative stela etc) fulfils in the above-cited process in the manner of a perceivable manifestation of the cultural memory.[2] The establishment of all *mnemotopoi* has a basic function: to partake in cultural memory. In fact, this achievement has not always been realised, and the failure that the excavator occasionally observes is not possible to explain in a monocasual way, rather with the help of an interaction of a wealth of direct and indirect factors.

For a better understanding, I propose an investigation of the "monument" from a communicative perspective. Similar to a textual analysis, I make a distinction between the role of an *experiencer* and an *agent*; two inseparable communicative functions, the difference being that of the focus and the function being realised in the sequence of relative past, actual present and relative future. The "monument" acts as an *experiencer* if it incorporates values from the past in the process of organising itself, and as an *agent* if it leaves certain features behind which prove to be effective and comprehensible enough to deserve a place in the "flow of tradition".

Sahurē's cult-complex embodies a unique case if interpreted from a communicative point of view. Although this pyramid-complex has often been cited as a successful *agent* (especially as far as the architectural as well as the iconographical features are concerned),[3] the later cult of Sakhmet of Sahurē inhibits us at first sight from presenting a case typical of this analysis. With regards to what we know about the maintenance of the cult of royalty, it is difficult to explain the emergence and long-term existence of such a kind of secondary cult. Moreover, in comparison with the kings from the protodynastic to the end of the IVth dynasty period, the researcher is provided with a very limited amount of material to glimpse into how people of the remote future handled the person of Sahurē and his "monuments". In 1969 WILDUNG published a detailed analysis of the topic under the title *Die Rolle ägyptischer Könige im Bewußtsein ihrer Nachwelt*, having covered the rulers of the first four dynasties. Despite the thorough and deep research into the field in individual instances, his ultimate conclusions – concerning the survival of the royal mortuary cult in particular – seem to be schematic.[4]

[1] J. ASSMANN, Kulturelle und literarische Texte, in: A. LOPRIENO (ed.), *Ancient Egyptian Literature: History and Forms*, PÄ 10, Leiden, New York, Köln 1996, pp. 71-72.

[2] ASSMANN, *Das kulturelle Gedächtnis. Schrift, Erinnerung und politische Identität in frühen Hochkulturen*, München 1992 (hereinafter referred to as: *Kulturelle Gedächtnis*), pp. 38-39; 50, 59-60. Cf. B.J. KEMP, *Ancient Egypt. Anatomy of a Civilization*, London, New York 1989, p. 30.

[3] E.g. M. LEHNER, *The Complete Pyramids*, London 1997, p. 143. " ... the 'conceptual beginning' of all subsequent Old Kingdom examples." Nevertheless, the complex cannot be termed as "canonic" in form (*contra* D. STOCKFISCH, Die Diesseitsrolle des toten Königs im Alten Reich, in: R. GUNDLACH, W. SEIPEL (eds.), *Das frühe ägyptische Königtum. Akten des 2. Symposiums zur Ägyptischen Königsideologie in Wien, 24.-26. 9. 1997*, ÄAT 36,2, Wiesbaden 1999, p. 5), since as ASSMANN put it: "Unter einem "Kanon" verstehen wir jene form von Tradition, in der sie ihre höchste inhaltliche Verbindlichkeit und äußerste formale Festlegung erreicht. Nichts darf hinzugefügt, nichts verändert werden." (ASSMANN, *Kulturelle Gedächtnis*, p. 103) In the development of the Old Kingdom royal mortuary enclosures the cult-complex of Djedkarē deserves the "canonic" epithet.

[4] D. WILDUNG, *Die Rolle ägyptischer Könige im Bewußt-*

In the following, I attempt to explore the presupposed role of topography in cultural memory as exemplified by the cult-complex of Sahurē, to draw attention to a phenomenon termed "the sacrilege of the cult-complex" and last but not at least, to detect a focal shift in the survival of the cult of Sahurē and to propose simultaneously an explanation for the occurrence of the cult of Sakhmet of Sahurē in its earliest attested form, during the Thutmoside Period. The ultimate aim of this paper is to prove that unless an intentional or non-intentional *damnatio memoriae* happens, the flow of tradition does not break off and finds its way to convey face values.

Sahurē in the Role of an *Experiencer*

From the remarkable amount of possibilities to analyse a cult-complex I would like to discuss the basic, however, still unsettled problem of pyramid-placement and pyramid-name, both strictly connected to identification. Before doing so, some observations have to be made concerning the way as we, human beings, perceive the space that surrounds us (**pl. 16**). The **perception of space** is a cognitive process independent of any temporal factors (era, period etc), and the referential point is always the factual present, the observer. In the eyes of the observer a **perceptible space** is a reflection of the **technosphere** (i.e. the effect of human activity on the natural landscape), which can further be divided into **architectural** as well as **cognitive space**; and the latter leads us towards a whole system of *mnemotopoi*, the **cultural topography**.[5]

Abusir, the royal cemetery established by Sahurē himself, should be observed in the wider (cultural) topography of the homogeneous Memphite necropolis extending southwards from the site of Abu Roash along the eastern escarpment of the desert plateau. Moreover, the effect of two further urbanistic factors must be taken into consideration as well: first, the movement of the town-nucleus in accordance with a shift of the bed of the Nile southwards and eastwards and the subsequent ribbon-development of the town;[6] second, the presence of early dynastic cemeteries all along the desert edge. A thorough study of these assemblages of Early Dynastic tombs revealed a list of regional and local factors which determined the placement of a cult-complex:

1. visibility;

2. accessibility;

3. orientation to another (archaeo-)topographical feature.

One cannot afford to ignore the residual branch of the ancient Nile currently known as the Bahr Libeini that apparently served as an ideal water-route for communication from the IIIrd dynasty on, and the chain of the Old Kingdom settlements along the desert escarpment.[7]

In the light of all of the above, one cannot avoid the question: why did Sahurē choose Abusir as a royal burial place?

Two theories have become widely accepted as answers to this question over the last decade of research:

1. The theory promoted by Miroslav VERNER: it was the sun temple of Userkaf that sacrilised the ter-

sein ihrer Nachwelt. Posthume Quellen über die Könige der ersten vier Dynastien, MÄS 17, Berlin 1969 (hereinafter referred to as: *Rolle ägyptischer Könige*), pp. 229-230. Beyond doubt, it is the presentation of the source material as a catalogue that makes it rather difficult to determine a multilinear relationship between the different types of evidence.

[5] The correspondence of cosmic and earthly spheres served as a basis for the semiotism of topographical units. ASSMANN, State and Religion in the New Kingdom, in: W.K. SIMPSON (ed.), *Religion and Philosophy in Ancient Egypt*, Yale Egyptological Studies 3, New Haven, Connecticut 1989 (hereinafter referred to as: State and Religion), pp. 64-65. As far as Egypt's cultural topography is concerned, the point of departure is still H. KEES, *Das alte Ägypten. Eine kleine Landeskunde*, Berlin 1955.

[6] L. GIDDY, Memphis and Saqqara during the late Old Kingdom: Some topographical considerations, in: C. BERGER, G. CLERC, N. GRIMAL (eds.), *Hommages à Jean Leclant* I. *Études Pharaoniques*, BdÉ 106/1, La Caire 1993 (hereinafter referred to as: Memphis and Saqqara), p. 195; D.G. JEFFREYS, *The Survey of Memphis* I, EES, London 1985 (hereinafter referred to as: *Memphis*), *passim*, especially pp. 48-51.

[7] GIDDY, Memphis and Saqqara, p. 194; H.S. SMITH, Uncharted Saqqâra: an Essay, in: BERGER, B. MATHIEU (eds.), *Études sur l'Ancien Empire et la nécropole de Saqqâra dédiéed à Jean-Philippe Lauer* II, Orientalia Monspelienia IX, Montpellier 1997 (hereinafter referred to as: Uncharted Saqqâra), p. 380.

ritory and "persuaded" Sahurē to establish his cult-complex in the immediate vicinity of his father's monument. Besides the difficulties of putting and discussing the two types of installations on the same ground, VERNER also leaves the question open – why Userkaf decided to build the first sun temple at that particular site hidden from the sight of Heliopolis.[8]

2. David JEFFREYS considered the visibility angle from the perspective of Heliopolis.[9] Our map makes it clear that due to the protruding cliff at Batn al-Bataqa (Old Cairo), only the cemeteries of Abu Roash, Giza, Zawiyet el-Aryan and Abu Ghurob are visible from the centre of the sun-cult, even Abusir remains hidden from the eye. In addition to this, GOEDICKE also supported JEFFREYS in the view that Abu Roash is in line with Heliopolis and that there probably existed a mythical axis between Heliopolis and Giza as an earthly reflection of the ecliptic.[10] Although of a preliminary character, I would like to note that Heliopolis is not at all in line with Abu Roash, but with another settlement, the significance of which seem not to have been recognised satisfactorily. This is Letopolis, the Egyptian *Ḫm* (west of modern Ausim) that constituted an axis with Heliopolis.[11] In order to render such a connection probable, I looked for archaeological and mythical links between Heliopolis and Letopolis as well as between Letopolis and Abu Roash. (**pl. 17**) At the edge of the escarpment lies the Early Dynastic cemetery 300 where tomb No 389 contained the following caption: one Hathor head (or Bat?) between two so-called "Min-emblems" which are closely associated with the name of the Old Kingdom Letopolis.[12] Some years ago M. JONES discovered traces of extensive Old Kingdom occupation (possible settlement) on the area between Abu Roash and Ausim by drilling on behalf of the Barakat Drain Improvements Project.[13] It is also worth considering that Djedefrē's pyramid was named after a celestial body (*sḥdw*), identical with one of the planets according to KRAUSS' proposal discussed in his distinguished work entitled *Astronomische Konzepte und Jenseitsvorstellungen in den Pyramidentexten*. Besides many attestations in the *Pyramid Texts*, *Coffin Texts* VI spell 350 claims that the deceased is a *sḥdw* and *Coffin Texts* II spell 117 declares that its setting point is located at *Ḫm*. Even later, the bipolar connection of the heliopolitan Rē-Horakhty and Horus Khenty-Irty, chief god of Letopolis, was paralleled in the two mythical hills of the ecliptic, the *M3nw* and the *B3ẖw*.[14]

Supra I enlisted the three factors which have, in my opinion, a crucial role in determining the placement of a cult-complex.

Visibility. Large-scale archaeological maps indicate a strong tendency to place pyramid-complexes on elevated sites, plateaus having connexions with a basin via natural approach routes, wadis. From a chronological point of view, all the prominent places from Abu Roash southwards had already been reserved by the time of the early Vth dynasty, let alone Saqqara-South.

Accessibility. Recent Egypt Exploration Society (EES) excavators suspect that the core of Memphis known as *inb(w)-ḥḏ* was located opposite to the Early Dynastic tombs of Saqqara-North proper, consequently the Abusir "Lake" and the Abusir Wadi served as the main approach route to the inner part of the cemetery[15] (**pl. 18**). The wadi

---

[8] As VERNER summarises a long-existent common Egyptological proposal: "Some Egyptologists believe that Abusir was chosen because it was still possible to glimpse the sun shining on the top of the obelisk of Re's temple in Heliopolis." (M. VERNER, *Forgotten Pharaohs, Lost Pyramids. Abusir*, Praha 1994 (hereinafter referred to as: *Abusir*), pp. 67-68; 102).

[9] JEFFREYS, The Topography of Heliopolis and Memphis: Some Cognitive Aspects, in: H. GUKSCH, D. POLZ (eds.), *Stationen. Beiträge zur Kultgeschichte Ägyptens. Rainer Stadelmann gewidmet*, Mainz 1998, p. 66.

[10] H. GOEDICKE, Giza: Causes and Concepts, *BACE* 6 (1995), pp. 39-40.

[11] For the ancient Egyptian settlement and her religious connotations see K. ZIBELIUS, *Ägyptische Siedlungen nach Texten des Alten Reiches*, TAVO Beiheft Reihe B 19, Wiesbaden 1978 (hereinafter referred to as: *Siedlungen*), pp. 186-9; F. GOMAÀ, *Die Besiedlung Ägyptens während des Mittleren Reiches. II. Unterägypten und die angrenzenden Gebiete*, TAVO Beiheft Reihe B 66/2, Wiesbaden 1987, pp. 67-75 with further literature.

[12] PM III², p. 8.

[13] M. JONES, A New Old Kingdom Settlement Near Ausim: Report of the Archaeological Discoveries Made in the Barakat Drain Improvements Project, *MDAIK* 51 (1995), pp. 87-88.

[14] R. KRAUSS, *Astronomische Konzepte und Jenseitsvorstellungen in den Pyramidentexten*, ÄA 59, Wiesbaden 1997, pp. 259-260.

[15] SMITH, Uncharted Saqqâra, p. 380; A. TAVARES, The Saqqara Survey Project, in: C.J. EYRE (ed.), *Proceeding of the Seventh International Congress of Egyptologists*,

itself is densely occupied by tombs ranging from Early Dynastic to Roman times, since it retained its status as the main entrance of the cemetery throughout the entire history of ancient Egypt.[16] The pyramid field occupies the large protruding cliff on the northern side of the continuously used route of the Abusir Wadi. This location implies that both principles (visibility and accessibility) operated at the same time.

Orientation. Instead of Heliopolis, the presence or vicinity of another cult-district could contribute to the nomination of Abusir to the status of a royal cemetery. In fact, one must bear in mind that *Pyramid Texts* spell 445 denotes two localities, namely *r-sṯ3w* and *pḏw(-š)* as areas sacred to Sokar, the latter often identified with the Abusir "lake".[17] An inscription on a statue base which defines Menkaurē as one "beloved of Sokar",[18] the presence of the Early Dynastic to the early Old Kingdom tombs south of Giza[19] and much more informative New Kingdom material concerning the topic supports EDWARD's suspicion that the extrasepulchral shabti depots (which had already been detected by PETRIE himself in some cases), which show remarkable similarity to depos unearthed at Abydos (cult-district of Osiris) as well as in the Serapeum area, may indicate the close vicinity of another significant cult installation, possibly that of Sokar.[20]

Without doubt, the ribbon development of Memphis constitutes another point of reference if the matter of orientation is to be taken seriously. The reconstruction of the Ramesside Memphis incorporating distinctive cult-districts helps us to imagine a similar rendering of that particular landscape even in the Old Kingdom times, since not only *inb(w)-ḥḏ* but *Ptḥ rsy inb=f, Nt mḥtt inb=s* and *Ḥwt-Ḥrw nbt nht*[21] can be attested among the toponims of such an early phase of Egyptian history, respectively. A setting, resembling the inner organisation of New Kingdom Thebes with a water route for communicational purposes, finds its way to several references in the Abusir archive, especially where navigational festivals of mortuary character (the festival of Min, Sokar, the Hathor-*bikt* and that of the sacred emblems etc) are mentioned.[22]

Before leaving the problem of orientation, I would like to render a few words on the so-called "Abusir diagonal" first observed by VERNER. Professor VERNER claimed that the northwestern corners of the pyramids of Sahurē, Noferirkarē and Noferefrē (this latter king was provided with a *i3t* and not a true pyramid)[23] constitute an axis pointing towards Heliopolis proper.[24] To date it was impossible to rec-

OLA 82, Leuven 1998, pp. 1135-42; JEFFREYS, TAVARES, The Historic Landscape of Early Dynastic Memphis, *MDAIK* 50 (1994), pp. 143-73; GIDDY, Memphis and Saqqara, p. 194.

[16] It may well be supported in the future by current Polish excavations under the direction of K. MYŚLIWIEC behind the Netjerikhet-complex, right at the edge of the wadi. (K. MYŚLIWIEC, Excavations 1997, *PAM* IX (1998), pp. 90-99; IDEM, *New faces of Sakkara. Recent discoveries in West Sakkara*, Warsaw 1999).

[17] Ro-setau as an extensive area south to the Sphinx of Giza: Ch.M. ZIVIE, *Giza au deuxième millénaire*, BdÈ 70, Caire 1976, pp. 218-219; I.E.S. EDWARDS, The Shetayet of Rosetau, in: L.H. LESKO (ed.), *Egyptological Studies in Honor of Richard A. Parker*, Hannover, London 1986 (hereinafter referred to as: Shetayet of Rosetau), pp. 28-29. Pedju-she taken to be identical with modern Abusir in VERNER, *Abusir*, p. 64; ZIBELIUS, *Siedlungen*, pp. 87ff.; C. GRAINDORGE-HÉREIL, *Le Dieu Sokar à Thèbes au Nouvel Empire*, I. *Textes*, Göttinger Orientforschungen 28,1, Wiesbaden 1994, pp. 34ff.

[18] *Egyptian Art in the Age of the Pyramids*, New York 1999, p. 277 n. 1; B. BEGELSBACHER-FISCHER, *Untersuchungen zur Götterwelt des Alten Reiches im Spiegel der Privatgräber der IV. und V. Dynastie*, OBO 37, Göttingen 1981, p. 187.

[19] For the early dynastic cemetery in the vicinity of the so-called 'Covington-tomb' see more in G..T. MARTIN, "Covington's Tomb" and Related Early Monuments at Gîza, in: C. BERGER, B. MATHIEU (eds.), *Études sur l'Ancien Empire et la nécropole de Saqqâra dédiées à Jean-Philippe Lauer* II, Orientalia Monspeliena IX, Montpellier 1997, pp. 279-288.

[20] EDWARDS, Shetayet of Rosetau, pp. 28ff.

[21] Not identical with *Ḥwt-Ḥrw nbt nht rsyt* which can be attested exclusively from the New Kingdom on.

[22] The solarised festival of Sokar is well attested in the Abusir-archive P. POSENER-KRIÉGER, J.L. de CENIVAL, *Hieratic Papyri in the British Museum. 5th Series: The Abu Sir Papyri*, London 1968 (hereinafter referred to as: *Hieratic Papyri*), pls. 13-14. Further information about the procession could be gained from the dedicatory inscription of Niuserrē's sun temple at Abu Ghurob: W. HELCK, Die "Weihinschrift" aus dem Taltempel des Sonnenheiligtums des Königs Neuserre bei Abu Gurob, *SAK* 5 (1977), p. 59, pl. II. The festival of the Hathor-falcon (*bikt*): POSENER-KRIÉGER, de CENIVAL, *Hieratic Papyri*, pl. 19; the festival of Min: *ibidem*, pl. 82.

[23] VERNER, *Abusir*, p. 139; G. CALLENDER, Report from Abusir 1997/98, *BACE* 9 (1998), p. 19.

[24] VERNER, *Abusir*, p. 135.

ognise such a direct orientation of the above-mentioned diagonal to Heliopolis as the situation at Giza. On the other hand, I find it far more interesting that the "Abusir diagonal" is determined by monuments of chronologically successive rulers, all of which containing the *b3* element in its own designation (a custom that never appeared afterwards).[25] Unfortunately, I am still not able to explore the relevance of this observation, if it has any at all.

Basically, under the early Vth dynasty, the cult-complex of Sahurē obtained the most prominent location on the Abusir plateau, even acting as an inner referential point for the placement of the royal complexes of Noferirkarē and Noferefrē in the following years. The pattern of pyramid placement along an imaginary axis, which can also be observed at Giza was broken by Niuserrē, whose large-scale building activities on the spot, highly influenced by economic factors as well, transformed the overall appearance of the royal pyramid field into an assemblage of tombs of the same bloodline.

The Sacrilege of the Cult-complex

The first trace of this process is the walled off secondary entrance which BORCHARDT dated to the late Old Kingdom; we are also informed that the work has been carried out by the *sḫm* subdivision of the *imy-nfrt* phyle.[26] The expansion of the dwelling place of the mortuary priests and the cult personnel entering and occupying sacred areas within the walls of the temple as well as making private use of the cult equipment and provision is a well demonstrated phenomenon not exclusively at Abusir, but at various places of the whole Memphite necropolis. Nonetheless, we can be certain that the mortuary cult of Sahurē himself was sustained at least until the end of the VIth dynasty, since at least eight mortuary priests served in the cult-complex of Sahurē under the reign of Pepi II.[27] The fragment that BORCHARDT came upon in the area of the valley temple is apparently a part of a royal decree, which might have also belonged to the second half of the VIth dynasty.[28]

Restoration of the Cult in the Middle Kingdom

Recent Czech excavations have revealed that central-Abusir ceased to be the cemetery of royalty and the upper class nobility from the Old Kingdom on.[29] Another feature worth mentioning is the revivification of the mortuary cults of the Old Kingdom rulers during the early XIIth dynasty. Typical Middle Kingdom hemispherical cups, and fragments of sealings were obtained from selected sectors of the funerary complexes (e.g. Khentikaus II, Pyramid Lepsius XXIV),[30] and the suspected family burials of the Middle Kingdom mortuary priests in the vicinity of the Noferirkarē and Niuserrē complexes have already been published by SCHÄFER.

In the case of Sahurē, the graffiti of Ameny and

[25] *Ḫꜥi-b3-S3ḥw-Rꜥ; Bꜥ-Nfr-ir-k3-Rꜥ; Nṯr-b3-Nfr.f Rꜥ.*

[26] L. BORCHARDT, *Das Grabdenkmal des Königs Sꜥa3ḥu-Rē* I. *Der Bau*, Leipzig 1910 (hereinafter referred to as: *Grabdenkmal des Sꜥa3ḥu-Rē* I), pp. 99-100.

[27] K. BAER, *Rank and Title in the Old Kingdom. The Structure of the Egyptian Administration in the Fifth and Sixth Dynasties*, Chicago 1960, pp. 109-159, Nos 360, 452, 458, 462, 523, 528, 600.

[28] BORCHARDT, *Grabdenkmal des Sꜥa3ḥu-Rē* I, pp. 100; GOEDICKE, *Königliche Dokumente aus dem alten Reich*, ÄA 14, Wiesbaden 1967, p. 226.

[29] VERNER, *Abusir*, p. 89; L. BAREŠ, Eine Statue des Würdenträgen Sachmethotep und ihre Beziehung zum Totenkult des Mittleren Reiches in Abusir, *ZÄS* 112 (1985), p. 117.

[30] The revivication of the cult extended to the whole of the royal cemetery. **Noferirkarē**: burials of the funerary priests at the eastern side of the pyramid temple (BORCHARDT, *Das Grabdenkmal des Königs Nefer-ir-ke3-reꜥ*, Leipzig 1909, pp. 72ff.; BAREŠ, *ZÄS* 112 (1985), p. 91; BAREŠ, A Note to the Thirteenth Dynasty at Abusir, *VA* 4/2 (1988), p. 117; VERNER, *Abusir*, pp. 89ff.), traces of cult activity from the rear part of the temple, from the area of the offering chapel (BAREŠ, *ZÄS* 112 (1985), p. 93). **Khentikaus II**: pottery characteristic of the early XIIth dynasty (*hemispherical cup*), burial of a child in the floor of the sarcophagus chamber (VERNER, *The Pyramid Complex of Khentkaus. Abusir* III, Praha 1995, pp. 19, 42). **Noferefrē**: burial of Huiankh inside the funerary temple (BAREŠ, *VA* 4/2 (1988), pp. 117, 119 footnote 3; BAREŠ, The Necropolis at Abusir (South Field) in Middle Kingdom, in: *Fifth International Congress of Egyptology. Abstracts of Papers*, Cairo 1988, p. 13; BAREŠ, *ZÄS* 112 (1985), p. 93), pottery fragments characteristic of the XIIth dynasty from the site of the northern-, or entrance-chapel (VERNER, Excavations at Abusir. Preliminary Report 1997/8, *ZÄS* 126 (1999), pp. 70-76 and p. 71 footnote 6). **Niuserrē**: cemetery of funerary priests including Herishefhotep inside and around the funerary temple and the causeway (H. SCHÄFER, *Priestergräber und andere Grabfunde vom Ende des Alten Reiches bis zur Griechischen Zeit von Totentempel des Ne-user-re*, Leipzig 1908; VERNER, *Abusir*, pp. 90-91). **Lepsius Pyr. XXIV**: pottery characteristic of the early XIIth dynasty

Apopy might well have originated prior to the Middle Kingdom,[31] though the restoration inscription, interpreted incorrectly as Ramesside by BORCHARDT, resembles the dedicatory inscription of Sesostris I on the Karnak-statue of Sahurē[32] to such a great extent that the question emerges whether we encounter another piece of evidence from roughly the same period (both inscriptions read as follows "*ir.n.f m mnw=f n it=f nswt-bity S3ḥw-Rꜥ*").[33] The unfortunate fact that the area surrounding the cult-complex of Sahurē is practically archaeologically unexplored makes it far more difficult to see the case clearly, but the remains of two tombs south-east of the complex as well as a fragment of a scarab from Middle Kingdom times suggest intensified Middle Kingdom activity.[34] As far as the Memphis ruin-field is concerned, a cemetery dated to the First Intermediate Period or early Middle Kingdom has been unearthed,[35] while the core of the actual settlement (*Ḏd-(i)swt-Tti*) as well as the majority of tombs were centred in and around the Teti-pyramid sector.[36]

It is still a matter of debate how we should handle the statues of Old Kingdom rulers from the *cachet* of Karnak.[37] Attacking WILDUNG's proposal, BAREŠ argued that they have nothing to do with an existing cult in the district of Memphis, as although the mortuary cult of Unis lasted till the end of the XIIth dynasty, there is not a single piece that could have originated from a possible Karnak statue of Unis at our disposal.[38] On the other hand, the establishment of an officially recognised cult for the royal ancestors might have well influenced the editors of Thotmes III when compiling the list of kings for the "Chamber of Ancestors" in the Akh-Menu.[39]

As a short summary, we can assert that the official maintenance of the royal mortuary cults at Abusir met their end not later than the First Intermediate Period. As the archaeological material suggests, the majority of the Middle Kingdom local population of Memphis – definitely middle-lower class people – preferred the area around the pyramid of Teti as their resting-place. The mortuary cults at Abusir came around due to official stimulus but in a roughly reduced form, nevertheless, whatever the inspiration of the later cult of Sakhmet of Sahurē was, it should have already been known at the time of establishing an ancestor-cult in the other religious centre, at Karnak. So far, we are not provided with any kind of source material concerning the fate of the Abusir Kings during the Second Intermediate Period, the next piece of information being a reference to the above-cited cult of Sakhmet of Sahurē.

The Medium

The communicative point of view implies the existence of a medium, or media, to convey a certain value from the dimension of the relative past through the actual present to the relative future. To trace it back, we cannot ignore the discussion of the question: why did the upper temple of Sahurē happen to accommodate a secondary cult of the feline goddess Sakhmet? One may argue that the well-known rep-

(*hemispherical cup*) as well as seal-fragments in the foreground of the pyramid entrance (VERNER, Excavations at Abusir. Season 1987 – Preliminary Report, *ZÄS* 115 (1988), p. 169).

[31] BORCHARDT, *Grabdenkmal des Sꜥa3ḥu-Rē* I, p. 120; BAREŠ, *ZÄS* 112 (1985), pp. 117, 119 footnote 5.

[32] CG 42004.

[33] BORCHARDT, *Grabdenkmal des Sꜥa3ḥu-Rē* I, p. 104 *contra* BAREŠ, *ZÄS* 112 (1985), p. 92; S.-E. HOENES, *Untersuchungen zu Wesen und Kult der Göttin Sachmet*, Bonn 1976 (hereinafter referred to as: *Sachmet*), p. 115.

[34] BAREŠ, *ZÄS* 112 (1985), p. 91 footnote 25.

[35] JEFFREYS, *Memphis*, pp. 28ff.

[36] J. MALEK, Saqqara. First Intermediate period and Middle Kingdom, *LÄ* V, col. 409; IDEM, King Merykare and his Pyramid, in: BERGER, CLERC, GRIMAL (eds.), *Hommages à Jean Leclant* IV, BdÉ 106/4, La Caire 1993, pp. 203-214; IDEM, The temples at Memphis. Problems highlighted by the EES survey, in: S. QUIRKE (ed.), *The Temple in Ancient Egypt. New discoveries and recent research*, London 1997, p. 93; MALEK, D.N.E. MAGEE, A Group of Coffins Found at Northern Saqqara, *Société D'Égyptologie Bulletin* 9-10 (1984-85), pp. 167-168; GIDDY, *The Anubieion at Saqqâra*, II. *The Cemeteries*, EES, London 1992, p. 2 and footnote 8; SMITH, Uncharted Saqqâra, pp. 385, 392 footnote 29.

[37] Fundamental to the problem: WILDUNG, *Rolle ägyptischer Könige*, pp. 60-63; IDEM, Zur Frühgeschichte des Amun-Tempels von Karnak, *MDAIK* 25 (1969), pp. 212-219; B.V. BOTHMER, The Karnak Statue of Ny-user-ra, *MDAIK* 30,2 (1974), pp. 165-170.

[38] BAREŠ, *ZÄS* 112 (1985), p. 93; cf. A.M. MOUSSA, Excavations in the Valley Temple of King Unas at Saqqara, *ASAE* 64 (1981), p. 76, pl. 4.

[39] For Sahurē's appearance in the Akh-Menu see WILDUNG, *Rolle ägyptischer Könige*, pp. 60-63; G. BJÖRKMAN, *Kings at Karnak. A Study of the Treatment of the Monuments of Royal Predecessors in the*

resentation of the royal offering to Bastet served as an inspiration,[40] though the Old Kingdom statuary program might well have included statues of sphinxes, the fragments of which were documented during BORCHARDT's excavation, one piece even bearing the titulatory of Sahurē himself.[41] I would like to draw attention to a frequently occurring lion-motive from the collection of the *Baugraffiti*, all of which come from the inner section of the mortuary temple bordered by the transverse corridor and the pyramid surface, respectively, in other words, from that particular part of the temple where the suspected statue cult could have taken place.[42] Do they refer to the presence of lion statues? Whatever may have happened, a relief with very much the same motif is also known from the temple of Niuserrē in the neighbourhood, moreover with a large granite lion-head has been discovered directly north of the so-called "statue-hall" with the five niches.[43] In my opinion, the ultimate reason for the late cult of Sakhmet being detected in the temple of Sahurē and not in that of Niuserrē should be looked for in the state of preservation. Every visitor is aware of the fact that the cult-complex of Sahurē is still the best-preserved monument on the whole pyramid-field. At the dawn of a new era, in the early New Kingdom, the landscape of the Memphite necropolis was characterised by hardly visible, sand-buried monuments; where a prevailing building could not escape the eye of the observer.[44] Consequently, it is not accidental at all that the first New Kingdom graffiti from the reign of Amenhotep I are made by visitors to the Step Pyramid.[45] The Ptahshepses mastaba, just a couple of metres from the pyramid of Sahurē, wears another graffito dated to the reign of Thotmes III which informs us that visitors came "to see the temple of King Sahurē and **speak of its beauty"**.[46] Despite rules governing how to compose the so-called *Besucherinschriften*, their attestations make it highly improbable that almost entirely collapsed monuments attracted visitors and induced their admiration; for this reason I tend to conclude that, similarly to the pyramid of Netjerikhet, the cult-complex of Sahurē endured in a quite well-preserved state.

The Early New Kingdom Cult

By way of some sort of introduction, I would like to remark that both the Thutmoside chapel immediately next to the *ka*-chapel of Khaemuaset on the high desert west of Abusir (currently excavated by a Japanese mission from the Waseda University)[47] as well as the occurrence of the phrase *š-pr ʿ3* in an inscription from the reign of Thotmes IV (identified as the "pool" of Abusir or the Abusir "lake") emphasise the sacred nature of that vast area of Abusir in the first half of the XVIIIth dynasty, although the tombs of the upper nobility were concentrated elsewhere.[48]

The emergence of the cult of Sakhmet of Sahurē is not a typical subject of personal piety,[49] since adding the cartouche of Thotmes IV to the scene entitled "Royal offering to Bastet" implies more an official recognition even at such an early stage, and a new upstairs was built of mudbrick to give easier access to the part of the temple dedicated to the veneration of Sakhmet. It is beyond doubt that the fact that no

Early New Kingdom, Uppsala 1971, pp. 41, 183; D.B. REDFORD, *Pharaonic King-Lists, Annals and Day-Books. A Contribution to the Study of the Egyptian Sense of History*, Mississauga 1986, pp. 32, 137 with extensive literature.

40 BORCHARDT, *Das Grabdenkmal des Königs Sʿa3ḥu-Rē*, II. *Die Wandbilder*, Leipzig 1913, Bl. 35, 36.

41 BORCHARDT, *Grabdenkmal des Sʿa3ḥu-Rē* I, p. 111, fig. 141; PM III², p. 329.

42 BORCHARDT, *Grabdenkmal des Sʿa3ḥu-Rē* I, pp. 88-89, 91 Graffiti M 23, M 32 and M 60.

43 VERNER, *Abusir*, pp. 82-83; PM III², p. 336.

44 The situation is discussed in detail by MALEK (MALEK, A Meeting of the Old and New Saqqâra during the New Kingdom, in: A.B. LLOYD (ed.), *Studies in Pharaonic Religion and Society in Honour of J.G. Griffiths*, EES 8, London 1992 (hereinafter referred to as: Saqqara during NK), p. 59).

45 WILDUNG, *Rolle ägyptischer Könige*, pp. 65-66.

46 J. BAINES, The Destruction of the Pyramid Temple of Sahure, *GM* 4 (1973), p. 12. (My emphasis).

47 S. YOSHIMURA, Recent Excavations of Waseda University in the Saqqara Area and on the West Bank at Luxor, in: *Eighth International Congress of Egyptologists. Abstracts of Papers*, Cairo 2000, p. 198.

48 *Urk.* IV, p. 1632, 2; HOENES, *Sachmet*, p. 113.

49 Definition with examples in ASSMANN, State and Religion, pp. 68ff.; U. LUFT, Religion, in: REDFORD (ed.), *The Oxford Encyclopedia of Ancient Egypt*, Oxford 2001, p. 144.

cult organisation can be attested from this phase and that the votive offerings including vessels, rings, beakers, ear-stele (the latter being a plain evidence of the intermediary role of the goddess) indicate that, ultimately, we should evaluate this cult as a manifestation of personal piety. With the Ramesside Period, one is faced with a new, slightly different phase of cult which falls out of our scope. Still, I intend to refer to two inscriptions (the second is of uncertain date) to exemplify the focal shift mentioned at the beginning of this paper. The inscription of Maya[50] (reign of Tutankhamun) dedicates the offering to *Sḫmt ḫrt-ib ḥwt* (*S3ḥw-Rꜥ*) with the sense that it is actually a guest/secondary cult (*ḫrt-ib*) in the area of the temple (*ḥwt*) of Sahurē, while on a stela of a certain Amenenhat[51] the name of the ruler is completely misspelt, and makes it obvious that it was the goddess Sakhmet and her cult that enjoyed the focus of veneration, and the person of a former ruler of the remote Old Kingdom had exclusively a specifying function from a cult-topographical point of view. Sakhmet is asked for a good life, a body full of joy, a good burial, a good age in the west of Memphis, favour and love etc, nothing to contribute to the regular vocabulary of personal piety.[52]

We can conclude that the New Kingdom cult of Sakhmet of Sahurē came into existence at a frequently visited site, and in this way similar to the pattern of veneration of Teti and Menkauhor as "local saints" from the New Kingdom onward, whose popularity is topographically based on the close vicinity of the Serapeum Way.[53]

The form of the cult in the Ramesside times as well as from the reign of Amasis onward constitute two further separate stages with minor and major modifications, additions and transformations, and discussion of them would stretch the limits of this or other papers.

Conclusions

The study of a royal cult-complex can be labelled as complete if the monument is explored in its wider historical dimensions, since from the very moment of its establishment it is part of the actual present. The fate of many monuments exemplifies that as soon as the organised administration of the royal cult ceased, some other factor(s) coincided to ensure the survival of the memory of particular royalty. This discussion has been aimed at demonstrating the crucial role of topography and cult-topography in maintaining the person of Sahurē in the memory of successive generations via a focal shift from the mortuary cult to the popular cult of a local goddess as well as in keeping the flow of tradition continuous from a purely theoretical perspective.

[50] BORCHARDT, *Grabdenkmal des Sꜥa3ḥu-Rē* I, pp. 121-122.

[51] *Ibidem*, p. 122. Possibly Ramesside.

[52] *ꜥḥꜥ nfrw, ẖt ḫry ršwt, ḥꜥ.w rnpy, ḥs.wt mrt, ḳrst nfrt m-ḫt sm3 t3 ḥr imntt Mn-nfr* occur in the inscriptions of Huy's bowl and Maya's stela, respectively. *Ibidem*, pp. 121-122.

[53] MALEK, Saqqâra during NK, pp. 67-72; for the New Kingdom cult of king Menkauhor see: J. BERLANDINI-GRENIER, Varia Memphitica I. (I), *BIFAO* 76 (1976), pp. 313-316 is of special importance.

Jozef Hudec
Bratislava

Some Scarabs from the Second Intermediate Period in the Bratislava Collection*

(Plates 19-20)

Scarab-beetles are a very characteristic feature of Ancient Egyptian culture and religion. Scarab-seals, on the other hand, are a characteristic feature of Egyptian material culture. They appeared as early as the Old Kingdom,[1] though the first scarabs decorated on their base are found in archaeological context in the First Intermediate Period.[2]

The scarabs were known also outside Egypt or Egypt-related areas in Syropalestine, Nubia or the Mediterranean.[3] They can be found in several other parts of the Roman Empire, in the areas to which the soldiers previously stationed in Egypt were moved and they are even known far beyond the *Limes Romanus*. For example, ŚLIWA[4] mentions scarabs found in Poland and there is a scarab found even on Ceylon (Sri Lanka).[5] There is also a piece found in 19th century Slovakia and another described in the early 60's,[6] though both were found under very obscure conditions.

Only a few of the about one hundred scarabs and scaraboids, today located in Slovak museums, are mentioned in this paper. The focus will be on three scarabs and one scaraboid (**pls. 19** and **20**). These four pieces are now deposited at the Archaeological Department of the Slovak National Museum, Bratislava. They were originally collected by Dr Daniel SCHIMKO,[7] probably before 1867. There is no further information on the origin of the scarabs and the scaraboid.

Description

Inventory No **AP 13 393**. The scarab is made of Egyptian faience.[8] Height – 0.8 cm, length – 1.9 cm, width – 1.3 cm. The scarab is provided with a stylised clypeus and a head with schematic eyes. This part is separated from the scarab's back, which has no division into prothorax and elytra. The legs are very stylised; there is only one short line depicting the pair of the most hind legs. There is a longitudinal aperture drilled into the scarab's body. On the flat base is carved the representation in an oval enclosure as follows: alongside the right edge of the base is depicted a crocodile, oriented towards the scarab's head. On the base's left side, behind the crocodile's back, there is a standing figure with a bird's head. The figure is stretching one hand up in front of its head and the other hand is hanging loosely down. The figure is probably wearing a wig and is dressed in a skirt. Below the figure is carved the *nb*-sign. There is a ribbed pattern on the crocodile's body, the skirt and the *nb*-sign. The core of the scarab is creamy coloured, without a glaze slip. The diameter of the scarab's longitudinal aperture is 0.2 cm.

* I would like to express here my thanks to the Andrew W. Mellon Foundation and to the W.F. Albright Institute of Archaeological Research in Jerusalem for having enabled me to conduct research necessary also for this paper.

1 R. GIVEON, Skarabäus, *LÄ* V, col. 973.

2 *Ibidem*, col. 974.

3 N.J. SKON-JEDELE, *"Aigyptiaka": A catalogue of Egyptian and Egyptianizing objects excavated from Greek archaeological sites, ca. 1100-525 B.C., with historical commentary*, Ann Arbor 1995.

4 J. ŚLIWA, *Skarabeusze egipskie. Uniwersytet Jagielloński*, Kraków 1995, pp. 29-32.

5 P. CHARVÁT, An Egyptian scarab from Sri Lanka (Ceylon), *GM* 70 (1984), pp. 19-26.

6 Z. ŽÁBA, Staroegyptské skaraby. Slovensko, *Časopis pre rozvoj humanitných vied* XV, part 7, Bratislava s.d., pp. 161-167.

7 J. HUDEC, Perspectives of research and publishing of Egyptian Collections in Slovakia, in: J. POPIELSKA-GRZYBOWSKA (ed.), *Proceedings of the First Central European Conference of Young Egyptologists. Egypt 1999: Perspectives of Research. Warsaw 7-9 June 1999*, Światowit Supplement Series E: Egyptology, vol. I, WES, vol. III, Warsaw 2001, p. 37.

8 A. LUCAS, J.R. HARRIS, *Ancient Egyptian Materials and Industries*, London 1962 (hereinafter referred to as: *Materials*), pp. 156-167.

Inventory No **AP 13 411**. The scaraboid is made of serpentine,[9] its back is undecorated. Height – 0.7 cm, length – 1.8 cm, width – 1.4 cm. Similar to scarabs there is a longitudinal aperture drilled in the scaraboid's core. The flat base in the shape of an irregular oval is decorated with interlocking S-shaped spiral scrolls and hieroglyphic signs. The decoration is divided into four parts oriented across the length of the base. In the upper left part of the base is carved an *ꜥnḫ*-sign. An S-shaped spiral scroll is on its right side. The lower left part is also decorated with an S-shaped spiral scroll, interlocking with the former one by curved lines, which border the base. Finally, there is a *ḏd*-sign, connected with the curved line, in the lower right part. The serpentine stone used for the scaraboid is soft and greenish in colour. The diameter of the scaraboid's longitudinal plugged hole is 0.25 cm.

Inventory No **AP 13 412.** The scarab is made of Egyptian faience. Height – 0.6 cm, length – 1.2 cm, width – 0.8 cm. The scarab is slightly damaged in its frontal part. Only two slant lines have survived from the original division of the clypeus and the head. Besides a trace of the head-to-prothorax division, there is no further division on the scarab's back. Legs are represented in a very stylised way; by two horizontal lines incised around the scarab's lateral sides. The space between the lines has further schematic divisions, one representing the hind legs. There is a longitudinal piercing through the scarab's body. The entire flat base is decorated by spiral scrolls and hieroglyphic signs, bordered by an oval enclosure. The scrolls are concentrated in eight points. Four of them are linked through a circle in the middle of the base. Others, close to the shorter ends of the base, are linked into tulip-shaped pairs with *wꜣḏ*-signs in the caps. The shabby glaze of the scarab was originally coloured green. On the damaged places is visible a light core. The diameter of the scarab's longitudinal aperture is 0.15 cm. There is a small old label stuck to the back.

Inventory No **AP 13 413**. The scarab is made of steatite.[10] Height – 0.7 cm, length – 1.7 cm, width – 1.15 cm. The scarab is very shabby, therefore only traces of the head have survived on its back. Legs are represented with a stylised plastic relief. The fore pair of legs is ribbed. There is a longitudinal aperture drilled through the scarab's body. The shabby flat base bears an undistinguished representation. There is a standing figure along the left longer side, turned to the right. The figure is wearing a skirt with an appendix(?). On the opposite side is a reared cobra (goddess), turned towards the figure. Underneath is a *nb*-sign. The cobra, the wig(?), the skirt and the *nb*-sign are ribbed. The representation is oriented across the length. The shabby scarab is made of green steatite. The diameter of the scarab's longitudinal plugged hole is 0.2 cm.

Commentary

Inventory No **AP 13 393**. The specimen belongs to the group of amulets bearing the figures of gods. The figure with the bird's head might depict several gods: the falcon headed god Horus, the god Hawron[11] of Near East or the ibis headed god Thot. There is also an analogy connected with the snake-headed goddess Wadjet[12] but this is not the case. The *nb*-sign, usually accompanying the representations on scarabs, probably has a particular meaning in this case – to stress the divine character of the bird-headed figure as compared to the *msḥ*-crocodile. It is displayed quite often on the scarabs of the XVth dynasty.[13] It seems, with regard to Ancient Egyptian myths, that the scene may represent the victory of Horus over the animal of Seth.[14] KEEL also suggests: "Der Falkenköpfige auf den Skarabäen der 15., der Hyksos-Dynastie, kann als ägyptischer Königsgott identifiziert werden".[15] The scarabs of this type occur very often in Palestinian sites.[16] In Tell

[9] *Ibidem*, pp. 420-421.

[10] *Ibidem*, p. 421.

[11] F.S. MATOUK, *Corpus du Scarabée égyptien* II. *Analyse thématique*, Beirut 1977 (hereinafter referred to as: *Scarabée égyptien* II), pp. 52-53, 377:189-190.

[12] *Ibidem*, pp. 86, 355.

[13] O. KEEL, *Corpus der Stempelsiegel-Amulette aus Palästine/Israel* I, OBO, Series Archaeologica 13, Freiburg, Schweiz 1997 (hereinafter referred to as: *Stempelsiegel-Amulette* I), pp. 86-7:24, 158-9:159, 282-3:526, 426-7:952, 460-1:1046, 1048, 1049.

[14] E. BRUNNER-TRAUT, Krokodil, *LÄ* III, col. 796.

[15] KEEL et al., *Studien zu den Stempelsiegeln aus Palästina/ Israel* II, OBO 88, Freiburg, Schweiz 1989 (hereinafter referred to as: *Stempelsiegeln aus Palästina* II), p. 276.

[16] W.M.F. PETRIE, *Hyksos and Israelite Cities*, London 1906, p. 24.

el-Far'a (South, i.e. Beth-Pelet)[17] a similar scarab was found in the tomb 1026 together with a scarab resembling AP 13 413. Both, typology (H-B2/3, B-PN/O, S-e5) and design (10A),[18] confirm the dating into the XVth dynasty. The scarab does not represent the *Scarabeus sacer L.* specimen but probably the *Gymnopleurus*.[19]

Inventory No AP **13 411** The scaraboid was originally probably incorporated into a ring, deduced from the shape of the piercing. It belongs to the group of amulets decorated with geometric designs. The hieroglyphic signs are connected with life and stability. The meaning of the spiral scrolls remains so far obscure. A similar design, but with two *ʿnḫ*-signs, covers the base of a scarab from Tell Fara-South.[20] It was set in the Hyksos Period, but it is not known in which tomb the scarab was found.[21] Typology can point to this dating in particular only; design 2B occurs on scarabs in the classical XIIth dynasty and then between the late XIIIth-XVth dynasty.[22]

Inventory No AP **13 412.** The scarab belongs to the group of amulets decorated with geometric patterns. The circle in the middle of the base may represent the sun, the hieroglyphic *w3ḏ*-signs symbolise youth and prosperity. The meaning of the spiral scrolls remains obscure. There are several similar patterns appearing on scarabs from Palestine/Israel, dated to the XIIIth-XVIIIth dynasty.[23] These scarabs are, however, dated without archaeological context. The cross design pattern class 5 and the typological features of the scarab (H-B2, B-PS/O, S-e7)[24] point to dating into the XIIth-XIIIth dynasty. Taking into consideration both dating periods, the conclusion of chronological setting would roughly correspond with the Second Intermediate Period.

Inventory No **AP 13 413**. The base is decorated with a frequently found representation,[25] depicting a falcon-headed god with ureaus in his hand.[26] The god is more likely to represent the Egyptian god Horus[27] than the Asian god Hawron.[28] The above-mentioned scarabs were in several cases found in an archaeological context, which allow a dating of the described scarab to the MBIIB/C, parallel with the Hyksos Period (XVth dynasty).[29] Typological features (H-?, B-PN/PS-?, S-d5, D-10A)[30] partly support this conclusion.

Conclusions

All the above-mentioned scarabs seem to be from the Second Intermediate Period, two of them are more exactly from the XVth dynasty. In the Second Intermediate Period the idea of scarab-seals was probably adopted also in Syropalestine in such a range that the local production of scarabs was exported even to Egypt.[31] Although we have no information on the origin of the scarabs and scaraboid, for the above-mentioned reason we cannot even reject their possible Syropalestinian origin.

Unfortunately, the scarabs from Bratislava are unable to contribute to the discussions on chronology because their archaeological context is, and will very probably stay, unknown. They can just adopt existing typological methods and more or less successfully prove their settings with parallels found in the archaeological context.

[17] E. MACDONALD, J.L. STARKEY, L. HARDING, *Beth-Pelet* II, London 1932, p. XLIV:69-70.

[18] W.A. WARD, W.G. DEVER, *Studies on Scarab Seals* III, Warminster 1994 (hereinafter referred to as: *Studies on Scarab Seals* III), pp. 5; 162-169; 180-186.

[19] WARD, *Studies on Scarab Seals* I, Warminster 1978, p. 91, fig. 33.

[20] PETRIE, *Beth-Pelet* I, London 1930, pl. XXII:223.

[21] *Ibidem*, p. 9.

[22] WARD, DEVER, *Studies on Scarab Seals* III, pp. 5, 166-167, 186.

[23] KEEL, *Stempelsiegel-Amulette* I, pp. 166-167:184; 440-441:989; 744-745:25

[24] WARD, DEVER, *Studies on Scarab Seals* III, pp. 5, 162-167, 180-186.

[25] J.E. QUIBELL, W. SPIGELBERG, *The Ramesseum*, London 1898, pl. XXX:33; GIVEON, *Egyptian Scarabs*, pp. 80f:59/L 954; F.V. RICHARDS, *Scarab Seals*, OBO 117, Freiburg, Schweiz 1992 (hereinafter referred to as: *Scarab Seals*), pp. 21, 96f:18; KEEL, *Stempelsiegel-Amulette* I, pp. 274f:502, 462f:1051.

[26] KEEL et al., *Stempelsiegeln aus Palästina* II, pp. 267-268.

[27] *Ibidem*, p. 276.

[28] MATOUK, *Scarabée égyptien* II, p. 377:186.

[29] RICHARDS, *Scarab Seals*, p. 43.

[30] WARD, DEVER, *Studies on Scarab Seals* III, pp. 5, 164-169, 182-188.

[31] For this remark I am indebt to Dr Baruch BRANDL from the Israel Antiquity Organisation, Jerusalem.

Jochem Kahl
Münster

Das Forschungsvorhaben „Frühägyptisches Wörterbuch"*

In dem von A. ERMAN und H. GRAPOW herausgegebenen *Wörterbuch der ägyptischen Sprache* (Band I-V aus den Jahren 1926-31; Belegstellen aus den Jahren 1935-53) sind fast keine Wörter aus der ägyptischen Frühzeit (0.-3. Dynastie; ca. 3150-2600 v.Chr.) aufgenommen. Die Gründe hierfür sind wohl zweierlei Art:

1. Im Jahre 1931, dem Zeitpunkt, zu dem Band V des *Wörterbuchs der ägyptischen Sprache* erschienen war, waren erst wenige frühzeitliche Fundplätze – und damit noch nicht alle heute bekannten Schriftträger – ausgegraben (z.B. waren die Stufenpyramiden von Djoser und Sechemchet, die Nekropolen von Saqqara-Nord, Helwan und Abu Roasch sowie die Festung und Stadt auf Elephantine noch nicht erforscht; ebenso erbrachten die seit 1977 unternommenen deutschen Nachgrabungen in Umm el-Qaab/Abydos zahlreiches neues Inschriftenmaterial, unter anderem mehr als 300 Inschriften aus Grab U-j,[1] das in die Zeitstufe Naqada IIIa2/ Naqada IIIA1 datiert[2] wird).

2. Die schwierige Lesbarkeit und das oftmals mangelnde Verständnis des Inhalts der Inschriften standen einer Aufnahme in ein Lexikon entgegen. Forschungsarbeiten, die in der zweiten Hälfte des 20. Jahrhunderts durchgeführt wurden, konnten diese Situation verbessern. Zu nennen sind vor allem die Arbeiten von Peter KAPLONY[3] und Wolfgang HELCK[4]. Allerdings bieten diese Arbeiten keine systematische lexikalische Aufbereitung des gesamten frühzeitlichen Materials.

Sind bis heute die Anfänge der schriftlichen Fixierung ägyptischer Wörter nicht übersichtlich dargestellt, so ist die Forschung auf dem Gebiet der frühen Schrift und Sprache doch so weit vorangeschritten, daß die Erstellung eines Wörterbuches der ägyptischen Frühzeit sowohl angemessen als auch durchführbar scheint.

Ein solches Wörterbuch wäre in mehrfacher Hinsicht von großem Nutzen:

– Es wäre die erste umfassende Zugangsmöglichkeit zum Wortschatz des greifbaren Anfangsstadiums schriftlich fixierter ägyptischer Sprache.

– Es diente der Vervollständigung des Wissens um das altägyptische Lexikon im allgemeinen (z.B. Erweiterung der im *Wörterbuch der ägyptischen Sprache* angegebenen Schreibungen und Belegzeiträume).

– Es böte sich als Hilfsmittel bei der Erforschung verschiedenster Bereiche der Frühzeit an (z.B. der Verwaltung oder des Königtums).

Aus der 0.-3. Dynastie sind derzeit ca. 4300 publizierte Inschriften überliefert:[5] Inschriften auf Ton- und Steingefäßen, Anhängetäfelchen, Stelen,

* Die Transkription folgt W. SCHENKEL, *Tübinger Einführung in die klassisch-ägyptische Sprache und Schrift*, Tübingen 1997, S. 29-33.

[1] G. DREYER, *Umm el-Qaab* I*: das prädynastische Königsgrab U-j und seine frühen Schriftzeugnisse*, Mainz 1998 (im folgenden zitiert als: *Umm el-Qaab* I).

[2] Datierung Naqada IIIa2 nach Werner KAISERS Chronologie (W. KAISER, Zur inneren Chronologie der Naqadakultur, *Archaeologia Geographica* 6 (1957), S. 69-77; G. DREYER, *Umm el-Qaab* I, S. 19-20); Naqada IIIA1 nach Stan HENDRICKX Chronologie (Stan HENDRICKX, La chronologie de la préhistoire tardive et des débuts de l'histoire de l'Egypte, *Archéo-Nil* 9 (1999), S. 31, 76).

[3] P. KAPLONY, *Die Inschriften der ägyptischen Frühzeit*, Wiesbaden 1963; IDEM, *Die Inschriften der ägyptischen Frühzeit.* Supplement, Wiesbaden 1964; IDEM, *Kleine Beiträge zu den Inschriften der ägyptischen Frühzeit*, Wiesbaden 1966.

[4] W. HELCK, *Untersuchungen zur Thinitenzeit*, Wiesbaden 1987.

[5] Vgl. J. KAHL, *Das System der ägyptischen Hieroglyphenschrift in der 0.-3. Dynastie*, Wiesbaden 1994 (im folgen-

Siegeln und deren Abrollungen ebenso wie Grab- und Tempelinschriften, Felsinschriften und andere mehr.

Die absolute Anzahl überlieferter Wörter dürfte grob geschätzt 22000-25000 betragen. Der Gesamtumfang der verschiedenen Lexeme beläuft sich auf ca. 1200, welche in ca. 3000 verschiedenen Schreibungen überliefert sind. Hierbei sind einige hundert Lexeme zwar als solche erkennbar, aber ihr exakter Lautwert bzw. ihre genaue Bedeutung sind nicht bestimmbar.

Geplant ist die Anlage eines Wörterbuches, in welchem die Lemmata nach der Reihenfolge des ägyptologischen Transkriptionsalphabetes angeordnet sind. Zudem ist ein Anhang vorgesehen, in dem Wörter unsicherer Lesart nach ihren Anfangshieroglyphen (in der Reihenfolge der frühzeitlichen Zeichenliste[6]) geordnet werden.

Hauptaufgabe des Projektes ist die Wiedergabe eines repräsentativen Querschnittes der Bezeugungen jedes einzelnen Wortes. Dabei muß das Wörterbuch nicht jeden Beleg für ein Lemma aufführen. Vielmehr muß redundantes Material aussortiert werden. Denn ein Wörterbuch sollte nur die Bezeugungen enthalten, die für die Bedeutung und den Gebrauch eines einzelnen Wortes relevant sind.

Die Seiten des frühägyptischen Wörterbuches werden mit dem Computer erstellt. Dazu wird ein eigens geschriebenes Programm benutzt,[7] welches die Eingabe der Daten in eine Datenbank (Typ Paradox) und deren Ausgabe auf den Bildschirm oder Drucker ermöglicht. D.h. das Wörterbuch kann bereits in publikationsfähigem Format erstellt werden.

Die Probleme, die bei der Erstellung eines derartigen Wörterbuches auftreten, sind mannigfaltig: Sie sind nicht nur lexikographischer, sondern auch epigraphischer und paläographischer Art. Um diesen speziellen Problemen gerecht zu werden, werden den einzelnen Lemmata folgende Informationen beigegeben:[8]

A. Lemmaeintrag in Transkription

B. Übersetzung (mit *Wb*-Verweis und weiteren klärenden Verweisen zu Lexikographie, Lesung und Grammatik)

C. Lemmaeintrag in Hieroglyphen (mit Angabe der häufigsten Schreibung)

D. Belegzeitraum (frühester – spätester Beleg)

E. Angabe der Lautformen und Flexionsformen sowie syntaktischer Parameter
Verwendung (Inschrift-/Textsorten, in denen das Lexem gebraucht wird) und Verweis auf Kollokationen, Gegensatzpaare etc.
Auswahl von Inschrift-/Textzitaten (in Transkription) mit Angabe der Inschrift-/Textträger und einer Auswahl von Belegstellen

F. die einzelnen Schreibungen (in Standardhieroglyphen) mit Belegzeitraum (chronologisch geordnet)

G. zu den einzelnen Schreibungen jeweils ein Beleg (unter Angabe der Belegstelle) in Faksimile oder als Umzeichnung nach Photo

---

den zitiert als: *System der Hieroglyphenschrift*), S. 169-417 und unter dem in jüngster Zeit publiziertem Material insbesondere DREYER, *Umm el-Qaab* I.
Bei der geschätzten Anzahl der Inschriften wurden mehrere erhaltene Abrollungen eines Siegels nur als eine Inschrift gezählt.

[6] KAHL, *System der Hieroglyphenschrift*, S. 419-906.

[7] Dieses Programm schrieb Herr stud. phil. Markus BRETSCHNEIDER.

[8] Die folgenden Anforderungen orientieren sich an denen, die W. SCHENKEL, Wörterbuch vs. Textkorpus oder: Wie und ob man überhaupt ein Wörterbuch machen kann, *ZÄS* 121 (1994), S. 154 aufgestellt hat.Im Gegensatz zu SCHENKEL sind die Forderungen nach hamitosemitischen Etymologien sowie demotischen und koptischen Äquivalenten im folgenden unberücksichtigt geblieben, dafür ist aber die Forderung nach Faksimile-Wiedergaben der einzelnen Belege aufgenommen worden, da gerade in der Frühzeit die Probleme der Lesungen mancher Wörter groß sind.

Zu A und B: Lemmaeintrag in Transkription und Übersetzung (mit *Wb*-Verweis und weiteren klärenden Verweisen zu Lexikographie, Lesung und Grammatik):
Beispiel: *ꜣbṯ* „Monat" (**Abb. 1**).
Bei diesem Lemma wird entgegen dem Eintrag im *Berliner Wörterbuch* (dort unter *ibd*) ein initiales *ꜣ* angesetzt. Als begründender Literaturverweis dazu ist Gardiner, *Egyptian Grammar*, 486 (N11) angegeben.

Zu C: Lemmaeintrag in Hieroglyphen (mit Angabe der häufigsten Schreibung):
Beispiel: *ꜣḫ* „Ach" (**Abb. 2**). Als häufigste Schreibung ist diejenige mit Gardiner-Nummer G25 angegeben, die zahlreich in der Frühzeit attestiert ist. Die phonographische Schreibung mit den Hieroglyphen G1 und Aa1 ist hingegen nur singulär bezeugt und wird deshalb nicht hier, sondern unter F. „Die einzelnen Schreibungen (in Standardhieroglyphen) mit Belegzeitraum (chronologisch geordnet)" aufgeführt.

Zu D: Belegzeitraum (frühester – spätester Beleg):
Beispiel: *ꜣpṯ* „Vogel" (**Abb. 3**). Dieses Lexem ist erstmals unter Den inschriftlich bezeugt. Ein weiterer Beleg ist nicht genau datierbar und stammt aus der 2. oder 3. Dynastie.

Zu E: Angabe der Lautformen, Flexionsformen und syntaktischer Parameter
Verwendung (Inschrift-/Textsorten, in denen das Lexem gebraucht wird) und Verweis auf Kollokationen, Gegensatzpaare etc.
Auswahl von Inschrift-/Textzitaten (in Transkription) mit Angabe der Schriftträger und einer Auswahl von Belegstellen:
Beispiel: *iyi̯ / iwi̯* „kommen" (**Abb. 4**) und *ꜣw.t-ib* (**Abb. 5**). Unter *iyi̯ / iwi̯* sind die Flexionsformen jeweils gesondert aufgeführt: Perfekt Aktiv *ś̂čm=f*, Partizip Perfekt Aktiv (mask. Sg. bzw. fem. Sg.) und Prospektiv Aktiv *ś̂čm=f*.
Unter *ꜣw.t-ib* ist auf den Gebrauch des Lexems in Kollokationen verwiesen (*ʿnḫ čṭ.t wꜣś ꜣw.t-ib*).
Textzitate bzw. Inschriftenzitate sind in Transkription mit ausgewählten Belegstellen unter Angabe der Schriftträger aufgeführt. So erfährt man beispielsweise von der Verwendung von *ꜣw.t-ib* in Tempelinschriften und Felsinschriften.

Zu F: einzelne Schreibungen (in Standardhieroglyphen) mit Belegzeitraum (chronologisch geordnet):
Beispiel: *ꜣś* „Asch" (**Abb. 6**). Hier sind alle verschiedenen Schreibungen dieses Gottesnamens in Standardhieroglyphen mit dem jeweiligen Belegzeitraum wiedergegeben.

Zu G: zu den einzelnen Schreibungen jeweils ein Belegbeispiel (unter Angabe der Belegstelle) in Faksimile oder als Umzeichnung nach Photo:
Beispiel: *ꜣmś* „Art Keule" (**Abb. 7**). Hier ist die Lesung des Wortes als *ꜣmś* nicht über jeden Zweifel erhaben.[9] Die beigefügten Faksimiles veranschaulichen die Problematik, ohne daß ein Zugriff auf die einschlägigen Publikationen sofort erfolgen müßte.

Perspektiven: Dank Unterstützung der Deutschen Forschungsgemeinschaft tragen zwei studentische Mitarbeiter (Markus Bretschneider und Barbara Kneißler) zum Gelingen des Projektes bei, so daß zu hoffen bleibt, daß die Arbeit am *Frühägyptischen Wörterbuch* im Jahre 2003 abgeschlossen sein wird.

[9] C. ZIEGLER, *Les Statues égyptiennes de l'Ancien Empire*, Paris 1997, S. 80-81 erwog auch eine Lesung *ś:ḥč mčḥ.ww*.

3bṭ

"Monat" (*Wb* I, 65.9; Gardiner, *Egyptian Grammar*, 486 (N 11))
(Netjerichet)
in der Datumsangabe:
3bṭ ḥmt.nw šmw (Architekturblock: Lauer, *PD*, III, 77, Abb. 9)

(Netjerichet)

Lauer, *PD* III, 77, Abb. 93

Fig. 1. Der Lemmaeintrag *3bṭ*

3ḫ

"Ach" (*Wb* I, 15.17-16.10; Sethe, *Dramatische Texte*, 193-194; Kaplony, *Inschriften* I, 370)
(Djer) - (2.-3. Dyn.)
in Titeln:
sḫn.w 3ḫ (Grabplatte: Smith, *Art and Architecture*, Taf. 13; Grabstelen: Petrie, *RT* I, Taf. 31.26,39; Grabwand: Petrie, *RT* I, Taf. 63 (W 62); Siegelabrollungen: Kaplony, *Inschriften* III, Abb. 111, 126, 181, 296; Siegelzylinder: Kaplony, *Inschriften* III, Abb. 483)
sḫn.w 3ḫ nsw (Grabplatte: Saad, *Ceiling Stelae*, Taf. 3)
sḫn.t 3ḫ (Grabstelen: Petrie, *RT* I, Taf. 32.14-15; Siegelzylinder: Kaplony, *Inschriften* III, Abb. 370)
ṯšn sḫn.ww 3ḫ (Grabplatten: Scharff, *Archaische Grabplatte*, Taf. 57; Saad, *Ceiling Stelae*, Taf. 16)

(Djer)

Kaplony, *Inschriften* III, Abb. 111

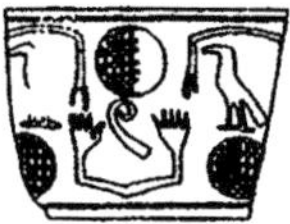

(Djer) - (2.-3. Dyn.)

Petrie, *RT* I, Taf. 31.39

Fig. 2. Der Lemmaeintrag *3ḫ*

ꜣpṯ

"Vogel" (*Wb* I, 9.5; Schenkel, *Aus der Arbeit an einer Konkordanz*, 212, 223; Godron, *Horus Den*, 63)
Den - (2.-3. Dyn.)
in annalistischer Notiz:
pl.: *ꜥmꜥꜣ ꜣpṯ.ww* (Anhängetäfelchen: Petrie, *RT*, I, Taf. 11.14 und 15.16)
in Inventaropferliste:
ꜣpṯ 2 (Grabplatte: Saad, *Ceiling Stelae*, Taf. 10)
evtl. auch in annalistischer Notiz: Anhängetäfelchen, Qaa (Dreyer, in: *MDAIK* 52, 1996, 74, Abb. 27, Taf. 14e)

Den

Petrie, *RT*, I, Taf. 15.16

(2.-3. Dyn.)

nach: Saad, *Ceiling Stelae*, Taf. 10

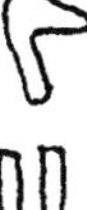

Fig. 3. Der Lemmaeintrag *ꜣpṯ*

iy(*i*) / *iw*(*i*) "kommen" (*Wb* I, 37.1-36, 44.1-45.6; Winand, *Le verbe iy/iw*, 374-384) 
Den - (Sechemchet)
Perf. Akt. *śč̣m=f*:
in PN:
iy-n=i (Steingefäß: Lacau - Lauer, *PD* V, Abb. 117)
iy-n=i-ẖnm.w (Steingefäße: Lacau - Lauer, *PD* V, Abb. 5-13, Taf. 2-6)
iy-n=i[...] (Anhängetäfelchen: Petrie, *RT* I, Taf. 15.18)
iy-śn=ś (Siegelzylinder: Kaplony, *Inschriften* III, Abb. 371)
iy-k3=i nčś (Steinblock: Fischer, *Scribe of the Army*, 262, Abb. 24, Taf. 11; Kahl - Kloth - Zimmermann, *Inschriften*, D3/Sa/32)
Part. Perf. Akt. mask. Sg.:
in PN:
iy-m-ḥtp (Königsplastik: Firth - Quibell, *Step Pyramid* II, Taf. 58; Kahl - Kloth - Zimmermann, *Inschriften*, Ne/Sa/50; Umfassungsmauer von Grabbezirk: Goneim, *Horus Sekhem-Khet*, Taf. 13; Kahl - Kloth - Zimmermann, *Inschriften*, Se/Sa/5)
Part. Perf. Akt. fem. Sg.:
in PN:
iy.t-n-k3=i (Steingefäß: Lacau - Lauer, *PD* IV.1, Taf. VII.1)
Prosp. Akt. *śč̣m=f*:
in PN:
iw-śn-č̣.t (Grabplatte: Saad, *Ceiling Stelae*, Taf. 23)

Den - (Sechemchet)

Lacau - Lauer, *PD* V, Abb. 10

(2.-3. Dyn.)

nach: Saad, *Ceiling Stelae*, Taf. 23

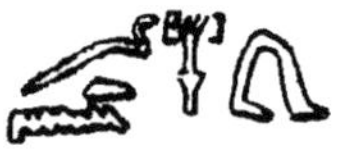

Fig. 4. Der Lemmaeintrag *iyi̯ / iwi̯*

ꜣw.t — "Länge" (*Wb* I, 4.15 - 5.1)

Netjerichet

in der Verbindung *ꜣw.t-ib* "Fröhlichkeit, Freude" (s.u.)

ꜣw.t-ib — "Fröhlichkeit, Freude" (*Wb* I, 4.17-19)

Netjerichet

als Gabe der Götter (Kollokation *ꜥnḫ č̣t.t wꜣš ꜣw.t-ib* u.ä.):

[...] *ꜥnḫ č̣t.t wꜣš ꜣw.t-ib* [...] (Tempelinschrift: Kahl - Kloth - Zimmermann, *Inschriften*, Ne/He/3 und Donadoni Roveri, *Passato e Futuro*, 19, Abb. 6)

č̣(i) ꜥnḫ č̣t.t wꜣš ꜣw.t-ib č̣.t (Tempelinschrift: Kahl - Kloth - Zimmermann, *Inschriften*, Ne/He/4 und Smith, *Sculpture*, 135, Abb. 50 und Donadoni Roveri, *Passato e Futuro*, 20, Abb. 7)

č̣(i) wꜣš č̣t.t ꜥnḫ ꜣw.t-ib č̣.t (Felsinschrift: Kahl - Kloth - Zimmermann, *Inschriften*, Ne/Ma/1 und Gardiner - Peet - Cerny, *Inscriptions Sinai* I, Taf. 1.2)

Netjerichet

Smith, *Sculpture*, 135, Abb. 50

Fig. 5. Der Eintrag *ꜣw.t-ib*

ꜣš 

"Asch" (GN; *Wb* I, 20.21)
Den - Netjerichet
als GN:
ꜣš (Siegelabrollungen: Kaplony, *Inschriften* III, Abb. 195, 196; Petrie, *RT* II, Taf. 19.151, 152)
als GN mit bildlicher Darstellung des Gottes:
ꜣš (Siegelabrollungen: Kaplony, *Inschriften* III, Abb. 283, 286, 291, 303, 307; Kahl - Kloth - Zimmermann, *Inschriften*, Ne/Be/12)

 Den - Peribsen

Kaplony, *Inschriften* III, Abb. 196 

 Hetepsechemui

Kaplony, *Inschriften* III, Abb. 307 

 Peribsen - Chasechemui

Kaplony, *Inschriften* III, Abb. 283 

 Peribsen - Netjerichet

Kaplony, *Inschriften* III, Abb. 286 

Fig. 6. Der Lemmaeintrag *ꜣš*

ꜣmś "Art Keule" (*Wb* I, 11.3-5; Helck, *Thinitenzeit*, 242)
(Netjerichet)
im Titel *mčḥ.w ꜣmś* (Lesung unsicher, evtl. *ś:ḥč mčḥ.ww*, vgl. Ziegler, *Statues égyptiennes*, 80-81):
ẖr.i ḥꜣb.t mčḥ.w ꜣmś (Siegelabrollung: Garstang, *Mahâsna and Bêt Khallâf*, Taf. 26.7 und Kahl - Kloth - Zimmermann, *Inschriften*, Ne/Be/43)
śmꜣ ḥr.w mčḥ.w ꜣmś (Privatstatue: Ziegler, *Statues égyptiennes*, 81, 296 (Cat. 22))

(Netjerichet)

Ziegler, *Statues égyptiennes* , 296 (Cat. 22)

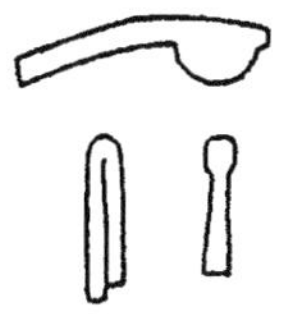

(Netjerichet)

Garstang, *Mahâsna and Bêt Khallâf*, Taf. 26.7

Fig. 7. Der Lemmaeintrag *ꜣmś*

Rafał Koliński
Poznań

Pottery Marks – Evidence for Early Writing Practices in Thinite Egypt and Early Dynastic Mesopotamia*

Terminology

Before the actual pottery marks are considered I should like to explain the reason why I use the term "pottery marks" instead of the more frequently used term "potters' marks". The term "potters' mark" originates from the Middle Ages when craftsman producing pottery used incised "marks" to identify their products. Marks were usually located on a part of a vessel that was not visible to its user after the pot was formed and prior to its firing. The "pottery marks" of the ancient Near East were also incised in the potters' workshop prior to firing pots but as they were usually located on a shoulder of the vessel and were easily observable they most probably served another purpose. I propose to use the term "pottery marks" to describe these signs because it allows for other interpretations of its purpose.

Early Dynastic Pottery Marks of Egypt

The custom of incising signs on pottery vessels is nearly as old as the use of pottery itself. It is known in Egypt from the Predynastic Period (Merimde Beni Salame) and continues throughout the Dynastic and Post-dynastic Periods of its history. Nevertheless, the pottery marks were never as abundant or as often applied on the pottery as during the relatively short period of dynasties 0 and I. In my description of the Early Dynastic pottery marks of Egypt I focus on a paper by Edwin van den BRINK, published in 1992.[1]

Signs on early Egyptian pottery were executed with a sharp-tipped tool, probably of flint or with a wide and blunt instrument of wood, sometimes 8 mm wide. No relation between the nature of the tool used and the shape of vessel was observed, although the marks executed with blunt instruments are rarer and are usually comprised of probably floral-related signs. Both groups were executed by prior firing. The only exception are imported vessels of Palestinian origin. More than twenty such pots are known, all of them with signs made after being brought to Egypt. A few of them, also bear "potters' marks" located on the base of the pot, evidently applied in potters' workshops.[2]

The corpus presented by van den BRINK comprised 3660 potmarks,[3] excluding *serekh* signs, city determinatives even when accompanied by other signs and floral-related signs executed with a blunt tool. It is certainly far from completeness, as no evidence from some important sites such as Buto or Hierakonopolis was included. The signs were applied to the pottery deposited in graves of the period corresponding to the 0 and Ist dynasties. They are relatively well dated by means of impressions of inscribed seals found in graves. Potmarks were rarely applied before the reign of Hor-Aha. During the reigns of subsequent rulers of the Ist dynasty the number of pottery marks increased to a peak during the reign of Den/Udimu. The number of marks decreased significantly during the reigns of Andjib and Semerkhet to disappear almost totally after the reign of Qaa, the last king of the Ist dynasty.[4] The most nu-

* This lecture was originally prepared for the conference "5000 years of the invention of writing", held in Baghdad in March 2001. For independent reasons I was not able to attend this conference. I am much obliged to Mrs Joanna POPIELSKA-GRZYBOWSKA for an invitation to the *Second Central European Conference of Young Egyptologists*, which gave me the opportunity to present the following paper to the audience of Egyptologists.

[1] E.C.M. van den BRINK, Corpus and Numerical Evaluation of the "Thinite" potmarks, in: R. FRIEDMANN, B. ADAMS, *The Followers of Horus. Studies dedicated to Michael Allen Hoffman 1944-1990*, Egyptian Studies Association Publication No. 2, Oxbow Monograph 20, Oxford 1992 (hereinafter referred to as: "Thinite" potmarks), pp. 265-296.

[2] van den BRINK, "Thinite" potmarks, p. 274 and footnote 6.

[3] *Ibidem*, p. 273, tab. 1.

[4] *Ibidem*, p. 272, fig. 5.

merous collection was found in the grave of Mer-neit, where 442 marks were identified. Unfortunately, in most of the older publications relations between the signs and pottery shapes could not be traced. Such an identification was possible in the case of the Abu Roash cemetery, where 188 of the total of 1679 vessels were incised with pottery marks (about 11%). The incised signs occurred most frequently on the so-called "wine jars", narrow jars with a tampering body and rounded bottom. They occurred on 88 out of 148 vessels of this type (58%). This group of vessels was reputedly most frequently marked on the other sites too. The other groups of vessels that were marked with remarkable frequency were ovoid jars with a blunt rounded base (42 out of 403, i.e. 10%), barrel shaped vessels with flat or rounded bottoms and sharp angles (15 out of 132, i.e. 11%) shallow bowls (10 out of 92, i.e. 11%) and bowls with convex sides and flat bases (21 out of 253, i.e. 8%).[5]

2474 potmarks were scrutinised in respect of the signs used and the composition of the marks. The signs occurred in groups composed of one to six signs, usually applied horizontally on the shoulder of the vessel. Some of the signs are similar to the signs of hieroglyphic writing and may (but not necessarily have to) be considered taken from Egyptian writing. There is also a group of signs which may be considered numerical ones, for instance combinations of horizontal strokes, one to four in number. Nevertheless, there is a relatively numerous group of signs which cannot be found among the hieroglyphs. The most often encountered were groups composed of two signs (56.1% of the marks). Single signs were less frequent, forming 28.7% of the corpus, groups of three signs formed 12.3% of all marks, and groups of four, five and six signs had only marginal significance, forming 2.9% of the corpus. Van den BRINK grouped all the signs according to a sign placed at the beginning (or the end) of the mark.[6] 77 groups composed of similar signs (like rectangles with different internal divisions, or quadrupeds of similar appearance) were formed. Only four signs out of 77 identified never occurred as a single sign. The triple groups are usually a development of a double group to which one more sign was added. In 71 cases of different triple groups only in 14 cases there is no double group composed of any of the signs used for composing a triple group known. In other cases there are one, two or even three such groups known. This frequent occurrence of the groups of signs instead of single signs (28.1%) gives a writing-like appearance to the pottery markings in ancient Egypt.

Several scholars had already considered the purpose of marking pots. PETRIE in 1896 proposed understanding them as property marks,[7] and in 1900 he identified them as a mixture of hieroglyphs and earlier prehistoric signs.[8] In 1897 de MORGAN proposed seeing them as indications of the content of the container.[9] In this proposition he was later joined by AMÉLINEAU (1899), SAAD (1938), EMERY (1949).[10] DARESSY proposed in 1905 explaining them as fantastic drawings done by the potter and deprived of any significance.[11] JUNKER in 1919 proposed seeing them as proper potters' marks, i.e. as identification of the craftsmen or workshop.[12] BRUNTON in 1927 interpreted them as determination of the volume of the pot.[13] SAAD in 1938 thought that marks may also determine the place a pot was bought (and made).[14] In 1985, HELCK proposed seeing them as the descriptions of the quality and origin of wine kept in the pots.[15] In 1990 he interpreted the pottery marks as a "writing" originating from Lower Egypt ("Butische Schrift") that was later replaced by Hie-

[5] *Ibidem*, p. 269 and fig. 3.

[6] *Ibidem*, pp. 271-4, tab. 2 and figs. 6-17.

[7] W.M.F. PETRIE, J.E. QUIBELL, *Naqada and Ballas*, BSAE 1, London 1896, p. 44.

[8] PETRIE, *The Royal Tombs of the First Dynasties* I, EES 18, London 1900, pp. 29-32.

[9] J. de MORGAN, *Recherches sur les origines d'Égypte: ethnographie préhistorique et tombeau royal de Négadah*, Paris 1897, p. 165.

[10] E. AMÉLINEAU, *Les Nouvelles Fouilles d'Abydos, 1985-1986* I, Paris 1989, pp. 199-200; Z. SAAD, The Tomb of Hemaka, in: W.B. EMERY, *Excavations at Saqqara 1937-38*, Cairo 1938 (hereinafter referred to as: Tomb of Hemaka), p. 53; W.B. EMERY, *Great Tombs of the First Dynasty* I, Cairo 1949, pp. 154-156.

[11] M.G. DARESSY, Une édifice archaïque Nezlet Batran, *ASAE* 6 (1905), pp. 6-7.

[12] H. JUNKER, *Bericht über die Grabungen der keiserlischen Akademie der Wissenschaften in Wien auf den Friedhofen von el-Kubaniek-Süd*, Wien 1919, pp. 80-82.

[13] G. BRUNTON, A. GARDINER, PETRIE, *Qau and Badari*, BSAE 44, London 1927, pp. 18, 68.

[14] SAAD, Tomb of Hemaka, p. 53.

[15] W. HELCK, Töpfaufschriften, *LÄ* VI, cols. 635-636.

roglyphic script invented in Upper Egypt.[16] Van den BRINK thought they served an administrative function related to collecting and redistribution of goods for funerary use.[17]

Numerous various interpretations of the purpose of pottery marks deserve at least a short comment. The hypothesis of DARESSY may be put aside. The marks were nearly always located in the same part of the pot and their character (repetitions of signs and groups of signs) testify that they were deliberately executed. Moreover, one could not expect meaningless signs to be allowed to be introduced into a grave, at least not in Egypt. The interpretation of pottery marks as potters' marks may be dismissed on grounds of the location of the signs on vessels. They are not located at the bottom of the pot or in other place where they could not be easily observed, as a rule. The marks are composed of more than one element. It is hard to believe that the pottery workshops would use such a developed system of naming the workshops or their owners. Moreover, there are some cases, when marks were applied on imported pots which are already marked at the bottom. In these cases the marks at the bottom have to be treated as real potters' marks and the signs introduced at the sides of the vessels had another purpose. The signs could be "labels" informing about the content of the vessel only on various conditions. First, the pots had to be highly standardised at least as far as their purpose is concerned. One can expect that in such a situation only a few different marks would be put on the same type of vessel. Van den BRINK identified over 900 different groups of signs, hence this is not the case. The other possible explanation is that the decision concerning the content of the vessels was taken prior to ordering them. This was certainly possible when a large number of pots was ordered for a grave. On the other hand, it is hard to believe that the marks were "Weingutmarken", as HELCK proposed. *Primo*, there is no reason to believe, that the labels referred to the wine only, *secundo*, making this assumption would mean that also open vessels were used as containers for wine, *tertio*, the number of over 900 combinations of signs had to relate to a corresponding number of the production centres, which is also difficult to accept. Many marks start with signs that in the later Hieroglyphic script denoted numerals, hence it was proposed that they were denoting the capacity of the vessel. However, an unpublished study by van den BERG, referred to by van den BRINK demonstrated that there is no relation between the capacity of the wine jars and the numeral signs used in the potmarks put on them.[18] Finally, the assumption that the pottery marks are the only preserved evidence for use of the "Butische Schrift" is impossible to accept as it is impossible to explain why the groups of pottery marks found in Upper and Lower Egypt did not differ, as should be the case if there were two centres responsible for invention of writing.

No satisfactory explanation of the role of the Egyptian pottery marks has been presented to date, although it seems that van den BRINK's proposition of considering them as "labels" used to help collection and administration of goods to be deposited in the graves is the most likely. Such labels written in hieroglyphic, referring to rural domains, are known from later royal graves, for instance from the pyramid of Djoser. A confirmation of this hypothesis would be possible only if we were able to understand the "labels" themselves, which seems to be unlikely at the moment.

The North Mesopotamian Pottery Marks

Pottery marks appear on Mesopotamian pottery already in the Prehistoric Period. They are quite popular during the first half of the 4th millennium (Middle Uruk culture). In the 3rd millennium they were used more extensively in the Middle Euphrates valley and in the territory east of it, reaching to the eastern boundary of the Khabur triangle. They occurred during a relatively short period of time, covering the later part of the EB III and EB IV periods (ca 2400-2200 BC). The marks were found both on vessels from graves and from settlements.

As in the case of Egyptian potmarks their Mesopotamian counterparts were executed after forming the pot and prior to its firing. The signs were made with a pointed tool of rounded or sharp tip, leaving an incision 1 to 2 mm in width. Sometimes a different

[16] HELCK, *Thinitische Töpfmarken*, ÄA 50, Wiesbaden 1990, p. 2.

[17] Van den BRINK, "Thinite" potmarks, p. 274.

[18] *Ibidem*, footnote 61.

tool was used to form circular impressions on the surface of the vessel. The signs were only in exceptional cases introduced after the firing of the pot.

The Mesopotamian potmarks were never collected into a corpus like that of van den BRINK. The most numerous assemblages from Tell al-Abd and Tell es-Sweyhat both located on Euphrates still await publication. On the first of these sites over 700 markings were registered,[19] on the second nearly 400 marks on an assemblage of about 5100 vessels and pottery sherds.[20] The most numerous published collection of pottery marks comes from Tell Mishrife/Qatna in central Syria. It amounts 66 examples.[21] Other assemblages came from two small settlements excavated by the Polish mission in the Khabur Triangle[22] as well as from some cemeteries located in the same part of the Euphrates valley as Tell Halawa,[23] Shams ed-Din, Djerniye[24] or Tell Tawi.[25] Each of them is between 5 and 30 potmarks in size. It seems that the potmarks found in burials got there accidentally, because they were incised on vessels that were reused as grave goods. Similarly, numerous sets of potmarks are known from contemporary settlements in Palestine (Tell el-Hesy, 68 marks[26]) and Iran (Tepe Yahya, 358 marks[27]).

The north Mesopotamian potmarks usually consist of a single sign, although in some cases this sign is composed of several repeated elements, for instance vertical strokes, arches or wavy lines. In the publication of Tell es-Sweyhat, now in print, the marks were divided into five groups. In the first of them, named "numerical", signs were composed of horizontal strokes from one to six in number, sometimes accompanied by shorter strokes (24 different combinations). The second group, called "curved lines", grouped 10 signs. The third, termed "alphabetic", grouped 21 signs similar to the Latin alphabet. A group called "symbols" was composed of 30 different signs, like flags or tridents. The last group consisted of two signs that were difficult to describe. These five groups accounted for 87 different signs. There were few cases listed when a sign from the group "alphabetic" or "symbolic" was accompanied with one or two vertical strokes. There is also no obvious relation between the shape of the marks and the cuneiform signs observed, even if the pictographic signs are taken into consideration. The marks are incised in different parts of the pot. The most frequent spot is the shoulder of a vessel, though the lower part of the vessel is nearly as often. Sometimes they are introduced on the rim of a vessel, or even inside it, in the upper part of the neck. Finally, there are several cases when the same drawing was incised several times, and marks located in the upper part of a vessel are upside-down versions of the drawings located in the lower part of the body. The above observations refer to all collections of pottery marks known from the Syrian and north Mesopotamian sites.[28] It is an interesting observation that pottery marks are used also in a later period, although the only more numerous collection known to me comes from the Late Bronze Age levels from Ugarit.[29]

[19] Dr Renate GUT, personal communication.

[20] T. HOLLAND, *Tell es-Sweyhat*, Syria, Vol. 2: Archaeology of the Bronze Age, Hellenistic and Roman Remains at an Ancient Town on the Euphrates River, Oriental Institute Publications, Chicago, in the press (hereinafter referred to as: *Tell es-Sweyhat*); cf. Chapter 6: Potters' marks.

[21] R. du MESNIL du BUISSON, *Le site archéologique de Mishrifé-Qatna* I, Collection de Textes et Documents d'Orient, Paris 1935, pl. 49.

[22] R. KOLIŃSKI, Early Dynastic Potter's Marks from Polish Excavations in Northern Syria, *Berythus* XLI (1993-94), pp. 5-27.

[23] W. ORTHMANN et al., *Halawa 1977-1979. Vorlaufiger Bericht über die 1. Bis 3. Kampagne. Saarbrücker Studien zur Vor- und Frühgeschichte* 31, Saarbrücken 1981, pls. 48:30; 56:4, 18, 61.

[24] J.-W. MEYER, *Gräber des 3. Jahrtausends im Syrischen Euphrattal. 3. Ausgrabungen in Šamseddin und Djerniye, Schriften zur Vorderasiatischen Archäologie* III, Saarbrücken 1991.

[25] I. KAMPSCHULTE, W. ORTHMANN, *Gräber des 3. Jahrtausends im Syrischen Euphrattal.* I. *Ausgrabungen bei Tawi 1975 und 1978*, Bonn 1984.

[26] F. BLISS, *The Mound of Many Cities or Tell el-Hasy Excavated, Palestinian Exploration Found*, London 1894, pp. 24-43 and V.M. FARGO, Early Bronze Age Pottery from Tell el-HESI, *BASOR* 236 (1980), pp. 23-40.

[27] D.T. POTTS, The Potter's Marks of Tepe Yahya, *Paléorient* 7/1 (1981), pp. 107-122.

[28] For a list of published pottery marks from this region cf. KOLIŃSKI, *Berythus* XLI (1993-94), p. 12, and IDEM, in: P. BIELIŃSKI (ed.), *Polish Excavations at Tell Rad Shaqrah 1991-1995*, Warsaw, in the press (hereinafter referred to as: *Tell Rad Shaqrah*), chapter Pottery Marks; cf. also HOLLAND, *Tell es-Sweyhat.*

[29] 121 marked vessels belonging to two groups: Aegean and local pottery, cf. N. HIRSCHFELD, Marked Late Bronze Age Pottery from the Kingdom of Ugarit, in: M. YON, V. KARAGHEORGHIS, HIRSCHFELD, *Céramiques*

Different explanations for the purpose of the marks have been proposed. The most often quoted is that of a label describing the content of the pot.[30] This is difficult to accept for several reasons. First, it does not seem very likely that the potter was able to predict what would be the contents of the vessels. Most of the pots signed were jars of different sizes (from storage containers over 1 m high to small fine ware jars 10 cm high) but they occurred on bowls as well as on one sieve, a vessel that could not be used for storage, (although they could be used for distributing or sieving products). It is the same with the interpretation of potmarks as property marks. It is possible that the potter marked a pot which was ordered, but a substantial number of different marks found in the single building at Tell Sweyhat cast doubt on this interpretation.[31] Finally, it was proposed considering them as designation of volume or price of the pot. Before the large pottery collections from Tell al-Abd and Tell es-Sweyhat are published an evaluation of this hypothesis will be difficult but it does not seem to be very likely, as in Tell es-Sweyhat, that the same mark was found on two vessels of different size.[32] Also a numerical sign composed of three strokes was found on a vessel that was larger than a jar bearing a mark composed of two strokes.[33] Another possibility is to interpret the pottery marks as referring to familial ownership[34] or marks that were technological signs used by potters during production.[35]

A hint to the role of pottery marks is offered by cuneiform sources of southern Mesopotamia, dating mainly from the Sargonic and Ur III Periods (later part of the 3rd millennium BC), thus slightly later than the pottery marks of Syria and northern Mesopotamia.[36] Several tablets describe marks used to mark animals, humans or boats. They may be executed by application of paint but more often by use of metal brandishing tools, made usually of copper or bronze. The descriptions of these marks, sometimes provided by the texts, fall into two categories. The first of them, less numerous, describes the appearance of the sign, the second informs whom or what the symbol represents. According to de MAAJER, marks of the second group represented deities or humans who are known to head local administration units. Unfortunately, they cannot be related to the known description of the marks (first group). Three marks, which were described in the texts were called: "thin boat", "turtle" and "fish", are all dated to the Sargonic Period.[37] These texts point directly to frequent use of the property marks in Mesopotamia, thus, despite all the reservations, such interpretations of the pottery marks have to be taken seriously into consideration.

Conclusion

A short review of Near Eastern potmarks demonstrates that they had different character in Egypt and Mesopotamia and that they served most probably different purposes. The Egyptian marks seem to form a coherent system. Their purpose was most probably to provide pots with necessary information before they were deposited in graves. This is evidenced by the fact that similar signs were scratched on the surface of some imported pots. In my opinion the marked pots were products meant exclusively for the funerary purposes, though it is impossible to prove this as we lack published pottery from the settlements of the Thinite Period. A much later ink inscription describing the contents of the pot known from the period of Pepi I on belong obviously to the same tradition.

The Mesopotamian potmarks are much more difficult to interpret. It is very likely that they served

Mycéniennes d'Ougarit, Ras Shamra – Ougarit XIII, Nicosie 2000, pp. 163-164.

[30] R.F.S. STARR, *Nuzi*, Cambridge, Mass. 1938, p. 411; S. MAZZONI, *Le impronte su giara eblaite e siriane nel Bronzo Antico*, Materiali e studi archeologici di Ebla, vol. I, Roma 1992, pp. 89-92; J. OATES, Some Late Early Dynastic Pottery from Tell Brak, *Iraq* 44 (1993), p. 207.

[31] In Areas IV and X (period F) in phase 2A) in 21 rooms fifty-nine pottery marks were identified appearing and in subsequent layer, in 23 rooms fifty two pottery marks were found (HOLLAND, in the press, tabs. 82-83).

[32] HOLLAND, *Preliminary Report on Excavations at Tell es-Sweyhat, Syria 1973-74*, Levant 8, figs. 9, 23 and 10, 4.

[33] HOLLAND, in the press, Marks A5 and A6.

[34] HOLLAND, in the press.

[35] KOLIŃSKI, *Berythus* XLI (1993-1994), pp. 13-15.

[36] Texts are collected and discussed by D. FOXVOG, Sumerian Brands and Branding-Irons, *Zeitschrift für Assyriologie* 85 (1995), pp. 1-7, R. de MAAIJER, Late Third Millennium Identifying Marks, in: W.H. van SOLDT, J.G. DERCKSEN, N.J.C. KOUWENBERG, Th.J.H. KRISPIJN (eds.), *Veenhof Anniversary Volume, Studies Presented to Klaas R. Veenhof on the Occasion of his Sixty-fifth Birthday*, Leiden 2001 (hereinafter referred to as: Identifying Marks), pp. 301-323.

[37] De MAAJIER, Identifying Marks, pp. 302-303, 310, tab. 1.

two or three different purposes. It is possible that some of them were put on the pots for technological reasons, while others may relate to the volume of vessels. It is also possible that at least some of them were used as potters' marks (for instance Palestinian ones). Finally, some may be labels of contents or property marks. The most important difference is that the pots on which they were incised served household purposes, thus the relation between the marks and their purpose is much more difficult to identify as the purpose of marking various vessels may vary.

Is there any analogy between the pottery marks of Ancient Egypt and Mesopotamia, besides that they were scratched on vessels? I believe it may be found at a higher level. Frequent use of potmarks both in Egypt and in Mesopotamia falls in a very similar stage of cultural development. Early hieroglyphic script occurred in Egypt several generations before the unification of Egypt, but it was not yet widely used prior to the period of the IInd dynasty. The situation in Mesopotamia was much the same around 2400 BC, specially in the north. Writing was already known in largest centres, like Ebla, Mari or Nagar (Tell Brak) but was not used at all in smaller settlements. Instead, other possibilities of noting information were offered, for instance by use of cylinder seals, frequent in both regions. Many Egyptian seals were decorated with hieroglyphic signs, on others as well as on Mesopotamian seals, floral, geometric and figural motives occurred. In the Nile valley and the Mesopotamian plain seals were used for sealings but were also impressed on the pottery. The location of the pottery sealings on the vessels (mainly on shoulders or rims of storage jars) suggests they were not used to decorate the pot. In Mesopotamia also a traditional system of tokens was still in use. The pottery marks seem to be just one more way of writing information, whatever was its purpose.

The proto-literate stage of the culture involves introducing much primitive information noting practices, some of which developed later in writing. They included, among others, use of tokens, use of clay discs covered with various impressions serving most probably as tallies,[38] use of seals for impressions on pottery vessels and use of signs scratched on the surface of the pots. These two last practices were known both in Early Dynastic Egypt and in Early Dynastic Period of yet proto-literate north Mesopotamia and Syria both dated to the early part of the 3rd millennium BC. The similar cultural setting of the appearance of the so-called potters' marks on early Egyptian pottery and on pottery from Palestine and north Mesopotamia allows for a comparison in the hope of some clues concerning their purpose.

It seems that at the verge of literacy both in northern Mesopotamia and in Egypt there existed means of noting information alternative to writing. Some of them may be considered as survivors of older tradition (tokens), other as innovations that were later abandoned when writing was more widely adopted. This situation resembles another important change in Near Eastern civilisation, namely domestication of animals several millennia earlier. Experiments with domestication were attempted most probably with all available species but worked only in the case of those which have a natural predisposition to be domesticated and attempts towards the other species were abandoned.

[38] For instance one shown in: R.J. MATTHEWS, Tell Brak in the Ninevite 5 period, in: K. van LERBERGHE, G. VOET (eds.), *Languages and Cultures in Contact at the Crossroads of Civilizations in the Syro-Mesopotamian Realm, Proceedings of the 42th RAI*, Orientalia Lovaniensia Analecta 96, Leuven 2000, fig. 5.

Piotr Laskowski
Warsaw

Meaning of the Verb *snfr* in the Building Records of the Thutmoside Period

"L'imprécision du terme *snfr* ne permet en aucune manière de mesurer l'ampleur des travaux effectués." This opinion was expressed by Roland TEFNIN in 1983.[1] It may seem like a discouraging introduction. Nevertheless one still may believe the problem of the meaning of the verb *snfr* has not been fully addressed and that a proper analysis of its occurrences may offer some interesting conclusions. The number of scholars who have paid some attention to the issue have been challenged to do so by research on XVIIIth dynasty material. Important remarks have been made by Gunn BJÖRKMAN in her study on XVIIIth dynasty activity in Karnak,[2] the above quoted Roland TEFNIN, and finally Dimitry LABOURY in his recently published study on the statuary of Thutmosis III.[3] There are others, of course, who have been obliged to suggest meanings for the verb in their translations of inscriptions.

The fact that it was in particular those scholars researching the XVIIIth dynasty who focused on the verb *snfr* does not seem accidental. The word, although rarely found in the Egyptian texts, seems to be quite popular in the Thutmoside Period. It occurs in a number of inscriptions that seem to follow one pattern and therefore may enable the scholar to forward some suggestions concerning its meaning.

The commonly accepted meaning of the verb *snfr* is to embellish, make beautiful.[4] FAULKNER, however, also suggests a meaning "to restore what is defective" while it refers to the statue of Thutmosis II *snfr*-ed by Thutmosis III.[5] *Wörterbuch* suggests "schön machen" and "gut machen" as well as "verschönern".[6] For *snfr* is a causative verb, it is obvious that its meaning is inseparably connected with the signification of the root *nfr*. While a number of meanings including "beautiful", "good", "happy", "fair" have been suggested, it seems that the English word "perfect" would be the most adequate. Thus the verb *snfr* should literally mean: "to cause sth., to be perfect". This, however, does not resolve the problems concerning the word. It was BJÖRKMAN who, having accepted the meaning "embellish" attempted to go further. She analysed the stela of Amenhotep II from Amada and noted: "exactly what kind of work the verb *snfr* 'to make beautiful' implies is hard to say. It may mean to complete an existing monument".[7] Henry BREASTED in his translation of the text from Amada suggested, but with no comments, the meaning: "to supply with inscriptions",[8] Thomas RITTER proposed: "renovieren".[9]

TEFNIN and LABOURY commented on the verb *snfr* inscribed on the colossal statues of Amenhotep I placed in front of the VIIIth pylon in Karnak. TEFNIN proposed it could mean: "soit l'achèvement du monument, soit la simple substitution d'une dedication personelle",[10] while LABOURY added: "Le verbe snfr signifie littéralement 'parfaire', et, appliqué à un monu-

---

[1] R. TEFNIN, Une statue de reine British Museum et Karnak et les paradoxes du portrait égyptien, *JEA* 69 (1983), pp. 96-107.

[2] G. BJÖRKMAN, *Kings at Karnak. A Study of the Treatment of the Monuments of Royal Predecessors in the Early New Kingdom*, Uppsala 1971 (hereinafter referred to as: *Kings at Karnak*), pp. 46-47.

[3] D. LABOURY, *La statuaire de Thoutmosis III*, Liège 1998 (hereinafter referred to as: *Statuaire*), pp. 30-32.

[4] Cf. A. GARDINER, *Egyptian Grammar*, Oxford [3]1957 (hereinafter referred to as: *EG*), p. 574; R.O. FAULKNER, *A Concise Dictionary of Middle Egyptian*, Oxford 1962, p. 232.

[5] Cf. *Urk.* IV, p. 605, 16.

[6] *Wb* IV, p. 163.

[7] BJÖRKMAN, *Kings at Karnak*, p. 47.

[8] J.H. BREASTED, *Ancient Records of Egypt* II, Chicago 1906-1907, p. 311 footnote f.

[9] T. RITTER, *Das Verbalsystem der königlichen und privaten Inschriften*, Wiesbaden 1995 (hereinafter referred to as: *Verbalsystem*), p. 218.

[10] TEFNIN, *JEA* 69 (1983), p. 106.

ment, il peut aussi bien désigner une restauration qu'un parachèvement".[11]

This short draft on the history of the research seems to me a satisfactory premise for the reconsideration of the problem. This may only start with a close look at the corpus of the inscriptions that include the verb in question. This paper is confined exclusively to the use of the verb during the Thutmoside Period. Thus the conclusions herein presented may only be considered preliminary and await future confrontation with earlier and later examples.

The corpus may be divided into two groups, namely the royal building records and the private autobiographical texts. The first group consists of eight inscriptions known to me, the latter of only two of them.

The royal building records that the verb *snfr* occurs in include:

1. The inscription of Thutmosis III carved on the limestone statue representing Amenhotep I, as well as on the limestone statue of Thutmosis II. Both were placed in front of the VIIIth pylon in Karnak. The action of *snfr*-ing was performed in the 22nd year of Thutmosis' reign.[12]

2. The inscription of Thutmosis III dated to the year 42 on the quartzite statue of Thutmosis II standing between the above-mentioned ones.

3. Rather obscure inscription on the statue of Thutmosis III from Asfun.[13]

4. The stelae of Amenhotep II from Amada and Elephantine.[14]

5. The inscription on the royal statue dedicated by Thutmosis IV found south of the IXth pylon in Karnak.[15]

6. The inscription of Thutmosis IV carved on the single obelisk of Thutmosis III.[16]

The private records known to me are:

1. The inscription of Intef from his tomb at Dra'Abu el-Naga, dated to the reign of Thutmosis III.[17]

2. The inscription of Amenhotep on his statue from Memphis dated to the reign of Amenhotep III.[18]

Let us then have a look on some of these inscriptions:

1-2. The complete inscription is preserved on the statue of Amenhotep I.

The particle *jst* introduces the background information that is semantically dependent on the preceding clause.[19] Translation would go as follows:

"The perfect god, lord of two lands, Djeser-ka-Re, son of Re of his body, Amenhotep is beloved of Amon-Re, lord of the thrones of two lands while the *snfr*-ing of this statue was made (*jst jrjj snfr twt pn*) on the 22nd year under the majesty of the king of Upper and Lower Egypt Men-kheper-Re, living forever."

3. The inscription of Asfun is badly damaged. It is arranged in two columns.

ꜥnḫ nṯr nfr nb tꜣwj {Mn-ḫpr-Rꜥ} dj ꜥnḫ [...]*jr.n=f m mnw=f n jt=f*

nṯr nfr nb tꜣwj {ꜥꜣ-ḫpr.n-Rꜥ} [...]
[*Jmn-Rꜥ ?*][a] *nb ḥwt snfr<t>=f*[b] *mrj dj ꜥnḫ mj Rꜥ*

a. The name of Amon-Re was not recognised by WEIGALL. The author would, regardless, suggest it had been written here, as it is the only explanation for the word *mrj*,

b. The verb *snfr* would be a relative form with *ḥwt* as an antecedent. In fact there is no feminine ending attached to the verb but the suffix *=f* makes it impossi-

[11] LABOURY, *Statuaire*, p. 30.
[12] Text: LABOURY, *Statuaire*, p. 31.
[13] A. WEIGALL, Upper Egyptian Notes, *ASAE* 9 (1908), p. 108.
[14] C. KUENTZ, *Deux steles d'Amenophis II*, Le Caire 1925.
[15] *Urk.* IV, p. 1561, 15.
[16] *Ibidem*, p. 1551, 8.
[17] *Ibidem*, p. 975, 7.
[18] *Ibidem*, p. 1795, 18.
[19] Cf. A. LOPRIENO, *Ancient Egyptian. A linguistic introduction*, Cambridge 1995, pp. 152-154, 165; also RITTER, *Verbalsystem*, p. 153.

ble that *snfr* is a participle here. It cannot be a *sḏm=f* form either for the verb *snfr* is a transitive verb.

The person described with the suffix must have been Thutmosis III for the phrase *dj ꜥnḫ mj Rꜥ* would indicate a living ruler. Thus we would have here another example of the *snfr*-ing performed in honour of Thutmosis III's father.

It is also important to note that the verb *snfr* cannot be considered here as part of a dedication formula, the infinitive specifying the character of the royal foundation.

Thus the translation would read: "May the perfect god, lord of Two Lands Men-kheper-Re live given life. It is as his *mnw* that he acted for his father, perfect god, lord of Two Lands Aa-kheperen-Re beloved by Amon-Re, lord of the temple which he [Thutmosis III] *snfr*-ed given life like Re."

4. The almost identical texts on the stelae of Amenhotep II from Amada and Elephantine.

"It is the king who satisfies his heart with building for all gods, being one who constructs their temples and fashions their images.

He gave (*rdj.n=f*) the house to its lord, supplied it with everything

[...]

in order that people should see, in order that everybody would know

[...]

while he *snfr*-ed the temple which his father, the King of Upper and Lower Egypt, Men-kheper-Re, had made for his fathers (*jst jn ḥm=f snfr ḥwt-nṯr tn jrt.n jt=f*)

[...]

in order that the great name (*n-mrt mn rn wr*) of his father Thutmosis may remain in this temple forever and ever. Then his majesty (*wn-jn ḥm n nṯr pn*) Amenhotep II stretched the cord and loosened the rope for all the fathers making for him a great pylon of hard stone in front of *wsḫt-ḫbjt*."

Here again the particle *jst* introduces the clause that, while syntactically independent, is in a kind of semantical dependency conveying the background information.

Certainly the act of *snfr*-ing precedes the erection of the pylon. The phrase *wn-jn* marks it clearly being the contingent tense form.

The analysis of this stela have led scholars to a number of suggestions concerning the actual meaning of the verb *snfr*. As it has already been mentioned, BJÖRKMAN suggested "complete", RITTER "renovate", BREASTED "supply with inscriptions". The temple of Amada could easily be a subject for an independent paper. Hopefully the conclusions herein presented will contribute to developing the problematic.

5. The translation of the inscription of Thutmosis IV on the statue found south of the IXth pylon is rather simple:

"It is his majesty who *snfr*-ed this foundation (*jn ḥm=f snfr mnw pn*) for his father Aa-kheperu-Re."

6. The inscriptions from the Lateran obelisk provide no new data for our research. The obelisk was *snfr*-ed in honour of Thutmosis III "in order that the name of his father might remain and endure in the house of Amon-Re".[20]

Analysis of the royal building records may lead to some conclusions. The action expressed with the verb *snfr* seems to be connected with the monuments of the royal predecessors. It is not, however, a spatial relationship only. Devotion towards the predecessor is strongly emphasised. While the king who simply rebuilds the pre-existing temple would use the phrase *m m3wt* – anew, the ruler that makes the *snfr*-ing makes it always in honour of his father – ancestor. It is the ancestor's name that should endure due to this act. In the light of these considerations the meaning "to complete" would seem the most adequate. It seems interesting that the rulers involved in this kind of activity are exactly those three kings whose succession might have been insecure. Thutmosis III was deposed for 20 years; it is possible, but by no means certain, that famous Dream Stela reflects Thutmosis IV problems of that kind. As for Amenhotep II one should recall the theory forwarded by Dimitry LABOURY who explained the late persecution of Hatshepsut with the suggestion that the rights of young Amenhotep might have been threatened.[21] The act of *snfr*-ing would then be a part of an attempt to make their rule legitimate.

[20] *Urk.* IV, p. 1549,18-19.

[21] LABOURY, *Statuaire*, pp. 497-511. The theory was first formulated by Ch. ROERIG and based on her research on the XVIIIth dynasty royal nurses.

Now we should turn to the private records that mention the act of *snfr*-ing. At first sight they appear to contradict these conclusions. However, it seems they may be incorporated into the wider scheme and contribute to a better understanding of the verb in question.

1. The autobiographical text of Intef describes the activity of that official in the oases and concludes:
"I supplied it.
I equipped it with every thing that was desired in the desert,
it being *snfr*-ed more than the palace (*ꜥḥ*) in Egypt."

In this text *snfr* should be considered a stative. The suffix pronoun of the first person singular is carefully written throughout the text, thus considering it a *sḏm=f* form does not seem likely. This stative is related to the *ꜥḥ*, which is indicated by the lack of the feminine ending and may also be deduced from the context.

This text clearly describes the activity of the official responsible for the royal residences. It is impossible to translate this verb as "to complete". The translation "to make beautiful" does not seem likely either. Intef was not occupied with the building activity. Moreover, even the boasting has its limits – certainly the provincial residence in the oasis could not have been more beautiful than the palace in Thebes. The text states clearly that it was excellently supplied. It should be suggested that Intef was proud of his efficiency as a royal supplier in the difficult, desert conditions. So the residence was better supplied than the palace in Thebes.

2. Second of the private inscriptions comes from Memphis. Amenhotep was an overseer of the works in the Mansion of Millions of Years erected by Amenhotep III in Memphis. He describes the temple – its enclosure, gates, furniture, sacred lake to conclude:
"After these works had been *snfr*-ed (*ḫr m-ḫt snfrw k3wt tn*) his majesty established (*ꜥḥꜥ.n w3ḥ.n ḥm=f*) the offerings anew."

It should be noted that there are works *snfr*-ed. This fragment would then summarise all the activities described above. It seems clear that *snfr* here means "to complete". However, no royal ancestor is mentioned in this text.

In thinking of a single scheme that would incorporate and explain all the above-mentioned examples, one should go back to the question of the meaning of the root *nfr*. The present author has already pointed to the fact that the English word "perfect" would seem most accurate. However, the notion of being perfect includes the concept of being finished, fully accomplished. When we say something is perfect we mean it needs no improvement or alteration. To make something perfect would then mean also to complete it.

The interesting feature of Egyptian that might be recalled to support these considerations is the use of *nfr* with the meaning of a negative verb.[22] It was already noted by GARDINER that *nfr* may signify "finished".[23] GARDINER compares it with the related nouns *nfrw* "lack", *nfrw* "end-room" and *nfryt* "end". This would explain why the phrase *nfr pw* was used as a negation. Something that has been completed is finished.

It seems to me that the verb *snfr* in the private records fits this interpretation. Intef's account of how the residence was supplied, and Amenhotep's description of the temple's erection were meant to be records of duties that were fully, perfectly fulfilled by the deceased official. The meaning perfect/completed – refers to their activity. It seems interesting that the verb *snfr* is employed in the passive forms – stative or *sḏmw=f* – it is a palace that was equipped; there are works that were completed.

The situation of the king is very different. The tasks of the king and the officials have nothing in common. It is a permanent activity – war outside, and erecting the temples inside the country – that is considered the duty of the king. If one pays attention to the context of the occurrences of the verb *snfr* he may observe that private texts are related to the deceased, while royal building records refer to the living ruler. Royal activity – including building activity – cannot be completed before the king is dead. It is only after his death that his foundation may finally be called perfect – completed. And it is a duty of the faithful son and heir to make it perfect.

[22] It was Professor L. ZONHOVEN who pointed this issue out to me.

[23] GARDINER, *EG*, § 351.

When the author analysed the dedication formula *jr.n=f mnw=f* he was trying to prove that its syntax would stress the significance of the king's activity rather than any specific object of this activity.[24] Some scholars have already suggested an understanding of the word *mnw* primarily as a royal act.[25] Moreover, one should note that the specification of the character of the royal *mnw* in the dedication formula is generally expressed by an infinitive, not by a noun.

It may seem strange that the verb *snfr* never occurs in the dedication formula. One should suggest that formula which emphasises the king's activity is not a proper place for it. The only ruler that may have his *mnw snfr*-ed is therefore the dead king – the royal ancestor. The living ruler by the act of *snfr*-ing makes the name of his predecessor everlasting in a perfect/completed – foundation. His own activity, however, may by no means be considered completed.

[24] Cf. P. LASKOWSKI, Some remarks on the dedication formula *jr.n=f m mnw=f*, *GM* 167 (1998), pp. 77-81.

[25] G. VITTMANN, Zum Verständnis der Weihformel jrjnf m mnwf, *WZKM* 69 (1977), pp. 22, 25.

Agnieszka Mączyńska
Poznań

Lower Egyptian Culture at Central Tell in Tell el-Farkha. Preliminary Report
(Plates 21-23)

1. Introduction

The site of Tell el-Farkha is situated in the eastern Nile Delta in the northern part of Ghazala village (Markaz el-Simbillawein). It consists of three tells (western, central and eastern) covering a total area of approximately 400 x 110 meters and rising 4.5 meters above the surrounding fields. The site was located in 1987 by the Italian Archaeological Mission of the "Centro Studi e Ricerche Ligabue" in Venice, which subsequently carried out excavations at the site between 1988-1990. The excavations supported the division into Predynastic, Protodynastic and early Old Kingdom occupational phases.[1]

In 1998 works at Tell el-Farkha were renewed by a Polish archaeological expedition headed by M. CHŁODNICKI from the Poznań Prehistoric Society and by K.M. CIAŁOWICZ from the Jagiellonian University in Cracow. During the three seasons of extensive fieldworks (1998-2001) a large assemblage, including pottery, flints, stones and bones, was found. In addition, geological core sample drilling together with a geophysical survey were applied at the site.[2] The results of the excavations carried out between 1998-2001, confirmed the occupation phase thesis proposed by the Italian mission. Thanks to the analysis of pottery we can distinguish seven occupational phases. The oldest can be associated with the culture of Lower Egypt dated back to NIIc-IId1. The second phase containing materials characteristic of the Lower and Upper Egyptian traditions can be dated back to NIId1. The third phase dated back to NIId2/NIIIa1 is entirely Naqadan in character. Phases 4 and 5 are connected with the period of the formation of the state in Egypt and the beginning of the Ist dynasty NIIIa2-NIIIc1 (the end of NIIIB to NIIIC1). Only at Central Tell were the 6th and 7th phases distinguished. They date back to the Early Dynastic Period and Old Kingdom period up to the IVth dynasty.

In this paper I would like to concentrate on the oldest phase in Tell el-Farkha, associated with Lower Egyptian Culture. Tell el-Farkha is one of the few Predynastic sites in the Nile Delta. Thanks to a lower level of underground water it was possible to reach the layers of Lower Egyptian culture without major problems. The first to reach the Lower Egyptian layers in Tell el-Farkha were members of the Italian mission to the Nile Delta that took place in the late eighties. They marked these layers as Ia and Ib, dating them back to NIIb and NIIc. They noted that these layers "shared strong direct links with the late Predynastic phase at Buto".[3] Now, we are sure that these layers belong to the oldest occupation phase at this site, which can be dated back to the NIIc period, or perhaps slightly earlier. This estimation is based on analogous Lower Egyptian ceramic assemblages from Buto (layer II),[4] Tell Ibrahim Iswid (phase A)[5] and Tell Ibrahim Awad (phase 7).[6] Nowadays, we know of only four typical of Lower Egyptian Culture settlements,

[1] M. CHŁODNICKI, R. FATTOVICH, S. SALVATORI, Italian Excavation in the Nile Delta: Fresh Data and New Hypotheses on the 4th Millennium Cultural Development of Egyptian Prehistory, *Rivista di Archeologia* 15 (1991), pp. 5-33; IIDEM, The Nile Delta in Transition: A View from Tell el-Farkha, in: E.M.C. van den BRINK (ed.), *The Nile Delta in Transition: 4th-3rd Millennium B.C.*, Tel Aviv 1992 (hereinafter referred to as: Nile Delta), pp. 171-190; IIDEM, The Italian Archaeological Mission of the C.S.R.L.–Venice to the Eastern Delta: A preliminary report of the 1987-1988 field season, *CRIPEL* 14 (1992), pp. 45-62.

[2] CHŁODNICKI, K.M. CIAŁOWICZ, Tell el-Farkha. Explorations 1998, *PAM* X (1999), pp. 63-70; IIDEM, Tell el-Farkha. Exploration 1999, *PAM* XI (2000), pp. 59-76.

[3] CHŁODNICKI, FATTOVICH, SALVATORI, Nile Delta, p. 183.

[4] T. von der WAY, *Tell el-Fara'in. Buto* I, Mainz 1997 (hereinafter referred to as: *Buto* I).

[5] van den BRINK, A Transitional Late Predynastic-Early Dynastic Settlement Site in the Northeastern Nile Delta, Egypt, *MDAIK* 45 (1989), pp. 55-108.

[6] van den BRINK, Preliminary Report on the Excavations at

namely, Maadi,[7] Buto,[8] Tell Ibrahim Iswid and Tell Ibrahim Awad[9] and also three cemeteries of Maadi, Wadi Digla[10] and Heliopolis.[11] The finds discovered coincidentally or finds from the surveys (Tura-Train Station, Giza, Es-Staff, Ezbet el-Qerdahi) are not mentioned here.[12]

2. Lower Egyptian Culture in Tell el-Farkha

This paper is a preliminary report including the results of excavations carried out in 1998 and 1999 at Central Tell where four trenches were located – on the southern, northern and western slopes. In each open trench we reached the layers associated with the settlement of Lower Egyptian Culture. The occupation traces left by the inhabitants of the settlement consist of the remains of the round shelter (**pl. 21** – pit 16; **pl. 22, fig. 2** – pit 16) of a diameter of about 3.5 meters, dug at a depth of ca 40-50 cm. There was a hearth of approximately 70 cm inside the shelter (**pl. 21** – pit 15).

We also recorded several round and oval storage pits (measuring 1,20-2,20 m in diameter) often intersecting each other, containing a black fill with a modest amount of small pot sherds (**pl. 22, fig. 1** – pit 18/24, 22, 23; **pl. 22, fig. 2** – pit 23). There were also concentrations of small, round pits (20-30 cm in diameter), probably post-holes lined with silt (**pl. 22, fig. 1** – pit 21, 26). Most of these smaller pits contained only isolated fragments of pottery occurring sporadically and a series of furrows about 10-20 cm wide formed into rectangular ground plans, which probably formed an indefinite structure built of organic materials above ground (**pl. 22, fig. 1** – F. 25, 27).

3. Lower Egyptian Pottery

a) Fabric

In all excavated trenches a large ceramic assemblage was discovered. Pottery from the layers of Lower Egyptian Culture in Tell el-Farkha was made from Nile alluvial clays. At this stage of our research there is still no specimen made from marl clay taken from these layers. According to a fabric type, most of the Lower Egyptian pottery was handmade from paste with fine to coarse sand and large amounts of straw (2-5 mm in size) (fabric IC1, IC2). There is also pottery made from paste with fine to medium sand and fine straw temper (fabric IB). Sometimes very fine and long organic temper which looks like hairlines was added to clay. The colour of this pottery is respectively brown, brownish-red, brownish-grey and brownish-black. Judging by a fabric type and surface treatment we have distinguished the following groups of pottery: the most abundant group is rough ware, containing coarse chaff and straw temper with a rough external surface. This characteristic rough appearance is given by the casts of burnt-out organic temper, which are clearly visible on the sur-

Tell Ibrahim Awad, Season 1988-1990, in: van den BRINK (ed.), *The Nile Delta in Transition: 4th-3rd Millennium B.C.*, Tel Aviv 1992 (hereinafter referred to as: Tell Ibrahim Awad), pp. 43-68.

[7] I. RIZKANA, J. SEEHER, *Maadi* I*: The Pottery of the Predynastic Settlement*, Mainz 1987 (hereinafter referred to as: *Maadi* I); IIDEM, *Maadi* II*: The Lithic Industries of the Predynastic Settlement*, Mainz 1988; IIDEM, *Maadi* III*: The Non-Lithic Small Finds and the Structural Remains of the Predynastic Settlement*, Mainz 1989.

[8] T. von der WAY, Tell el-Fara'in – Buto. 1 Bericht, *MDAIK* 42 (1886), pp. 242-257; IDEM, Tell el-Fara'in – Buto. 2 Bericht, *MDAIK* 43 (1986), pp. 241-257; IDEM, Tell el-Fara'in – Buto. 3 Bericht, *MDAIK* 44 (1986), pp. 283-306; IDEM, Tell el-Fara'in – Buto. 4 Bericht, *MDAIK* 45 (1986), pp. 275-307; IDEM, Excavation at Tell el-Fara'in/Buto in 1987-1989, in: van den BRINK (ed.), *The Nile Delta in Transition: 4th-3rd Millennium B.C.*, Tel Aviv, 1992, pp. 1-10; IDEM, *Untersuchungen zur Spätvor- und Frühgeschichte Unterägyptens*, SAGA 8, Heidelberg 1993; von der WAY, *Buto* I; D. FALTINGS, Recent Excavation in Tell el-Fara'in/Buto: New Finds and their Chronological Implication, in: C.J. EYRE (ed.), *Proceeding of the Seventh International Congress of Egyptologists*, OLA 82, Leuven 1998, pp. 365-375.

[9] van den BRINK, *MDAIK* 45 (1989), pp. 55-108; IDEM, Tell Ibrahim Awad, pp. 43-68.

[10] RIZKANA, SEEHER, *Maadi* IV. *The Predynastic Cemeteries of Maadi and Wadi Digla*, Mainz 1990 (hereinafter referred to as: *Maadi* IV).

[11] F. DEBONO, B. MORTENSEN, *The Predynastic Cemetery at Heliopolis. Season March-September*, Mainz 1950 (hereinafter referred to as: *Predynastic Cemetery at Heliopolis*).

[12] H. JUNKER, *Bericht über die Grabungen der Kaiserlichen Akademie der Wissenschaften in Wien, auf dem Friedhof in Turah*, Wien 1912; H. von LABIB, W. KAISER, Ein Friedhof der Maadikultur bei es-Staff, *MDAIK* 41 (1985), pp. 43-41; MORTENSEN, Four Jars from the Maadi Culture found in Giza, *MDAIK* 41 (1985), pp. 145-147; A. el-SANUSSI, M. JONES, A Site of the Maadi Culture near Giza Pyramids, *MDAIK* 53 (1997), pp. 241-253; J. von WUNDERLICH, von der WAY, K. SCHMIDT, Neue Fundstellen der Buto-Maadi-Kulture bei Ezbet el-Qerdahi, *MDAIK* 45 (1989), pp. 309-318.

face of the vessels. Sometimes the upper parts of vessels were wet smoothed.

About 92% of pottery from Lower Egyptian layers belongs to a finer type of rough ware, characterised by less coarse paste and thinner walls than the coarser type.

The remaining 8% of this pottery includes red slip ware, dark red (plum) slip ware, light red slip ware, brownish-red or brown slip ware and hard smoothed ware. These groups come only from the upper layers of Lower Egyptian Culture. At the lower layers only pottery from the rough ware group was collected.

b) Shapes

The most characteristic shapes of Lower Egyptian Culture in Tell el-Farkha are rather small globular jars with a roll rim, an undistinguished neck and an irregular surface. They amount to approximately 36% of the rough ware (**pl. 23:1-2, 9-10, 14**).

Other abundant shapes of the rough ware from this period are small, irregular truncated conical bowls with rims rounded or formed into a small lip (about 40%) and medium-depth bowls with a simple or rounded rim (about 5%) (**pl. 23:19-24, 28**).

Some other very distinctive shapes from Lower Egyptian Culture are jars with an almost vertical neck and sometimes a roll rim and small jars with an outturned neck. Their bases are flat or pointed, though, lemon shaped bases were also collected (about 19%) (**pl. 23:25-27, 29-30**).

c) Decoration

Only a small amount of pottery from Lower Egyptian Culture in Tell el-Farkha was decorated. Decorated pottery amounts to about 15% of the assemblage. The most typical kind of pottery decoration from this period is an incised continuous zigzag made by means of the rocker technique, and a dotted zigzag. It occurs on small jars with an everted rolled rim and undistinguished neck (**pl. 23:2-18**).

Other, less common, motives of decoration from this period are oblique lines on jars and impressed semi-circles on bowls (**pl. 23:19-21**).

In the upper levels of Lower Egyptian Culture in Tell el-Farkha, apart from the rough ware, there are simple, open bowls with a burnished surface and jars with a rolled rim and smoothed upper part belonging to the red slip ware (approximately 3%), as well as dark, red slip bowls and jars with a distinct neck and a fabric similar to that used for the rough ware (approximately 3%). Other wares, such as the light red slip ware, the half polished light red slip and the hard smoothed ware amount to only about 1% and their sherds do not allow a precise recognition of vessel shapes. They pertain probably to different kinds of jars and bowls and they are only secondarily found in Predynastic layers.

d) Others

Apart from pottery we discovered other interesting Lower Egyptian artefacts like a clay bead or amulet, a perforated clay disc with an impressed fingerprint which may have served as a seal. A large flint assemblage was also discovered. Sickle blades are the most common, with knives occurring in smaller quantities.

4. Social Aspects of Pottery Production in Tell el-Farkha

The fabric, modes of production and conditions of firing characteristic of Lower Egyptian pottery in Tell el-Farkha indicate the lack of a specialised system of pottery production. E.Ch. KÖHLER[13] refers to this stage as "*household production*". It is characteristic of rather simple production conditions. Pottery is handmade and fired in uncontrolled oxidising conditions. As a result the pots have soft, thick and uneven walls, contain huge amounts of organic and mineral temper and the colour is not solid with plenty of stains and accidental arrangement of colours on the surface. According to KÖHLER,[14] potters in this period were not economically dependent on their craft. The production was connected with just a few technical problems and economical expenses and had a seasonal character due to climatic conditions in the Delta.[15] Moreover, the agricultural character of Lower Egyptian society,

[13] E.Ch. KÖHLER, Socio-economic Aspects of Early Pottery Production in the Nile Delta, *BACE* 8 (1997), pp. 81-89.

[14] *Ibidem, loc. cit.*

[15] Because of the cold winter period from October to March with pouring rains, high humidity (a. 80%) and low temperatures, pottery production was possible only during the summer period, when the dry and warm climate makes good conditions for production, drying and storage of pots (KÖHLER, *BACE* 8 (1997), p. 82).

involving each man in the periods of the highest social activity (e.g. harvest), led to a situation in which pottery could be made only by women staying at home for the purpose of taking care of the children and performing other household duties.

5. Chronology

In conclusion I would like to summarise what has been said above from a chronological point of view. The oldest pottery from Tell el-Farkha is similar to the ceramic assemblage in other Lower Egyptian sites. We notice the most striking convergence between the following sites: Tell el-Farkha (phase 1), Tell el-Fara'in/Buto (level II),[16] Tell el-Iswid (phase A)[17] and Tell Ibrahim Awad (phase 7).[18] The pottery from these sites has similar fabric and surface treatment (the most numerous pots belong to rough ware), vessel forms (bowls and jars) and decoration (zigzag, semi-circles). Taking under consideration comparable material we can date the Lower Egyptian levels in Tell el-Farkha back to NIIc-IId1, the second phase of Lower Egyptian Culture (Buto II NIIc-IId1,[19] Tell el-Iswid A NIIc-IId1,[20] Tell Ibrahim Awad NIId1[21]). The pottery from the remaining known sites such as Maadi (settlement and cemetery), Heliopolis, Wadi Digla and Buto (level I) is less similar to the oldest Tell el-Farkha pottery. This situation is caused by a different chronology of these sites. Maadi, Heliopolis, Wadi Digla and Buto (level I) represent the older – first phase of Lower Egyptian Culture dating back to NI-NIIb or even NIIc (for example Buto – NIIa/b or earlier or NIIb/c,[22] Maadi settlement – second half of NI to NIIc,[23] Maadi cemetery – second half of NI,[24] Wadi Digla – second half of NI to NIIa/b or possibly until NIIc,[25] Heliopolis – NIIa-b[26]). Among the pottery coming from these sites there is no zigzag pattern and semi-circle pattern on vessels and there are more vessel forms which are missing in the second phase of this culture (jars on a raised base, bowls of a wave-shaped rim, T-shaped bowls). Fabric and surface treatment in the first phase are also more differentiated. Apart from rough ware there are other ceramic classes, for example, in Maadi: Red Burnished Ware, Yellowish Washed Ware, Local Blacktopped Ware; in Buto: Ware 1b and 1c with red and brown slip, Ware 1d-f with yellow slip).[27]

6. Conclusion

In spite of these differences, all these sites belong to Lower Egyptian Culture, a cultural complex which spread all over the Nile Delta as far as Faium in the south in the early Predynastic Period. The differences are caused by different chronology and local phenomena. There are still a considerable number of unanswered questions and the information collected so far remains insufficient. We need new discoveries to enrich our knowledge of Lower Egyptian Culture.

In July 2000 we started excavations at the top of the central hill. We reached Old Kingdom and Early Dynastic levels, but we need at least three seasons to reach Lower Egyptian levels. We hope that further works will bring answers to all our questions and Lower Egyptian Culture will become less of a mystery than it is today.

[16] von der WAY, *Buto* I, pp. 81-101, pls. 5, 31, 39.

[17] van den BRINK, *MDAIK* 45 (1989), pp. 67-71, figs. 8-12.

[18] IDEM, Tell Ibrahim Awad, pp. 53-55, fig. 10.

[19] D. FALTINGS, Recent Excavation in Tell el-Fara'in/Buto: New Finds and their Chronological Implication, in: *Proceeding of the Seventh International Congress of Egyptologists*, OLA 82, Leuven 1998 (hereinafter referred to as: Excavation in Tell el-Fara'in), p. 373.

[20] van den BRINK, *MDAIK* 45 (1989), p. 78.

[21] IDEM, Tell Ibrahim Awad, p. 53.

[22] FALTINGS, Excavation in Tell el-Fara'in, pp. 372-373.

[23] *Ibidem*; Thematical Discussions. 4. Harbors and Colonization, in: van den BRINK (ed.), *The Nile Delta*, p. 483.

[24] RIZKANA, SEEHER, *Maadi* IV, pp. 97-104.

[25] *Ibidem*, *loc.cit.*

[26] DEBONO, MORTENSEN, *Predynastic Cemetery at Heliopolis*, pp. 34, 49-51.

[27] *Ibidem*, pp. 23-34; RIZKANA, SEEHER, *Maadi* I, pp. 23-76; IIDEM, *Maadi* IV, pp. 26-27, 76-89.

Dariusz Niedziółka
Warsaw

Were Queen Hatshepsut's Eastern Obelisks at Karnak Erected Twice?

(Plates 24-27)

It is commonly assumed that the eastern obelisks of Queen Hatshepsut at Karnak were executed under Senenmut's supervision and then erected at the beginning of her reign as a King, most probably on the occasion of her enthronement.[1] It is also well known, that in the foundations of the southern obelisk of the pair, blocks decorated with the names of Thutmose II and Thutmose III were reused.[2] Recently, blocks decorated with names of Hatshepsut herself were discovered in the foundations of these obelisks.[3] Since it was impossible to insert these blocks while the monoliths stood on their bases, one might reject such an early date for the erection of these obelisks in this case at least, if not of their execution.

It is well known that Hatshepsut erected three pairs of obelisks in the precinct of Amon-Re at Karnak: they were the monoliths erected in the festival court of Thutmose II in front of the IVth pylon of the temple,[4] those which once stood in the eastern part of the precinct,[5] and the obelisks introduced by the Queen into the hall between the IVth and the Vth pylons of the temple.[6] The most famous pair in the *wadjit* hall was executed in the 16th regnal year of Thutmose III, as Hatshepsut's inscription at the base of the still standing northern monolith of the pair attests:[7]

[1] See D. NIEDZIÓŁKA, Some Remarks on the Graffito of Senenmut at Aswan, in: J. POPIELSKA-GRZYBOWSKA (ed.), *Proceedings of the First Central European Conference of Young Egyptologists. Egypt 1999: Perspectives of Research. Warsaw 7-9 June 1999*, Światowit Supplement Series E: Egyptology, vol. I, WES, vol. III, Warsaw 2001 (hereinafter referred to as: Graffito of Senenmut), pp. 100-104, with an older bibliography concerning this issue.

[2] See A. VARILLE, Description sommaire du sanctuaire oriental d'Amon-Rê à Karnak, *ASAE* 50 (1950), p. 140 and pl. V.

[3] Regarding unpublished blocks of Hatshepsut, see D. LABOURY, L'évolution des relations politiques entre Thoutmosis III et Hatshepsout à travers l'analyse de leur programmes architecturaux dans la région thébaine, *Revue des historiens de l'art, des archéologues, des musicologues et des orientalistes de l'Université de Liège* 14 (1995), pp. 9 and 17 note 26.

[4] L. GABOLDE, À propos de deux obélisques de Thoutmosis II, dédiés à son père Thoutmosis I et érigés sous le règne d'Hatshepsout-pharaon à l'ouest du IVe pylône, Cahiers de Karnak VIII, Paris 1987 (hereinafter referred to as: Deux obélisques de Thoutmosis II), pp. 143-158.

[5] PM II[2], p. 218; see also NIEDZIÓŁKA, Pyramidia of Queen Hatshepsut's Eastern Obelisks at Karnak and their Attribution to Particular Bases, *GM* 175 (2000), pp. 39-58 and bibliography therein, p. 40 footnote 3.

[6] PM II[2], pp. 81-83; see also W.C. HAYES, *Internal Affairs from Tuthmosis I to the Death of Amenophis III.* Part 1, CAH II, Cambridge 1962 (hereinafter referred to as: CAH), pp. 21-22; W. WESTENDORF, *Altägyptische Darstellungen des Sonnenlaufes auf der abschüssigen Himmelsbahn*, MÄS 10, Berlin 1966, p. 15; G. BJÖRKMAN, *Kings at Karnak. A Study of the Treatment of the Monuments of Royal Predecessors in the Early New Kingdom*, Uppsala 1971 (hereinafter referred to as: *Kings at Karnak*), pp. 66-67, 74-75; W. SEIPEL, Hatschepsut I., *LÄ* II, col. 1046; K. MARTIN, *Ein Garantsymbol des Lebens. Untersuchung zu Ursprung und Geschichte der altägyptischen Obelisken bis zum Ende des Neuen Reiches*, HÄB 3, Hildesheim 1977 (hereinafter referred to as: *Garantsymbol*), pp. 137-147; L. HABACHI, *Obelisks of Egypt. Skyscrapers of the Past*, New York 1977 (hereinafter referred to as: *Obelisks*), pp. 60-66, 68-70; S. RATIÉ, *La reine Hatchepsout: sources et problèmes*, Orientalia Monspeliensia I, Leiden 1979 (hereinafter referred to as: *Hatchepsout*), pp. 205-207, 209-210; Ch. MEYER, *Senenmut: eine prosopographische Untersuchung*, HÄS 2, Hamburg 1982 (hereinafter referred to as: *Senenmut*), pp. 131-132, 135-136; GABOLDE, Deux obélisques de Thoutmosis II, pp. 149-150; P. DORMAN, *The Monuments of Senenmut. Problems in Historical Methodology*, London 1988 (hereinafter referred to as: *Monuments of Senenmut*), pp. 50, 61-62, 64; A.-K. SELIM, *Les obélisques égyptiens. Histoire et archéologie*, CASAE 26, Le Caire 1991 (hereinafter referred to as: *Obélisques*), I, pp. 82-112, II, pp. 21-46; J.-Cl. GOLVIN, Hatchepsout et les obélisques de Karnak, *Les Dossiers d'Archéologie* 187 (1993), pp. 36-40; Chr. WALLET-LEBRUN, Contribution à l'étude de l'histoire de la construction à Karnak, in: M. DEWACHTER, A. FOUCHARD, *L'égyptologie et les Champollion*, Grenoble 1994, pp. 236-237; LABOURY, *Revue des historiens de l'art, des archéologues, des musicologues et des orientalistes de l'Université de Liège* 14 (1995), pp. 9 and 11; IDEM, *La statuaire de Thoutmosis III. Essai d'interprétation d'un portait royal dans son contexte historique*, Ægyptiaca Leodiensia 5, Liège 1998 (hereinafter referred to as: *Statuaire de Thoutmosis III*), pp. 21-24, 47-49, 55, 134, 554, 567-568, 591 footnote 1747, 594.

[7] *Urk.* IV, p. 367, 3-5.

š3.n ḥm=j k3.t r=s	"My Majesty has ordained works concerning it (= obelisks),
m rnp.t zp 15 3bd 2 pr.t sww 1	beginning on the regnal year 15, 2nd month of the *peret*-season, first day,
nfry.t r rnp.t zp 16 3bd 4 šmw ʿrḳy sww	ending with regnal year 16, 4th month of the *shemu*-season, last day,
jr.n=ø 3bd 7 m š3.t m ḏw	while (this)[8] has made seven months as those ordained in the mountain (= quarries)."

Thus, one cannot identify those obelisks with the monoliths mentioned in Senenmut's graffito at Aswan. This also implies that the text might concern the pair in the eastern Karnak, or obelisks in the festival court of Thutmose II.

In Luc GABOLDE's opinion, Senenmut's graffito was a reference to the pair in the festival court.[9] It seems, however, that such an attribution mainly results from GABOLDE's a priori assumption of a relation between each of Hatshepsut's officials involved in execution and decoration of her obelisks – that is Senenmut, Djehuti and Amenhotep – and a different pair of monuments. Such an assumption is not firmly founded since both Amenhotep and Djehuti were beyond any doubt concerned with the obelisks erected in the hall between the IVth and the Vth pylon at Karnak. Amenhotep's relation to that pair has found almost universal acceptance,[10] but Djehuti was connected with the eastern pair by some scholars,[11] and with the one erected in *wadjit* by others.[12] There are three important factors, however, which attest the identification of obelisks mentioned in the Northampton stela of Djehuti with those erected in the *wadjit* hall. They are: firstly – an almost perfect agreement in the height of 108 cubits, mentioned by Djehuti, with the double height of the still standing obelisk; secondly – the covering of the upper halves of these monoliths, at minimum, with an electrum foil, attested both in Djehuti's and Hatshepsut's inscriptions and by archaeological data as well. The third factor would be the position of the obelisks in the chronologically arranged list of monuments referred to in the Djehuti's stela. This position implies a relatively late date of the monoliths mentioned in the Northampton stela, which

[8] There is an evident subject omission under relevance in this clause, as regards this issue see M. COLLIER, The Relative Clause and the Verb in Middle Egyptian, *JEA* 77 (1991), pp. 36-37; A. LOPRIENO, *Ancient Egyptian. A linguistic introduction*, Cambridge 1995 (hereinafter referred to as: *Ancient Egyptian*), p. 161. The omitted pronoun =*s* should most probably be identified with the duration of the works referred to in the preceding clause.

[9] See GABOLDE, Deux obélisques de Thoutmosis II, p. 149 footnote 9.

[10] See HABACHI, Two Graffiti at Sehel from the Reign of Queen Hatshepsut, *JNES* 16 (1957), p. 99 and IDEM, *Obelisks*, pp. 69-70; W. HELCK, *Zur Verwaltung des Mittleren und Neuen Reichs*, Leiden, Köln 1958 (hereinafter referred to as: *Verwaltung*), p. 364 and IDEM, *Materialien zur Wirtschaftsgeschichte des Neuen Reiches* I, Abhandlungen der Geistes- und Sozialwissenschaftlichen Klasse, Jahrgang 1960, Nr. 10, Wiesbaden 1961 (hereinafter referred to as: *Materialien*), p. 807; HAYES, CAH II, pp. 22-23; SEIPEL, *LÄ* II, col. 1050 footnote 37; MARTIN, *Garantsymbol*, p. 153 with footnote 4; RATIÉ, *Hatchepsout*, p. 266; GABOLDE, Deux obélisques de Thoutmosis II, p. 149 footnote 9; GOLVIN, *Les Dossiers d'Archéologie* 187 (1993), p. 38. MEYER, who identifies the obelisks mentioned by Amenhotep with the Hatshepsut's eastern pair, is the single exception in this respect, see her *Senenmut*, p. 138.

[11] See P. LACAU, L'or dans l'architecture égyptienne, *ASAE* 53/2 (1956), p. 247; HABACHI, *JNES* 16 (1957), p. 99; HAYES, CAH II, p. 21; MARTIN, *Garantsymbol*, p. 153; GABOLDE, Deux obélisques de Thoutmosis II, p. 149 footnote 9; and Cl. VANDERSLEYEN, *L'Égypte et la vallée du Nil. II. De la fin de l'Ancien Empire à la fin du Nouvel Empire*, Paris 1995 (hereinafter referred to as: *Égypte et la vallée du Nil* 2), p. 293 footnote 1.

[12] See W. SPIEGELBERG, Die Northampton Stele, *RecTrav* 22 (1900), pp. 123-124. His opinion has been followed by J.H. BREASTED, *Ancient Records of Egypt* II, Chicago 1906 (hereinafter referred to as: *AR* II), p. 156 footnote h; HELCK, *Verwaltung*, p. 398 footnote 9 and IDEM, *Materialien*, p. 807; P. BARGUET, *Le temple d'Amon-Rê à Karnak: Essai d'exégèse*, RAPH 21, Le Caire 1962 (hereinafter referred to as: *Temple d'Amon-Rê*), p. 100 footnote 1; RATIÉ, *Hatchepsout*, p. 271 footnote 49; MEYER, *Senenmut*, p. 136 and NIEDZIÓŁKA, On the Obelisks Mentioned in the Northampton Stela of Djehuti, in: *Eight International Congress of Egyptologists, Cairo, 28 March-3 April 2000, Late Abstracts*, Cairo 2000 (hereinafter referred to as: *8th ICE Late Abstracts*), pp. 9-10 and the

accords with the 16th year recorded in the Hatshepsut's inscription.[13] Thus, one of GABOLDE's arguments relating Senenmut's graffito to the obelisks in the festival court of Thutmose II loses its validity.

As GABOLDE has remarked, one of the faces of an obelisk once erected in the festival court of Thutmose II is decorated with an original Horus name of that King,[14] while on the remaining two decorated sides his names are evidently in palimpsest, secondary carved most probably by Thutmose III, after erasing of Hatshepsut's names.[15] GABOLDE concludes from this that the obelisks were executed already in the reign of Thutmose II and their decoration was begun still in his reign. Then, the remaining sides were decorated after the enthronement of Hatshepsut, who would have been responsible for their erection.[16] Assuming such an interpretation, it is impossible to identify the obelisks referred to in Senenmut's graffito at Aswan with Thutmose II's monoliths, since the graffito was engraved on rocks at Aswan immediately before Hatshepsut's enthronement.[17] Such a dating of the graffito is attested – it seems – by the occurrence of the epithet relating to Hatshepsut *dj.t.n n=s Rꜥ nzy.t* "one to whom Re has given the kingship" and the circumstantial phrase *mꜣꜥ ḥr-jb psḏ.t nṯr.w*, qualifying her investiture with kingship as righteous in the opinion of the divine Ennead. The epithet is attested only in relation to rulers who had already assumed the kingship, the royal protocol, and thus were considered legally valid. The case of Senenmut's graffito would be the only exception. The same also concerns the phrase *ḫpr.n n bꜣ.w ḥm.t=s* "and it was because of the power of her majesty that (it) happened".[18] An argument against dating the graffito to Thutmose II's reign might in turn be the possession of her own estate by Nefrure, mentioned in Senenmut's title *jmj-rꜣ pr wr nj zꜣ.t nzw Nfrw-Rꜥ* "great steward of royal daughter Nefrure", and the lack of any mention of Thutmose II in the text.[19]

GABOLDE has put forward an alternative hypothesis, that works on the obelisks in the Aswan quarries were begun during Thutmose II's reign, then they might have been continued in Hatshepsut's regency period, their decoration finished after her enthronement, and eventually were erected in the court by Hatshepsut's order.[20]

In the opinion of Dimitri LABOURY, who does not attempt to relate definitely to which pair of obelisks Senenmut's graffito might be concerned,[21] the monoliths in the court of Thutmose II were Hatshepsut's work from the very beginning, and they should be dated to the turn of the regency and the coregency period,[22] similarly to her statue from the Elephantine Island dedicated to her late husband Thutmose II.[23] Thus, in LABOURY's opinion, both the eastern obelisks and those from the festival court might have been executed and erected in the same time approximately.

It seems that scenes and inscriptions decorating the Portico of Obelisks in Hatshepsut's temple at Deir el-Bahari might be decisive in this issue.

In the scene representing the dedication of the obelisks on the wall of the southern lowermost portico of Hatshepsut's temple at Deir el-Bahari, two pairs of monoliths are depicted.[24] Based on the dedication formulas occurring on the representations of obelisks at Deir el-Bahari, the left pair had the pyramidia covered with electrum:[25]

jr.n=s m mnw=s n jt=s [*Jmn* +1 gr.+	"That she has acted is her foundation for her father [Amon......,

same entitled paper in the Proceedings of the Congress (in the press).

[13] See NIEDZIÓŁKA, *8th ICE Late Abstracts*, pp. 9-10 and the paper in the Proceedings of the Congress (in the press).

[14] GABOLDE, Deux obélisques de Thoutmosis II, pp. 144, 145, 149.

[15] *Ibidem*, pp. 146, 147, 149.

[16] *Ibidem*, p. 149.

[17] As regards the date of Senenmut's graffito, see NIEDZIÓŁKA, Graffito of Senenmut, pp. 100-104.

[18] See *ibidem*, pp. 88, 100-101, 103-104.

[19] See *ibidem*, p. 103.

[20] See GABOLDE, Deux obélisques de Thoutmosis II, p. 149 footnote 9.

[21] LABOURY, *Statuaire de Thoutmosis III*, p. 554.

[22] *Ibidem*, pp. 23 footnote 134, 554, 588 and 626 footnote 1890.

[23] See G. DREYER, Eine Statue Thutmosis'II. aus Elephantine, *SAK* 11 (1984), pp. 489-499, pls. 19-22.

[24] E. NAVILLE, *The Temple of Deir el Bahari* VI, London 1906 (hereinafter referred to as: *Deir el Bahari* VI), pl. 156.

[25] *Ibidem*, pl. 156 – left pair. The actual facsimile of this text kindly provided to the present author by Dr Zbigniew E. SZAFRAŃSKI, the Director of the Polish-Egyptian

sʿḥʿ] n=f ṯḫn.wj wr.wj m mꜣṯ bnbn.(w)t m ḏʿm

jr=s dj.(tj) ʿnḫ nb mj Rʿ ḏ.t

(namely) the erecting] for him of two great obelisks with pyramidia of electrum, that she might act being given all life like Re forever."[26]

In the case of the other dedication, the space is insufficient to restore any mention of gold or electrum in the text:[27]

jr.n=s m mnw=s n jt=s J[mn]-Rʿ nb ns.wt [tꜣ.wj......]

sʿḥʿ [n=f ṯḫn.wj wr.wj

jr=s] dj.<tj> ʿnḫ mj Rʿ ḏ.t

"That she has acted is her foundation for her father Amon-Re, the lord of the thrones [of the Two Lands.......], (namely) the erecting [for him of two great obelisks, that she might act] being given life like Re forever."

Thus, it would be difficult to identify the obelisks depicted in Deir el-Bahari temple with those erected in the hall between the IVth and the Vth pylons, for the latter were decorated with electrum at least on their upper halves, which is evident from both archaeological and epigraphic sources.[28]

As observed by Pierre LACAU,[29] inside the *p.t*, *tꜣ* and *wꜣs* signs framing the shaft sides of Hatshepsut's obelisks erected in the *wadjit*, there are rather deep and thin grooves, which were most probably intended for fixing electrum foil adorning more than a half of the monoliths' sides, from the pyramidia down to the

Mission at Deir el-Bahari, contributes nothing to the reading published by NAVILLE. The lacuna is exactly 3 sign-groups high, thus one should therein reconstruct the name of Amon in the first group, an epithet of the god in the second, and the infinitive *sʿḥʿ* (*jr.t* is much less probable) in the third.

[26] As regards various interpretations of the dedication formula's grammatical structure see most recently LOPRIENO, *Ancient Egyptian*, p. 198; T. RITTER, *Das Verbalsystem der königlichen und privaten Inschriften: XVIII. Dynastie bis einschließlich Amenophis III.*, GOF.IV 30, Wiesbaden 1995, pp. 139-141; J.-M. KRUCHTEN, Deux cas particuliers de phrase coupée sans l'opérateur énonciatif *in*, *JEA* 82 (1996), pp. 51-60; K. JANSEN-WINKELN, Hervorgehobenes Objekt und königliche Widmungsformel, *Or* 66 (1997), pp. 15-33; P. LASKOWSKI, Some Remarks on the Dedication Formula *jr.n=f m mnw=f*, *GM* 167 (1998), pp. 77-81. As regards the final clause *jr=f/s* (*n=f/s/sn*) *dj.w/tj ʿnḫ* see most recently E. TEETER, *The Presentation of Maat. Ritual and Legitimacy in Ancient Egypt*, SAOC 57, Chicago 1997, pp. 55-69; P. BEYLAGE, Die Formel *jr(j)=f ḏ(j) ʿnḫ* in den Texten der 18. Dynastie, *GM* 181 (2001), pp. 19-26.

[27] NAVILLE, *Deir el Bahari* VI, pl. 156 – right pair. Thanks to the facsimile kindly provided by Dr SZAFRAŃSKI, one can ascertain that the lacuna, which is almost six sign-groups high in NAVILLE's publication, actually contains almost eight groups. Fortunately, there are some signs partly preserved allowing a reconstruction, in some degree, of the missing part of the text. Immediately below *jt=s* there are traces of the name *Jmn-Rʿ* and this god's epithet *nb ns.wt [tꜣ.wj]*, that jointly fills two groups and a half. Then, one missing group, which once had undoubtedly contained another epithet of the god, is followed by traces of *sʿḥʿ*, which combined gives another two sign-groups. The remaining part of the lacuna, which is a little higher than 3 sign-groups, should be filled with *n=f ṯḫn.wj* (one uppermost sign-group and a half) and *jr=s* (half of the lowermost sign-group). Since one cannot insert the phrase *m ḏʿm*, or *m nbw* into the still missing part of the lacuna, which should have filled two groups, the epithet *wr.wj* should be considered the one possible candidate to be reconstructed therein.

[28] Such an interpretation has been already pertinently advocated by R. TEFNIN, *La statuaire d'Hatshepsout. Portrait royal et politique sous la 18e Dynastie*, MonAeg 4, Bruxelles 1979, pp. 51-53; see also NIEDZIÓŁKA, in: *Proceedings of the 8th ICE* (in the press).

[29] LACAU, *ASAE* 53/2 (1956), p. 244 and fig. 8.

lowermost register of their decoration. This is confirmed beyond doubt by the texts adorning these obelisks.[30]

The gilding of these monoliths is also twice referred to in inscriptions decorating Hatshepsut's Red Chapel: in the text accompanying the scene of the gold offering to Amon,[31] and in the text accompanying the scene of obelisk presentation to the god.[32] The text of the Djehuti's stela also attests a rich gilding of these obelisks.[33]

tḫn.wj wr.wj k3=sn mḥ 108	"two great obelisks, which are 108 cubits high,
b3k.(w) r 3w=sn m ḏʿmw	being worked entirely with electrum,
mḥ.n t3.wj m st.wt=sn	while the Two Lands have become full of their rays"

Therefore, considering the dedication formulas on the representation of the obelisks at Deir el-Bahari, the lack of mention of a more extensive gilding of Hatshepsut's eastern monoliths, and those from the festival court, and concurrently the very well attested rich adorning with electrum of her western pair of monuments, it seems almost certain that the obelisks in the scene of dedication represent Hatshepsut's eastern obelisks at Karnak (probably the left pair), and the ones decorated and erected by Hatshepsut in the festival court in front of the IVth pylon at Karnak (probably the right pair).[34]

Secondly, as is widely known, the transport of obelisks is shown in the most spectacular representation of the same portico of the temple.[35] Despite some attempts to recognise in it a depiction of the transport of four monoliths,[36] both the representation and especially the text above it clearly attest that two obelisks only, and not four, are shown and mentioned.[37] The apparent inconsistency in the number of monuments depicted in the scene of transport (two obelisks) and the scene of dedication (four obelisks) seems to be easy to explain. Most probably, Hatshepsut's eastern obelisks at Karnak are depicted in the former representation, and the same ones together with those of Thutmose II in the latter. This might suggest that up to the moment of decorating the portico, the Queen executed and transported to Karnak one pair of monuments only, surely the eastern ones, that is, those depicted in the scene of transport. She might have, however, erected two pairs of obelisks, namely the eastern ones and those already executed and transported to Karnak by Thutmose II, that is four monuments shown in the scene of dedication. This in turn would mean that Senenmut's graffito at Aswan must refer to the eastern obelisks, since the text was executed at the very end of the regency of Hatshepsut. Concurrently, this would testify that the pair from the festival court had been executed and transported to Karnak already in the reign of Thutmose II, as GABOLDE has suggested.

Since the obelisks mentioned by Senenmut were executed at the end of Hatshepsut's regency, and concurrently blocks decorated with names of Thutmose II, Hatshepsut and Thutmose III were reused in their foundations, one should reconsider the problem of their erection.

One cannot exclude the possibility that the obelisks in question were executed in quarries at the turn of the regency period, as Senenmut's graffito attests, then transported to Karnak at the beginning of Hatshepsut's reign as a King, as the scene from Deir el-Bahari shows, and then abandoned for some period. Their erection, however, might have occurred much later, possibly in the sole reign of Thutmose III, who might have reused in their foundations some blocks originating from the dismantled (by himself) predecessor of Akhmenu. Rejecting this solution, one should rather

---

[30] *Urk.* IV, pp. 357, 4-9; 362, 10-14; 364, 16-365, 5; 365, 10-13; 366, 13-367, 2; 367, 8-9 and 367, 14-368, 1.

[31] LACAU, H. CHEVRIER, *Une chapelle d'Hatshepsout à Karnak* I, Le Caire 1977 (hereinafter referred to as: *Chapelle d'Hatshepsout*), p. 230 § 365.

[32] LACAU, CHEVRIER, *Chapelle d'Hatshepsout*, p. 232 § 369.

[33] *Urk.* IV, pp. 425, 16-426, 2.

[34] This was already suggested by NIEDZIÓŁKA, Die Bauten der Königin Hatschepsut, in: *Geheimnisvolle Königin Hatschepsut. Ägyptische Kunst des 15. Jahrhunderts v. Chr.*, Warschau 1997, p. 32; see also LABOURY, *Statuaire de Thoutmosis III*, p. 23 footnote 134.

[35] NAVILLE, *Deir el Bahari* VI, pl. 154.

[36] E.g. LACAU, CHEVRIER, *Chapelle d'Hatshepsout*, pp. 233-234 § 373; LABOURY, *Statuaire de Thoutmosis III*, p. 554.

[37] See e.g. MEYER, *Senenmut*, p. 135; GOLVIN, *Les Dossiers d'Archéologie* 187 (1993), p. 38; as regards the representation see recently A. WIRSCHING, Das Doppelschiff

assume that it was Hatshepsut herself who was responsible for dismantling a building decorated with names of Thutmose II, Thutmose III and hers as well, and reused some blocks taken from this building in foundations of her obelisks. One should not, moreover, overlook the evidence provided by the scene of the dedication of obelisks in the temple at Deir el-Bahari, which seems to exclude the former possibility.

It seems, however, that there are some factors supporting the former solution.[38] The names and representations of Hatshepsut were hammered out on the whole surface of her eastern obelisks, including their pyramidia, on which Queen's images were substituted by representations of offering tables.[39] One should concurrently notice that in the case of Hatshepsut's obelisks in the hall between the IVth and the Vth pylons, on the southern obelisk of the pair the names of the Queen were erased only to the height of 3.50 m above the roof of the hall. They were totally intact in the higher portion of its shaft and the same concerns the Queen's images on its pyramidion, despite the fact that the latter was only 10 m above the roof.[40] Moreover, on the northern obelisk of the pair, hammering out of Hatshepsut's images and names occurred only on the western and southern face of the monolith, and this concerns only her names in side scenes of the shaft in the fifth and sixth registers. The central column of the text was not touched at all, even at the height immediately above the roof.[41] Bearing in mind that the eastern obelisks were most probably higher than those in *wadjit*,[42] the hammering out of images and names of the Queen, and then replacing Hatshepsut's representations with the offering tables, was more difficult to do than in the case of her western monuments. Moreover, one should also bear in mind that Thutmose III frequently contented himself with hammering out the names of the Queen, without any attempt to replace them with Thutmose II's names or his own, and with effacement of her images without redecorating a wall even in easily accessible places.[43] Thus, one should assume that in this particular case the effacement of his former coregent from memory was particularly important for Thutmose III. Even if the redecorating of the standing high obelisks was possible, as the post-Amarna restorations of Amon's images and names on obelisks well attest,[44] it was much easier to do on the lying monuments.

Problems with maintaining the stability of the eastern obelisks during the works on the foundations of

– die altägyptische Technologie zur Beförderung schwester Steinlasten, *SAK* 27 (1999), pp. 401-407.

[38] This was already suggested by NIEDZIÓŁKA, *Sektor wschodni Karnaku w czasach Totmesa III* (= *The Eastern Sector of Karnak in the Reign of Thutmose III*) unpublished MA thesis, Institute of Archaeology, Warsaw University, Warszawa 1989 (hereinafter referred to as: *Sektor wschodni*), pp. 85-88; see also Di. ARNOLD, *Die Tempel Ägyptens. Götterwohnungen, Baudekmäler, Kultstätten*, Zürich 1992 (hereinafter referred to as: *Tempel Ägyptens*), p. 119.

[39] See Ch. KUENTZ, *Obélisques*, CGC, Le Caire 1932, pp. 20-24 and pls. VII-IX.

[40] *LD* III, 24; L. BORCHARDT, *Zur Baugeschichte des Amonstempels von Karnak*, UGAÄ 5/1, Leipzig 1905 (hereinafter referred to as: *Baugeschichte*), p. 25; *Urk.* IV, pp. 359-360; BARGUET, *Temple d'Amon-Rê*, p. 100 footnote 3; BJÖRKMAN, *Kings at Karnak*, pp. 74-75; MARTIN, *Garantsymbol*, fig. 15; RATIÉ, *Hatchepsout*, p. 306; DORMAN, *Monuments of Senenmut*, p. 61 footnote 80; SELIM, *Obélisques* I, p. 109, II, pp. 41-42; LABOURY, *Statuaire de Thoutmosis III*, p. 48.

[41] *LD* III, pls. 22-23; *Urk.* IV, pp. 357-358; HABACHI, *Obelisks*, pp. 61-63; RATIÉ, *Hatchepsout*, p. 304; DORMAN, *Monuments of Senenmut*, p. 61; SELIM, *Obélisques* I, pp. 93-97, II, pp. 23-27; LABOURY, *Statuaire de Thoutmosis III*, p. 48.

[42] This was first suggested by HABACHI (*JNES* 16 (1957), p. 99). His hypothesis was based, among others, on comparison of measurable elements of Hatshepsut's eastern and western obelisks. For example, the width of the northern obelisk socle in the eastern pair is ca 3.90 m (as results from the plan published by VARILLE, *ASAE* 50 (1950), pl. XLI), and the northern monolith socle in the western pair is 3.77 m wide (see M. AZIM *et al.*, *Karnak et sa topographie* I. *Les relevés modernes du temple d'Amon-Rê 1967-1984*, Paris 1998, 3); the original height of the Cairo pyramidion was 3.92 m (KUENTZ, *Obélisques*, p. 21 fig. 25), and the pyramidion of the southern monolith in the western pair is 2.96 m high (R. ENGELBACH, *The Aswân Obelisk*, Le Caire 1922 (hereinafter referred to as: *Aswân Obelisk*), p. 9); the base of the former pyramidion is 1.805-1.83 m wide (KUENTZ, *Obélisques*, p. 21 fig. 25), and the width of the base of the latter is 1.78 m (ENGELBACH, *Aswân Obelisk*, p. 9). Subsequently, many scholars, e.g. MARTIN (*Garantsymbol*, p. 149), GOLVIN (*Les Dossiers d'Archéologie* 187 (1993), p. 40), VANDERSLEYEN (*Égypte et la vallée du Nil* 2, pp. 287 and 293 footnote 1), and the present author (*Sektor wschodni*, pp. 86 and 101; see also in: *Geheimnisvolle Königin Hatschepsut*, p. 32 and the forthcoming paper in the *Proceedings of the 8th ICE*), were of the opinion that the eastern obelisks were higher than the western ones.

[43] DORMAN, *Monuments of Senenmut*, p. 64; see also numerous cases at Deir el-Bahari.

[44] See BARGUET, *Temple d'Amon-Rê*, p. 100 footnote 3; HABACHI, *Obelisks*, p. 62 pl. 14 – restored figure and

the eastern section of the wall enclosing the temple of Amon-Re together with Akhmenu seem to be another factor which would support the erection of the eastern obelisks in the reign of Thutmose III. The same problems might have occurred during works on the eastern sanctuary of that King. It is well known the wall in question was built during the sole reign of Thutmose III. There is much controversy, however, regarding a more precise dating of its erection. LABOURY suggested a date in the second half of the third decade, common for Akhmenu and the wall.[45] In Paul BARGUET's opinion the wall was built at the turn of the third decade, based on the contemporarity of the wall and the Eastern Sanctuary, the latter dated by him to the first jubilee of the King.[46] Jean LAUFFRAY was rather inclined to date the wall to the last decade of the reign of Thutmose III,[47] that is after the *damnatio memoriae* of Hatshepsut had begun.[48] Thus, the redecorating of the eastern obelisks might have been executed on the lying monuments, which then were erected after foundations of the eastern section of the wall had been completed.

Trying to reconcile these mutually exclusive factors, it seems that one should rather take into account the hypothetical possibility of the erection of these obelisks twice. This might have been done for the first time on the occasion of Hatshepsut's enthronement, then the obelisks might have been removed from their bases by Thutmose III during his works on Akhmenu, to be eventually erected later in his reign, after the works on the foundation of the wall enclosing this temple together with that of Amon-Re were completed and the proscription of Hatshepsut begun. In such a case these obelisks foundations might be dated to the reign of Thutmose III, and this would be the reason why blocks decorated with names of his father Thutmose II, his coregent Hatshepsut and himself could have been reused there. The predecessor of Akhmenu, connected with Thutmose II, Hatshepsut, and Thutmose III as well, seems to be the most probable source of these blocks. Consequently, these obelisks might have been even erected somewhere else for the first time, probably on the area then occupied by the newly built Akhmenu.

One should note, however, that the process of removing the obelisk from its base was rather complicated from the technical point of view. It is well known that Egyptian obelisks were transferred to be erected in another place in the Roman Period.[49] The first such an operation, well attested, carried out in 13/12 BC,

name of Amon on the pyramidion of the northern Hatshepsut's obelisk from the *wadjit*; see also DORMAN, *Monuments of Senenmut*, p. 61 and LABOURY, *Statuaire de Thoutmosis III*, p. 48. Restoration of Amon's figures and names on the pyramidia of Hatshepsut's eastern obelisks from Karnak is evident as well.

[45] LABOURY, *Statuaire de Thoutmosis III*, pp. 37-38, 48, 56, 197, 202 footnote 660, 527 and 552-553. It seems that the mere fact of use both of limestone and sandstone blocks in the construction of the wall and Akhmenu cannot be proof of the same early date of erection of the former and the latter. This method of mixing building material is equally well attested in the case of the temple of Thutmose III at Deir el-Bahari, built in the last decade of his reign; as regards this method of construction at Deir el-Bahari, see J. LIPIŃSKA, *Deir el-Bahari* II. *The Temple of Tuthmosis III. Architecture*, Warsaw 1972, pp. 13-14; as regards the date of its building see *ibidem*, p. 62, see also LABOURY, *Statuaire de Thoutmosis III*, pp. 37, 45 with footnote 261 (previous discussion on the issue), 51, 57-58 and 71 footnote 362.

[46] *Temple d'Amon-Rê*, p. 220. The wall and the sandstone rooms of the Eastern Sanctuary were evidently constructed in the same time. There is no evidence, however, to date the latter to the 30th regnal year of Thutmose III, as mentions of *zp tpj ḥb sd* on the pillars contribute nothing to the date of its building and decorating. Concurrently, the only preserved potrait of Thutmose III in the reliefs of the Eastern Sanctuary occurs on the northern face of the travertine naos which might have been earlier than the rest of this temple. Thus, the representation and its style cannot be considered evidence for the date of the whole Eastern Sanctuary and, consequently, for the date of the wall of Thutmose III enclosing Akhmenu and the temple of Amon-Re, contrary to LABOURY's opinion (*Statuaire de Thoutmosis III*, pp. 202 and 527-528).

[47] J. LAUFFRAY, Le secteur nord-est du temple jubilaire de Thoutmosis III à Karnak. État des lieux et commentaire architectural, *Kêmi* 19 (1969), p. 182.

[48] As regards the date of the beginning of the *damnatio memoriae* of Hatshepsut see DORMAN, *Monuments of Senenmut*, pp. 46-65; Van SICLEN, New Data on the Date of the Defacement of Hatshepsut's Name and Image on the Chapelle Rogue, *GM* 107 (1989), pp. 85-86; LABOURY, *Statuaire de Thoutmosis III*, pp. 44-47, 57 and 483-511. An earlier date suggested by MEYER (Zur Verfolgung Hatschepsuts durch Thutmosis III., in: H. ALTENMÜLLER, R. GERMER (eds.), *Miscellanea Aegyptologica, Wolfgang Helck zum 75. Geburtstag*, Hamburg 1989, pp. 119-126) seems hard to defend.

[49] See e.g. E. IVERSEN, *Obelisks in Exile*. I. *The Obelisks of Rome*, Copenhagen 1968; HABACHI, *Obelisks*, pp. 109-151.

was the removing the obelisks of Thutmose III from the temple of Atum-Re at Heliopolis and their re-erection in Alexandria in the monument dedicated to Julius Caesar.[50] There are sufficient data, however, attesting operations of that kind carried out already in the pharaonic times. The best known example is the transfer of Ramesses II's obelisks from Pi-Ramesses to Tanis in the Third Intermediate Period.[51] The highest obelisk found in Tanis, however, was less than 17 m high,[52] and that is incomparable to the eastern obelisks of Hatshepsut at Karnak, which were circa 30 m high.[53] The monument of Senuseret I at Heliopolis[54] is another obelisk which might have been re-erected in the pharaonic times. Such a hypothesis was first suggested by Essam el-BANNA,[55] and subsequently taken into account, with reservations however, by Dietrich RAUE[56] and David JEFFREYS.[57] Unfortunately, until the excavations on the Atum-Re-Horakhty temple area are resumed, which might possibly define the exact location and orientation of the temple(s), there is no possibility of ascertaining if the obelisk was re-erected or not,[58] and, if this occurred, when the operation happened.[59] The height of this obelisk is 20.41 m only,[60] that is again much less than the height of the eastern obelisks of the Queen.

It seems however, that the obelisk re-erection might have taken place already in the XVIIIth dynasty. And this might concern the obelisks of Thutmose III which once stood in the festival court of his father in front of the IVth pylon at Karnak.[61] Four important fragments of their shafts are still preserved, some smaller fragments of them, and also their foundations and fragments of their socles included partly in the IIIrd pylon of Amenhotep III. Works of the French-Egyptian mission carried out at the end of the sixties of the last century revealed that the foundations of this pylon, adjoining those of the obelisks, reached not less than 3 m below the base of the obelisk socles.[62] Thus, it does not seem very probable that the monoliths could remain stable during works on the pylon foundations.

Moreover, analysis of decoration of the available large preserved fragments of these obelisks seems to support the hypothesis that they also might have been erected twice. In the case of the southern monolith of the pair, in Merenptah's reign one column of inscription was added on both sides of the central one of Thutmose III on the northern face of the shaft (see **pl. 24, figs. 1-2**).[63] On the southern face of the monolith there are two addi-

50 IVERSEN, *Obelisks in Exile*. II. *The Obelisks of Istanbul and England*, Copenhagen 1972, p. 91.

51 See M. RÖMER, Tanis, *LÄ* VI, col. 196.

52 Obelisk No IV, see P. MONTET, Les obélisques de Ramsès II, *Kêmi* 5 (1935-37), pp. 108-109, pl. 6.

53 As regards the height of these monoliths see NIEDZIÓŁKA, *Proceedings of the 8th ICE*, in the press; and where the older bibliography concerning this problem has been also referred to.

54 PM IV, p. 60; see also MARTIN, *Garantsymbol*, pp. 65-69; HABACHI, *Obelisks*, pp. 46-49; E. el-BANNA, L'obélisque de Sésostris I à Héliopolis a-t-il été déplacé?, *RdE* 33 (1981), pp. 8-9; SELIM, *Obélisques* I, pp. 65-68, II, p. 5; Di. ARNOLD, *Tempel Ägyptens*, p. 206; VANDERSLEYEN, *Égypte et la vallée du Nil* 2, p. 71; D. RAUE, *Heliopolis und das Haus des Re. Eine Prosopographie und ein Toponym im Neuen Reich*, ADAIK 16, Berlin 1999 (hereinafter referred to as: *Heliopolis und das Haus des Re*), pp. 83 and 465; D. JEFFREYS, Joseph Hekekyan at Heliopolis, in: A. LEAHY, J. TAIT (eds.), *Studies in Ancient Egypt in Honour of H.S. Smith*, EES Occasional Publications 13, London 1999 (hereinafter referred to as: *Studies Smith*), pp. 166-168.

55 el-BANNA, *RdE* 33 (1981), pp. 8-9.

56 RAUE, *Heliopolis und das Haus des Re*, p. 83.

57 JEFFREYS, *Studies Smith*, p. 168.

58 As regards orientation of this temple, see JEFFREYS, *Studies Smith*, pp. 166-168.

59 Late Period date has been taken into account by RAUE, *Heliopolis und das Haus des Re*, p. 83.

60 See Di. ARNOLD, *Lexikon der ägyptischen Baukunst*, München, Zürich [2]1997, p. 180.

61 PM II[2], pp. 59 and 74-75; see also HAYES, *Internal Affairs from Tuthmosis I to the Death of Amenophis III*. Part 2, CAH II, Cambridge 1962, p. 32; BARGUET, *Temple d'Amon-Rê*, pp. 103-104; BJÖRKMAN, *Kings at Karnak*, p. 105; MARTIN, *Garantsymbol*, pp. 154-155; HABACHI, *Obelisks*, pp. 72-73; GABOLDE, Deux obélisques de Thoutmosis II, pp. 149 and 152; LABOURY, *Statuaire de Thoutmosis III*, pp. 32 footnote 183, 35 footnote 199, 43 footnote 251, 541 footnote 1527, 578 footnote 1717 and pp. 581-582.

62 See S. SAUNERON, J. VÉRITÉ, Fouilles dans la zone axiale du IIIe pylône à Karnak, *Kêmi* 19 (1969), figs. 3, 13, 15.

63 As results from the distribution of crowns worn by the King on the pyramidion, the fragment had once been the uppermost part of the southern obelisk, see Cl. TRAUNECKER, Estimation des dimensions de l'obélisque ouest du VIIe pylône, Cahiers de Karnak VII,

tional representations flanking Horus above the *serekh* of Thutmose III (see **pl. 25, fig. 1**).[64] This side of the shaft, however, was not provided with Merenptah's additional inscriptions (see **pl. 25, fig. 2**).[65] The eastern side of the monolith was, beyond any doubt, not additionally inscribed by any later king following Thutmose III, as results from the attribution of the fragment shown on **pl. 26, figs. 1-3** to the southern monolith.[66] Consequently, the front side (= western one) was inscribed by Merenptah, as results from information published by GABOLDE,[67] according to whom three sides of the southern monolith were decorated in the Ramesside Period. Thus, the obelisk would be additionally inscribed on the face bordering the central axis of the temple (= northern face) and on the face against the IIIrd pylon (= western face), and adorned with additional depictions on the upper part of the southern face of the shaft.

In the case of the northern monolith, the northern face of the shaft was surely not provided with any additional inscription (see **pl. 27, fig. 1**).[68] The eastern face, that is the back one, and not front side as suggested by MARTIN,[69] was beyond doubt inscribed by Merenptah (see **pl. 27, fig. 2**).[70] Thus, based on GABOLDE's remark on two additionally inscribed sides of this obelisk,[71] the western or southern face was also provided with Merenptah's inscriptions. Consequently, the shaft of the northern obelisk would be additionally inscribed on the face bordering the transversal axis of the temple (= eastern one), and on the face against the pylon (= western one) or on that bordering the main axis of the temple (= southern one). This is in evident contradiction to the location of additional inscriptions on the southern obelisk. One should note that Merenptah's inscriptions, if they were added on the sides flanking the pylon could be hardly visible when the pylon was standing. Thus, it would be tempting to suggest that in Merenptah's reign the southern monolith at least, was oriented in an unconventional manner, which in turn could imply that this obelisk was re-erected this way after completion of the pylon, or at least its foundations.

Paris 1982, p. 205. As regards published photos of this side see also MARTIN, *Garantsymbol*, fig. 17b.

[64] See also BARGUET, *Temple d'Amon-Rê*, pl. VII.D and MARTIN, *Garantsymbol*, fig. 17c.

[65] See also MARTIN, *Garantsymbol*, fig. 17a.

[66] Assuming this fragment once belonged to the southern monolith, and based on the direction of hieroglyphs on particular sides, it is evident that **pl. 26, fig. 1** shows the southern, **pl. 26, fig. 2** the eastern, and **pl. 26, fig. 3** the northern side of the shaft. Assuming attribution of this fragment to the northern monolith, **pl. 26, fig. 1** would show the western, **pl. 26, fig. 2** the southern, and **pl. 26, fig. 3** the eastern side of the shaft. The latter solution is excluded, however, since the eastern side of the northern obelisk was decorated with the *Nebty* name (see **pl. 27, fig. 2**) of the third set of the so-called "jubilee" names of Thutmose III (see *Urk.* IV, p. 600, 6) and the allegedly eastern side of the northern obelisk (**pl. 26, fig. 3**) would be decorated with the Golden name *ḥr-ḥr-nḫt-ḥw-ḥḳ3.w-ḫ3s.wt-pḥ.w-sw* of the first set of the so-called "jubilee" names (see *Urk.* IV, p. 599, 8). Because there is no evidence for mixing together of names from different sets in one string of Thutmose III's protocol, the former solution is the only possible, thus the fragment represented on **pl. 26, figs. 1-3** once belonged to the southern obelisk.

[67] GABOLDE, Deux obélisques de Thoutmosis II, p. 149 footnote 7.

[68] See also MARTIN, *Garantsymbol*, fig. 16d.

[69] *Garantsymbol*, p. 155. The additionally decorated upper fragment of the shaft of the northern obelisk published by MARTIN on his fig. 16c has to represent the eastern (= back) side of the northern monolith as results from the orientation of scenes on this monument.

[70] Since the fragment shown on **pl. 27, fig. 2** cannot belong to the southern monolith (as results from the state of preservation of the fragment shown on **pl. 24, fig. 1**), and because the northern side of the northern monolith is uninscribed (see **pl. 27, fig. 1**), it is evident, based on the direction of signs of the inscriptions preserved on the fragment on **pl. 27, fig. 2**, that it once constituted the eastern side of the northern obelisk. See also the fragment published by MARTIN, *Garantsymbol*, fig. 16c.

[71] GABOLDE, Deux obélisques de Thoutmosis II, p. 149 footnote 7.

Joanna Popielska-Grzybowska
Warsaw

Some Introductory Remarks on *Topoi* and Sacred Word-Symbols in the Pyramid Texts*

In olden days it was said that a certain PARMENIDES from Egypt devoted his entire life spent on a rock in contemplation of the logical *topoi*, and this is what him famous. This very legend suggests a lifelong interest in this rhetorical term, which means stating some specific "rules or formula for efficient reasoning, which should be an effective instrument in dialectical discussions". J. BRUNSCHVIG wrote in an introduction to the Paris edition of ARISTOTLE's "Les Topiques" that it is the "Vademecum du parfait dialecticien, risquent des nos jours d'apparaître comme un art de gagner à un jeu personne joue plus."[1]

As mentioned above, the original term *topos* is connected with rhetorical terminology, in contrast to the definition based on a diverse understanding of the notion *topos* introduced in the theory of literature by Ernst Robert CURTIUS in his work "Europäische Literatur und lateinisches Mittelalter".[2] CURTIUS maintained that not all of the *topoi* could be derived from the rhetorical genres. According to him, many of them descended from poetry and were then adopted into rhetoric. Originally *topoi* were used to help compose an oration, as KWINTYLIAN called them "argumentorum sedes" ("seats of mental threads"). However, finally *topoi* assumed a different function and became current notions, clichés which could be incorporated in every literary form. That way they spread to all spheres of life, somehow connected with or shaped by literature, as for example: "beauty of nature", "dream world" or "golden age". Analysis of *topoi*, in CURTIUS' view,[3] could broaden our knowledge about "the 'genetics' of formal elements of literature", as well as enabling us to understand hints of changes in the spiritual state and in this way increase the thoroughness of our understanding of the spiritual history of the West.

For CURTIUS, the concurrence of concepts and evidence arising from various, worldwide literary sources such as e.g. the *topos* of an "*old* boy" or in other words "a boy with grey hair", indicated that we were dealing with an archetype, with an image belonging to the collective unconscious – the psychological term introduced by C.G. JUNG.[4] Introducing such an understanding of *topos*, CURTIUS provoked "everlasting discussion". However difficult it is to agree with the presumption of CURTIUS, one should state what JUNG meant by archetype. For JUNG, archetype was a primareview model existing in the human mind since time immemorial, determining one's conception of the world, religious experience and behaviour.

However important this primary definition is, let us focus on the term as it functioned and functions in literary research.

It should be emphasised that although *topos* is a specific kind of motive,[5] these two terms should not be mixed or falsely identified, especially as there exists a tendency, at least in colloquial perception, to perceive the two terms as synonyms.

The most significant and most widely accepted interpretation is the comprehension of archetype presented by Northrop FRYE.[6] Archetypes are understood in his works as perdurably prevailing in literature motives, deriving from myth and ritual. According to FRYE, archetypes are not linked to the collec-

* I would like to express my deep indebtedness to Professor Karol MYŚLIWIEC for commenting on this article and stimulating discussions. No less cordially I acknowledge my debt to Professor Teresa DOBRZYŃSKA (Institute of Literary Research Polish Academy of Science) for her remarks after a paper delivered in March 2001, for her inestimable support and encouragement.
This article is an excerpt of the author's dissertation.

[1] J. BRUNSCHVIG, *Topiques* vol. 1, Paris 1967, p. IX.

[2] E.R. CURTIUS, *Europäische Literatur und lateinisches Mittelalter*, Bern-München [6]1967, pp. 79 ff.

[3] *Ibidem*.

[4] Cf. eg C.G. JUNG, *Grundwerk*, vol 1: Archetyp und Unbewusstes, Olten 1984.

[5] On the themes and the motives in the Pyramid Texts cf. H. ROEDER, Themen und Motive in den Pyramidentexten, *LingAeg* 3 (1993), pp. 81-119.

[6] N. FRYE, *Anatomy of Criticism*, Princeton 1957, p. 365.

tive unconscious, and he emphasises the fact that changes in archetypes depend on transformations in literature itself.

The next conception of *topos* is a view formulated by the Polish theorist of literature, Janina ABRAMOWSKA,[7] in her article on *topoi* and commonplaces in literary research. ABRAMOWSKA maintained that E.R. CURTIUS artificially and venturesomely linked revived philological method and elements of older rhetorical theories with the conception of a culture adopted from psychology, which has led to the identification of a *locus* with an archetype.

According to ABRAMOWSKA, *topos* remains a way of speaking, of expressing oneself. It is a result of petrifaction of a traditional motive which becomes persistently linked with a certain meaning, or use, and an easily "recognisable 'half-ready' linguistic form". Thus *topos*, for ABRAMOWSKA, is a stereotype, a "fossil", a well-known symbol, very important in propaganda, and as a stimulus and incentive for action used to some degree automatically.

However, on the other hand, she agrees that these are the *topoi* that constitute the clearest determinant of a cultural commonwealth.

Finally, in ABRAMOWSKA's view, that which is eternal and symbolic is an archetype as defined by Northrop FRYE. She does, however, admit that archetypes could also become *topoi*.

Significant for this research is the definition of *topos* expressed by Antonio LOPRIENO.[8] He understands *topos* as to some extent an anonymous, literary figure, which explains in any given society "a form of thinking by existence, over reality". In other words, LOPRIENO perceives the term under discussion as: "die literarische Übertragung einer im kulturellen Kon-Text verankerten Grundaussage über die Realität, ein Bezugsschema."[9] Moreover, he places the notion *topos* in "ideationalen Dimension der Sprache". Thus it is derived from the whole cultural context and, furthermore, it is based on "Aesthetics of Identity" (a phrase coined by J. LOTMAN and used *inter alia* by J. ASSMANN and A. LOPRIENO).

Such an explication appears to support the attempt undertaken herein to formulate the definition of *topos* applicable to studies of ancient Egyptian religious literature. However, before presenting this definition, one more conception will be outlined.

While examining the historical development of such terms as *topos* and archetype, Philip WHEELWRIGHT's say in the matter[10] obviously cannot overlooked. He defined a symbol on two levels. Firstly, "the expressive symbol – the living and organic one", e.g. in poetry: ELIOT's "Wasteland". Secondly, the "steno-symbol", namely the inert and formalised one, e.g. "the mathematical square root sign (or for that matter any arithmetical digit) and the symbols of symbolic logic. Semantic congruity, plurisignation, soft focus and contextual variability are the traits of the expressive symbol. "Some symbols have more universality and durability than others [it refers only to the expressive ones, for the degree of universality of steno-symbols is beyond doubt]. [...] And such Symbols are found to be universal or nearly so, in their broadly human manifestations, are called archetypes."[11] WHEELWRIGHT states clearly, however, that the word "archetype" is independent of JUNG's clinical psychoanalytical theories. The foundations of his study are "ancient evidences ... drawn mainly from ancient literary sources, amplified and sometimes interpreted by philology, archaeology, and anthropology."[12]

However approximate and tentative the methods of defining archetypes are, some symbols are "indubitably archetypal", namely, wrote WHEELWRIGHT: "the sky father, the earth mother, the serpent, the eye of the sun, the ear of grain, the vine, the sprouting tree, ritualistic bathing, the road or path and the pilgrimage along it, kingly power as both blessing and threat, the soaring bird, the circle or sphere, and

[7] J. ABRAMOWSKA, *Topos* i niektóre miejsca wspólne badań literackich (=*Topos* and Some Common Places of Literary Research – English translation of the title J.P.-G.), *Pamiętnik Literacki* 73 (1982, part 1/2), pp. 3-23.

[8] A. LOPRIENO, *Topos und Mimesis. Zum Ausländer in der ägyptischen Literatur*, ÄA 48, Wiesbaden 1988 (hereinafter referred to as: *Topos und Mimesis*), pp. 10, 11. Compare, however, this book's detailed criticism in: Hannes BUCHBERGER, Zum Ausländer in der altägyptischen Literatur – Eine Kritik, *WdO* XX/XXI (1989/1990), pp. 5-34.

[9] LOPRIENO, *Topos und Mimesis*, p. 10.

[10] P. WHEELWRIGHT, The Archetypal Symbol, *Perspectives in Literary Symbolism, Yearbook of Comparative Criticism*, vol. 1, University Park & London 1968 (hereinafter referred to as: Archetypal Symbol), pp. 214-243.

[11] IDEM, pp. 221, 222.

[12] IDEM, p. 223.

so on – these symbols are not the products of a single culture, as the Christian cross is, but are to be found exercising their powers in cultures widely separated in time and in historical trends of influence."[13]

Most significant for the present analysis is that those archetypal symbols listed above are very often identical with *topoi*, and make phrases constructed in a parallel way as e.g. the *topos* of peregrination – so thoroughly depicted by WHEELWRIGHT, the image of the Pilgrim. Both, *topoi* and archetypes, are provided with value qualification, e.g. the native land-mother (or earth-mother); the sky-father, or finally defined by the interpretative context, namely kingly power as both blessing and threat etc.

All of this suggests that *topos* in religious texts cannot be devoid of symbolic implications. It seems also evident that one should not perceive it as a formalised "fossil", as ABRAMOWSKA did.

Inasmuch as *topoi* show so many relevant traits, for the purposes of this study it appears well-founded to see in them archetypal symbols as described by Philip WHEELWRIGHT.

Consequently, *topos* is a long-lasting symbol based on a commonwealth of thought, on a kind of knowledge universal within a certain culture.

Of course it would be preposterous to say that people worship symbols, notions, archetypes or *topoi*. In the rituals all of them constitute real actions and are not conventional motives, but naturally they became so for unbelievers and scholars.

Archetypal is – and in accordance with the statement made above – creates a *topos*, the concept of the god creator – in the case of the Pyramid Texts – Atum. Studying principles of Egyptian and different religions e.g. the Buddhist tradition, one comes across an idea of the god's nothingness, as well as his plenitude, completeness. Both aspects of the creation bear extreme import. The primareview god-demiurge overcomes non-existence. But non-existence is perceived as something that does not exist, being nothing negative, being simply a formless, undifferentiated boundlessness, the Abyss. This would appear to make sense of the matter, to be the essence of the word *tm* – the embodiment of the creation the complete world from nothingness. The best examples of this *topos* make spells in which the king[14] is identified with Atum (*tm*), e.g. **spell 213**,[15] **215**[16] (see

[13] IDEM, p. 222.

[14] Cf. the author's discussion about the problem of the king's and Atum's identification: J. POPIELSKA-GRZYBOWSKA, Atum in the Pyramid Texts, in: J. POPIELSKA-GRZYBOWSKA (ed.), *Proceedings of the First Central European Conference of Young Egyptologists. Egypt 1999: Perspectives of Research. Warsaw 7-9 June 1999*, Światowit Supplement Series E: Egyptology vol. I, WES vol. III, Warsaw 2001 (hereinafter referred to as: Atum in PT), pp. 115-124.

[15] Cf. publications and translations of the spell: G. MASPERO, La pyramide du roi Ounas, *RecTrav* 3 (1881-1882), pp. 200-201; G. JÉQUIER, *La Pyramide d'Oudjebten*, Le Caire 1928 (hereinafter referred to as: *Oudjebten)*, pl. XXVI, 214-215; IDEM, *Les Pyramides des Reines Neit et Apouit*, Le Caire 1933 (hereinafter referred to as: *Neit et Apouit)*, pl. VII, pp. 493-494; IDEM, *La Pyramide d'Aba*, Le Caire 1935 (hereinafter referred to as: *Aba)*, pl. VII, pp. 261-262; IDEM, *Le Monument Funéraire de Pépi II*, Le Caire 1936 (hereinafter referred to as: *Pépi II)*, pl. VIII, p. 709+ 51; L. SPELEERS, *Traduction, index et vocabulaire des Textes des pyramides égyptiennes*, Bruxelles 1934 (hereinafter referred to as: *Traduction)*, pp. 24-25; K. SETHE, *Die altägyptischen Pyramidentexte*, Leipzig 1908-1922 (hereinafter referred to as: *Pyramidentexte)*, vol. I/1, pp. 80-81; IDEM, *Übersetzung und Kommentar zu den altägyptischen Pyramidentexten*, Glückstadt 1935-1939 (hereinafter referred to as: *Übersetzung*), vol. 1, pp. 1-4; S.A.B. MERCER, *The Pyramid Texts in Translation and Commentary*, New York-London-Toronto 1952 (hereinafter referred to as: *Pyramid Texts)*, vol. 1, pp. 58-59, vol. 2, pp. 74-75; T. ANDRZEJEWSKI, *Dusze boga Re. Wśród egipskich świętych ksiąg*, Warszawa 1967, p. 78 (see the discussion on the Polish translation of the spell 213: POPIELSKA-GRZYBOWSKA, Zaklęcie 213 z egipskich Tekstów Piramid, *Światowit* vol. II (XLIII) part A, Warszawa 2000, pp. 176-183); A. PIANKOFF, *The Pyramid of Unas*, Princeton 1968 (hereinafter referred to as: *Unas*), p. 59; R.O. FAULKNER, *The Ancient Egyptian Pyramid Texts*, Oxford 1969 (hereinafter referred to as: *Egyptian PT)*, pp. 40-41; J. SPIEGEL, *Das Auferstehungsritual der Unas-Pyramide*, ÄA 23, Wiesbaden 1971 (hereinafter referred to as: *Unas-Pyramide)*, pp. 46, 50-51, 78, 102, 105, 160-162, 171, 177, 199, 288, 376, 389; J.P. ALLEN, *The Inflection of the Verb in the Pyramid Texts*, BA 2, Malibu 1984 (hereinafter referred to as: *Inflection*), pp. 272 (§ 134a only), 664; L. BAREŠ, *Abusir* IV, *The Shaft Tomb of Udjahoresnet at Abusir*, Prague 1999, p. 52; POPIELSKA-GRZYBOWSKA, Some Preliminary Remarks on Atum and Jackal in the Pyramid Texts, *GM* 173 (1999), pp. 143-153; C. BERGER-EL NAGGAR, J. LECLANT, B. MATHIEU, I. PIERRE-CROISIAU, *Les Textes de la pyramide de Pépy I*[er], MIFAO 118, vol. 1, Le Caire 2001 (hereinafter referred to as: *Textes de Pépy I*[er]), p. 44 (P/F/Se 1).

[16] Cf. publications and translations of the spell: MASPERO, *RecTrav* 3 (1881-1882), p. 205; JÉQUIER, *Oudjebten*, pl. XXVI, 218-223; IDEM, *Neit et Apouit*, pl. VII, 493-494; IDEM, *Aba*, pl. VII, 265-271; IDEM, *Pépi II*, pl. VIII, p. 709+53 à + 58; SPELEERS, *Traduction*, p. 26; SETHE, *Pyramidentexte*, vol. I/1, pp. 82-85; IDEM, *Übersetzung*, vol. 1, p. 18; MERCER, *Pyramid Texts*, vol. 1, p. 60, vol. 2,

also below in the text), as well as **spells 537,**[17] **690.**[18] The translations run as follows:

§ 135 a-b spell 213: "Your arms are those of Atum, Your shoulders are those of Atum, Your belly is that of Atum, your back is that of Atum, Your hinder-parts are those of Atum, your legs are those of Atum."
§ 1298 spell 537: "O King, stand up and sit on the throne of Osiris! Your entire flesh is that of Atum, your face is that of Jackal."

§ 2097a-2098b spell 690: "This King comes provided as a god, his bones are knit together as those of Osiris, having followed after [him]. **This King comes(?) to you in On, you being protected, and your heart being placed in your body for you. Your face is that of Jackal, your entire flesh is that of Atum, your soul is within you, your power is about you,** Isis is before you and Nephthys is behind."

In all these fragments presented, *topoi* are formed by enumeration of body members, which is a classic trope used to do so.

Alive means complete, whole, having all elements, hence parts of the deceased's body are identified with the god's equivalents with the use of *m* of predication in contrast to *mr* (means of comparison). This indicates the identity of the subject with the predicate in this case expressed by means of an adverbial phrase *m tm*. One may interpret the assumption of other gods' names or parts of their body as metamorphosis.[19]

The *topos* of completeness was expressed not only by the word *tm*, sometimes *de facto* meaning Atum (in ANTHES' definition: "der, welcher vollzählig ist an denen (scil. den verschiedenen Urwesen nach vorzeitlicher Vorstellung), die als einzelne vergangen sind und sich ihm eingeordnet haben" = "the completed one who has absorbed all the first living beings",[20] i.e. the gods), but one also finds it when parts of the deceased's body are identified with any god's equivalent body parts.[21] Compare **spell 215 (§ 148 a-149)**[22] or **spell 556 (§ 1380 c-d)**:[23] "Your feet are those of Jackal, so stand up! Your arms are those of Jackal, so stand up!"

Thus the deceased becomes complete to the extent required in a particular mythical or ritual situation. When the pharaoh names himself or is named by someone else: "This King is Osiris,

p. 80; PIANKOFF, *Unas*, p. 61; FAULKNER, *Egyptian PT*, p. 42; SPIEGEL, *Unas-Pyramide*, pp. 167-177; ALLEN, *Inflection*, p. 331 § 492 (§ 142c-43a), p. 395 § 578 (§ 145a), p. 232 § 361A (§ 145b-46), p. 402 § 586C (§ 147b), p. 504 § 719D (§ 148a), p. 138 § 236 (§ 149a-b); BERGER-EL NAGGAR, LECLANT, MATHIEU, PIERRE-CROISIAU, *Pépy Ier*, p. 45 (P/F/Se 3-6).

[17] Cf. publications and translations of the spell: MASPERO, La pyramide du roi Pepi Ier, *RecTrav* 7 (1886), p. 176; IDEM, La pyramide du roi Pepi II, *RecTrav* 12 (1892), p. 156; SPELEERS, *Traduction*, pp. 158-159; SETHE, *Pyramidentexte*, vol. II/2, pp. 225-226; IDEM, *Übersetzung*, vol. V, pp. 227-231; MERCER, *Pyramid Texts*, vol. 1, pp. 212-213, vol. III, pp. 648-649; FAULKNER, *Egyptian PT*, pp. 205-206; SPIEGEL, *Unas-Pyramide*, p. 362; ALLEN, *Inflection*, p. 389 § 569B (PT § 1298 N); BERGER-EL NAGGAR, LECLANT, MATHIEU, PIERRE-CROISIAU, *Textes de Pépy Ier*, p. 50 (P/F/Se 80-82).

[18] Cf. publications and translations: MASPERO, *RecTrav* 12 (1892), p. 190-192; JÉQUIER, *Oudjebten*, pl. XXIX J (2093-2095); IDEM, *Neit et Apouit*, pl. XXII, 582-601; pl. XXIV, 655-657; IDEM, *Pépi II*, pl. XI, 990 à 1000; SPELEERS, *Traduction*, pp. 224-226; SETHE, *Pyramidentexte*, vol. II/3, p. 510-516; MERCER, *Pyramid Texts*, vol. I, pp. 307-309, vol. III, pp. 928-935; FAULKNER, *Egyptian PT*, pp. 298-301; ALLEN, *Inflection*, pp. 201-202 § 313 (PT § 2097-2098 Nt), p. 173 § 281A (PT § 2099b), p. 253 § 381B (PT § 2107a), p. 409 § 592 (PT § 2110c-d N), p. 587 § 746 (PT § 2114a-b), p. 213 § 329 (PT § 2117-2118a N), p. 408 § 591B (PT § 2119a N); BERGER-EL NAGGAR, LECLANT, MATHIEU, PIERRE-CROISIAU, *Textes de Pépy Ier*, p. 50 (P/F/Se 82-89).

[19] Cf. POPIELSKA-GRZYBOWSKA, Atum in PT, p. 119 footnote 26.

[20] R. ANTHES, Egyptian Theology in the Third Millenium B.C., *JNES* 18 (1959), p. 209-210 ("the one who has been completed by absorbing the other first living beings"); IDEM, Der König als Atum in den Pyramidentexten, *ZÄS* 110 (1983), p. 3.

[21] See, for instance, spells: 213, 215, 539. ANTHES, Atum, Nefertem und die Kosmogonien von Heliopolis: ein Versuch, *ZÄS* 82 (1957), pp. 1-8; IDEM, *JNES* 18 (1959), pp. 209-210; IDEM, *ZÄS* 110 (1983), pp. 3-4; Compare the discussion of the problem in: POPIELSKA-GRZYBOWSKA, Atum in PT, pp. 117, 119, 122.

[22] See above footnote 16.

[23] Cf. publications and translations of the spell: MASPERO, La pyramide du roi Pepi Ier, *RecTrav* 8 (1886), p. 95; JÉQUIER, *Pépi II*, pl. XVIII, 1297 à 1298; SPELEERS, *Traduction*, p. 167; SETHE, *Pyramidentexte*, vol. II/2, pp. 253-254; IDEM, *Übersetzung*, vol. V, pp. 314, 317; MERCER, *Pyramid Texts*, vol. I, pp. 222-223, vol. III, pp. 682-

Horus etc"[24] the *topos* under discussion is concerned as well.

On the other hand, the sense of a *topos* is likewise comprised in the destructive aspect of the creator. At the end of the world he, who is all and gave beginning to everything, will annihilate the world. In the Book of the Dead (**chapter 175; L. b. col. 16**) Atum says: "(I will)... destroy everything that I have created, the earth shall return to the Abyss..."[25]

Spell 213[26] is constructed of another very weighty *topos,* namely the *topos* based on an antithesis between life and death, namely life despite death.[27] Hence the deceased was said to "pass away" alive: "O *Wnjs*, it is not dead but alive that you have gone away." (**§ 134 a**).

In the spells depicting the pharaoh, this opposition, crucial for an understanding of the Pyramid Texts, is prevalent. "Rise up, O King, for you have not died!" (**§ 657 e spell 373**).[28]

Movement – very often an ascending one, with or without the help of other beings – a distinctive feature of life, is contrasted with the inertness of death. Death is defined by means of euphemism, such as "to sleep". Therefore the King's "detestation is sleep, his detestation is inertness. O flesh of the King, do not decay, do not rot, do not smell unpleasant!" (**§ 721-722 b spell 412**);[29] "earth is this King's detestation, the King will not enter into Geb lest he perish lest he sleep in his mansion upon earth." (**§ 308 b-c spell 258**).[30] Such an image creates another *topos* of death as a sleep commonly attested even in European culture.

No less prevailing is the *topos* of peregrination. Strange though it may seem, both life and death are described as a wayfaring state.[31]

684; FAULKNER, *Egyptian PT*, p. 216; BERGER-EL NAGGAR, LECLANT, MATHIEU, PIERRE-CROISIAU, *Textes de Pépy Ier*, p. 184 (P/V/E 11-15 = P 616-620).

[24] See, for instance, spells: 259, 260.

[25] É. NAVILLE, *Das aegyptische Todtenbuch der XVIII. bis XX. Dynastie. Aus verschiedenen Urkunden zusammengestellt und her*, Berlin 1886, p. CXCIX. Compare also: P. BARGUET, *Le Livre des Morts des anciens Égyptiens*, Paris 1967, p. 260; T.G. ALLEN, *The Book of the Dead or Going Forth by Day, Ideas of the ancient Egyptians Concerning the Hereafter as Expressed in Their Own Terms*, Studies in Ancient Oriental Civilization No 37, Chicago-Illinois 1968, p. 184; FAULKNER, *The Ancient Egyptian Book of the Dead*, London 1985 (edited by C. ANDREWS), p. 175.

[26] See above footnote 15.

[27] On conceptions of life and death in Ancient Egypt cf. e.g.: A.H. GARDINER, *The Attitude of the Ancient Egyptians to Death and the Dead*, Cambridge 1935; C.E. SANDER-HANSEN, *Der Begriff des Todes bei den Ägyptern*, Historisk-Filologiske Meddelelser, vol. XXIX No 2, København 1942; J. ZANDEE, *Death as an Enemy. According to Ancient Egyptian Conceptions*, Leiden 1960; H. ALTENMÜLLER, *Die Texte zum Begräbnisritual in den Pyramiden des Alten Reichs*, Ägyptologische Abhandlungen 24, Wiesbaden 1972; ALLEN, The Cosmology of the Pyramid Texts, in: *Religion and Philosophy in Ancient Egypt*, YES 3, New Haven, Connecticut 1989, pp. 1-28; A.B. LLOYD, Psychology and Society in the Ancient Egyptian Cult of the Dead, *Religion and Philosophy in Ancient Egypt*, YES 3, New Haven, Connecticut 1989, pp. 117-133; J. ASSMANN, Death and Initiation in the Funerary Religion of Ancient Egypt, *Religion and Philosophy in Ancient* Egypt, YES 3, New Haven, Connecticut 1989, pp. 135-159; IDEM, Egyptian Mortuary Liturgies, in: *Studies in Egyptology presented to M. Lichtheim*, vol. 1, Jerusalem 1990, pp. 1-45; IDEM, *Tod und Jenseits im Alten Ägypten*, München 2001.

[28] Cf. publications and translations of the spell: MASPERO, La pyramide de Mirinrî Ier, *RecTrav* 9 (1887), p. 184; IDEM, *RecTrav* 12 (1892), p. 70; SPELEERS, *Traduction*, p. 91; SETHE, *Pyramidentexte*, vol. I/3, p. 362; IDEM, *Übersetzung*, vol. III, p. 202, 206-207; MERCER, *Pyramid Texts*, vol. I, p. 130, vol. II, p. 321; FAULKNER, *Egyptian PT*, p. 124; SPIEGEL, *Unas-Pyramide*, p. 303; ALLEN, *Inflection*, p. 219 § 334 (PT § 657e).

[29] Cf. publications and translations of the spell: MASPERO, *RecTrav* 12 (1892), p. 75; JÉQUIER, *Pépi II*, pl. I, 172 à 179; IDEM, *Neit et Apouit*, pl. XVII, 468-478; pl. XXIV, 640-652; SPELEERS, *Traduction*, p. 98; SETHE, *Pyramidentexte*, vol. I/3, p. 395; IDEM, *Übersetzung*, vol. III, p. 334, 338-340; MERCER, *Pyramid Texts*, vol. I, p. 139, vol. II, pp. 357-358; FAULKNER, *Egyptian PT*, p. 135; SPIEGEL, *Unas-Pyramide*, pp. 305, 392, 454; ALLEN, *Inflection*, p. 190 § 303 (PT § 721d), p. 106 § 203 (PT § 722b N); BERGER-EL NAGGAR, LECLANT, MATHIEU, PIERRE-CROISIAU, *Textes de Pépy Ier*, p. 41 (P/F/Sw B 27-37).

[30] Cf. publications and translations of the spell: MASPERO, La pyramide du roi Ounas, *RecTrav* 4 (1883), p. 51; SPELEERS, *Traduction*, p. 47; SETHE, *Pyramidentexte*, vol. I/2, p. 166; IDEM, *Übersetzung*, vol. I, p. 377-378; MERCER, *Pyramid Texts*, vol. I, p. 82, vol. II, pp. 144-145; PIANKOFF, *Unas*, p. 35, pls. 18, 19; FAULKNER, *Egyptian PT*, pp. 67-68; SPIEGEL, *Unas-Pyramide*, p. 229-232 (See also Indexes, p. 479); ALLEN, *Inflection*, p. 182 § 291A (PT § 308b-c W).

[31] On the motive of the way and the use of metaphors concerned with it in Egyptian texts cf. G. VITTMANN,

Life could be a journey, sailing by barque, going to and fro: "I have gone and returned." (**§ 316 b spell 260**)[32] or "...for the King is one who goes to and fro, going and coming with Ra" (**§ 310c-d spell 258**).[33] In **spell 215** Atum is invoked to help the deceased ascend to the sky and to embrace him in his arms: "O Atum, raise him up to you, embrace him in your arms" (**§ 140b**).[34] Not only was Atum invoked to raise the pharaoh up, but also such gods as Nut, Shu, Horus, Set, Ra, Osiris, Imperishable Stars or the Great Wild Cow: "You are a son of the Great Wild Cow. She has conceived you, she has given birth to you and she has put you within (on) her wing (?). She has crossed the lake with you, she has traversed the *sjw*-waterway with you." (**§ 1370a-c spell 554**).[35] Finally, even the monarch's own hand is what will raise him up (**§ 537c spell 328**).[36]

The King's peregrination could be performed by going up the stairs or ladder. The way he moves is described as going, running or flying. Very often the verbs are used in the imperative mood: Go! Run! Come into being! Rise up! Live! or Wake up! etc. A thought provoking example is provided by **§ 810a-b spell 438**:[37] "Live! Live, according to the command of the gods that you live!" These instructions use the magical power of a word understood as a natural sign – magical creation of reality.

Death, on the contrary, was depicted as descending to the tomb, a motion downwards or to the Abyss, a journey into darkness: "What *Wnjs* detests is to travel in darkness, he will not see those who are upside down." (**§ 323a-b spell 260**).[38]

As for a king's propaganda, it is present rather in non-religious texts. In this respect the Pyramid Texts would serve only to create possibly the most desirable image of the pharaoh in the eyes of his subjects and perhaps of gods – as it was in the case of rhetorical commonplaces which, being simply a practice of persuasion, served to "manipulate" the listeners.

The language of the Pyramid Texts, as every religious language, is filled with sacred word-symbols which happen to be, unfortunately for scholars, understandable only for believers and those who know the specific system of beliefs of a given religion. It may be comprehensible only on the basis of faith.

It ought to be remembered that some verities of a religion for unbelievers could be meaningless and incongruous. Religious language is highly symbolic, which one has to accept at the primary stage of research. Sometimes, unequivocal meaning is unattainable on the basis of a modern way of thinking. It

---

Altägyptische Wegmetaphorik, Beiträge zur Ägyptologie 15, Wien 1999.

[32] Cf. publications and translations of the spell: MASPERO, *RecTrav* 4 (1883), p. 52; SPELEERS, *Traduction*, p. 48; SETHE, *Pyramidentexte*, vol. I/2, p. 172; IDEM, *Übersetzung*, vol. I, p. 391, 394-396; MERCER, *Pyramid Texts*, vol. I, p. 83, vol. II, p. 149; PIANKOFF, *Unas*, p. 36, pls. 18, 19; FAULKNER, *Egyptian PT*, p. 69; SPIEGEL, *Unas-Pyramide*, p. 235-236 (See also Indexes, p. 479); ALLEN, *Inflection*, p. 245 § 373A (PT § 316b-d), p. 424 § 608C (PT § 316b-c), p. 429 § 614 (PT § 316b).

[33] Cf. publications and translations of the spell: MASPERO, *RecTrav* 4 (1883), p. 51; SPELEERS, *Traduction*, p. 48; SETHE, *Pyramidentexte*, vol. I/2, p. 168; IDEM, *Übersetzung*, vol. I, p. 374, 387-388; MERCER, *Pyramid Texts*, vol. I, p. 82 , vol. II, p. 147; PIANKOFF, *Unas*, p. 36, pl. 19; FAULKNER, *Egyptian PT*, p. 68; SPIEGEL, *Unas-Pyramide*, p. 229-233 (See also Indexes, p. 479); ALLEN, *Inflection*, p. 174 § 282A (PT § 310c-d W), p. 250 § 376 (PT § 310c-d).

[34] See above footnote 16.

[35] Cf. publications and translations of the spell: MASPERO, *RecTrav* 8 (1886), p. 94; SPELEERS, *Traduction*, p. 166; SETHE, *Pyramidentexte*, vol. II/2, pp. 248-249; IDEM, *Übersetzung*, vol. V, p. 301-303; MERCER, *Pyramid Texts*, vol. I, p. 221, vol. III, p. 678; FAULKNER, *Egyptian PT*, p. 214; ALLEN, *Inflection*, p. 284 § 422A (PT § 1370a-b); BERGER-EL NAGGAR, LECLANT, MATHIEU, PIERRE-CROISIAU, *Textes de Pépy Ier*, p. 184 (P/V/E 8-9 = P 613-614).

[36] Cf. publications and translations of the spell: SPELEERS, *Traduction*, p. 75; SETHE, *Pyramidentexte*, vol. I/2, p. 274; IDEM, *Übersetzung*, vol. III, p. 8, 10; MERCER, *Pyramid Texts*, vol. I, p. 112, vol. II, p. 257; FAULKNER, *Egyptian PT*, p. 106.

[37] Cf. publications and translations of the spell: MASPERO, La pyramide du roi Pepi Ier, *RecTrav* 5 (1884), p. 170; SPELEERS, *Traduction*, p. 108; SETHE, *Pyramidentexte*, vol. I/3, p. 447; IDEM, *Übersetzung*, vol. IV, p. 41, 43-44; MERCER, *Pyramid Texts*, vol. I, p. 152, vol. II, p. 409; FAULKNER, *Egyptian PT*, p. 145; ALLEN, *Inflection*, p. 490 § 697B (PT § 810a-b).

[38] Cf. publications and translations of the spell: MASPERO, *RecTrav* 4 (1883), p. 53; IDEM, *RecTrav* 12 (1892), p. 59; SPELEERS, *Traduction*, p. 49; SETHE, *Pyramidentexte*, vol. I/2, p. 174; IDEM, *Übersetzung*, vol. I, p. 392, 408-409; MERCER, *Pyramid Texts*, vol. I, p. 84, vol. II, p. 152; PIANKOFF, *Unas*, p. 37, pls. 20, 21; FAULKNER, *Egyptian PT*, p. 69; SPIEGEL, *Unas-Pyramide*, p. 235-239 (see

seems that the arrangement of words is helpful and diagnostic for contemporary scholars. Very often the words are arranged according to their homophony creating puns, plays on words, as for example in **spell 587 (§ 1587)**[39] or **600**.[40]

Notwithstanding the difficulties, it is necessary to study *topoi* in religious literature, but with the intention of a possibly thorough and overall analysis.

The Pyramid Texts as the first known collection of ancient Egyptian religious utterances were the inspiration for ensuing modified collections.

Not only is it possible to find variants of some spells originating from the Pyramid Texts in the Coffin Texts or the Book of the Dead, but one can also observe the motives outlined and developed in both later collections of religious texts. However the focus of this paper were the Pyramid Texts, the concepts presented are omnipresent and conventional enough in Egyptian religious literature to be easily recognised in the Coffin Texts and the Book of the Dead as well. These analyses constitute a base for a further study.

When talking about the archetypal symbols as *topoi* in religious literature, one has to bear in mind that they are formed by different conceptual metaphors.[41] The sacred context ensures that they assume traits of reality. However tempting it is to interpret every single sacred symbol, one should stick to the semantic methods, even though:

"A study of archetypal symbols tends to raise the hauntingly futile question. 'Symbols of what?' The question is futile because it seems to express a hope of getting beyond symbols altogether and grasping cleanly their non-symbolic purport. Such escape from semantics is roughly possible where empirical meanings are involved – meanings either digital, where one can point, or practical, where one can exemplify in action. Where meanings are expressive, on the other hand, and particularly where they have archetypal status, there is no exit from semantics. To elucidate a Symbol is to replace it with a set of words, which are symbolic operators of another kind."[42]

Discovering material culture should always be complemented by an "archaeology of thought," which reveals primaeval conceptual systems, "primary" schemes of thought and the way of the articulation of the beliefs – archaic *topoi*, which sometimes, paradoxically, prove to be identical to the schemes of thinking or picturing that are vital also today.

also Indexes, p. 479); ALLEN, *Inflection*, p. 231 § 360A (PT § 323a-b).

[39] Cf. publications and translations of the spell: MASPERO, *RecTrav* 12 (1892), p. 160; JÉQUIER, *Aba*, pl. XV A; SPELEERS, *Traduction*, pp. 191-192; SETHE, *Pyramidentexte*, vol. II/2, p. 344; MERCER, *Pyramid Texts*, vol. I, p. 246, vol. III, p. 762; PIANKOFF, *Unas*, p. 5; FAULKNER, *Egyptian PT*, p. 238; ALLEN, *Inflection*, p. 248 § 375C (PT § 1587), p. 180 § 290 (PT § 1587b); BERGER-EL NAGGAR, LECLANT, MATHIEU, PIERRE-CROISIAU, *Textes de Pépy Ier*, p. 194 (P/D ant/W 25-56), p. 199 (P/D ant/E 75-102(?) = P 827-835 sq.).

[40] Cf. publications and translations of the spell: MASPERO, La pyramide de Mirinrî Ier, *RecTrav* 10 (1888), pp. 7-8; IDEM, *RecTrav* 12 (1892), pp. 144-146; JÉQUIER, *Aba*, pl. XIII, 774-778 (§ 1656-1659); SPELEERS, *Traduction*, pp. 191-192; SETHE, *Pyramidentexte*, vol. II/2, p. 372-II/3, p. 377; MERCER, *Pyramid Texts*, vol. I, pp. 253-254, vol. III, pp. 779-783; PIANKOFF, *Unas*, p. 4, 5; FAULKNER, *Egyptian PT*, pp. 246-247; SPIEGEL, *Unas-Pyramide*, p. 25; ALLEN, *Inflection*, p. 480 § 687B1 (PT § 1655c-1656a N), p. 305 § 454 (PT § 1659).

[41] G. LAKOFF, M. JOHNSON, *Metaphors we live by*, Chicago 1980.

[42] Ph. WHEELWRIGHT, Archetypal Symbol, p. 241.

Sławomir Rzepka
Warsaw

An Old Kingdom Cloaked Statue

According to the title of our conference we present here research perspectives in the field of Egyptology. Development of our discipline depends on new discoveries, made each season on various sites in Egypt. But beside this newly excavated material a huge resource of new information is the material discovered long ago, which can – and should – be rediscovered. This is obvious for material which was excavated, but never published in a proper way. But it is true also for the material which was published (in a better or worse manner), but was left without any attempt to interpret it. This is the case of the monument which is the subject of this paper.

Selim HASSAN in the nineth volume of his *Excavations at Giza* published a rock-cut tomb of a certain *Nst-ṯmꜣt*, one of the numerous rock-cut tombs in the Central Field of Giza Necropolis.[1] HASSAN described the tomb rather briefly: he published only 3 pages of text, 2 drawings and 3 photos. One of these photos shows a quite unusual statue (**fig. 1**). The statue is placed in a niche in the west wall of the chapel. The niche is carved in the rock, but its sides are lined with white Turah limestone. The niche is 120 cm high, 37 cm deep and 36 cm wide. Inside is a statue representing a striding man, wearing a broad wig and dressed in a cloak completely concealing the figure from its shoulders to the knees. Two features of this statue are original:

– its technique of execution;
– its iconography – more precisely the dress of the figure.

The Technique of Execution

As mentioned above the tomb of *Nst-ṯmꜣt* has a rock-cut chapel. The statue is also cut in the rock, but not entirely. In the rock was carved only the torso, the part which is concealed under the cloak, while the head and legs were carved separately of white Turah limestone and attached to the corpus. Thus we are dealing here with a kind of composite statue, produced of several separate pieces made of different materials. It is the only example known to me of a joining together of rock and limestone in one statue. We know, however, of statues composed of several separately carved parts. This is the usual technique for sculpting wooden statues, which have their arms, feet and bases carved of separate pieces of wood. Sometimes a similar technique was used also in stone statuary: we know of statues with separate bases, and group statues with separate figures (e.g. family groups with figures of children carved from separate blocks of stone);[2] we even find statues with heads carved separately.[3] In all these cases, however, the mixing of different materials in one statue is very limited. It is only the base of the statue which could have been made of another material than the statue proper: in the case of wooden statues it was made of a cheaper kind of wood;[4] in the case of statues made of hard stones (granite or diorite) the bases were made sometimes of limestone.[5] We should also mention that some statues (wooden, as well as made of stone) have inlaid eyes made of copper, white limestone and rock crystal (in later statues – of black obsidian).

---

[1] S. HASSAN, *Excavations at Giza* IX, Cairo 1960, pp. 75-77, pl. XXXI A-C.

[2] E.g. Hildesheim 16 (E. MARTIN-PARDEY, *Plastik des Alten Reiches* I, CAA Hildesheim 1, Mainz 1977, pp. 30-38).

[3] E.g. Cairo CG 95 (L. BORCHARDT, *Statuen und Statuetten von Königen und Privatleuten* I, Catalogue général du Musée du Caire, Berlin 1911 (hereinafter referred to as: *Statuen und Statuetten*), p. 75, pl. 21).

[4] E.g. statues of *Mṯṯj* (P. KAPLONY, *Studien zum Grab des Metheti*, Bern 1976 (hereinafter referred to as: *Grab des Metheti*), pp. 55-70).

[5] E.g. granite scribe statue placed in wooden and limestone bases, Louvre E 12629, 12631 (Ch. ZIEGLER, *Les statues égyptiennes de l'Ancienne Empire. Catalogue Louvre*, Paris 1997, pp. 64-68, Nos 17-18); granite scribe statue installed in a wooden base, Cairo JE 65907 (PM III^2,

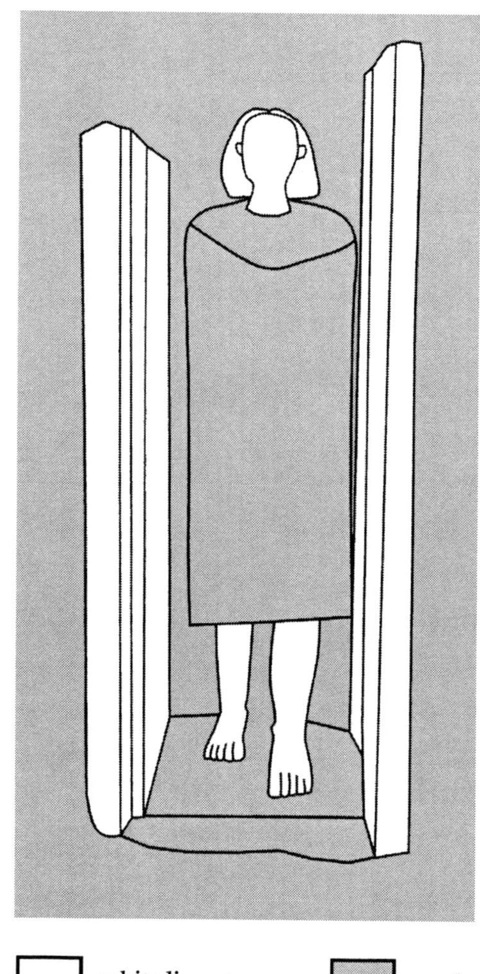

Fig. 1. Statue of *Nst-ṯmꜣt* (drawn by S.RZEPKA based on HASSAN, *Giza* IX, pl. XXXI C)

Fig. 2. *ḥꜣtj-ꜥ* during *heb-sed* celebrations (based on von BISSING, *Das Re-Heiligtum des Königs Newoser-re.* II, pl. 6 [13])

Fig. 3. *jrj nṯr* (*r nṯr*) during *heb-sed* celebrations (based on von BISSING, *Das Re-Heiligtum des Königs Ne-woser-re.* II, pl. 19 [45a])

The only Old Kingdom examples comparable to our case – that is to say a case where large parts of the sculpted human figure are made of various materials – belong to the corpus of the royal statuary. These are two copper statues, of which the larger represents Pepi I and the smaller one is commonly identified as Merenra.[6] Garments of both figures and the head-dress of the larger one were made of different, probably precious, material.

Selim HASSAN suggested that the limestone parts of the *Nst-ṯm3t*'s statue are reused fragments of an older statue. If he is right, we would be dealing here with a very specific case of usurpation. Usurpation of statuary during the Old Kingdom is, however, not unequivocally attested[7] and the supposition of HASSAN seems to be pure speculation.

Why in the *Nst-ṯm3t*'s statue was a composite technique used? The explanation is probably quite simple: the tomb owner wanted to have a large statue. But a life-size statue made of good Turah limestone must have been expensive – the cost of the material must have been very high. The rock in which the chapel is hewn was free, but its quality was rather poor. Thus *Nst-ṯm3t* decided to have a statue in which the parts deserving detailed modelling (the head and legs) are made of good limestone, while the block of the corpus is carved of cheap rock.

The Dress

The technique by which the statue was made is unusual, but even more surprising is the garment of the figure – a long cloak completely concealing the figure from the shoulders to the knees. It is commonly stated that this type of cloaked **private** statues was not known before the Middle Kingdom.[8] The statue of *Nst-ṯm3t* proves that it is not absolutely true.

The repertory of garments attested in the Old Kingdom private statuary is not especially rich. The most common are three kinds of kilts:

1. The so-called half-goffered kilt or "Galaschurz".[9]

2. A simple, plain short kilt.[10] Usually it was short (above the knee), but longer examples also occur.[11]

3. A kilt with a triangular front part.[12] Shorter and longer versions are known. During VIth dynasty this kind of kilt is often pleated.

One could expect that each of this basic kinds of dress was related to the specific field of activities of the person who is represented wearing it. One could be restricted to official occasions, the other to a more private sphere or to religious ceremonies. This is, however, not the case – there is no consistent rule. Each kind of dress could occur in each context.

The majority of male Old Kingdom non-royal statues is represented in one of the above-mentioned garments. But there are of course also some rare examples of other kinds of dress:

– a kilt resembling the royal *šnḏwt* (3 examples, all belonging to the same man).[13] We are dealing here with a clear attempt of a private person to use insignia reserved for the king,

– the "royal kilt with a triangular front part" (1 example).[14] This dress is in its general form quite

p. 724); diorite seated statue installed in a limestone base, Brooklyn 37.23E (T.G.H. JAMES, The Northampton Statue of Sekhemka, *JEA* 49 (1963), pp. 9-12, pl. iii).

[6] Cairo JE 33034, JE 33035 (J.E. QUIBELL, *Hierakonpolis* II, London 1902, pls. 50-54; the smaller figure after claening: W.S. SMITH, *The Art and Architecture of Ancient Egypt* [revised by W. Kelly Simpson], New Haven, London 1998, p. 77, fig. 144).

[7] M.A. SHOUKRY, *Die Privatgrabstatue im Alten Reich*, CASAE 15, Le Caire 1951, p. 93; cf. however A.M. ROTH, *A Cemetery of Palace Attendants Including G 2084-2099, G 2230+2231, and G 2240. Giza Mastabas* 6, Boston 1995, pp. 151-152, fig. 81.

[8] E.g. E. RUSSMANN, *Egyptian Sculpture*, Cairo 1989, pp. 69-71; cf. also R. SCHULZ, *Die Entwicklung und Bedeutung des Kuboiden Statuentypus. Eine Untersuchung zu den Sogenannten „Würfelhockern"* II, HÄB 34, Hildesheim 1992, pp. 728-735.

[9] E. STAEHELIN, *Untersuchungen zur ägyptischen Tracht im Alten Reich*, MÄS 8, Berlin 1966 (hereinafter referred to as: *Tracht*), pp. 11-31.

[10] STAEHELIN, *Tracht*, pp. 6-8.

[11] E.g. Cairo CG 34 (BORCHARDT, *Statuen und Statuetten* I, pp. 32-33, pl. 9).

[12] STAEHELIN, *Tracht*, pp. 9-11.

[13] Cairo CG 37, 196 and 201 (BORCHARDT, *Statuen und Statuetten* I, pp. 35-36, 133-134, 136, pl. 10, 41, 42).

[14] Cairo JE 72218 (S. HASSAN, *Excavations at Giza* VI [3],

similar to the regular "private" kilt with a triangular front part (mentioned above, among the most common private dresses). Its characteristic, radially ordered pleating is however restricted only for royal users.[15] As in the case of *šndwt* we are dealing here with a kind of usurpation of royal insignia by a private man:

– the dress of *ẖrj-ḥbt* priest (2 examples).[16] This kind of garment is in direct connection to the function of its owner – "lector priest" or "ritualist" *ẖrj-ḥbt*,

– a dress made of panther skin or skins (2 examples known).[17] The panther skin is connected with the function of *sm* priest, which played an important role in the *heb-sed* rituals. In reliefs on the walls of private funerary chapels the tomb owner is often represented in this kind of dress,

– a long tunic with the *b3t* emblem (1 example).[18] This dress was apparently connected with the function of the tomb owner as a priest of *b3t*,

– a cloak concealing one arm (1 example).[19] This kind of cloak covers not both, but only one arm and leaves the other arm free – thus it is different from the garment which is represented on the statue of *Nst-ṯm3t*. This is attested relatively often in reliefs,[20] but only a single example in sculpture in the round is known, and it belongs to the Archaic Period and not to the Old Kingdom.

Finally, it should be mentioned that since the late Vth dynasty naked statues of tomb owners occur. They became relatively popular during VIth dynasty.

After the review of various arts of garments attested in Old Kingdom private statuary we can propose three different interpretations of the cloak of the *Nst-ṯm3t*'s statue:

1. This kind of cloak was just commonly used in everyday life, like the different kilts or the cloak covering only one arm. The tomb owner wanted to be dressed in the afterlife in the same way as he was during his life on earth.

2. The other possibility: the tomb owner imitated a royal dress – similar to the case of *šndwt* or the pleated kilt with a triangular front part mentioned above.

3. And the third possibility – this cloak was strictly related to a specific function performed by the tomb owner: similarly as in the case of the *ẖrj-ḥbt* garment, a dress made of panther skins or the tunic with the *b3t* emblem.

Ad. 1

Let us start with the first hypothesis – the cloak covering both arms as a common, popular dress. Such a cloak is well attested in the Old Kingdom (and even earlier) – however not as a **male** but a **female** gar-

Cairo 1950, pp. 93-110, pls. xxxviii-lii, especially 106, pls. li and lii; PM III², pp. 244-245).

[15] This dress is well attested in relief representations of kings in funerary temples of Sahura and Neuserra (L. BORCHARDT, *Das Grabdenkmal des Königs Sʿa3ḥu-Rē* II, Leipzig 1913, pls. 17, 39 and 40; IDEM, *Das Grabdenkmal des Königs Ne-user-Reʿ*, Leipzig 1907, p. 84, pls. 33-36 and 39). We should note that private kilts with triangular front parts are also sometimes pleated (especially during VIth dynasty), but the pleats are ordered in a completely different way, cf. e.g. statue Brooklyn 51.1 (KAPLONY, *Grab des Metheti*, pp. 62-64).

[16] Cairo CG 25 (BORCHARDT, *Statuen und Statuetten* I, p. 26, pl. 7; statue of *3ḫtj-ḥtp* (Ch. ZIEGLER, Les statues d'Akhethetep, propriétaire de la chapelle du Louvre, *RdE* 48 (1997), pl. XVIII, fig. 1).

[17] Leyden D 93 (M. EATON-KRAUSS, Two Masterpieces of Early Egyptian Statuary, *OMRO* 77 (1997), pp. 7-21); statue of *Jpj* (H. SOUROUZIAN, La statue du musicien Ipi jouant de la flûte et autres monuments du règne de Snofrou à Dahchour, in: *L'art de l'Ancien Empire égyptien. Actes du colloque organisé au musée du Louvre par le Service culturel les 3 et 4 avril 1998*, Paris 1999, p. 165, figs. 8-11).

[18] Statue of *3ḫtj-ḥtp* (ZIEGLER, *RdE* 48 (1997), pl. XIX, figs. 2, 3).

[19] Berlin, Ägyptisches Museum 21839 (H. SOUROUZIAN, Concordances et écarts entre statuaire et représentations à deux dimensions des particuliers de l'époque archaïque, in: *Kunst des Alten Reiches*, SDAIK 28, Mainz 1995, pp. 317-318, fig. 21).

[20] Cf. *ibidem*, figs. 38, 39a, 41b.

ment. We find it in several ivory statuettes from Hierakonpolis,[21] in a limestone statue of the so-called "city god", which in reality represents rather a queen.[22] We also have, later, Old Kingdom examples.[23] According to Biri FAY, this kind of garment was typical of royal women.[24] But it was not reserved only for them – we can find it in the famous statue of Nofret,[25] who was not of royal blood (though she was married to a royal son).

We are, however, interested in male garments.[26] As already stated, our statue is the only example of this kind of garment in the Old Kingdom private statuary. As far as I know this kind of garment is also not attested in the wall decoration of private chapels. Such cloaks were thus most likely not a popular, commonly used, male dress. They came into fashion much later, during the Middle Kingdom and are well attested in the iconography of this period. Thus the first interpretation cannot be accepted.

Ad. 2

Could *Nst-ṯm3t*'s cloak have imitated a royal garment? As the "original" of this "imitation" may have served only one royal garment: the *heb-sed* cloak. This kind of dress has been known since the Archaic Period in different versions, which vary in length. Generally it is very similar to the garment of our statue.

We know a number of examples of "usurpation" of royal insignia by private persons. Already mentioned are examples of private persons using such royal kinds of dress as *šnḏwt* or the pleated kilt with a triangular front part. As another example may be quoted a tripartite wig, which was reserved for queens, gods and goddesses, but sometimes also a private person could have been represented in it.[27] All these examples show that already during the Old Kingdom iconographic elements reserved for royal or divine sphere were usurped by non-royal figures (this process intensified during the First Intermediate Period). In this context interpretation of the garment on our statue as an imitation of a royal *heb-sed* cloak seems to be quite convincing.

Ad. 3

Let us presently turn to the third hypothesis, according to which the cloak is strictly connected with a specific function of the tomb owner (similar to the case of the dress of *ẖrj-ḥbt* or the tunic with the *b3t* emblem). As mentioned above, in wall decoration of private tombs no cloaked male figures are attested. But we have at our disposal another category of sources: reliefs from royal temples. In the decoration of the sun-temple of Neuserra, among the reliefs showing *heb-sed* rituals, we find representations of non royal figures wearing the garment in which we are interested. Among the numerous people accompanying the king during the rituals, two figures are represented several times, identified by inscriptions: *ḥ3tj-ꜥ* and *jrj nṯr* (or *r nṯr*).[28] They wear cloaks which completely conceal their figures – only one hand, holding various attributes, is visible (**figs. 2, 3**). In some cases the cloaks have additional, protruding front parts, but these are apparently just variants of the same kind of dress. It is clearly the same kind of cloak in which the king is dressed.

Did *Nst-ṯm3t* play the role of *ḥ3tj-ꜥ* or *jrj-nṯr* during the celebrations of *heb-sed* and to commemorate this fact placed in his tomb the statue with the appropriate dress? This cannot be excluded, but is impossible to prove. The title *jrj-nṯr* is attested only in *heb-sed* representations[29] and is absent among strings of titles inscribed in private chapels. The fact that we do not find it in the chapel of *Nst-ṯm3t* is thus meaningless.

---

[21] *Ibidem*, fig. 3.

[22] *Ibidem*, fig. 6.

[23] B. FAY, Royal Women as represented in Sculpture during the Old Kingdom, in: N. GRIMAL (ed.), *Les critères de datation stylistiques à l'Ancien Empire*, BdE 120, Le Caire 1998, p. 128, fig. 6.

[24] *Ibidem*, p. 102.

[25] Cairo CG 4 (BORCHARDT, *Statuen und Statuetten* I, pp. 5-6, pl. 1).

[26] The statue in *Nst-ṯm3t*'s tomb surely represents a male figure – the full, striated wig partly covering the ears was used exclusively by men. The figure is striding (and not standing with feet together), which is a posture usual in statues representing men and very exceptional in those representing women.

[27] E.g. *Sšm-nfr* IV, represented in two statues flanking the entrance of his mastaba (H. JUNKER, *Giza* XI, Wien, Leipzig 1953, pl. I).

[28] F.W. von BISSING, *Das Re-Heiligtum des Königs Ne-woser-re.* II: *Die kleine Festdarstellung*, Berlin, Leipzig 1923, pl. 6 [13, 14], pl. 19 [45a], pl. 21 [50b], pl. 22 [53].

[29] W. HELCK, *Untersuchungen zu den Beamtentiteln des ägyptischen Alten Reiches,* ÄF 18, Glückstadt, Hamburg, New York 1954, p. 93.

Neither does he have the title *ḥ3tj-ʿ*, which was during this period a rather high honorific title. Actually only two titles of *Nst-ṯm3t* are attested in two lintel inscriptions from his chapel: *rḫ njswt* (King's Relative), *jmj-r3 st nj pr-ʿ3* (Overseer of the Department of the Palace) and an epithet *nb jm3ḫ ḫr nb.f* (Possessor of Honour in the Presence of his Master). His titles testify that *Nst-ṯm3t* was an official of middle rank, who was active in palace administration. They say, of course, nothing about his possible participation in the celebration of *heb-sed*. Thus the third interpretation, connecting the unusual dress with a specific function (namely the participation in the *heb-sed* celebrations), cannot be excluded, though is impossible to prove.

Recapitulation

The original statue from the tomb of *Nst-ṯm3t*, unique as it is, can be interpreted in the following way:

1) The strange technique of execution is a result of an attempt to produce a large statue using as little of the valuable material (white Turah limestone) as was possible.

2) The unique dress is an imitation of the royal *heb-sed* cloak. Usurpation of royal insignia should have given royal aspects to *Nst-ṯm3t*'s afterlife.

An alternative explanation is that during the royal *heb-sed Nst-ṯm3t* played the role of *ḥ3tj-ʿ* or *jrj-nṯr*, who were dressed with similar kind of cloak. To commemorate this fact he ordered such an original statue.

Teodozja Izabela Rzeuska
Warsaw

Some Remarks on the Old Kingdom White Painted Funerary Cult Pottery from West Saqqara

(Plates 28-31)

The joint Polish-Egyptian archaeological mission of Polish Centre for Mediterranean Archaeology in Cairo and the Supreme Council of Antiquities under the direction of Professor Karol MYŚLIWIEC working in Saqqara since 1987 on the western side of the mortuary complex of Netjerykhet has brought to light a necropolis dated to the late Old Kingdom.[1]

Some years ago G.A. REISNER noted that every tomb or grave has two functions:

1. to house the body and the *ka,* i.e. burial place;

2. to provide means of supplying the *ka* with its daily necessities, i.e. a place of cult.[2]

Both functions, i.e. burial and place of cult, are reflected in the architecture of the tomb/grave, where the former function corresponds to the substructure (shaft and burial chamber) and the later to the superstructure (offering place – chapel or merely false door). This division should follow the inventory from a tomb, for example pottery. Hence, pots directly connected with the second function is expected in the place of cult, inside the chapels or in their vicinity.

During the work on the necropolis at West Saqqara one has observed that pottery from the chapels differs in character, quality and quantity from the pottery found outside the chapels. This was the reason behind dividing these vessels from the site into two groups:

– pottery nearby the place of offering, next to the entrances to the chapels or in their vicinity;

– pottery found in the place of offering: chapels, on or beside offering tables, and false doors.

To the first group belong miniature vessels (see **fig. 1**), beer jars (see **fig. 2**), stoppers, bread moulds and trays (see **fig. 3**). The pots were made of poor quality Nile silt B2 or Nile silt C according to the *Vienna System*,[3] with a roughly treated surface, often badly fired. This type of pots is most common on Old Kingdom necropoleis. The West Saqqara cemetery is no exception to this rule. There are large deposits of complete vessels or sherds, some of which add up to hundreds of objects. G. REISNER found a lot of beer jars at Giza necropolis and called this type the "traditional offering jar".[4] They were the cheapest, most carelessly made vessels found at Giza. A great number of these vessels were used in the chapel services.[5] After the offering was presented to the dead the pots, used only once, were deposited outside the chapels, hence the deposits of pots outside places of cult. This group shall be termed *offering pottery.*

To the second group belong potstands (see **fig. 4**), bowls, dishes of different shapes (see **fig. 5**). The pottery is usually of higher quality. All are made of fine Nile silt B1 or marl clay A2, red slipped, pol-

[1] K. MYŚLIWIEC, T. HERBICH, with contribution by A. NIWIŃSKI, Polish Research at Saqqara in 1987, *ET* XVII (1995), pp. 177-203; MYŚLIWIEC, Saqqara, Excavations 1996, *PAM* VIII (1997), pp. 103-109; IDEM, Saqqara. Excavations 1997, *PAM* IX (1998), pp. 90-99; IDEM, Saqqara. Excavations 1998, *PAM* X (1999), pp. 81-89, IDEM, Saqqara. Excavations 1999, *PAM* XI (2000), pp. 89-99, IDEM, Saqqara. Excavation 2000, *PAM* XII (2001), pp. 107-119.

[2] G.A. REISNER, *The Development of the Egyptian Tomb down to the Accession of Cheops*, Cambridge 1936, p. 1.

[3] H.-Å. NORDSTRÖM, J. BOURRIAU, Ceramic Technology: Clays and Fabrics, Fascicle 2, in: Do. ARNOLD, BOURRIAU (eds.), *An Introduction to Ancient Egyptian Pottery*, Mainz 1993, pp. 171-174.

[4] REISNER, *Mycerinus. The Temples of the Third Pyramid at Giza*, Cambridge Massachusetts 1931, Type IV, p. 212, fig. 4; IDEM, *A History of the Giza Necropolis* II (completed and revised by W.S. SMITH), Cambridge-Massachusetts 1955 (hereinafter referred to as: *Giza Necropolis* II), pp. 70ff., fig. 85, type A-IV.

[5] REISNER, *Giza Necropolis* II, p. 70.

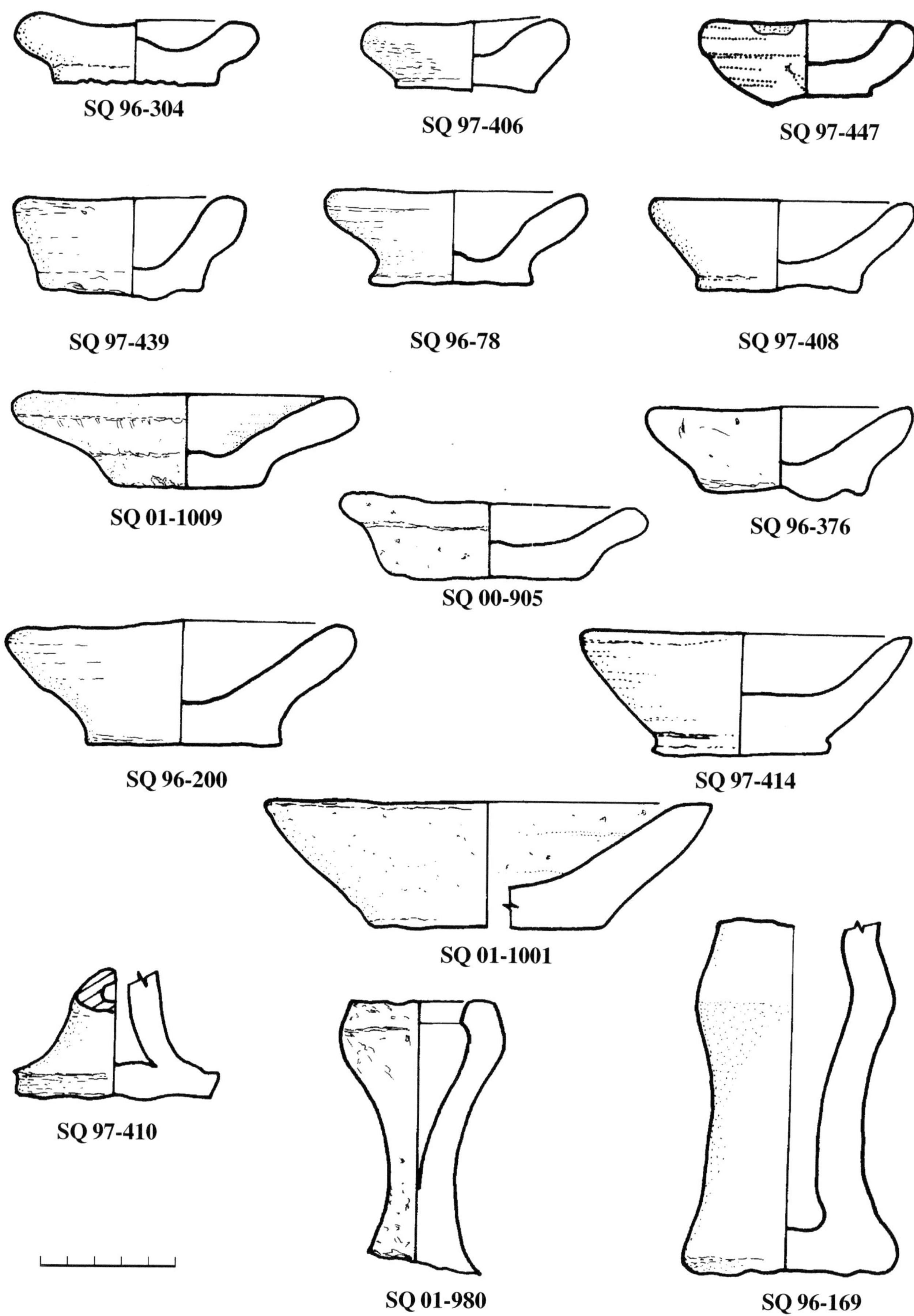

Fig. 1. Miniature vessels used as offering in funerary cult (scale 1:1)

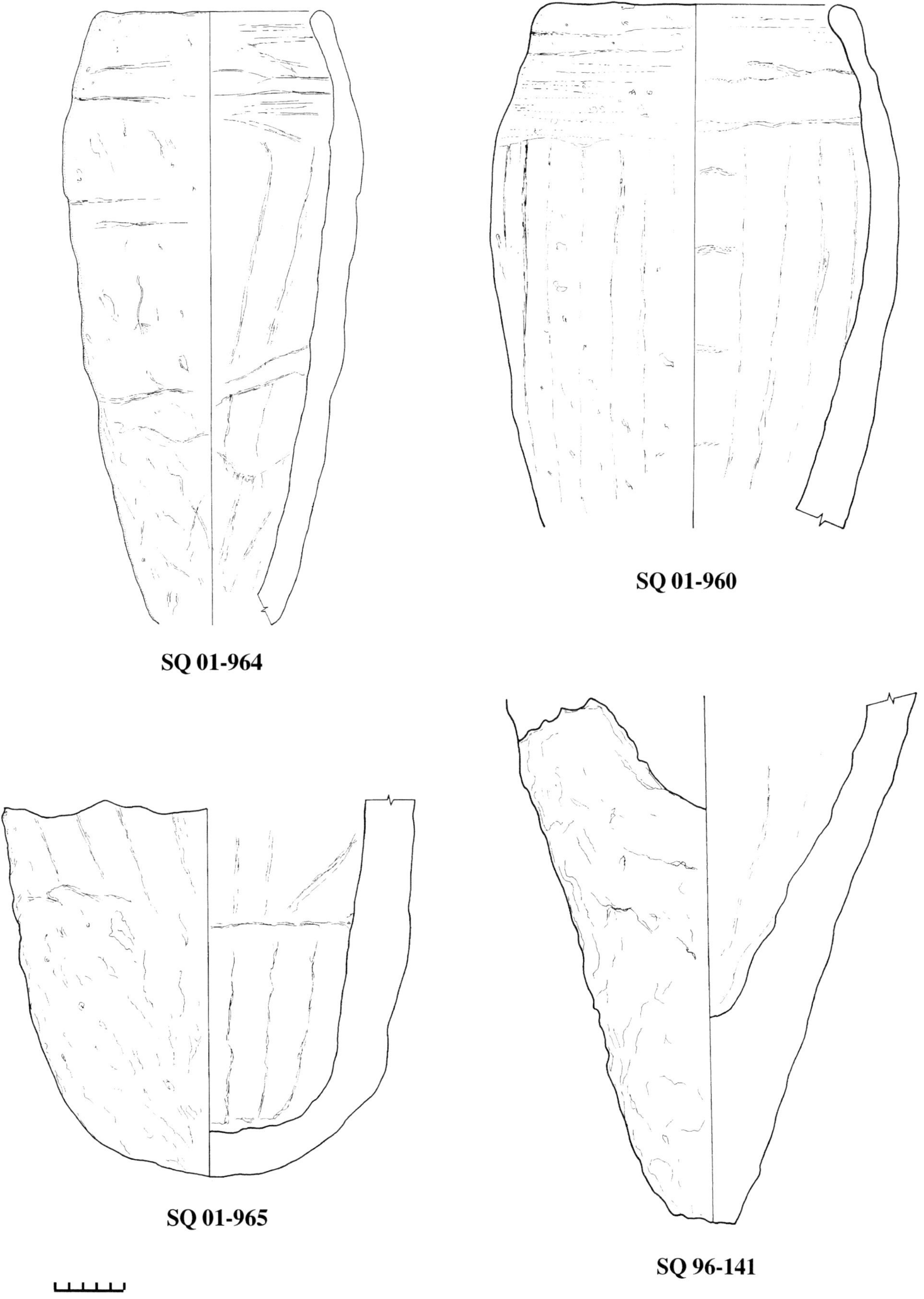

Fig. 2. Beer jars used as offering in funerary cult (scale 1:2)

ished. Sometimes such pots were found in front of a false door (see **pl. 28**).[6] In relation to the *offering pottery* these pots are rare. Hence the supposition that these pots most likely were in long-term use. They were replaced by the next batch after they had been broken. The potstands with bowls standing on them were placed in front of the false door. They were called *ḫ3w.t*. The word is attested already in the Pyramid Texts.[7] At the beginning it meant only a bowl, especially if standing on a tall potstand, then it signified both: a bowl and a high stand used in offering.[8] They are well known from the tomb scens, some were found standing in front of false doors.[9] This second group shall be termed *funerary cult pottery*.

Observations of the two different groups allow one to propose a new classification of pottery connected with the cult of the dead.[10]

According to this there are two distinctive groups of ceramics connected with the cult of the dead: *offering pottery* and *funerary cult pottery*. (see **fig. 6**)

Apart from the differences between the offering and funerary cult pottery, that have been mentioned above, there is another one. The *cult pottery* from the necropolis of West Saqqara is usually covered with white painting: both surfaces – interior and exterior (see **pl. 29**). Sometimes there are several layers of white substance, which allow one to suppose that the pots were white painted several times (see **pl. 30** and **31**). None of the *offering pots* bear traces of such white painting.

White painted pots used in the cult of the dead were found at other necropoleis as well. In front of the false door of Gegi at Abusir South (Tomb II) stood two biconical pottery stands covered with a thick coat of white plaster.[11] From the Old Kingdom tomb of Kaaper at Abusir (Vth dynasty) are two high, white painted potstands that were found *in situ* in front of a false door.[12] From the sun temple of Userkaf at Abusir comes the next example of a white painted stand. All stands from the sun complex, mainly from the valley temple, were made of medium fine, well fired clay. Some pots were polished. One stand (type 249) bears white painting.[13]

From the First Intermediate Period until the beginning of the New Kingdom there is no evidence of white painted cult pottery. The next examples date from the New Kingdom confirming the practice of white painting of *funerary cult pottery*.

From Amarna white painted cult pottery is known not only from the necropolis, but also from the place of cult in a sanctuary in the village. To the cult pots from the necropolis belong pots from the chapel No 524: "the pottery vessels used in the cult still remain near, if not actually in their original places. Like all vases found in the chapels they were whitewashed, as were the walls and, probably even the floors of the chapels themselves."[14] Another potstand was

---

[6] T.I. RZEUSKA, The Pottery from the Funerary Complex of Vizier Merefnebef (West Saqqara). The Evidence of a Burial and Cult of the Dead in the Old Kingdom, in: J. POPIELSKA-GRZYBOWSKA (ed.), *Proceedings of the First Central European Conference of Young Egyptologists. Egypt 1999: Perspectives of Research, Warsaw 7-9 June 1999*, ŚWIATOWIT Supplement Series E: Egyptology, vol. I, WES, vol. III, Warsaw 2000 (hereinafter referred to as: Pottery from the Funerary Complex of Vizier Merefnebef), pp. 165-167, pls. 29, 34-36.

[7] *PT* § 1552b.

[8] Wb. III, p. 225; H. BALCZ, Die Gefäßdarstellungen des Alten Reiches, *MDAIK* 3 (1932), p. 101.

[9] T. RZEUSKA, Pottery from the Funerary Complex of Vizier Merefnebef, pp. 165-166.

[10] It is contrary to REISNER's typology. He divided ceramics from the Giza necropolis taking into account above all else their shape. There are pots he terms "ordinary traditional offering jars" (REISNER, *Giza Necropolis* II, p. 70), namely common beer jars, ring stands (REISNER, *Giza Necropolis* II, p. 88) or "ceremonial vessels" (REISNER, *Giza Necropolis* II, p. 88), namely bread mould or trays. This may lead to misunderstanding, since some of his "traditional offering jar" (=beer jars) may have been found not only in chapels or deposits of offering pots, but also in burial shafts and chambers (i.e. substructure = burial) as well. This suggests their connection with burial, i.e. with the first function of tomb rather than with the cult. Therefore it is not shape, but first of all place of finding of ceramic, when it is *in situ*, and also the function of the ceramic group that should play more important role in interpreting pottery from a necropolis.

[11] M. BÁRTA, *The Cemeteries at Abusir South* I, Abusir V, Prague 2001 (hereinafter referred to as: *Cemeteries at Abusir South*), p. 126, pl. XLIVb-c.

[12] Lecture of Dr Miroslav BÁRTA on "Czech Excavations on the Necropolis at Abusir" on the 20th of April 1999, Warsaw.

[13] W. KAISER, Die Tongefäße, in: H. RICKE (ed.), *Das Sonnenheiligtum des Königs Userkaf* II, BeiträgeBf 8, Wiesbaden 1969, p. 76.

[14] T.E. PEET, C.L. WOOLLEY, *The City of Akhenaten* I, 38th of Memoir of the EES, London 1923, p. 100, pl. XXVII, fig. 1.

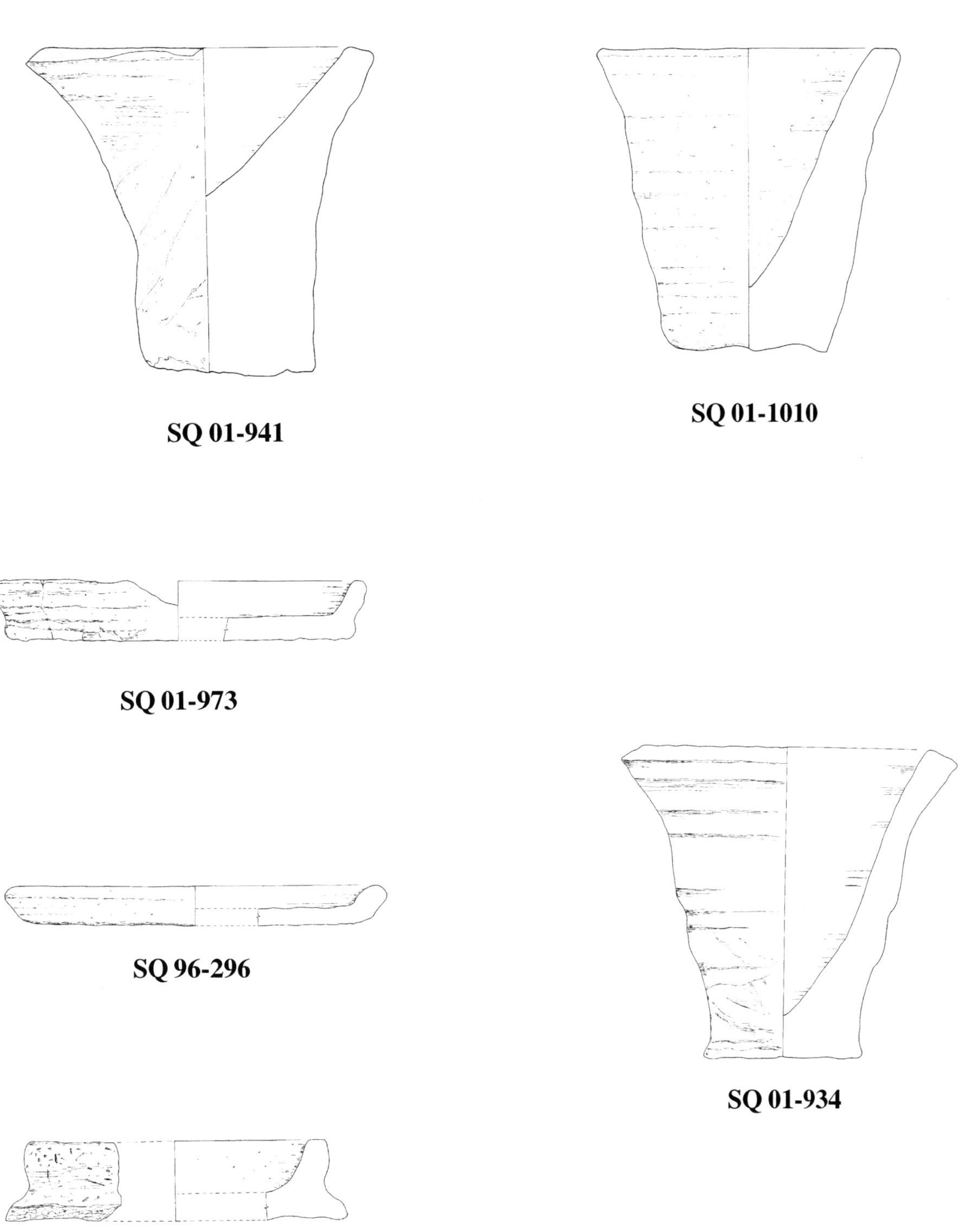

Fig. 3. Bread moulds and trays used as offering in funerary cult (scale 1:4)

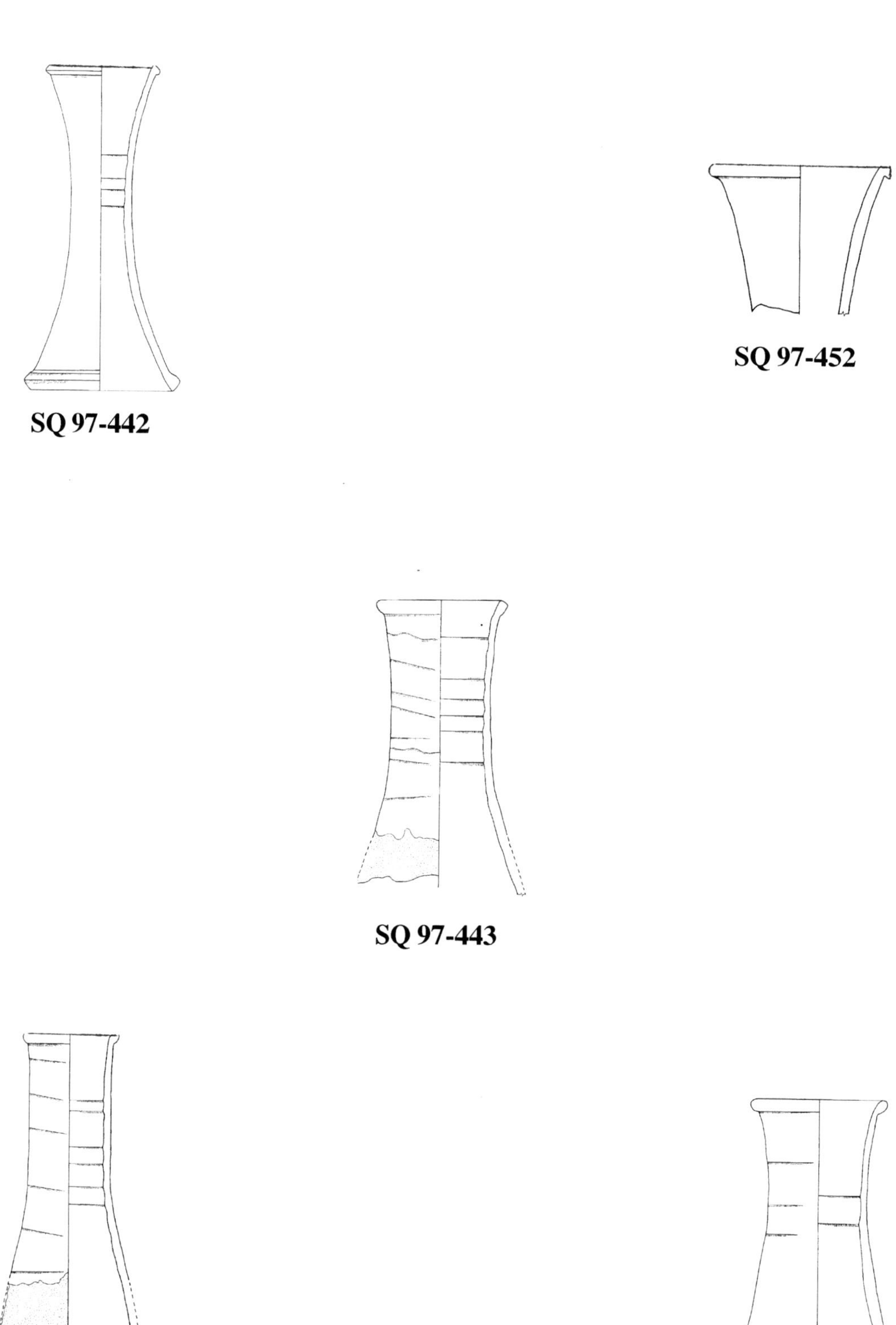

Fig. 4. Red slipped and white painted high stands used in funerary cult (scale 1:4)

found in Tomb 28. The whole vessel was encrusted with gypsum plaster.[15] In the Tomb 29 bowls were found, some bear signs burned on the interior. One polished bowl was coated internally and externally with gypsum plaster.[16] Other examples come from the Workmen's Village.

Important observations on pottery cult vessel were made by Linda C. HULIN. Tall potstands and bowls without pre-fired surfaces treatment were coated with gypsum on the outside surface and on the interior. Gypsum had also been poured into the stem. Inside the stem there is a small hole from top to bottom, apparently formed around a stick, or created by a stick being forced into the gypsum before it set. Similar potstands were found in the place of cult in sanctuary, i.e. in the Main Chapel. These are a tall offering stand with gypsum plaster on the exterior surface (No 51973) and a small foot bowl with a thin layer of gypsum with remains of burnt incense inside.[17]

Some parallels are known from Thebes as well. In the tombs of Amenhotep, Khnummose and Amenmose (TT Nos 294, 253, 254) among the pots there was a potstand coated on the exterior and rims with gypsum.[18]

Some white painted potstands were found in tombs or chapels at Deir el-Medina as well.[19]

From Tod came a fragment of a censer covered on all surfaces with a white substance.[20] Since it was found in the vicinity of a chapel, it is likely that it belonged to the equipment of the chapel.

The most widespread explanation of the practice of white painted pots in the Old Kingdom was that they imitate more expensive stone vessels.[21] This theory may seem convincing. But a comparison between the Old Kingdom *funerary cult pottery* and the New Kingdom ceramics opens up various questions, for example: Is this true "imitation"? Why should the Egyptians imitate only white stone when they made pots or other artefacts imitating various types of stone?[22] The idea of "stone imitation" has no sense from the ceramological point of view either. Why should luxury ceramics, like the Old Kingdom red slipped and polished bowls and potstands from the Merefnebef chapel, have been covered with a white substance? Polished or burnished surfaces look much nicer and shine more than a surface covered with a white substance. There is no evidence of a practice of treating the pot surface in such a way i.e. covering the well elaborated surface with a white substance. In fact, white painting has nothing to do with the surface treatment of pots at all. It seems to be secondary. The finds from the Old Kingdom mastabas show clearly that, if stone potstands and bowls were used in the funerary cult, they were made almost always exclusively of white limestone.[23] The basic ancient Egyptian term for limestone was *inr ḥḏ*,[24] which means "white stone". It seams probably, that the white painting on the red slipped pottery did not imitate white stones. This intend the cultic funerary cult pottery to be white i.e. ritually purified.

The next problem to solve was whether or not these types of white painted pots were known from settlements of the Old Kingdom times. There is, however, no information on this in scholarly literature.[25]

So one is dealing here with the practice of covering the pots with white paint, and not with the pots that imitate white stone. This practice is known from

[15] P. ROSE, The Pottery, in: A. el-KHOULY, G.T. MARTIN, *Excavations in The Royal Necropolis at el-'Amarna 1984*, Supplément aux ASAE, Le Caire 1989, p. 24.

[16] *Ibidem*, p. 27.

[17] ROSE, Pottery from the Main Chapel, in: B. KEMP, *Amarna Reports* III, London 1986, p. 101, fig. 7.2.

[18] ROSE, Pottery, in: N. and H. STRUDWICK, *The Tomb of Amenhotep, Khnummose, and Amenmose (Nos. 294, 253 and 254)*, Oxford 1996, p. 176, No 93, pl. 65.

[19] G. NAGEL, *La céramique du Nouvel Empire à Deir el-Médineh*, Le Caire 1938, e.g. from tomb 1169, pp. 91-92, fig. 72, Nos 24-25; from chapel 1193, pp. 111-112, figs. 97-98, Nos 3-4, 6, 12, 13.

[20] G. PIERRAT-BONNEFOIS, *La céramique dynastique et ptolémiaque des fouilles du Louvre à Tôd*, CCE 6, Le Caire 2000, p. 312, fig. 122.

[21] M. BÁRTA, *Cemeteries at Abusir South*, p. 167.

[22] R. BALDASSARI, *Proposte di classificatione e di interpretazione dei vasi imitanti del Regno Nuovo, EVO* IV (1981), pp. 143-175.

[23] L. BORCHARDT, *Denkmäler des Alten Reiches (ausser den Statuen) im Musem von Kairo Nr. 1295-1808*, part I *Catalogue Géneral des Antiquités Égyptiennes du Musée du Caire*, Berlin 1937, pp. 1-4, pl. 1, Nos 1295-1303. H.G. FISCHER, Offering Stands from the Pyramid of Amenemhet I, *MMJ* 7 (1973), pp. 125-126, fig. 6, footnote 7. He quoted taht in the offering niche of Giza tomb 1453 stood two limestone stands with bowls.

[24] *Wb* I, p. 97.

[25] The author asked her colleagues working on the Old Kingdom pottery from the settlements at Giza and on the Elephantine whether they had any white painted stands

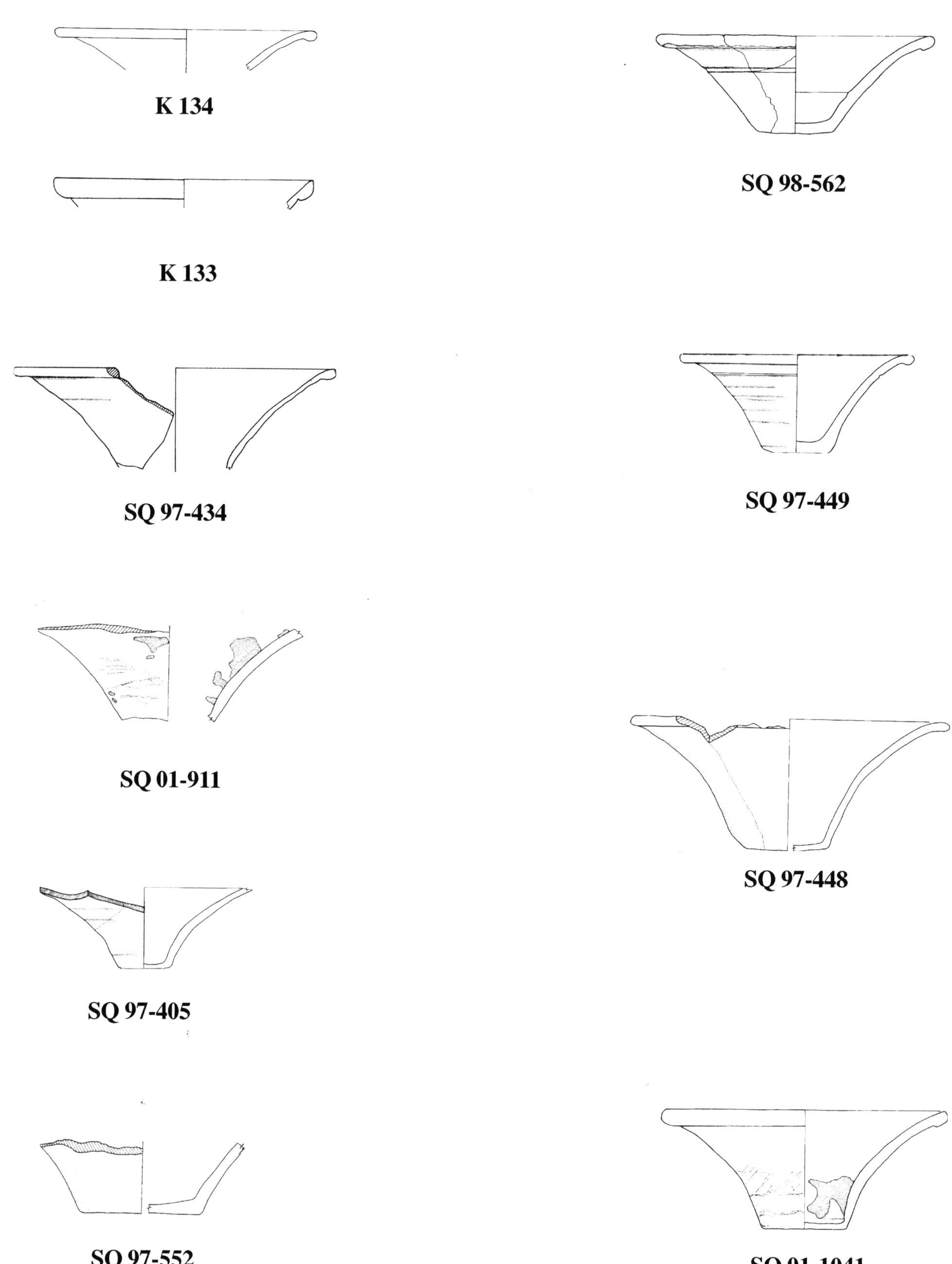

Fig. 5. Red slipped and white painted bowls used in funerary cult (scale 1:4)

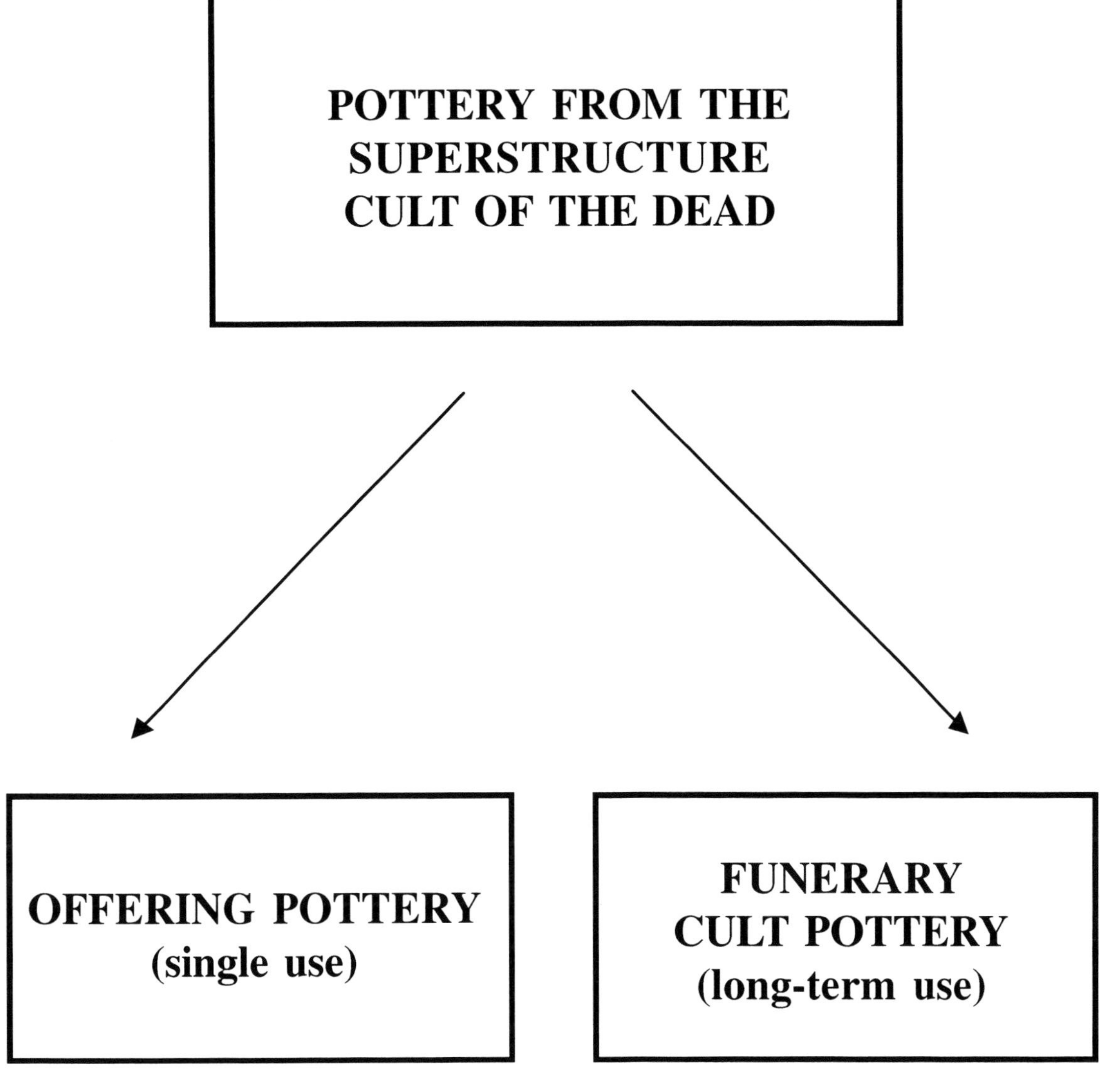

Fig. 6. Diagram showing two groups of pottery connected with cult of the dead

necropoleis or other places of cult, but not from settlements.[26]

In spite of the fact that the analogies are from distant periods it is likely that in both cases one is dealing with the same practice. In the Old Kingdom as well as in the New Kingdom the cult pottery hosted in places of cult was painted white.

This *funerary cult pottery* seems to be evidence of real cultic practice. The amount and the dating of *funerary cult pottery* found at a place of cult may indicate how long and how intensive the cult of the dead person was. This seems to be very important, especially in the case of a complete lack of written sources concerning funerary cults.

The last question to answer is, what substance was used for painting? In almost all cases, especially those dating from the New Kingdom, the white substance covering pots has been identified as gypsum. Was it really gypsum used for painting? Without chemical analysis this problem cannot be solved. In West Saqqara there are hundreds of limestone pieces with traces of drilling.[27] The powder obtained by drilling limestone fragments may serve this purpose well. Similar drilled fragments of limestone were also found on other necropoleis.[28] But to verify the theory that the white pigment originated from limestone not gypsum further analyses are needed.

To sum up, it seems probable that *funerary cult pottery,* such as potstands and bowls used in the cult of the dead, stood in places of cult and formed part of the offering. White painting probably made the pots purified, as they belonged to the *sacrum*, not *profanum* sphere.

---

or bowls. They did not have. I am thankful to Mrs Anna WODZIŃSKA (Giza Plateau Mapping Project, Warsaw University) and Dr Dietrich RAUE (Elephantine, Deutsches Archäologisches Institut) for their information concerning the Old Kingdom pottery.

[26] As L. HILIHAN pointed out, there are some indications that such cult vessels were used in the Village of Amarna, but still in the cult sphere, i.e. probably for household cults. L. HULIN, *op.cit.*, p. 175.

[27] A. ĆWIEK, West Saqqara. Addendum, *PAM* XI (2000), p. 117, fig. 5. In the author's opinion this is evidence of obtaining limestone powder. One could suggest that the process of pot painting took place most probably at the necropolis, if not in a tomb itself, given that the walls and the false doors were white painted as well. K.O. KURASZKIEWICZ, Inscribed Objects from the Old Kingdom Necropolis West of the Step Pyramid (with remarks on their coating), Archiv Orientální 70 No 3 (August 2002), pp. 351-376.

[28] Examples dated to the Archaic Period from Helwan cf. Z.Y. SAAD, *Royal Excavations at Saqqara and Helwan (1941-1945)*, Supplément aux ASAE, Le Caire 1947, p. 5, pl. Via; dated to the IIIrd dynasty from the Step Pyramid cf. C.M. FIRTH, J.E. QUIBELL, *Excavation at Saqqara. The Step Pyramid* II, Cairo 1935, pl. 93, 1 and 2; dated to the IVth dynasty from Meidum cf. A. el-KHOULI, *Meidum*, Sydney 1991, pl. 41; S. HASSAN, *Giza* II, Cairo 1936, p. 31.

Anna Wodzińska
Warsaw

Pottery from the Tomb of Khafraankh (G 7948)*

(Plates 32-41)

The rock-cut tomb of Khafraankh is located at the eastern edge of the Giza plateau.[1] The tomb and its decoration were first documented by LEPSIUS (tomb number LG75).[2] Since 1996 the study of the tomb has been carried out by the Russian Archaeological Mission under the direction of Eleonora KORMYSHEVA.

During the cleaning of the tomb of Khafraankh (during the 1997-1998 seasons) a number of pot sherds were discovered. All together there were 1086 fragments including 154 diagnostic pieces, the latter representing parts of rims, parts of bases, handles and decorated sherds, as well as pieces bearing potmarks. Eighty of the diagnostic pieces were drawn.

Following is the breakdown of the sherds in numbers, types of clay used (in percentages), and dates:

Sherds..........................**1086**
body sherds......................**931**
rims........................ ....**88**
bases...............................**41**
complete profiles........... ....**13**
handles.............................**12**
stopper..............................**1**
Clay:
imported clay.................**0.3%**
marl clay.........................**4.4%**
Nile alluvial clay..............**95.3%**
Dating:
Old Kingdom sherds..........**81%**
Later pottery (Middle Kingdom, Late Period, Ptolemaic Period, Late Roman Period): **19%**

Pottery sherds were found in (see **pl. 32, fig. 1** – plan of the tomb):[3]

- the shaft leading to the burial chamber of the tomb owner (3);
- the burial chamber of Khafraankh (11);
- the burial shaft of Herenka, Khafraankh's wife (4);
- the burial shaft of Herimerw and Ishepet (5);
- the so-called "X" grave (7, 8);
- the entrance to the tomb of Khafraankh (6);

The ceramic material found in the tomb of Khafraankh seems to come from perturbed strata and can be dated to the Old Kingdom, Middle Kingdom, Late Period, Ptolemaic Period and Roman Times. The predominant Old Kingdom types date from IVth dynasty.

Old Kingdom

Many fragments of a single big pot (**pl. 33, fig. 2**)[4] were found on the burial bed of Khafraankh in his burial chamber. A few sherds of this pot were also found above a layer of stones covering the Khafraankh burial. The tall (38.3 cm), slender jar was made of very fine, marl group clay, of foreign origin. Two vertical handles were added to the vessel, roughly half-way up. The surface was decorated in the so-called "comb" pattern. The ancient potter had drawn, in the still wet clay on the shoulder of the jar, a small, square-like potmark. This jar belongs to a very well known group of similar pots found at Giza during excavations led by H. JUNKER,[5] S. HASSAN[6] and G.A. REI-

* I would like to express my gratitude to Professor Karol MYŚLIWIEC, Mrs Teodozja RZEUSKA and Mr Hratch PAPAZIAN for their help with work on this article.

[1] PM III[1], pp. 207-208.

[2] *Ibidem*, p. 207.

[3] For details see: E. KORMYSHEVA, Report on the Activity of the Russian Archaeological Mission at Giza, Tomb G 7948, East Field, During the Season 1998, *ASAE* 74 (1999), pp. 23-37, pls. I-II.

[4] *Ibidem*, p. 36, pl. II b.

[5] H. JUNKER, *Bericht über die Grabungen auf dem Friedhof von Giza* I, Vienna-Leipzig 1929 (hereinafter referred to as: *Friedhof von Giza* I), figs. 13, 16.

[6] S. HASSAN, *Excavations at Giza, 1930-1931*, Cairo 1936, p. 147, fig. 173 [4].

SNER;[7] some of those jars are a little bit taller, sometimes smaller and wider. REISNER described this kind of jar as the B-LIV type: "a two-handled 'oil jar' of special ware: height ranges from 23 to 43 cm, all with combed-ware decoration, usually both in horizontal and vertical lines".[8] These jars, used as containers for a certain kind of oil, seem to be of special significance since they were placed only in tombs of exceptionally prominent individuals. According to JUNKER and REISNER, jars of this kind possibly date back to the IVth dynasty. This dating seems to be correct if we rely on the work of S. MAZZONI.[9] Shape and, for most of them, combed pattern can determinate the dating. Plain horizontal parallel combed bands are common for the IVth dynasty. A jar from Giza,[10] dated by REISNER also to the IVth dynasty, is decorated with horizontal, but also vertical, combed stripes as well.[11] This jar is in fact the closest comparable piece to the jar from the tomb of Khafraankh. Similar pots were also found in other places in Egypt: Abusir,[12] Ballas,[13] Buto,[14] Matmar[15] and Nezlet Batran (at Giza).[16]

In the burial chamber of Khafraankh, next to the sherds of the jar just described, some fragments of a "Meidum" bowl were found (**pl. 33, fig. 3**).[17] Other fragments of the bowl were located also in the burial shaft of Herenka. The bowl was made of fine local alluvial silt including only very small grains of sand. The surface of the pot is covered with a very fine red slip, and polished. There are three diagnostic features to the piece: a relatively long distance between the rim and the shoulder; a round shoulder; the 22 cm diameter of the pot. Such properties are characteristic of "Meidum" bowls from the late IVth dynasty.[18] REISNER also found similar bowls in Giza. In *A History of the Giza Necropolis* II he categorised them as C-XXXII type (a type of carinated bowls[19]).

In the burial shaft and burial chamber of Khafraankh other fragments of "Meidum" bowls were found. Only one example of this assemblage comes from the Vth dynasty[20] (**pl. 34, fig. 7**); the rest belongs to the IVth dynasty (**pls. 33, fig. 4; pl. 34, figs. 5-6**).

Five pieces of bread moulds (**pl. 34, fig. 8-10; pl. 35, fig. 11**) and the so-called ledge bowls (**pls. 35, figs. 12,**[21] **13,**[22] **14**) were located in the shafts of Khafraankh's and Herenka's burials, and in the grave "X". We can date back both groups of pots to the IVth dynasty as well. Bread moulds may be divided into two groups: medium – approximately 20-25 cm

---

[7] G.A. REISNER, *A History of the Giza Necropolis* I, Cambridge-Massachusetts 1942, p. 437, fig. 256; p. 461, fig. 279, below; p. 467, fig. 282, below right; p. 269, fig. 283; p. 472, fig. 285, below; p. 476, fig. 287; p. 489, fig. 297b; p. 493, fig. 299; p. 509, fig. 312; type: B-LIV. Compare also: G.A. REISNER, W.S. SMITH, *A History of the Giza Necropolis* II, Cambridge-Massachusetts 1955 (hereinafter referred to as: *Giza Necropolis* II), pp. 75-76, figs. 80, 96-98.

[8] REISNER, SMITH, *Giza Necropolis* II, p. 75.

[9] S. MAZZONI, The Diffusion of the Palestinian Combed Ware, in: *Studies in the History and Archaeology of Palestine. Proceedings of the First International Symposium on the Palestine Antiquities* II, Aleppo 1986 (hereinafter referred to as: Diffusion of the Palestinian Combed Ware), pp. 145-157.

[10] REISNER, SMITH, *Giza Necropolis* II, fig. 18, No 34-6-17j.

[11] MAZZONI, Diffusion of the Palestinian Combed Ware, p. 147.

[12] W. KAISER, Die Tongefäße, in: H. RICKE (ed.), *Das Sonnenheiligtum des Königs Userkaf* II, BeiträgeBf 8, Wiesbaden 1969 (hereinafter referred to as: Tongefäße), p. 54, VII: 63.

[13] J.E. QUIBELL, *Ballas*, London 1896, pl. XLV [7].

[14] E.Ch. KÖHLER, *Tell el-Fara'in Buto*. III. *Die Keramik von der späten Naqada-Kultur bis zum frühen Alten Reich (Schichten III bis VI)*, AV 94, Mainz 1998 (hereinafter referred to as: *Buto* III), pl. 68 [9].

[15] In the context of tombs from IVth and Vth dynasties see G. BRUNTON, *Matmar*, London 1948, pl. XXXVII [2].

[16] K. KROMER, *Nezlet Batran. Eine Mastaba aus dem Alten Reich bei Giseh (Ägypten), Österreichische Ausgrabungen 1981-1983*, Vienna 1991, pl. 38 [4].

[17] KORMYSHEVA, *ASAE* 74 (1999), p. 36, pl. II a.

[18] Compare S. MARCHAND, M. BAUD, La céramique miniature d'Abou Rawash. Un dépôt à l'entrée des enclos orientaux, *BIFAO* 96 (1996), p. 277, fig. 7,1; JUNKER, *Friedhof von Giza* I, figs. 12, 15.

[19] REISNER, SMITH, *Giza Necropolis* II, fig. 110 [33-1-59c, 14-3-44].

[20] Compare KAISER, Tongefäße, p. 57, No 97, type: XIV: 92-97; B. KEMP, The Locations of the Early Town at Dendera, *MDAIK* 41 (1985), fig. 4 [2-4]; REISNER, *Giza Necropolis* I, fig. 227b, type: C-XXXII; S.J. SEIDLMAYER, Beispiele nubischer Keramik aus Kontexten des hohen Alten Reiches aus Elephantine, in: *Afrikanistische Arbeitspapiere (AAP), Sondernummer, Gedenkschrift Peter Behrens,* Cologne 1991, p. 341, fig. 2 [8].

[21] Compare REISNER, SMITH, *Giza Necropolis* II, fig. 121, No 14-1-100.

[22] *Ibidem*, fig. 105.

in diameter and small – 12-16 cm in diameter. These types are known from other tombs,[23] as well as from a settlement located south of the Wall of the Crow at Giza.[24] Ledge bowls are typical of the IIIrd and IVth dynasties and they are also known from Buto,[25] Dahshur,[26] Elephantine,[27] Saqqara[28] and El-Tarif.[29] The ones presented in this paper are typical of Giza from the late IVth dynasty.[30]

Large amounts of beer jar fragments (**pls. 35, figs. 15-17; pl. 36, figs. 18-24; pl. 37, figs. 25-31; pl. 38, figs. 32-36; pl. 39, fig. 37**) were found in the mortar bonding stones on the funerary bed of Khafraankh and also in other parts of the tomb (see Appendix below). After an analysis of the surviving rims, one may presume that they can be most probably dated to the IVth dynasty[31] as well. One fragment of a beer jar stopper (**pl. 39, fig. 38**) was found during the clearing of the shaft leading to the burial chamber of Khafraankh.

Simple bowls with straight walls (**pl. 39, fig. 39**)[32] and flaring walls (**pl. 39, figs. 40-42**)[33] were located inside the tombs – in particular in the so-called X grave. They are also known from Giza in the Old Kingdom context, especially of late IVth – early Vth dynasties.[34]

Also from the X grave comes a bowl with relief walls (**pl. 39, fig. 43**). This kind of bowl is common to the VIth dynasty.[35]

The jar with the round rim (from the burial chamber of Khafraankh) (**pl. 39, fig. 44**) is most probably part of a small flat bottomed jar known from the Giza cemetery.[36] Also, the storage jar made of fine marl clay with a triangular rim (from X grave) (**pl. 40, fig. 45**) is typical of the Giza area in general.[37] Part of a large jar with a potmark on its horizontal shoulders found (**pl. 40, fig. 46**) in the X grave is similar to large spherical jars used probably for water storage.[38]

Small miniature vessels: jars (**pl. 40, figs. 47** and **48**[39]) and plates (**pl. 40, figs. 49-52**)[40] were present almost everywhere inside the tomb.

Part of a stand (**pl. 40, fig. 53**) made of fine Nile silt coated with very fine red slip (both surfaces) and polished came from the X grave. The rim diameter and surface treatment are typical of tall stands even a meter in height.[41] This kind of pot can be dated to the Old Kingdom in general. It is not possible to give a more precise dating.

Middle Kingdom

A simple hemispherical bowl (**pl. 40, fig. 54**) was located in the burial shaft of Herenka. The bowl was made of very fine Nile silt and covered by a thin red slip. Its surface was additionally nicely smoothed. These features are characteristic of the early Middle Kingdom,[42] more specifically the later years of Senwoseret I.[43]

Late Period

Among other pot sherds, parts of a big marl clay

[23] *Ibidem*, fig. 132, No 35-8-58.

[24] The author's personal experience.

[25] KÖHLER, *Buto* III, p. 128, pl. 34 [12-14].

[26] D. FALTINGS, Die Keramik aus den Grabungen an der nördlichen Pyramide des Snofru in Dahschur. Arbeitsbericht über die Kampagnen 1983-1986, *MDAIK* 45 (1989), p. 144, fig. 8e.

[27] According to the results of Dietrich RAUE's work on the Elephantine island (personal communication, spring 1999); S. SEIDLMAYER, Die staatliche Anlage der 3. Dynastie in der Nordweststadt von Elephantine. Archäologische und historische Probleme, in: M. BIETAK (ed.), *Haus und Palast im Alten Ägypten*, Vienna 1996, p. 201, fig. 4 [left side at the top].

[28] J.E. QUIBELL, *Excavations at Saqqara (1911-1912). The Tomb of Hesy*, Cairo 1913, pl. XXVII [19].

[29] H. KAMMERER-GROTHAUS, Keramik des Alten Reiches, in: B. GINTER et al., *Frühe Keramik und Kleinfunde aus El-Tarif*, AV 40, Mainz 1998, p. 77, fig. 39 [1,2].

[30] According to the results of work on material from a settlement located south of the Wall of the Crow at Giza (the author's personal experience).

[31] FALTINGS, *MDAIK* 45 (1989), p. 148, fig. 12c [A54, A55]; see also: K. KROMER, *Siedlungsfunde aus dem frühen Alten Reich in Giseh. Österreichische Ausgrabungen 1971-1975*, Wien 1978, pl. 19, 4 and 5; see also REISNER, SMITH, *Giza Necropolis* II, fig. 85.

[32] REISNER, SMITH, *Giza Necropolis* II, fig. 121, No 14-3-64.

[33] *Ibidem*, fig. 75, Nos 34-4-70 and 34-4-71.

[34] *Ibidem*, p. 85.

[35] S. MARCHAND, Le survey de Dendera (1996-1997), *CCE* 6 (2000), fig. 12.

[36] REISNER, SMITH, *Giza Necropolis* II, fig. 93.

[37] *Ibidem*, fig. 58, especially Cairo No 67755.

[38] D. FALTINGS, *Die Keramik der Lebensmittelproduktion im Alten Reich*, SAGA 14, Heidelberg 1998, pp. 5-20.

[39] REISNER, SMITH, *Giza Necropolis* II, fig. 100, No 29-2-45 from tomb: G 7650 C.

[40] *Ibidem*, fig. 127; MARCHAND, BAUD, *BIFAO* 96 (1996), p. 273, also fig. 6A, Nos 8-11 and fig. 9, Nos 15-19.

[41] FALTINGS, *MDAIK* 45 (1989), p. 150.

[42] E. CZERNY, Eine Plansiedlung des frühen Mittleren Reiches, *Tell el Dab'a IX* (1999), p. 136; MARCHAND, *CCE* 6 (2000), fig. 17.

[43] Do. ARNOLD, Pottery, in: Di. ARNOLD (ed.), *The South Cemeteries of Lisht. I. The Pyramid of Senwoseret I*, New York 1988, pp. 140-142 and 128, fig. 65.

imported amphora (**pl. 41, fig. 55**) with two vertical handles have been found in the burial shafts of Khafraankh and Herenka. The so-called "transport amphora"[44] belongs to the foreign Levantine pottery group.[45] The shape of the amphora found in Khafraankh's tomb is similar to pots from: Kurru,[46] and Thebes (Medinet Habu[47] and Mortuary Temple of Seti I[48]). According to D.A. ASTON, the pot found in Medinet Habu is "somewhat similar to A. SAGONA's type 7c".[49] Original jars with a pointed base began to appear around 1200 BC and continued down to the end of the 5th century BC.[50] Those found in Egypt may be dated back from the Late Period up to the Ptolemaic Period.[51] The pot presented here probably dates from the 6th century BC.[52]

The jar with a double rim and straight neck (**pl. 41, fig. 56**) from the X grave is probably from the XXVth dynasty.[53] We can also assign the jar with the simple straight rim and long straight neck (**pl. 41, fig. 57**) found in the burial shaft of Herenka, and the small pointed base (**pl. 41, fig. 58**)[54] to the same time.[55]

Ptolemaic Period

A small ring base (**pl. 41, fig. 59**) dated to the mid-Ptolemaic Period (a similar pot from Tod has been dated to Ptolemy IV – 221-203 BC[56]) was found in the X grave.

Late Roman Period

A jar with straight rim and short neck made of fine Nile silt was found in the burial chamber of Khafraankh (**pl. 41, fig. 60**). Similar pots are dated to the 5th-7th centuries AD.[57]

Potmarks

In the X grave three potmarks were found. Two of them were probably incised on walls of an Old Kingdom beer jar (**pl. 41, figs. 61-62**). The third is part of a marl jar of unknown date (**pl. 41, fig. 63**). Its surface is also much worn.

Conclusions

Observing the complete and well preserved pots found in the tomb of Khafraankh (especially in the burial chamber of the tomb owner) we can discern two periods of utilisation of the tomb. First, during the Old Kingdom – especially in the late IVth dynasty. Second, around 6th/7th centuries BC (XXVth/XXVIth dynasty). The rest of the pottery is very fragmentary and dates from different periods. This material has probably fallen over from the top of the edge of the Giza plateau during the work of the first archaeologists who worked around this area.

Description of pots on the plates:[58]

Fig. 2. "Oil jar" with a small potmark (made before firing) on the shoulder;

NR 98/11/23;
Con- 11;

---

[44] See D.A. ASTON, *Egyptian Pottery of the Late New Kingdom and Third Intermediate Period (Twelfth – Seventh Centuries BC). Tentative Footsteps in a Forbidding Terrain*, SAGA 13, Heidelberg 1996 (hereinafter referred to as: *Egyptian Pottery*), p. 85.

[45] *Ibidem*, pp. 84-86, 336, fig. 234.

[46] D. DUNHAM, *El Kurru. The Royal Cemeteries of Kush* I, Cambridge Massachusetts 1950, pp. 81, 84, fig. 28c.

[47] U. HÖLSCHER, *Excavations at Medinet Habu* V. *Post Ramesside Remains*, Chicago 1954, pl. 47 [I-J]; ASTON, *Egyptian Pottery*, p. 336, fig. 234 c.

[48] MYŚLIWIEC, *Keramik und Kleinfunde aus der Grabung im Tempel Sethos' I in Gurna*, Mainz am Rhein 1987 (hereinafter referred to as: *Keramik*), pp. 60-61, figs. 394-396.

[49] ASTON, *Egyptian Pottery*, p. 85, basing on: A.G. SAGONA, Levantine Storage Jars of the 13th to 4th Century BC, *Opuscula Atheniensia* 14 (1982), pp. 83-84, fig. 2 [7].

[50] SAGONA, *Opuscula Atheniensia* 14 (1982), p. 84.

[51] MYŚLIWIEC, *Keramik*, pl. XII [3,5].

[52] Peter FRENCH – personal communication.

[53] From Amarna – see ASTON, *Egyptian Pottery*, p. 215, fig. 113 [SJ1.6.1(W)].

[54] MYŚLIWIEC, *Keramik*, pp. 49, 52, figs. 290, 291.

[55] Pots of XXVth-XXVIth dynasties from Elephantine – ASTON, *Egyptian Pottery*, p. 282, fig. 180 (18853A:1); from Amarna – see *ibidem*, p. 215, fig. 113 [SJ1.1.4 (H1)].

[56] G. PIERRAT-BONNEFOIS, La céramique dynastique et ptolémaïque des fouilles du Louvre à Tôd, 1989-1991, *CCE* 6 (2000), pp. 327, 328, fig. 187.

[57] R. D. GEMPLER, *Die Keramik römischer bis früharabischer Zeit, Elephantine* X, AV 43, Mainz 1992, p. 179, figs. 111-118, 10.

[58] The description of each pot consists of the following data:
kind of pot;
NR – number of pot;
Con – context;
Pr – percent of preserved pot;

Pr- 100%;
Rd- 9.4 cm;
Bd- 11.3 cm;
CH- 38.3 cm;
Wl- 0.5-1.5 cm;
Cl- foreign marl group clay;
PM- WM;
Bs- Kn, Sm;
Br- beige; **Bp**- dense, **Bt**- fine;
Ms- 4;
Inc- WP round-1, also visible on the surface;
Sf- ex- "comb" pattern, in- traces of wheel;
Col- beige.

Fig. 3. "Meidum" bowl;
NR 97-98/3/4;
Con- 3;
Pr- 60%;
Rd- 22 cm;
PH ~ 8.5 cm;
Wl- 0.3-0.5 cm;
Cl- alluvial silt;
PM- WT;
Br- light brown, **Bp**- medium dense, **Bt**- fine;
Ms- 3;
Inc- S (0.5 mm)-1;
Sf- RC very carefully P (in, ex);
Col- brownish red.

Fig. 4. "Meidum" bowl;
NR 97-98/3/2;
Con- 3;
Rd- 17.3 cm;
PH- 3.7 cm;
Wl- 0.4 cm;
Cl- alluvial silt;
PM- WT;
Br- brown-red-brown; **Bp**- medium dense, **Bt**- fine;
Ms- 3;
Inc- S-1;
Sf- RCP (in, ex);
Col- red.

Fig. 5. "Meidum" bowl;
NR 98/3/3;
Con- 3;
Rd- 24 cm;
PH- 2.4 cm;
Wl- 0.3-0.4 cm;
Cl- alluvial silt;
PM- WT;
Br- brown-red-brown, **Bp**- medium dense, **Bt**- fine;
Ms- 3;
Inc- S- a few grains;
Sf- RCP (in, ex);
Col- red.

Fig. 6. "Meidum" bowl;
NR 98/11/17;
Con- 11;
Rd- 16 cm;
PH- 2 cm;
Wl- 0.4 cm;
Cl- marl clay;
PM- WT;
Br- pink, **Bp**- dense, **Bt**- smooth;
Ms- 4;
Inc- S-1, WP- a few grains;
Sf- RCP (in, ex);
Col- red.

Fig. 7. "Meidum" bowl;
NR 97-98/3/1;
Con- 3;
Rd- 20 cm;

Rd – diameter of rim;
Bd – diameter of bottom;
PH – height of the preserved fragment, **CH** – complete height;
Wl – wall thickness;
Cl – clay;
PM – method of manufacture (**HM** – handmade, **WT** – wheel-turned, **WM** – wheel-made);
Bs – base shaping (**M** – moulded, **Sr** – string cut, **Kn** – knife cut, **Sm** – smoothed, **WM** – wheel-made);
Br – break sections; **Bp** – break porosity (open, medium, dense); **Bt** – break texture (smoothed, fine, irregular, hackly);
Ms – Mohs hardness: **1** – soft (finger nail), **2** – middle (knife blade), **3** – hard (not knife blade), **4** – very hard (usually to very hard marl clay sherds);
Inc – inclusions: **St** – straw (fine < 2 mm, medium: 2-5 mm, coarse > 5 mm), **S** – sand, **Sh** – shell, **M** – mica, **G** – grog, **BP** – black particles, **RP** – red-brown particles, **WP** – white particles, **D** – dung;
Sf – surface treatment – ex – exterior, in – interior, **Sm** – smooth, **P** – polish, **U** – untreated, **Ro** – rough, **C** – coated, **Wh** – washed (**R** – red, **O** – orange, **Pi** – pink, **Br** – brown, **Bl** – black, **W** – white);
Col – colour.

PH- 2.6 cm;
Wl- 0.4-0.6 cm;
Cl- alluvial silt;
PM- WT;
Br- red-dark grey-red, **Bp**- medium dense, **Bt**- fine;
Ms- 4;
Inc- S-1, St-1;
Sf- RCP (in, ex);
Col- red.

Fig. 8. Bread mould;
NR 97-98/3/12;
Con- 3;
PH- 6.5 cm;
Wl- 1.7-2.8 cm;
Cl- alluvial silt;
PM- HM;
Br- light brown, **Bp**- open, **Bt**- irregular;
Ms- 2;
Inc- S-3, St (1-2 mm)-2, WP(1-3 mm)-1;
Sf- well Sm (in, ex);
Col- light brown.

Fig. 9. Bread mould;
NR 97/5/4;
Con- 5;
Rd- 25 cm;
PH- 4.4 cm;
Wl- 1.9-2.1 cm;
Cl- alluvial silt;
PM- HM;
Br- brown-pink-red-pink-brown, **Bp**- open, **Bt**- regular;
Ms- 2;
Inc- S-2, St- (1-2 cm)-3;
Sf- Sm;
Col- light brown, grey.

Fig. 10. Bread mould;
NR 97/8/13;
Con- 8;
Rd- 16 cm;
PH- 2.7 cm;
Wl- 1.5-1.6 cm;
Cl- alluvial silt;
PM- HM;
Br- brown-black-brown, **Bp**- open, **Bt**- irregular;
Ms- 1;
Inc- S-3, St-1, WP- (1mm)-1;
Sf- Sm;
Col- light brown.

Fig. 11. Bread mould;
NR 97/8/12;
Con- 8;
Rd- 26 cm;
PH- 5 cm;
Wl- 1.5-1.6 cm;
Cl- alluvial silt;
PM- HM;
Br- ex- light brown, black, red- in, **Bp**- open, **Bt**- irregular;
Ms- 2;
Inc- S-3, St-2, WP- (1-5 mm)- a few grains;
Sf- Sm;
Col- brown, yellowish white.

Fig. 12. Ledge bowl;
NR 97/8/34;
Con- 8;
Rd- 19 cm;
PH- 3 cm;
Wl- 0.8 cm;
Cl- alluvial silt;
PM- WT;
Br- light brown-red-light brown, **Bp**- medium,
Bp- regular;
Ms- 2;
Inc- S- (1 mm)-2; WP-1;
Sf- RCP (in – to the ledge);
Col- ex- red, in- red and light brown.

Fig. 13. Ledge bowl;
NR 97-98/3/13;
Con- 3;
Rd- 23 cm;
PH- 3 cm;
Wl- 0.6-0.8 cm;
Cl- alluvial silt;
PM- WT;
Br- light brown, **Bp**- medium, **Bt**- regular;
Ms- 1;
Inc- St- 1, S- 1;
Sf- Sm;
Col- light brown.

Fig. 14. Ledge bowl;
NR 98/6/5;

Con- 6;
Rd- 11 cm;
PH- 2.3 cm;
Wl- 0.4-0.9 cm;
Cl- alluvial silt;
PM- WT;
Br- brown, **Bp**- medium, **Bt**- fine;
Ms- 2;
Inc- S-1;
Sf- Sm;
Col- light brown.

Fig. 15. Beer jar base;
NR 97-98/11/10;
Con- 11;
Pr- 5%;
Cl- alluvial silt;
Br- red-black-red, **Bp**- open, **Bt**- irregular;
Ms- 3;
Inc- S-3; St-2;
Sf- ex- eroded, in- traces of fingers;
Col- light brown.

Fig. 16. Beer jar base;
NR 97-98/11/11;
Con- 11;
PH- 13 cm;
Wl- 1.2-2 cm;
Cl- alluvial silt;
PM- HM;
Bs- HM;
Br- orange-red-black-red-orange, **Bp**- open, **Bt**- irregular;
Ms- 1;
Inc- S-2, St- (1-2 cm)-3;
Sf- U rather;
Col- light brown.

Fig. 17. Beer jar base;
NR 97-98/3/6;
Con-3;
PH- 8cm;
Wl –1.2-5 cm;
Cl- alluvial silt;
PM- HM;
Bs- HM;
Br-red-black-red, **Bp**- open, **Bt**- irregular;
Ms- 1;
Inc- S-2, St- (1 cm)-3, WP- (1-4 mm)-1;
Sf- U;
Col- red.

Fig. 18. Beer jar;
NR 97-98/11/20;
Con- 11;
Rd- 10 cm;
PH- 5 cm;
Wl- 0.7-0.9 cm;
Cl- alluvial silt;
PM- HM;
Br- red-black-red, **Bp**- open, **Bt**- irregular;
Ms- 1;
Inc- S-2, St-2, WP- (1-3 and 6mm)-1;
Sf- well Sm;
Col- light brown.

Fig. 19. Beer jar;
NR 98/3/8;
Con- 3;
Pr- 5%;
Rd- 10 cm;
Cl- alluvial silt;
Br- red-brown-red, **Bp**- open, **Bt**- irregular;
Ms- 3;
Inc- S-2, St-2;
Sf- Es and IS: smoothed;
Col- brownish orange.

Fig. 20. Beer jar;
NR 97-98/11/18;
Con- 11;
Rd- 10.3 cm;
PH- 2.4 cm;
Wl- 0.6-0.8 cm;
Cl- alluvial silt;
PM- HM;
Br- red, **Bp**- open, **Bt**- irregular;
Ms- 3;
Inc- S-2, St-2;
Sf- Sm;
Col- light brown.

Fig. 21. Beer jar;
NR 97-98/11/2;
Con- 11;
Rd- 10 cm;
PH- 2.9 cm;
Wl- 0.8 cm;

Cl- alluvial silt;
PM- HM;
Br- red-black-red, **Bp**- open, **Bt**- irregular;
Ms- 1;
Inc- S-2, St-2, WP-1;
Sf- Sm;
Col- light brown.

Fig. 22. Beer jar;
NR 97-98/11/3;
Con- 11;
Rd- 14 cm (on the top);
PH- 5.3 cm;
Wl- 0.7-1 cm;
Cl- alluvial silt;
PM- HM;
Br- red-black-red, **Bp**- open, **Bt**- irregular;
Ms- 1;
Inc- S-1, St-2, WP-1;
Sf- Sm;
Col- red.

Fig. 23. Beer jar;
NR 97-98/11/9;
Con- 11;
Rd- 11.5 cm;
PH- 2.5 cm;
Wl- 0.5-0.8 cm;
Cl- alluvial silt;
PM- HM;
Br- red-black-red, **Bp**- open, **Bt**- irregular;
Ms- 1;
Inc- S-2, St- (2-4 cm)-2;
Sf- Sm;
Col- light brown.

Fig. 24. Beer jar;
NR 97-98/11/12;
Con- 11;
Rd- 10 cm;
PH- 5.1 cm;
Wl– 1 cm;
Cl- alluvial silt;
PM- HM;
Br- brown, **Bp**- open, **Bt**- irregular;
Ms- 1;
Inc- S-2, St-3;
Sf- Sm;
Col- red.

Fig. 25. Beer jar;
NR 97-98/11/13;
Con-11;
Rd- 14.5 cm;
PH- 5 cm;
Wl- 1-1.2 cm;
Cl- alluvial silt;
PM- HM;
Br- light brown, **Bp**- open, **Bt**- irregular;
Ms- 1;
Inc- St-3, S-2;
Sf- Sm;
Col- light brown.

Fig. 26. Beer jar;
NR 97-98/11/14;
Con- 11;
Rd- 10.5 cm (on the top);
PH- 5 cm;
Wl- 0.6-0.9 cm;
Cl- alluvial silt;
PM- HM;
Br- red-black-red, **Bp**- open, **Bt**- irregular;
Ms- 1;
Inc- S-2, St-3;
Sf- Sm;
Col- red.

Fig. 27. Beer jar;
NR 97-98/11/15;
Con- 11;
Rd- 12.5 cm;
PH- 3.5 cm;
Wl- 0.6-0.7 cm;
Cl- alluvial silt;
PM- HM;
Br- light brown, **Bp**- open, **Bt**- irregular;
Ms- 1;
Inc- S-2, St-2;
Sf- Sm;
Col- light brown;

Fig. 28. Beer jar;
NR 97-98/11/16;
Con-11;
Rd- 11 cm;
PH- 3.2 cm;
Wl- 0.8-1 cm;
Cl- alluvial silt;

PM- HM;
Br- red-grey-red; **Bp**- open, **Bt**- irregular;
Ms- 1;
Inc- S-2, St-2, WP- a few grains;
Sf- Sm;
Col- red.

Fig. 29. Beer jar;
NR 97-98/11/17;
Con- 11;
Rd- 12 cm;
PH- 4.4 cm;
Wl- 0.9-1 cm;
Cl- alluvial silt;
PM- HM;
Br- red-black-red, **Bp**- open, **Bt**- irregular;
Ms- 1;
Inc- S-2, St-2;
Sf- Sm;
Col- light brown.

Fig. 30. Beer jar;
NR 97-98/11/21;
Con- 11;
Rd- 11.5 cm (on the top);
PH- 4.2 cm;
Wl- 0.7-1 cm;
Cl- alluvial silt;
PM- HM;
Br- light brown, **Bp**- open, **Bt**- irregular;
Ms-1;
Inc- S-2, St-2, WP- (1- 4 mm)- 1;
Sf- Sm;
Col- light brown.

Fig. 31. Beer jar;
NR 97/8/1;
Con- 8;
Rd- 12 cm;
PH- 2.6 cm;
Wl- 0.6-1 cm;
Cl- alluvial silt;
PM- HM;
Br- brown- red- brown, **Bp**- open, **Bt**- regular;
Ms- 1;
Inc- S-2, St-2;
Sf- Sm;
Col- light brown.

Fig. 32. Beer jar;
NR 97/8/2;
Con- 8;
Rd- 10.5 cm;
PH- 9 cm;
Wl- 0.8-1 cm;
Cl- alluvial silt;
PM- HM;
Br- red-black-red, **Bp**- open, **Bt**- irregular;
Inc- S-2, St- (1 cm)-2, WP- (1- 3 mm)-1;
Sf- Sm;
Col- light brown.

Fig. 33. Beer jar;
NR 97/8/33;
Con- 8;
Rd- 9 cm;
PH- 7.2 cm;
Wl- 0.7-1.1 cm;
Cl- alluvial silt;
PM- HM;
Br- brown, **Bp**- open, **Bt**- irregular;
Ms- 1;
Inc- S-2, St-3;
Sf- Sm;
Col- light brown.

Fig. 34. Beer jar;
NR 97/4/5;
Con- 4;
Rd- 12.5 cm;
PH- 6.5 cm;
Wl- 0.6-1.2 cm;
Cl- alluvial silt;
PM- HM;
Br- brown-red-brown, **Bp**- open, **Bt**- irregular;
Ms- 1;
Inc- S-2; St- (1-3 cm)-2, WP- (2 mm)-1;
Sf- Sm;
Col- light brown.

Fig. 35. Beer jar;
NR 97/4/6;
Con- 4;
Rd- 10 cm;
PH- 7.5 cm;
Wl- 0.8-1.1 cm;
Cl- alluvial silt;

PM- HM;
Br- brown, **Bp**- open, **Bt**- irregular;
Ms- 1;
Inc- S-2, St-3;
Sf- Sm;
Col- light brown.

Fig. 36. Beer jar;
NR 97-98/3/9;
Con- 3;
Rd- 10.5 cm;
Wl- 0.7-0.9 cm;
Cl- alluvial silt;
PM- HM;
Br- brown, **Bp**- open, **Bt**- irregular;
Ms- 1;
Inc- S-2, St- (1 cm)-2, WP- (1 mm)-1;
Sf- Sm;
Col- light brown.

Fig. 37. Beer jar;
NR 97-98/3/10;
Con-3;
Rd- 11 cm (on the top);
PH- 3 cm;
Wl- 0.9-1.1 cm;
Cl- alluvial silt;
PM- HM;
Br- red-black-red, **Bp**- open, **Bt**- irregular;
Ms- 1;
Inc- S-2, St- (1 cm)-2, WP (1 mm)-1;
Sf- Sm;
Col- red.

Fig. 38. Stopper;
NR 97-98/3/11;
Con- 3;
Cl- Nile mud;
PM- HM;
Col- dark grey.

Fig. 39. Simple bowl with straight walls, white contents – in;
NR 97/8/44;
Con- 8;
Rd- 22 cm;
PH- 7.5 cm;
Wl- 0.8-0.9 cm;
Cl- alluvial silt;
PM- WT;
Br- brown-red-brown, **Bp**- medium, **Bt**- regular;
Ms- 2;
Inc- S-2, St- (1 cm)-1, WP- a few grains;
Sf- ex- eroded, in- not visible;
Col- red?

Fig. 40. Bowl with flaring walls;
NR 97/7/1;
Con- 7;
Rd- 26 cm;
PH- 3.2 cm;
Wl- 0.8-1 cm;
Cl- alluvial silt;
PM- HM;
Br- light brown, **Bp**- open, **Bt**- irregular;
Ms- 1;
Inc- S-2, St-1, WP- (0.5-1 mm)-1;
Sf- Sm;
Col- light brown.

Fig. 41. Bowl with flaring walls;
NR 97/8/15;
Con- 8;
Rd- 23 cm;
PH- 4.2 cm;
Wl- 0.8-1 cm;
Cl- alluvial silt;
PM- WT;
Br- red; **Bp**- medium; **Bt**- regular;
Ms- 2;
Inc- S-2; St-1;
Sf- Sm;
Col- red.

Fig. 42. Bowl with flaring walls;
NR 97/8/16;
Con- 8;
Rd- 23 cm;
PH- 2.5 cm;
Wl- 0.7-0.8 cm;
Cl- alluvial silt;
PM- WT;
Br- light brown-red-light brown, **Bp**- medium, **Bt**- regular;
Ms- 2;
Inc- S-2, St-2;
Sf- RCP (in, ex);
Col- red.

Fig. 43. Bowl with relief walls;
NR 97/8/39;
Con- 8;
Rd- 15 cm;
PH- 4.2 cm;
Wl- 0.4-0.6 cm;
Cl- marl clay;
PM- WT;
Br- pink, **Bp**- dense, **Bt**- fine;
Ms- 4;
Inc- none;
Sf- RCP (in, ex);
Col- red.

Fig. 44. Round rim jar;
NR 98/11/4;
Con- 11;
Rd- 10 cm;
PH- 1.8 cm;
Wl- 0.5 cm;
Cl- alluvial silt;
PM- WT;
Br- light brown, **Bp**- rather dense, **Bt**- regular;
Ms- 2;
Inc- S-2, WP- a few grains;
Sf- Sm;
Col- light brown.

Fig. 45. Triangular rim jar;
NR 97/8/45;
Con- 8;
Rd- 10.7 cm;
PH- 5.3 cm;
Wl- 0.6-1 cm;
Cl- marl clay,
PM- WT;
Br- greyish brown, **Bp**- dense, **Bt**- regular;
Ms- 4;
Inc- WP-3;
Sf- Sm;
Col- very light brown.

Fig. 46. Jar with a pot mark, after firing – ex;
NR 97/8/36;
Con- 8;
Rd- 10 cm;
PH- 3.2 cm;
Wl- 0.8-1.5 cm;
Cl- alluvial silt;
PM- WT;
Br- grey, **Bp**- medium dense, **Pt**- fine;
Ms- 2;
Inc- S-1, St-1;
Sf- Sm;
Col- brown.

Fig. 47. Miniature jar;
NR 97/8/10;
Con- 8;
Pr- 30%;
Rd- 3.7 cm;
PH- 3 cm;
Wl- 0.6-0.8 cm;
Cl- alluvial silt;
PM- WM;
Br- light brown, **Bp**- medium, **Bt**- regular;
Ms- 3;
Inc- S-2, St-1;
Sf- well Sm;
Col- light brown.

Fig. 48. Miniature jar;
NR 97/8/9;
Con- 8;
Pr- 80%;
Rd- 4.6 cm;
Bd- 2.8 cm;
CH- 5.9 cm;
Wl- 0.5-0.8 cm;
PM- WM;
Bs- St;
Cl- alluvial silt;
Br- red-black-red, **Bp**- medium, **Bt**- regular;
Ms- 3;
Inc- S-2, St-1, WP- (1 mm)-1;
Sf- well Sm;
Col- light brown.

Fig. 49. Miniature plate;
NR 97/4/4;
Con- 4;
Pr- 100%;
Rd- 4.5 cm;
Bd- 2.8 cm;
CH- 1.5 cm;
Wl- 0.5-0.8 cm;
Cl- alluvial silt;

PM- WM;
Bs- St;
Br- without break;
Ms- 2;
Inc- S-2, St-1, WP- (1-3 mm)-1;
Sf- Sm;
Col- light brown.

Fig. 50. Miniature plate;
NR 97/4/11;
Con- 4;
Rd- 5.6 cm;
Bd- 3.8 cm;
CH- 1.8 cm;
Wl- 0.4-0.7 cm;
Cl- alluvial silt;
PM- WT;
Bs- Sr;
Br- homogenous-brownish orange, **Bp**- medium, **Bt**- fine;
Ms- 3;
Inc- S-2, St-1, WP- (1-4 mm)-1;
Sf- well Sm;
Col- light brown.

Fig. 51. Miniature plate;
NR 97/7/3;
Con- 7;
Rd- 6 cm;
Bd- 3.5 cm;
CH- 1.7 cm;
Wl- 0.4-0.6 cm;
Cl- alluvial silt;
PM- WM;
Bs- St;
Br- brown, **Bp**- medium, **Bt**- regular;
Ms- 2;
Inc- S-1, St-1;
St- Sm;
Col- light brown.

Fig. 52. Miniature plate;
NR 97/8/35;
Con- 8;
Rd- 6.5 cm;
Bd- 5 cm;
CH- 2 cm;
Wl- 0.4-0.6 cm;
Cl- alluvial silt;
PM- WM;
Bs- St;
Br- light brown, **Bp**- medium, **Bt**- regular;
Ms- 2;
Inc- S-1, St-1;
Sf- Sm;
Col- light brown.

Fig. 53. Stand;
NR 97/8/17;
Con- 8;
Rd- 20 cm;
PH- 3 cm;
Wl- 0.6-0.7 cm;
Cl- alluvial silt;
PM- HM;
Br- brown-red-violet-red-brown, **Bp**- medium, **Bt**- regular;
Ms- 2;
Inc- S-2, St- (1 cm)-2, WP- (1 mm)- a few grains;
Sf- RCP;
Col- red.

Fig. 54. Hemispherical bowl;
NR 97/4/10;
Con- 4;
Rd- 13 cm;
PH- 6 cm;
Wl- 0.3-0.4 cm;
Cl- alluvial silt;
PM- WM;
Br- red-grey-red, **Bp**- dense, **Bt**- fine;
Ms- 1;
Inc- S-1; St- (1 mm)-1;
Sf- Sm;
Col- red.

Fig. 55. Levantine amphora;
NR 97-98/3/19;
Con- 3;
Pr- 30%;
PH- 35 cm;
Wl- 0.7-1.3 cm;
Cl- foreign marl group clay;
PM- WM;
Br- pink-grey-pink, **Bp**- dense, **Bt**- fine;
Ms- 4;
Inc- WP (1 mm)-2, S-1;

Sf- ex- well Sm, in: Sm, clear traces of work on the wheel;
Col- pink.

Fig. 56. Double rim jar;
NR 97/8/38;
Con- 8;
Rd- 8 cm;
PH- 6 cm;
Wl- 0.7-1.2 cm;
Cl- alluvial silt;
PM- WM;
Br- brown, **Bp**- medium, **Bt**- regular;
Ms- 2;
Inc- St-1, S-1;
Sf- Sm;
Col- brown.

Fig. 57. Straight rim jar;
NR 97/4/9;
Con- 4;
Rd- 9 cm;
PH- 6.3 cm;
Wl- 0.5-0.7 cm;
Cl- alluvial silt;
PM- WM;
Br- grey, **Bp**- dense, **Bt**- fine;
Ms- 3;
Inc- St-1;
Sf- Sm;
Col- brown.

Fig. 58. Pointed base;
NR 97/7/2;
Con- 7;
PH- 2 cm;
Wl- 0.5-1.1 cm;
Cl- alluvial silt;
PM- WM;
Bs- WM;
Br- brown-red-brown, **Bp**- medium, **Bt**- regular;
Ms- 2;
Inc- S-2, St-1;
Sf- Sm;
Col- light brown.

Fig. 59. Small ring base;
NR 97/8/42;
Con- 8;
Bd- 6 cm;
PH- 1 cm;
Wl- 0.3 cm;
Cl- marl clay;
PM- WM;
Bs- WM;
Br- pink, **Bp**- dense, **Bt**- smooth;
Ms- 4;
Inc- none;
Sf- BlCP- ex;
Col- black.

Fig. 60. Straight rim jar;
NR 98/11/6;
Con- 11;
Rd- 16 cm;
PH- 2.6 cm;
Wl- 0.3-0.5 cm;
Cl- alluvial silt;
PM- WM;
Br- red-black-red, **Bp**- medium, **Bt**- fine;
Ms- 2;
Inc- S-1, St- a few blades;
Sf- eroded;
Col- red ?

Fig. 61. Potmark, after firing- ex;
NR 97/8/49;
Con- 8;
Wl- 0.6-0.9 cm;
Cl- alluvial silt;
PM- HM (?);
Ms- 2;
Inc- S-2, St- (1 cm)-1, WP- (0,5 mm)- a few grains;
Sf- Sm;
Col- red.

Fig. 62. Potmark, before firing- ex;
NR 97/8/43;
Con- 8;
Wl- 0.6-0.8 cm;
Cl- alluvial silt;
PM- HM (?);
Br- ex- pink, in- yellowish white, **Bp**- dense, **Bt**- fine;
Ms- 4;
Inc- S-2;
Sf- Sm;
Col- beige.

Fig. 63. Potmark (before firing);
NR 97/8/20;
Con- 8;
Wl- 0.6-0.7 cm;
Cl- marl clay;
PM- WM;
Br- pink-light brown-pink, **Bp**- dense, **Bt**- fine;
Ms- 4;
Inc- S-1, WP-2, RP-1;
Sf- very good Sm;
Col- pink.

APPENDIX
POTTERY COUNT[59]

Context: the burial chamber of Khafraankh (11)

TYPE AND FABRIC	FORM GENERAL	DATING
Beer jars (**figs. 15, 16, 18, 20-30**)	W- 550, R- 26, B- 12	Old Kingdom
Bowl, NB2 RCP	W- 1	Old Kingdom
Bowl, NB1 RCP	W- 2	Old Kingdom
Bowl, NB2	B- 1	Old Kingdom
Bread moulds, NC	W- 11	Old Kingdom
Canaan jar (**fig. 2**)	Cpot- 1	Old Kingdom (IVth dynasty)
Bowl,	W- 5	? (much worn)
Jar, NB1 RCP (**fig. 44**)	R- 1	Old Kingdom
Jar, NA	R- 1	Late Period
Jar	B- 1	End of Ptolemaic/ Beginning of Roman Period (probably)
Jar, NA (**fig. 60**)	R- 1	Late Roman Period
Ledge bowl, NB2	W- 1, R- 1	Old Kingdom
Meidum bowl, M RCP (**fig. 6**)	R- 1	Old Kingdom (IVth dynasty)

Context: the shaft leading to the burial chamber of the tomb owner (3)

Ring base, NE RCP (?)	B- 1	Old Kingdom?
Amphora, NB2	H- 1	Late Period
Amphora, NA	B- 1	Late Period
Beer jar, NC (**figs. 17, 19, 36, 37**)	W- 61, R- 5, B- 4	Old Kingdom
Beer jar stopper (**fig. 38**)	Cpr- 1	Old Kingdom
Base, M	B- 3	Late Period
Bowls, NB2	W- 2	Old Kingdom
Bowls, NB1, RCP	W- 8	Old Kingdom
Bread mould, NC (**fig. 8**)	W- 1, R- 1	Old Kingdom
Jar, NB1, RCSm	W- 1	?

[59] In the tables other abbreviations were used: W – wall, R – rim, B – base, Cpot – complete pot, Cpr – complete profile, H – handle, PM – potmark; also NA, NB1, NB2, NC, NE, M – clay description according to the Vienna System after: H.A. NORDSTRÖM, J. BOURRIAU, in: Do. ARNOLD, J. BOURRIAU (eds.), *An Introduction to Ancient Egyptian Pottery*, SDAIK 17, Mainz 1993.

Jar, M	R- 1	Old Kingdom?
Ledge bowl, NB2 (**fig. 13**)	R- 1	Old Kingdom (IVth dynasty)
Meidum bowl, NA RCP (**figs. 4**, **5** and **7**)	R- 3	Old Kingdom (IVth-Vth dynasty)
Miniature bowl, NB1	B- 1, Cpr- 1	Old Kingdom
Stand, NB1	W- 1	Old Kingdom
Bread mould, NC	R- 1	Old Kingdom

Context: the shaft leading to the burial chamber of Khafraankh and the burial chamber of Khafraankh (3, 11)

Meidum bowl, NA RCP (**fig. 3**)	Cpr- 1	Old Kingdom (IVth dynasty)

Context: the shaft leading to the burial chamber of Khafraankh and burial shaft of Herenka (3, 4)

Amphora, M (foreign) (**fig. 55**)	B- 1, H- 1	XXVth dynasty
Beer jar, NC	R- 1	IVth dynasty
Bottle, NB2 WWh + PM band handle	B- 1	Late Period

Context: the burial shaft of Herenka (4)

Beer jar, NC (**figs. 34**, **35**)	W- 15, R- 5, B- 2	Old Kingdom (IVth dynasty)
Base, M	B- 1	Late Period
Bowl, NA (**fig. 54**)	R- 1	Early Middle Kingdom (Senwoseret I)
Bread mould, NC	W- 1	Old Kingdom
Jar, M	W- 3	Late Period?
Jar, NB1 (**fig. 57**)	W- 4, R- 1	XXVth dynasty
Miniature bowl, NB1 (**fig. 49** and **50**)	Cpr- 2	Old Kingdom

Context: the burial shaft of Herimerw and Ishepet (5)

Amphora?, NA	W- 1	Late Period
Beer jar, NC	W- 9, R- 4	Old Kingdom
Bowl, NB1	W- 1	Old Kingdom
Bread mould, NC (**fig. 9**)	R- 1	Old Kingdom
Jar, NB1	W- 4	Late Period
Jar, NB1 RCP	W- 1	Late Period
Cooking pot, NE	W- 1	Late Period

Context: the entrance to the tomb (6)

Beer jar, NC	W- 30	Old Kingdom
Bowl, NB1	R- 2	Old Kingdom
Bread mould, NC	W- 2	Old Kingdom
Jar, M RCP	W- 1	Late Period

Jar, M	W- 3	Late Period
Jar, NB1	R- 1	Old Kingdom
Jar, M	R- 2	Late Period
Ledge bowl, NB2 (**fig. 14**)	R- 1	IVth dynasty
Miniature bowl, NB1	Cpr- 1	Old Kingdom
Miniature jar, NB1	B- 1	Old Kingdom
Bowl, NB1 RCP	R- 1	Old Kingdom

Context: the so-called X-grave (7)

Beer jar, NC	W- 16, R- 2, B- 1	Old Kingdom
Base, NB1 (**fig. 58**)	B- 1	XXVth dynasty
Bowl, NB1 RCP + handle	W- 1	Old Kingdom
Bowl, NB2 (**fig. 40**)	R- 1	Old Kingdom
Jar, NB1	W- 51	Late Period
Jar, M	W- 10	Late Period
Jar, NB1 RCP	W- 1	Old Kingdom
Jar, NC (S- 3)	R- 1	Late Period
Miniature bowl, NB1 (**fig. 51**)	Cpr- 1	Old Kingdom

Context: the so-called X-grave (8)

Amphora, NB1	H- 1	Late Period
Amphora + handle, M	W- 3	Late Period
Amphora, NE	R- 1	Late Roman
Amphora, M	W- 6	Late Period
Beer jar NC (**figs. 31-33**)	W- 109, R- 10, B- 1	Old Kingdom
Base, NB1	B- 4	Late Period
Base, M (**fig. 59**)	B- 2	Beginning of Ptolemaic Period
Bowl, NB1	R- 2	Old Kingdom
Bowl, NB1 RCP (**figs. 41-43**)	R- 3	Old Kingdom
Bowl, NB2 (**fig. 39**)	R- 1	Old Kingdom
Bowl, M	R- 1	Late Period
Bread mould, NC (**figs. 10** and **11**)	W- 7, R- 3	Old Kingdom
Jar, M (one with pot mark **fig. 63**)	W- 8	Late Period
Jar, NB1 (two with a pot mark **figs. 61, 62**)	W- 52	Old Kingdom
Jar, NB1 RCP	W- 6	Old Kingdom
Jar, M (**fig. 45**)	R- 1	Old Kingdom
Jar with pot mark, NB1 (**fig. 46**)	R- 1	Old Kingdom
Jar, NB2	R- 2	Late Period
Jar, NB1 (**fig. 56**)	R- 1	XXVth dynasty
Ledge bowl, NB2	R- 1	Old Kingdom
Ledge bowl, NB2 RCP- in (**fig. 12**)	R- 1	Old Kingdom (IVth dynasty)
Miniature bowl, NB1 (**fig. 52**)	Cpr- 2, B- 2	Old Kingdom
Miniature jar, NB1 (**figs. 47** and **48**)	R- 1, Cpr- 1	Old Kingdom
Tub, NB2 NC	W- 5, R- 2, B- 2	Old Kingdom
Bowl/ jar?, M	W- 1	Late Period
Stand, NB1 RCP (**fig. 53**)	R- 1	Old Kingdom

Louis Zonhoven
Leiden

Continuity and Change in the *sḏm.n=f*-forms in Old Egyptian

That Classical Egyptian forms a language continuum encompassing Old and Middle Egyptian is demonstrated by the fact that the narrative verbal system that is generally called "Middle Egyptian" has its roots in Old Egyptian. Old Egyptian has witnessed a change that most clearly surfaces in the corpus of texts treated by DORET in his "Narrative Verbal System".[1] With regard to the rhematic narrative verb forms, Later Old Egyptian is in better tune with Middle Egyptian than with Earlier Old Egyptian.

Single versus Compound Forms in Old Egyptian Narrative

That major change is that the active Simple Past Old Perfect 1st ps. sing. *sḏm.k / pr.k* as well as the Independent (/Indicative) *sḏm=f* 3rd ps. used in the main clause of Earlier Old Egyptian narrative were giving way to the compound forms *jw sḏm.n=j/=f* and the Pseudoverbal construction *jw=j pr.kj / jw=f pr.w*, which were to become common in Middle Egyptian.[2] The latter construction functions as the counterpart of *jw sḏm.n=j/=f* with the verbs of motion because this class of intransitive verbs cannot form a Circumstantial *sḏm.n=f*.[3]

The compound form *jw sḏm.n=j* is generally agreed to contain the form morphologically known as the "Circumstantial *sḏm.n=f*", though, in my opinion, the compound form as a whole is best considered as a unity in its own right consisting of a bound particle and a verb form which cannot function in the main clause without the particle. With justification GARDINER labelled it a "compound verb form".[4]

The "Perfect" *sḏm.n=f*-complex

This compound form is part of the *sḏm.n=f*-complex, which represents the "Perfect" in the suffix-conjugation. As the 'New' Perfect it stands in contrast to the "Old Perfect".

The latter term I prefer to other names of the form, such as the "Stative", the "Pseudoparticiple" or GARDINER's "Old Perfective". The first two names cover the uses and the meanings of the form only in part, and, from the aspectual point of view, the term "Perfect" as a general denominator for the form seems to me preferable to "Old Perfective", which

---

[1] E. DORET, *The Narrative Verbal System of Old and Middle Egyptian*, Cahiers d'Orientalisme, Genève 1986 (hereinafter referred to as: *NVS*).

[2] *Ibidem*, pp. 108 and 145.

[3] *Ibidem*, p. 98.

[4] A.H. GARDINER, *Egyptian Grammar*, Oxford 1957, pp. 382-384 (§ 460), under my assumption that GARDINER used this word in its strict sense of a whole composed of at least two elements, for which see also under "compound" in the Concise Oxford Dictionary (Oxford, many editions). For example, G. LEFÈBVRE, *Grammaire de l'Égyptien classique*, Le Caire 1955, p. 157 (§308) too uses the term "formes composées", while J. POLOTSKY, Les transpositions du verbe en égyptien classique, *IOS* 6 (1976), p. 32 (3.8.1) speaks of "temps composés". Opposed to these views of a compound form seems to be M. COLLIER, The Circumstantial *sḏm(.f)/sḏm.n(.f)* as Verbal Verb-Forms in Middle Egyptian, *JEA* 76 (1990), pp. 73-85, especially 74, footnote 7, where it is claimed, without further exposition, that in *jw/ꜥḥꜥ.n sḏm.n=f* the role of the particles (in COLLIER's terms "auxiliaries") is to be viewed in the same way as the particles focused upon by him, i.e. *mk* and *jsṯ*. On the basis of my studies of the *sḏm.t=f* as a relative future tense, I have pointed out (ZONHOVEN, Studies on the *sḏm.t=f* verb form in Classical Egyptian, V: The relative future tense *sḏm.t=f*, *BiOr* 55 (1998), cols. 604-605 (§ 4)), in contrast to COLLIER's view, that from the viewpoint of how these main clause compound verb forms semantically work GARDINER's term seems most appropriate. The verb forms they contain, which have been identified by POLOTSKY as the Circumstantial *sḏm=f/sḏm.n=f*, fulfil all the requirements of belonging to a set of finite relative tenses at work in Classical Egyptian, as appears from their use in the circumstantial-temporal clause. In all probability, such finite relative tenses can only function in Classical Egyptian in the main clause – for which absolute time reference is typical – when anchored to a Reference Point representing the speaker's present, i.e. *jw* "here-now-(and mostly)-I" (see footnote 27 below) and *ꜥḥꜥ.n* with approximately the Perfect meaning "as it has come to stand (and stands now)", to

term cannot easily be reconciled with the stativity the form so often denotes: stativity is strongly associated with Imperfectivity.[5] From the form's originally being a Perfect its very frequent use as a Stative as well as its rarer use as a narrative form in the 1st ps. sing. only can easily be explained.

The Text Material of Old Egyptian Considered Here

The text material considered here I divide into three text types:
Autobiography in the sense of Real Lifestory;
Ideal Autobiography with its formulaic phraseology in general terms;
Administrative Documents, above all letters, which actually are written speech acts of a 1st ps. addressing a 2nd ps.

jw sḏm.n=f in Earlier Old Egyptian

Beginning with Earlier Old Egyptian, I should like to present first some examples of this form *jw sḏm.n=f* in the 1st ps. sing.: *jw sḏm.n=j*.
Ex. 1: *Urk.* I, 179,13 (Vth dynasty; letter of king Isesi to his vizier). *jw m3.n ḥm=(j) sš pn nfr nfr rdj.n=k jn.t(j)=f m stp-s3* "My Majesty has seen this very fine letter which you caused to be brought in the Palace".[6]

The use of the Compound form is paralleled in another letter of this king, though this time in the 2nd ps. masc.
Ex. 2: *Urk.* I, 63,8; emended DORET, *NVS*, ex. 184 (Vth dynasty; letter of king Isesi to Senedjemib). *jw ḥm jr.n=k* [...] *ḥḥw n* [*sp*] "You have indeed done [something excellent] millions of times".[7]

Indeed, our Present Perfect is a common tense in letters. With regard to Ex. 1: "I have received your message [and am now aware of its contents]; with regard to Ex. 2, the speaker expresses as his present judgment that "you have done excellent things [of presently enduring value]".

This Present Perfect value of *jw sḏm.n=j* is confirmed by its use in an Autobiography which, though written in a period that the above described change of system was well underway, still uses the old system.
Ex. 3: *Urk.* I, 139,1 (reign of Pepi II; Autobiography of Sabni son of Mekhu). *jw ḳrs.n=(j) jt=(j) pn m js=f n ẖr.t-nṯr* "I have buried this father of mine in his tomb of the necropolis".[8]

The compound verb form used to describe the burial of the speaker's father, which, of course, is of major present significance for the son as the person responsible for the funerary cult of his father, stands in clear contrast to that used to describe another burial of just some other person not related to the speaker, which he took care of too.
Ex. 4: *Urk.* I, 140,8 (reign of Pepi II; Autobiography of Sabni son of Mekhu). *ḳrs.k s pn m js=f mḥ n Nḫb* "I buried this man in his tomb north of El-Kab".[9]

In this case, it is not the Present Perfect tense that is used, but the more detached narrative tense of the Simple Past, in Earlier Old Egyptian the Old Perfect, since the funerary cult of this other man is of no special present relevance to the speaker.

Active Verb Forms Used in the Autobiography in Earlier Old Egyptian

Indeed, the Old Perfect 1st ps. sing. and the Independent (/Indicative) *sḏm=f* 3rd ps. are the common tenses used in Simple Past narrative, as is apparent from the first line of the next examples from the well-known autobiography of Weni, which is written as well in Earlier Old Egyptian.
Ex. 5: *Urk.* I, 104,4 (reigns of Teti to early Merenre; Autobiography of Weni). *ḥs w(j) ḥm=f ḥr=s r ẖ.t-nb* "His Majesty praised me exceedingly on account of it".
Ex. 6: *Urk.* I, 104,14 – 105,3 (reigns of Teti to early Merenre; Autobiography of Weni). *ḏ3.k m nmj.w ḥnʿ ṯs.wt jptn. jr.n=(j) wd-r-t3 m pḥwj k3w.w n ṯs.t*

which the relative verb form is related. In other words, without these particles (/auxiliaries) the verb forms cannot operate in the main clause and they are bound to them, differently from *mk/jsṯ*, which are unbound particles that may assume the bound role in 'substitution'. In my view, there is insufficient justification for COLLIER's regarding the Circumstantial *sḏm=f/sḏm.n=f* after auxiliaries in main clause forms as syntactically 'verbal' in their own right, thus in separation from the particles; it is the main clause compound form as a unity that should be regarded as 'verbal'.

[5] B. COMRIE, *Aspect*, Cambridge Textbooks in Linguistics, Cambridge 1976 (hereinafter referred to as: *Aspect*), p. 51: "Given the naturalness of the combination of stativity and imperfectivity...".

[6] DORET, *NVS*, p. 103, footnote 1314.

[7] *Ibidem*, p. 104, Ex. 184.

[8] *Ibidem*, p. 100, Ex. 175.

[9] *Ibidem*, p. 65, Ex. 102.

ḥr mḥ.t tꜣ ḥr.j.w-šꜥ, sṯ gs-t(w)t m mšꜥ pn m ḥrtj. jj.n=(j), nḏr.n=(j) sn mj-ḳd=sn "I crossed in ships with these troops. I made a landing in the back of the hills of the mountain-ridge, to the north of the land of the Bedouin, [*nota bene*], while half of the army went overland. I returned, [*nota bene*] after I had grabbed them in their entirety".[10]

The latter example was selected to illustrate the difference in the choice of verb forms for pragmatic reasons. As can be noticed, *dꜣ.k* functioning as a Simple Past active narrative tense is not followed by the verb form *jr.k*, but by a bare *sḏm.n=f*-form *jr.n=(j)* opening an Emphatic Sentence, i.e. the Substantival *sḏm.n=f*. This form equally functions as a Simple Past narrative tense. Thus it is with the third line, in which the circumstantial-temporal clause with the Circumstantial *sḏm.n=f* is emphasised.

What can be learned from this example is the following. Firstly, the Old Perfect 1st ps. sing. (as well as the Independent (/Indicative) *sḏm=f* 3rd ps. in Ex. 5) are not used in the Emphatic Sentence, obviously because they are rhematic verb forms that cannot be used in the pragmatic role of thematic verb forms. Secondly, the Substantival *sḏm.n=f* belonging to the Perfect complex is used in the Simple Past narrative style of the Autobiography.

The Verb Forms in the Ideal Autobiography in Earlier Old Egyptian

Bare *sḏm.n=f*-forms also occur in the Ideal Autobiography of Earlier Old Egyptian.

Ex. 7: Urk. I, 198,13 – 199,8 (reign of Teti; Ideal Autobiography of Neferseshemre-Sheshi). *pr.n=(j) m njw.t=(j), hꜣ.n=(j) m spꜣ.t=(j), jr.n=(j) mꜣꜥ.t n nb=s, sḥtp.n=(j) sw m mrr.t=f. ḏd.n=(j) mꜣꜥ.(w), jr.n=(j) mꜣꜥ.t. ḏd.n=(j) nfr, wḥm.n=(j) nfr, jṯ.n=(j) tp-nfr, mr=(j) nfr jm n rmṯ. wp.n=(j) sn.wj r ḥtp=sn, nḥm.n=(j) mꜣr m-ꜥ wsr r=f <n> sḫm.t.n=(j) jm. rdj.n=(j) t n ḥḳr ḥbs <n ḥꜣj> smꜣ-tꜣ m jw. ḳrs.n=(j) jwtw sꜣ=f, jr.n=(j) mẖn.t n jwtw mẖn.t=f. snḏ.n=(j) <n> jt=(j), jmꜣ.n=(j) n mw.t=(j), šd.n=(j) ẖrd.w=sn, ḫr=f rn=f nfr Ššj* " I have gone out from my town and I have come down from my nome, [*nota bene*], after I had done Maat for its lord and satisfied him with what he loves. I have spoken truthfully, I have done Maat. I have spoken good, I have repeated good, I have set a good example, as I wished good through it for the people. I have judged two persons, so that they were satisfied, I have saved the wretched from the one stronger than him, with respect to that over which I possessed power. I have given bread to the hungry, clothes [to the naked] and a landing to the boatless. I have buried the one who had no son, I have made a ferry for the one who had no ferry. I have shown respect to my father, I have been kind to my mother, I have raised their children. So says he whose good name is Sheshi".

In my translation the *sḏm.n=f* forms that occur in the main clauses are rendered as Present Perfects because in the Ideal Autobiography the deceased recalls his lasting achievements in generalising terms. There can be little doubt that the opening statement is an Emphatic Sentence consisting of a main clause with two thematic Substantival *sḏm.n=f*-forms and two emphasised circumstantial-temporal clauses with two Circumstantial *sḏm.n=f*-forms having Relative Past meaning. This is in full accordance with one of POLOTSKY's rules concerning the two *sḏm.n=f*-forms recognised by him: a bare sentence-initial *sḏm.n=f* is always the Substantival, and the "vedette" may be the Circumstantial *sḏm.n=f* of a transitive verb.

As appears from his discussion of the inscription, POLOTSKY identifies all *sḏm.n=f*-forms following *pr.n=(j)* and *hꜣ.n=(j)* as the emphasised Circumstantial form.[11] By doing that, POLOTSKY falls onto the sword of his own rules because of another rule of his theory: the intransitive verbs, among which the Verbs of Motion are the most common, cannot form the Circumstantial *sḏm.n=f*.[12] In his translation, however, the *sḏm.n=f*-forms of the intransitive verbs *snḏ* "to fear for, to show respect for" and *jmꜣ* "to be kind to" are rendered in relative-past circumstantial clauses as if they were the Circumstantial variety.[13] While, given POLOTSKY's own rules, these forms cannot be the Circumstantial *sḏm.n=f*, they are for two rea-

---

[10] *Ibidem*, p. 83, Ex. 140 and 93, Ex. 93.

[11] J. POLOTSKY, Egyptian Tenses, in: *The Israel Academy of Sciences and Humanities, Proceedings* II.5, Jerusalem 1965, pp. 15-16 (§§ 31-2) = IDEM, *Collected Papers*, Jerusalem 1971, pp. 85-86.

[12] J. POLOTSKY, *IOS* 6 (1976), p. 27 (§ 3.2).

[13] In his study of *sḏm.n=f*-forms of adjective verbs P. VERNUS, Études de philologie et de linguistique (III), *RdE* 35 (1984), p. 136 (Ex. 14) translates *jmꜣ.n=j* as a main clause form.

sons most unlikely to be the Substantival either. First, for want of a decent "vedette", since being respectful towards one's father and kind to one's mother is all too natural to be especially emphasised. Second, the clauses in which they occur cannot be coupled as a Balanced Sentence "as I have (always) shown respect for my father, so I have (always) been kind to my mother", because the following statement concerning taking care of the children contextually belongs to these statements as a third member. Furthermore, as I shall attempt to make plausible in a study in preparation and give here as my provisional view, the stem of the suffix-conjugation forms of the verb *rdj* when occurring in the circumstantial-temporal clause seems to be consistently *dj* (*dj=f*, *dj.n=f*, Passive *dj.w=(f)*).

Thus, in this inscription there are two bare *sḏm.n=f*-forms that can, in my view, not be the Substantival. I suggest that the inscription be translated as given above, in accordance with EDEL,[14] and that POLOTSKY's generally accepted couple of *sḏm.n=f*-forms is to be extended, in addition to the Compound *sḏm.n=f* as a form in its own right (the best witness is, in my opinion, *jw/ꜥḥꜥ.n rdj.n=f/ dj.n=f*), with a fourth variety: the Independent (/Indicative) *sḏm.n=f*, in favour of the existence of which in Middle Egyptian I have already argued in an article of several years ago.[15]

What now is the value of this Independent (/Indicative) *sḏm.n=f*, which in Old Egyptian seems to occur only in the Ideal Autobiography using the older system, but which, unfortunately, is very rare, owing to the scarcity of the Ideal Autobiography texts before the late Vth and VIth dynasties. There can be no doubt that the form has the true Present

[14] E. EDEL, *Hieroglyphische Inschriften des Alten Reiches*, Abh. d. Rheinisch-Westfälischen Ak. d. Wiss. 67, Opladen 1981, pp. 77-84, part. 78-79, reconstructed and translated the almost identical Ideal Autobiography of Neferseshemptah (which deviates from SETHE's reconstruction in *Urk.* I, pp. 200,9-201,9). See also the brief, in part similar Ideal Autobiography from the contemporary tomb of Hesi at Saqqara, studied in D.P. SILVERMAN, The Threat-Formula and Biographical Text in the Tomb of Hezi at Saqqara, *JARCE* 37 (2000), pp. 2-3 and observe his footnote 7 on the *sḏm.n=f*-question. Unfortunately, this Ideal Autobiography does not provide further good evidence for the issue of the existence of the Independent *sḏm.n=f*, though the fact that SILVERMAN translates the bare *sḏm.n=f*-form *wp.n=(j)* after Hesi's opening statement, which is nearly identical to that of Neferseshemre and Neferseshemptah, as independent "I have judged" might betray his view on the existence of the Independent *sḏm.n=f*. His translation in the same way as EDEL's (see above in this footnote) might have been triggered by the occurrence of the expression *n sp ḏd=(j) ḫ.t ḏw.(t)* "never have I said an evil thing" immediately after the opening statement, since this construction is usually translated as (and considered to be?) a main clause construction. Although the negative constructions *n sḏm=f / n sḏm.n=f /n sḏm.t=f* are on principle capable of functioning as (/in the) circumstantial-temporal clause, the *n sḏm=f*-derivative *n sp sḏm=f* might indeed be an exception. An indication for this might come from the stela of Tjetji (B.M. 614), A,13-14, which lines read: *jw šms.n=(j) sw r s.wt=f nb.t nfr.t nt sḫmḫ-jb n sp ṯs ḏbꜥ=f ḫ.t jm=(j) n-ꜥꜣ.t-nt rḫ-ḫ.t=(j) dj.n=f n=(j) šm.t nb.(t) wn.t m-ꜥ=(j) m rk jt=f ḥr sḏꜣ.t=s ḫr ḥm=f n jw ḫ.t-nb jm=(j)*. Under the assumption that it is unlikely that, if *dj.n=f* were used continuatively, the immediately preceding *n sp sḏm=f*-construction would be embedded in between two main clauses in a complex sentence, the form *dj.n=f* is better taken as the Substantival heading a new Emphatic Sentence and, consequently, the negative construction *n jw ḫ.t-nb jm=(j)* is then the candidate for being the rheme in the form of a circumstantial-temporal clause. It seems as if this construction is here used instead of the much more common expression *n sp jw.t ḫ.t-nb jm=(j)* to avoid the latter being used in a circumstantial-temporal clause. Thus, my translation is: "I followed him to all his good places of heart's content. Never did his finger raise objection against me because of the excellence of my knowledge. He gave to me every commission that was in my hand in the time of his father, whilst making it continue under his reign, [*nota bene*] without that any fault against me occurred".

[15] I now prefer the term "Independent" to "Indicative", since the new term clearly distinguishes the form syntactically from: (1) the "Circumstantial" as a subordinate clause form dependent on a main clause; (2) the "Substantival" either as a thematic form not occurring without a rheme located further on in the sentence or as dependent 'that'-form in the subordinate clause (the latter is quite rare); (3) the Compound Form which is obligatorily headed by a particle. I have argued in favour of the occurrence of this form in Sinuhe, where certain sentence-initial narrative *sḏm.n=f* forms cannot be explained as either the Circumstantial or the Substantival *sḏm.n=f*-forms; see ZONHOVEN, Polotsky, Sinuhe, Negation and the *sḏm.n=f*. On the existence of an indicative *sḏm.n=f* in Middle Egyptian, *JEOL* 33 (1993-1994), pp. 53-84. For examples where a circumstantial-temporal clause as protasis precedes the Independent (/Indicative) in the main clause as apodosis see, among many more, Shipwrecked Sailor, 62 (*gm.n=j*) and 76 (*ḫm.n=j*); Hatnub 14, 6 (2 x *pḥ.n=j*). Note that this syntactically independent form is not to be confused with COLLIER's "Verbal *sḏm=f/ sḏm.n=f*" (see footnote 4 above), which term refers to the Circumstantial *sḏm=f/sḏm.n=f* that, in his opinion, are used as syntactically independent 'verbal' verb forms in the main clause.

Perfect value of enduring relevance, well known from the use of the Present Perfect tense in English, not only to judge from the translation but more so on account of the fact that the typical Simple Past narrative tenses do not occur in the Ideal Autobiography, while vice versa the Independent (/Indicative) *sḏm.n=f* seems unattested in the Autobiography using Simple Past narrative, as no bare *sḏm.n=f*-forms could be detected by me that cannot be explained as the Substantival in the Emphatic Sentence.

In this connexion, it is worth noting that, given the typical Present Perfect value of the Ideal Autobiography, which focuses on the lasting achievements of the speaker, the Substantival and Circumstantial *sḏm.n=f*-forms of the opening line of the Ideal Autobiography of Neferseshemre also have Perfect value, whereas these forms have Simple Past and Relative Past value, respectively, in the Autobiography.

The Situation in Later Old Egyptian

After having dealt in the following with the situation in Later Old Egyptian, which, essentially, is the Middle Egyptian system, I shall return to the Perfect, in particular the Present Perfect.

All following examples are from the inscription of Harkhuf, which incorporates an Ideal Autobiography, an Autobiography, and a royal letter. Harkhuf's career runs from Merenre to early Pepi II.

Ex. 8: *Urk.* I, 122,6 (Ideal Autobiography). *jw rdj.n=(j) t n ḥkr* "I have given bread to the hungry".

We see that the bare *rdj.n=(j) t n ḥkr* of the inscription of Neferseshemre has now been replaced with the Compound *sḏm.n=f*, no doubt still with the meaning of a Present Perfect. The replacement of bare *rdj.n=j* in Earlier Old Egyptian with the undoubtedly main clause form *jw rdj.n=j* may be taken as support for the view that the bare form also is a main clause form instead of being a Circumstantial *sḏm.n=f* in a circumstantial-temporal clause. It makes, in my opinion, more sense to assume that an expression which almost always unambiguously occurs in (/as) an independent main clause also does so in the few more ambiguous instances.

With regard to the Autobiography of Harkhuf, we notice that the Old Perfect 1st ps. sing. and the Independent (/Indicative) *sḏm=f* 3rd ps. are being replaced with that same compound verb form *jw sḏm.n=j/=f*, but here with Simple Past meaning, as appears from the two next examples.

Ex. 9: *Urk.* I, 124,13 (Autobiography). *jw jr.n=(j) s(j) n ꜣbd 7* "I did it in seven months".[16]

Ex. 10: *Urk.* I, 124,9-10 (Autobiography). *jw hꜣb.n w(j) ḥm n Mr-n-rꜥ nb=(j) ḥnꜥ jt=(j)* "the Majesty of Merenre, my lord, sent me out together with my father".[17]

This replacement with the Compound *sḏm.n=f* is not possible for the Old Perfect 1st ps. sing. of the Verbs of Motion (compare *ḏꜣ.k* in Ex. 6), since this verb class cannot form a Circumstantial *sḏm.n=f*; instead, the compound form with the Old Perfect 1st ps. is used, which is generally called the "Pseudoverbal Construction".

Ex. 11: *Urk.* I, 126,2-3 (Autobiography). *jw=(j) pr.k(j) m-sꜣ=f r tꜣ Ṯmḥ sḥtp.n=(j) sw* "I set out after him to the land of the Tjemeh and I appeased him". In this example the *sḏm.n=f*-form is interpreted by me as being used continuatively, thus dependent on the initial *jw*.[18]

Whereas both these compound forms replace the single forms of Earlier Old Egyptian as rhematic Simple Past forms, the Substantival *sḏm.n=f* of both the transitive verbs and the verbs of motion simply continues to function in the Autobiography of Later Old Egyptian in the same way as in the earlier system, thus as thematic Simple Past forms in the Emphatic Sentence.

Ex. 12: *Urk.* I, 125,5-6 (Autobiography). *hꜣ.n=(j) jn.n=(j) jn.w m ḫꜣs.t tn r ꜥꜣ wrt* "I came down, [*nota bene*] after I had collected products in this land, very many".

The inscription of Harkhuf also contains a specimen of the third text type under discussion, a letter.

Ex. 13: *Urk.* I, 128,5 (letter of Pepi II). *jw sjꜣ.w md.t nt šꜥ.t=k tn* "Notice has been taken of the matter of this letter of yours".[19]

Here we encounter the Passive *sḏm.w(=f)* as the passive counterpart of the Circumstantial *sḏm.n=f* in the compound verb form, like in the letters of king Isesi again with Present Perfect value.

[16] DORET, *NVS*, p. 110, Ex. 201.

[17] See the preceding footnote.

[18] DORET, *NVS*, p. 113 interprets the form as the Substantival.

[19] *Ibidem*, p. 81, Ex. 136.

The Perfect *sḏm.n=f*-complex Compared with the Perfect in English

After this brief review of verb forms used in three text types of Earlier and Later Old Egyptian, I should like to turn to some remarks on the Perfect *sḏm.n=f*-complex in Classical Egyptian as a language continuum.

Though the Perfect complex in English is generally divided into three, that is, the Present Perfect, the Pluperfect and the Future Perfect, the *sḏm.n=f*-complex of Classical Egyptian has a different division which covers four varieties: (1) the Independent (/Indicative), (2) the Substantival, (3) the Circumstantial, which last variety is part of the main clause (4) Compound form.

Remarkably, the Pluperfect and the Future Perfect are united in the Circumstantial *sḏm.n=f*, the Relative Past tense which, in contrast to the English tenses being absolute-relative tenses – which means that in them also the speaker's present is involved –,[20] functions as a genuine relative finite tense in the circumstantial-temporal clause, that is, quite independently from the absolute time reference of the Reference Point, mostly the tense expressed in the main clause verb form.

To clarify this point, I refer to the above Exs. 6 and 12, which have absolute past time reference in the main clause: the translation of the following circumstantial clauses requires the use of the Pluperfect, "after I **had** grabbed" and "after I **had** collected", respectively. Compare these with the translation of the following example.
Ex. 14: Hekanakhte Papers XVI, vso 2.[21] *jmj jw.t tꜣ wsḫ.t pḥ.n=s wj* "let this boat return, after it **will have** reached me".

Note that a strict translation with the Future Perfect "will have reached" is possible in English, though it is not obligatory, as also "has reached" may be used. This is possible because both express the absolute non-past. Indeed, "had reached" would be ungrammatical, since this form can only be used when the event is located in the absolute past.

For Classical Egyptian it suffices, in dealing with both time situations, to use only one verb form, the genuine Relative Past tense Circumstantial *sḏm.n=f*!

To reduce complexity somewhat, I concentrate in the following on the Pluperfect rather than on the Future Perfect with respect to the presence of Perfect value and will then relate the situation to the Circumstantial *sḏm.n=f*. The following example from English containing the Pluperfect admits of two interpretations of that form, either the strict Perfect-in-the-Past, which expresses continuing relevance, or the more common Past-in-the-Past, which simply locates a situation prior in time to another one.
Ex. 15: "Bill had arrived at 6 o'clock".[22]
First, interpreted as Perfect-in-the-Past: Bill had arrived before 6 o'clock and was still there at that time point, in the sense of "John arrived at 6 o'clock. By then Bill had arrived".

Second, interpreted as Past-in-the-Past: Bill's arrival at 6 o'clock just preceded some other past, but later situation, in the sense of "John arrived at 7 o'clock. Bill had arrived at 6 o'clock".

This latter interpretation of simply relating a situation to some earlier situation applies to most uses of the Pluperfect.[23]

Relating these two possible interpretations to the meaning of the Circumstantial *sḏm.n=f*, it seems fair to state that undoubtedly the form as used in the Present Perfect context of the Ideal Autobiography of Earlier Old Egyptian (see Ex. 7) is meant as Perfect-in-the-Past, in paraphrase "I have gone into my tomb after having practised Maat all my life up to my death".

However, it seems obvious that already in the perfective-oriented Simple Past narrative of Earlier Old Egyptian the Circumstantial *sḏm.n=f* had lost its Perfect value, there simply denoting the location of the situation described in a circumstantial-temporal clause as prior to that in the main clause, such as in Ex. 6 ("after I had grabbed") and in Ex. 12 ("after I had collected").

Thus, dependent on context, the Circumstantial *sḏm.n=f* may retain its original Perfect value of continuing relevance.

---

[20] B. COMRIE, *Tense*, Cambridge Textbooks in Linguistics, Cambridge 1985 (hereinafter referred to as: *Tense*), pp. 64-82.

[21] T.G.H. JAMES, *The Hekanakhte Papers and Other Early Middle Kingdom Documents*, Publications of the Metropolitan Museum of Art Egyptian Expedition 19, New York 1962, pls. 25-25a. Thus also in the stela of Ikhernofret (Berlin 1204), 9 (*jr.n=k* "after you (will) have acted").

[22] The example is taken from COMRIE, *Aspect*, p. 56 (3.0).

[23] Hence the treatment of the Pluperfect (and the Future Perfect) as 'tenses' (in the strict sense) in COMRIE, *Tense*, pp. 65-69.

The Value of the Independent (/Indicative) *sḏm.n=f*

So far we have seen that three of the *sḏm.n=f*-forms, namely the Substantival, the Circumstantial and the Compound, are freely used in the three text types selected to study the situation in Old Egyptian and may, dependent on context, lose or retain their Perfect value.

Remarkably, however, the Independent (/Indicative) *sḏm.n=f* only occurs in the typically Present Perfect context of the Ideal Autobiography of Earlier Old Egyptian, thus with exclusively genuine Present Perfect value.

Interestingly, it may well be a certain semantic feature of the Present Perfect form Independent (/Indicative) *sḏm.n=f* that may have elicited POLOTSKY's identifying as the Circumstantial *sḏm.n=f* all the forms in the Ideal Autobiography of Ex. 7 that I identify as the Independent (/Indicative) variety: all these forms refer to situations in real life, which, of course, are prior to those in the statement in the opening line, the Passing from Life to Death formula, which indicates that the speaker has entered into his tomb after ending his life on earth.

Here the two main values of the Present Perfect may well have come into play, for which compare the following examples in English:[24]

Ex. 16: "Bill has gone to America". The verb form expresses the Present Perfect of Result.

Ex. 17: "Bill has been to America". The form expresses the Experiential (/Existential) Present Perfect.[25]

In the Present Perfect of Result a present state is referred to as being the result of some past situation, thus in the Egyptian statement: the deceased speaker has entered his tomb and will remain there forever.

The Experiential (/Existential) Present Perfect indicates that a given situation has held at least once during some time in the past leading up to the present, in principle under the requirement of present relevance being still important, as, e.g., in the Egyptian statement "I have (always) given bread to the hungry" as a deed in accordance with Maat to be proud of and helping to ensure paradise in the Hereafter.

Indeed, the use of the Present Perfect form Independent (/Indicative) *sḏm.n=f* in the Ideal Autobiography context of Ex. 7 for describing verbal situations in real life that evoke the interpretation of the Experiential (/Existential) Present Perfect gives the false impression that these verb forms themselves explicitly express as part of their meaning – thus, grammaticise – that these situations are located in the past relative to the opening statement concerning the present situation of having entered the tomb. Since, accidentally, this is the well-known typical performance of the Circumstantial *sḏm.n=f* in the circumstantial-temporal clause, identification as this form is quite understandable. Closer observance of certain rules, however, would have revealed that, on their account, this identification cannot be correct and that, therefore, we are confronted here with a case of implicature inferred from certain verbal situations instead of that the verb form used to describe them has this meaning.[26] The fact that this Independent (/Indicative) *sḏm.n=f* does not occur in Simple Past narrative contexts of Old Egyptian corroborates its functioning, in that phase, exclusively as a genuine Present Perfect.

What is clear in any case from the occurrence in Middle Egyptian of a bare *sḏm.n=f*-form that can neither be the Substantival nor the sentence-initial Circumstantial is that the Independent (/Indicative) *sḏm.n=f* has made a come-back in Middle Egyptian, though now, like the other varieties, also in Simple Past narrative as a rhematic alternative to the Compound *sḏm.n=f*. Thus, in Middle Egyptian even the last form of the *sḏm.n=f*-complex that exclusively functioned as the Present Perfect has given up this value, having come to be used as a Simple Past tense too.

The Two Forms for Expressing the Present Perfect in Earlier Old Egyptian

Returning to the Independent (/Indicative) *sḏm.n=f* as a rhematic Present Perfect in Earlier Old Egyptian, we must draw attention to its rival in that stage, the Compound *sḏm.n=f*. In the beginning of this paper we have seen that in letters the Compound form is used as a rhematic Present Perfect of Result, and not the Independent (/Indicative) *sḏm.n=f*, which is found in the Ideal Autobiography.

[24] Both following examples are taken from the discussion in COMRIE, *Aspect*, pp. 56-59, especially 59 top.

[25] The term "Existential" is preferred by J.D. McCAWLEY; see under this name in the bibliography of COMRIE, *Aspect*.

[26] See COMRIE, *Tense*, pp. 23-26 (3.1 on "meaning and implicature"). About his view of implicature being involved in the Luganda 'not yet'-tense (see pp. 54-55) I have serious doubts; see ZONHOVEN, *BiOr* 55 (1998), cols. 633-637.

The Compound form derives from the Relative Past tense Circumstantial *sḏm.n=f*, which as a relative tense approximately meaning "relative to a reference point in the context he had already heard" is related to the Reference Point *jw* representing the Here and Now of the speaker (Ego).[27] If taken as one form – as I do –, the Compound form thus acquires the value of an absolute past tense: Present Perfect "he has heard" or Simple Past "he heard" (the latter not yet in Earlier Old Egyptian).

To explain this phenomenon in Earlier Old Egyptian of the mutually exclusive occurrences of the Independent (/Indicative) variety in the Ideal Autobiography and the Compound variety in administrative documents such as letters, I suggest that in letters, in which, of course, the Here and Now of the speaker/writer (Ego) is most overtly present, the Compound variety as an **explicit** Present Perfect of Result in which Ego's Here and Now is represented by the particle *jw* is preferred to the Independent (/Indicative) *sḏm.n=f*. In the latter form the Present Perfect of Result is only **implicitly** contained, since the form also allows interpretation as the Experiential (/Existential) Present Perfect of " a situation valid at least once in a lifetime and felt by the user of the verb form to be of some relevance up to the present".

It seems to me that the administrative-juridical aspect of pointing out the continuous validity of a decree, royal edict or even the contents of a royal letter, thus continuing present relevance as expressed in the Present Perfect of Result, requires the use of the in this respect most overt verb form, the Compound verb form with its explicit expression of the Present through *jw*.

The Development of the Compound Form *jw sḏm.n=f*

In Later Old Egyptian, the Compound verb form *jw sḏm.n=j/=f* replaces, where possible (thus not with the verbs of motion), the single Simple Past forms with rhematic force of Earlier Old Egyptian. It may retain its Present Perfect value in typically Present Perfect contexts such as the Ideal Autobiography where it replaces the rhematic Independent (/Indicative) *sḏm.n=f* used in Earlier Old Egyptian, but it is now also used in Simple Past narrative, where it has 'degraded' into a Narrative Perfect, used as a Simple Past tense without Present Perfect value.

In Later Old Egyptian it is only compounding with *jw* that we meet, but in Middle Egyptian the compound with *ꜥḥꜥ.n* has become the regular Simple Past narrative tense, while then the compound form with *jw* is primarily found in the context of speech situations and with the 1st ps., which context indeed evokes in translation use of the Present Perfect rather than the Simple Past. Thus, generally speaking, the Present Perfect *jw sḏm.n=j* stands in clear contrast to the Simple Past narrative *ꜥḥꜥ.n sḏm.n=f*. Clearly, Middle Egyptian felt the need to distinguish by this means between a Present Perfect form and a Simple Past form.

The Development of the Substantival *sḏm.n=f*

Finally, we are left with the Substantival *sḏm.n=f*. We have seen it functioning in the Present Perfect context of the Ideal Autobiography in the passing from Life to Death-formula opening with *pr.n=j / hꜣ.n=j / jj.n=j*, which continues to function in Later Old Egyptian and Middle Egyptian. We have further seen it functioning in Simple Past narrative of both Earlier and Later Old Egyptian, as the thematic equivalent to the rhematic Simple Past tenses, in which context the verb form has lost its genuine Present Perfect value and functions as the Narrative Perfect with Simple Past value.

Conclusion

Concerning the four forms seen as varieties in the *sḏm.n=f*-complex it can be concluded that in Middle Egyptian none of them still exclusively grammaticises the original Present Perfect value, which, however, may surface, dependent on context. This loss of genuine Perfect value and shift towards functioning as a simple narrative tense is in accordance with a trend seen in other languages too with respect to the Perfect.[28]

[27] Compare POLOTSKY's "nynégocentrisme" (using the term coined by DAMOURETTE & PICHON) in *IOS* 6 (1976), p. 36 (3.8.4).

[28] For this development in some Indoeuropean languages see the remarks in COMRIE, *Aspect*, p. 53.

PLATES

PLATE 1

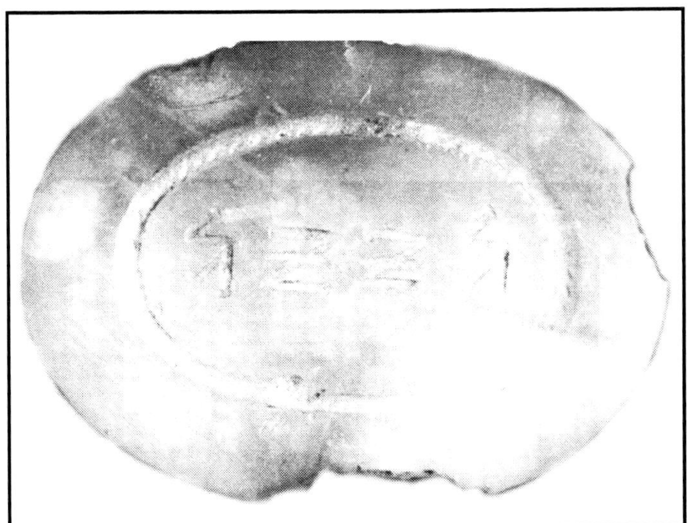

Magical gem. National Museum in Poznań, Inv. No V 188 (photo by B. DRZEWIECKA)

PLATE 6

Fig. 1.

Fig. 2.

Tell el-Farkha. **Fig. 1.** Bottom layer of the structure (presumably a place for brewing beer) with visible supports for vats and brick sticking out an angle; **Fig. 2.** Older phase of great Naqadian building (photo by R. SŁABOŃSKI)

PLATE 7

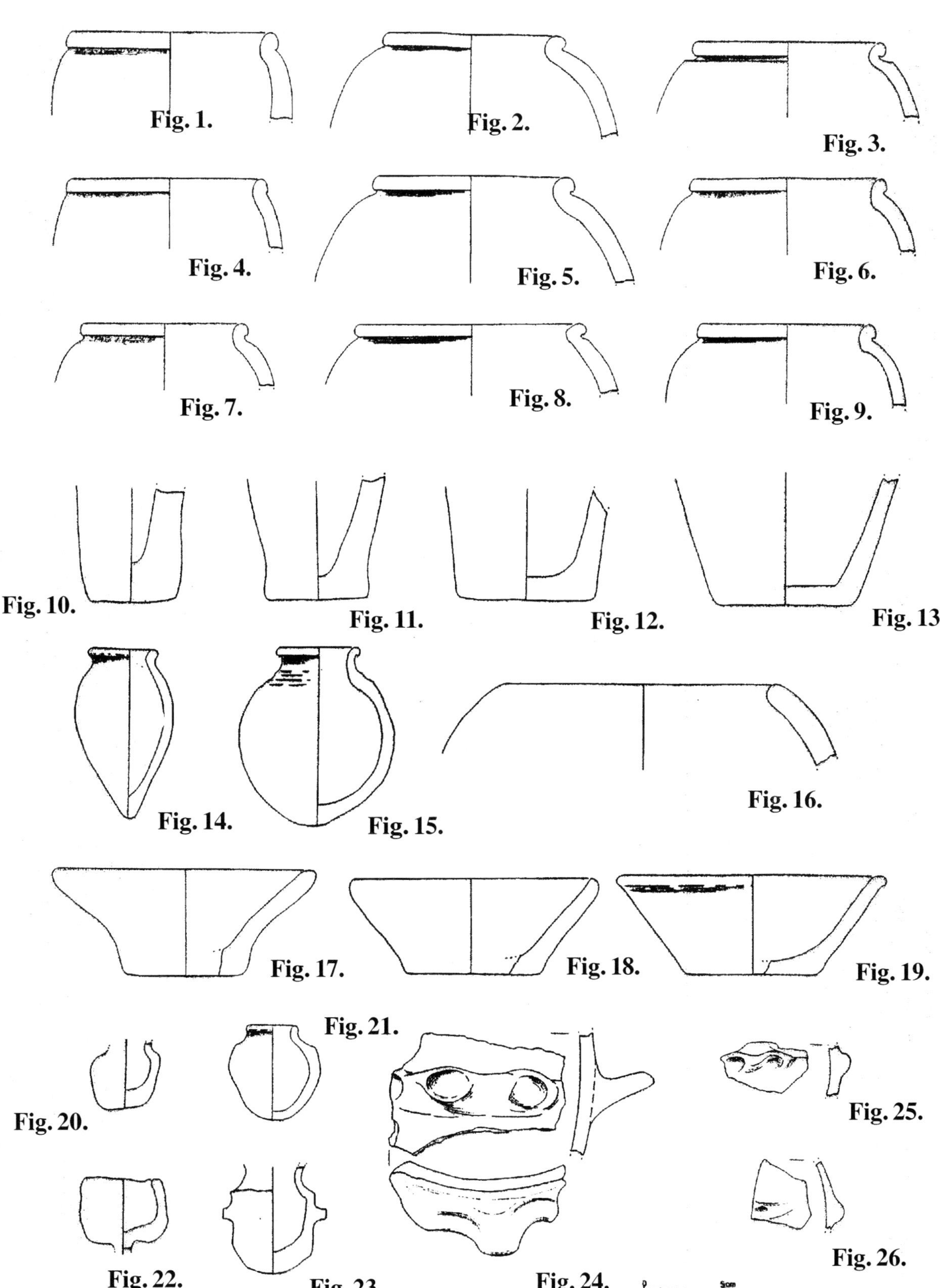

Tell el-Farkha. Pottery of phase 3

PLATE 8

Fig. 1. Younger phase of great Naqadian building (photo by R. SŁABOŃSKI)

Fig. 2. Room with vessels uncovered in 2000 north-east of the great Naqadian building (photo by R. SŁABOŃSKI)

PLATE 9

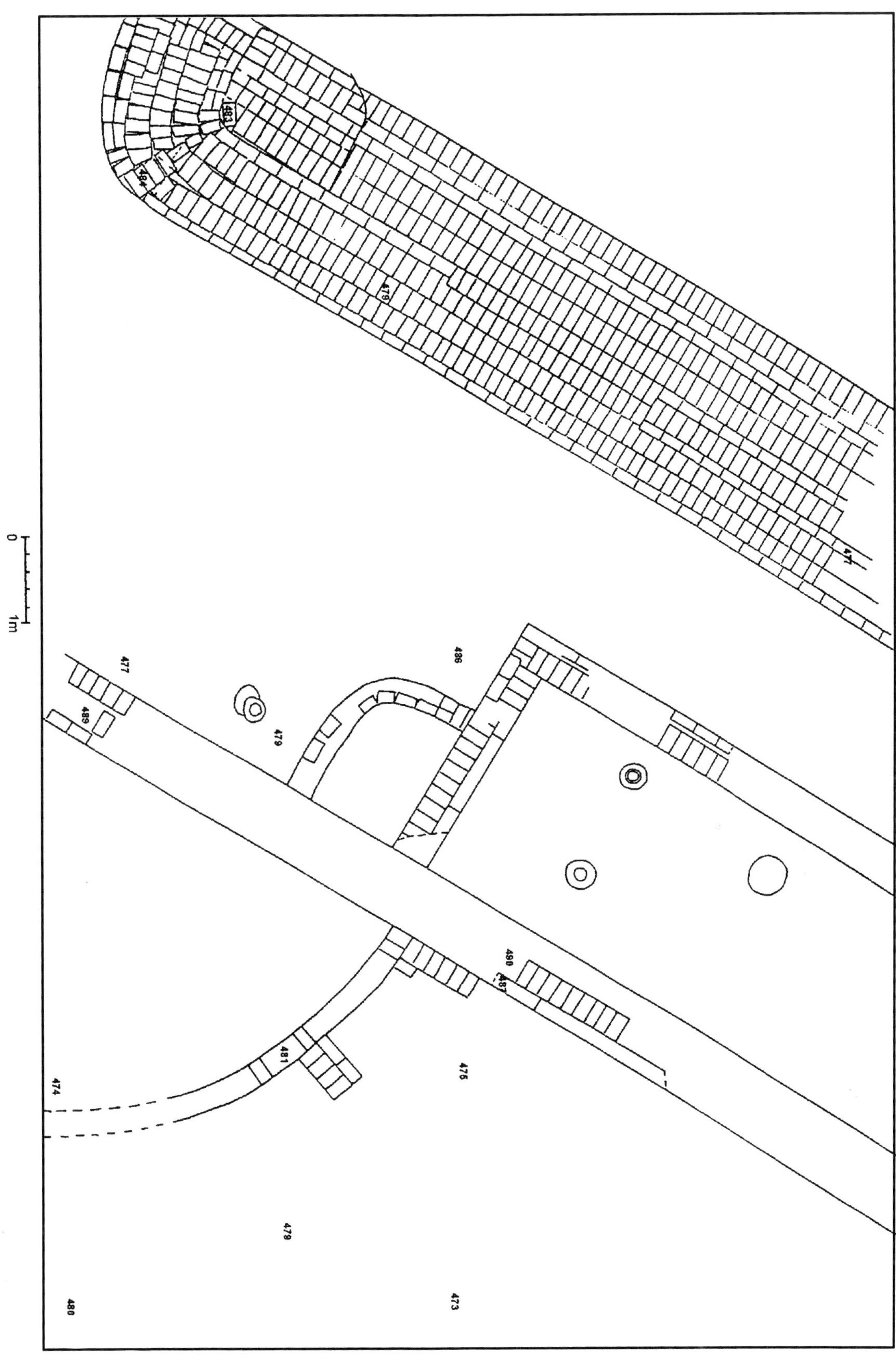

Tell el-Farkha. Younger phase of great Naqadian building discovered in 2000 and storage rooms discovered in 1999

PLATE 10

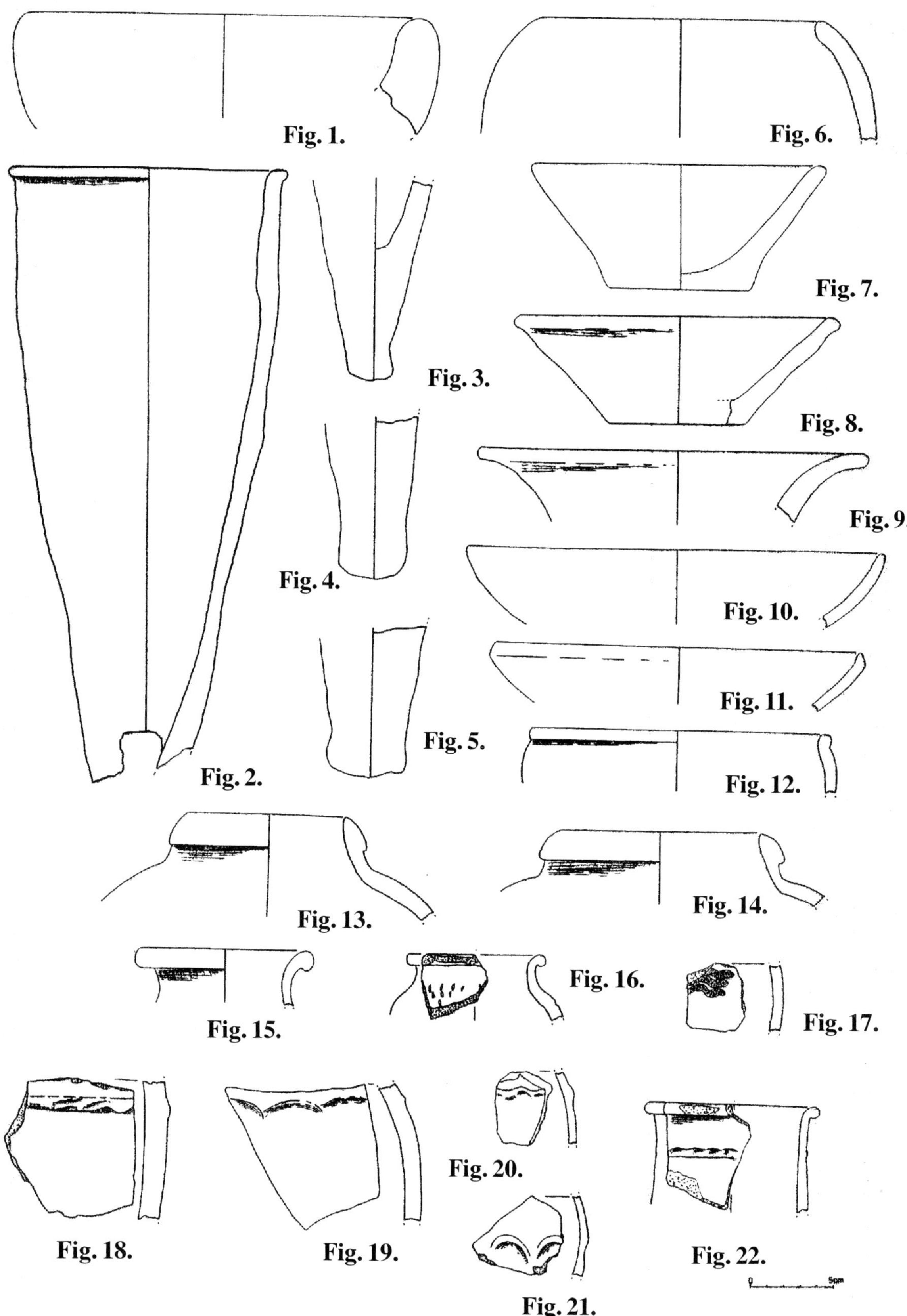

Tell el-Farkha. Pottery of phase 4

PLATE 11

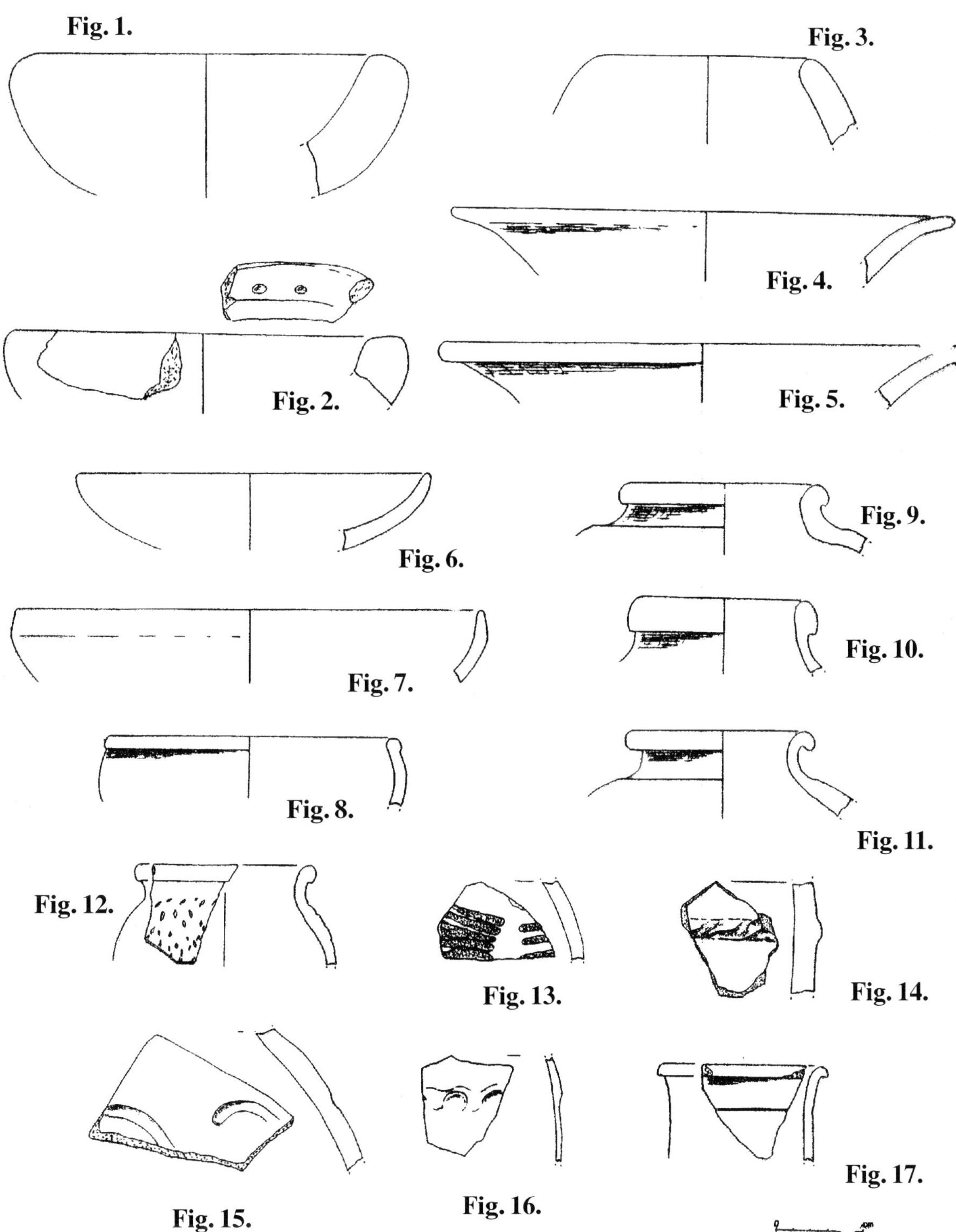

Tell el-Farkha. Pottery of phase 5

PLATE 16

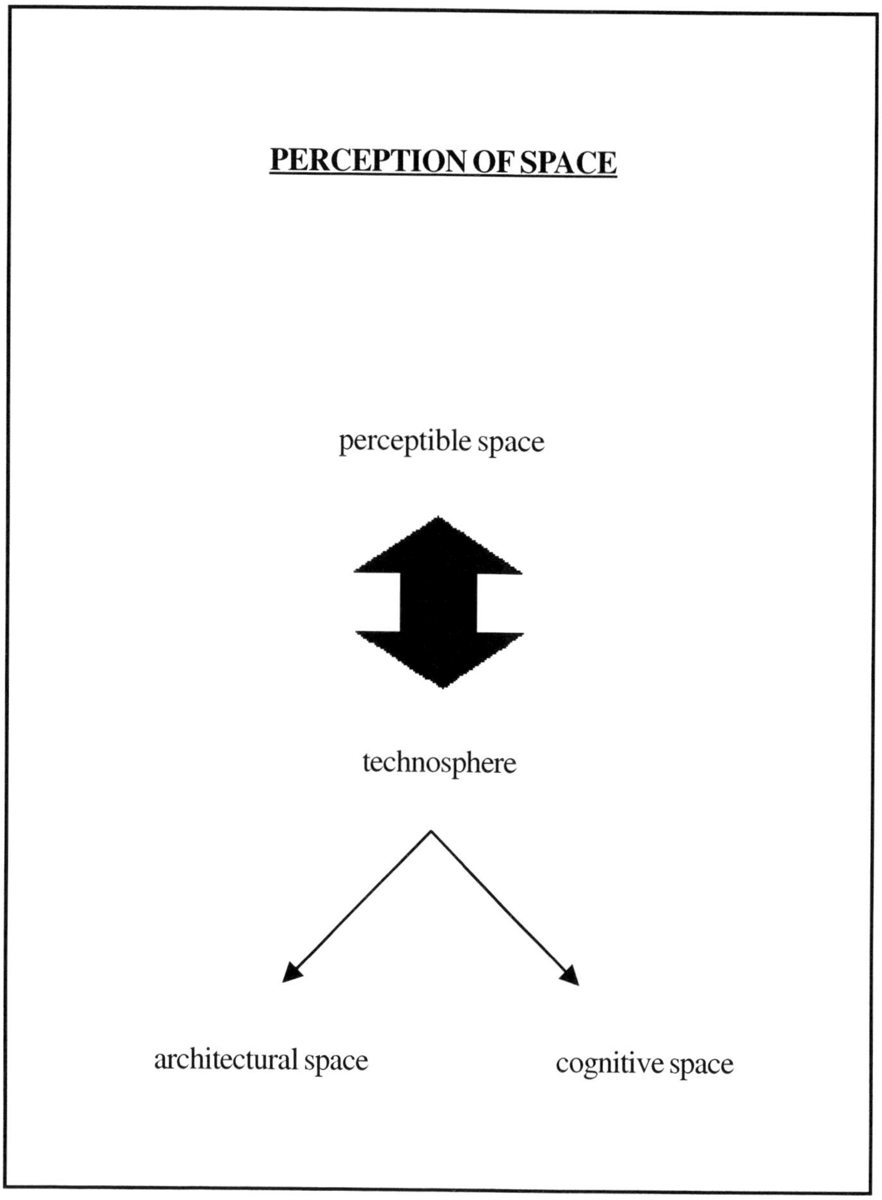

PERCEPTION OF SPACE

perceptible space

technosphere

architectural space

cognitive space

PLATE 17

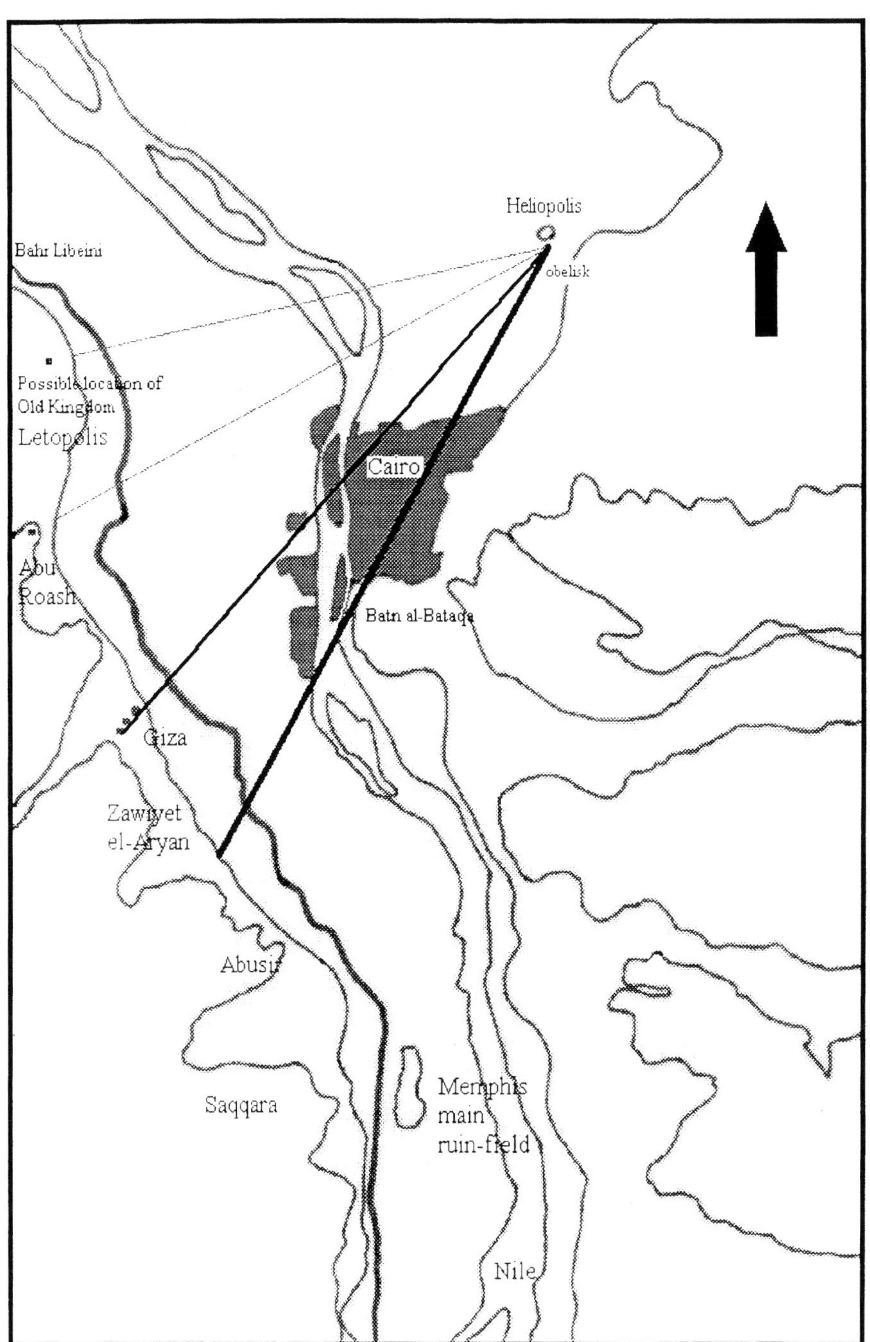

Diagonals in the Memphite Cemeteries

(drawn by Z. HORVÁTH based on A.el-SANUSSI, M. JONES, A Site of the Maadi Culture near the Giza Pyramids, *MDAIK* 53 (1997), pp. 241-253)

PLATE 18

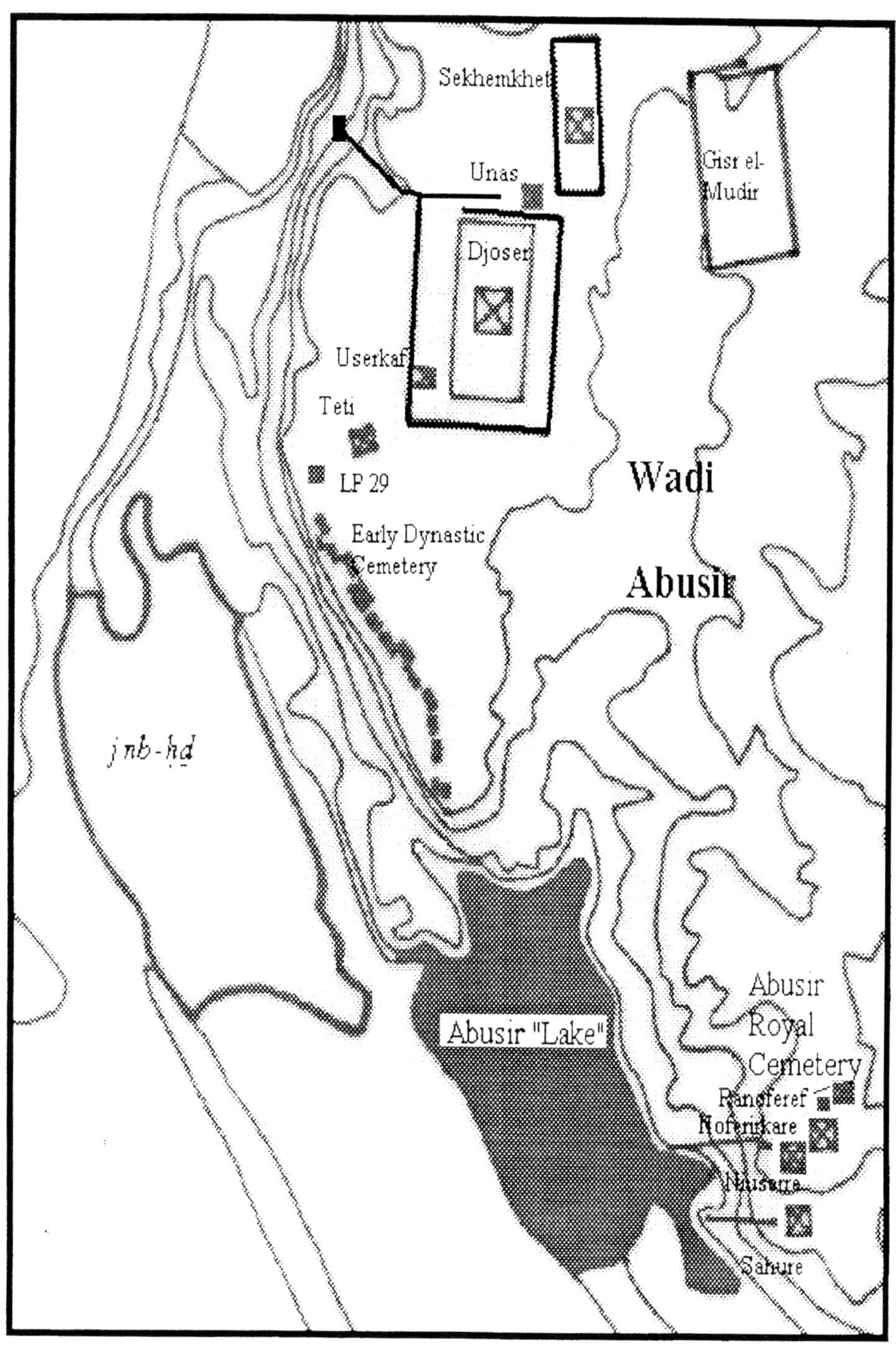

Abusir and Saqqara-North

(drawn by Z. HORVÁTH based on M. LEHNER, *The Complete Pyramids*, London 1997, p. 83)

PLATE 19

AP 13 393

AP 13 411

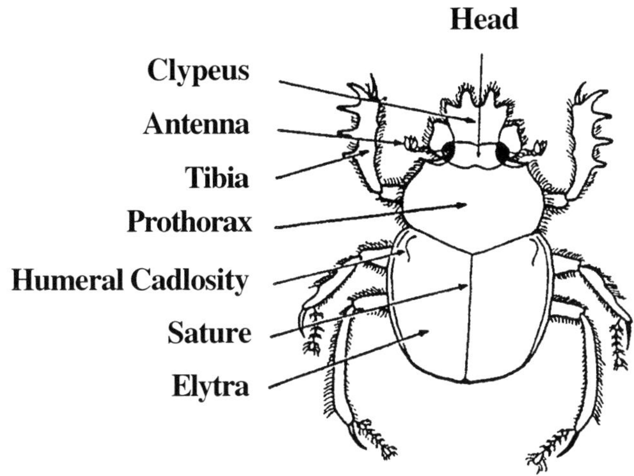

SCARABEUS SACER L.

AP 13 412

AP 13 413

PLATE 24

Fig. 1. Northern face of the southern obelisk of Thutmose III in the court in front of the IVth pylon at Karnak – an upper part of the shaft with an inscription of Thutmose III to the right and an additional inscription of Merenptah in the left column of the text (photo by J. LIPIŃSKA)

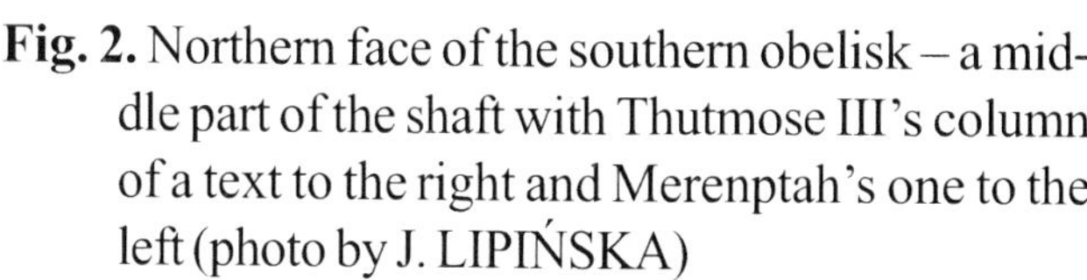

Fig. 2. Northern face of the southern obelisk – a middle part of the shaft with Thutmose III's column of a text to the right and Merenptah's one to the left (photo by J. LIPIŃSKA)

PLATE 25

Fig. 1. Southern face of the southern obelisk – the uppermost part of the shaft with the pyramidion (photo by J. LIPIŃSKA)

Fig. 2. Southern face of the southern obelisk – a middle part of the shaft with Thutmose III's inscription (photo by J. LIPIŃSKA)

PLATE 26

Fig. 1. Southern face of the southern obelisk – a middle part of the shaft with Thutmose III's inscription (photo by D. NIEDZIÓŁKA)

Fig. 2. Eastern face of the southern obelisk – a middle part of the shaft with Thutmose III's inscription (photo by D. NIEDZIÓŁKA)

Fig. 3. Northern face of the southern obelisk – a middle part of the shaft with Thutmose III's column of a text to the right and Merenptah's one to the left (photo by D. NIEDZIÓŁKA)

PLATE 27

Fig. 1. Northern face of the northern obelisk of Thutmose III in the court in front of the IVth pylon at Karnak – the uppermost part of the shaft (photo by J. LIPIŃSKA)

Fig. 2. Eastern face of the northern obelisk – an upper part of the shaft with Thutmose III's column of a text in the middle, Merenptah's one to the right and the rest of another column of the text of the latter king to the left (photo by D. NIEDZIÓŁKA)

PLATE 36

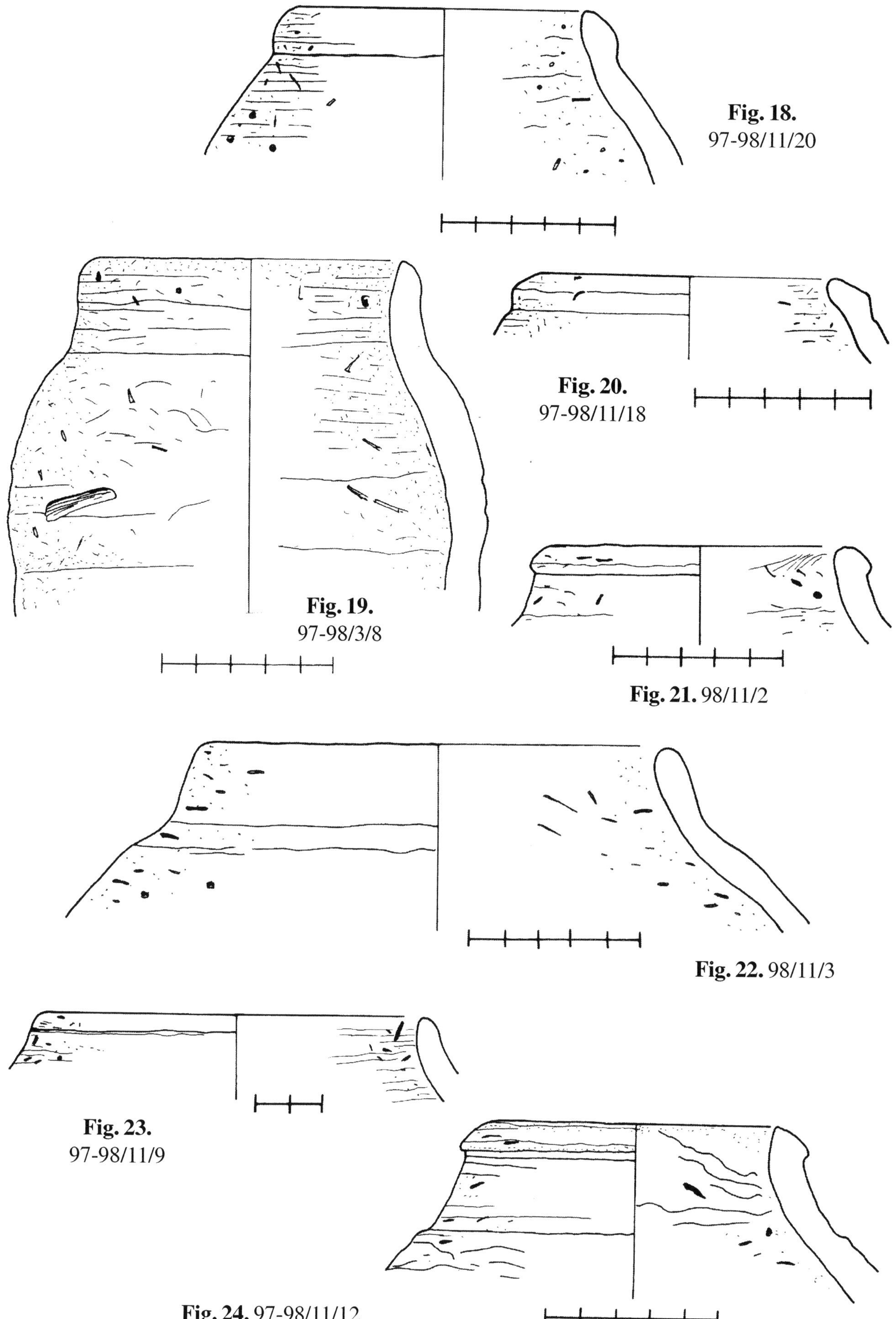

Fig. 18. 97-98/11/20

Fig. 19. 97-98/3/8

Fig. 20. 97-98/11/18

Fig. 21. 98/11/2

Fig. 22. 98/11/3

Fig. 23. 97-98/11/9

Fig. 24. 97-98/11/12

PLATE 37

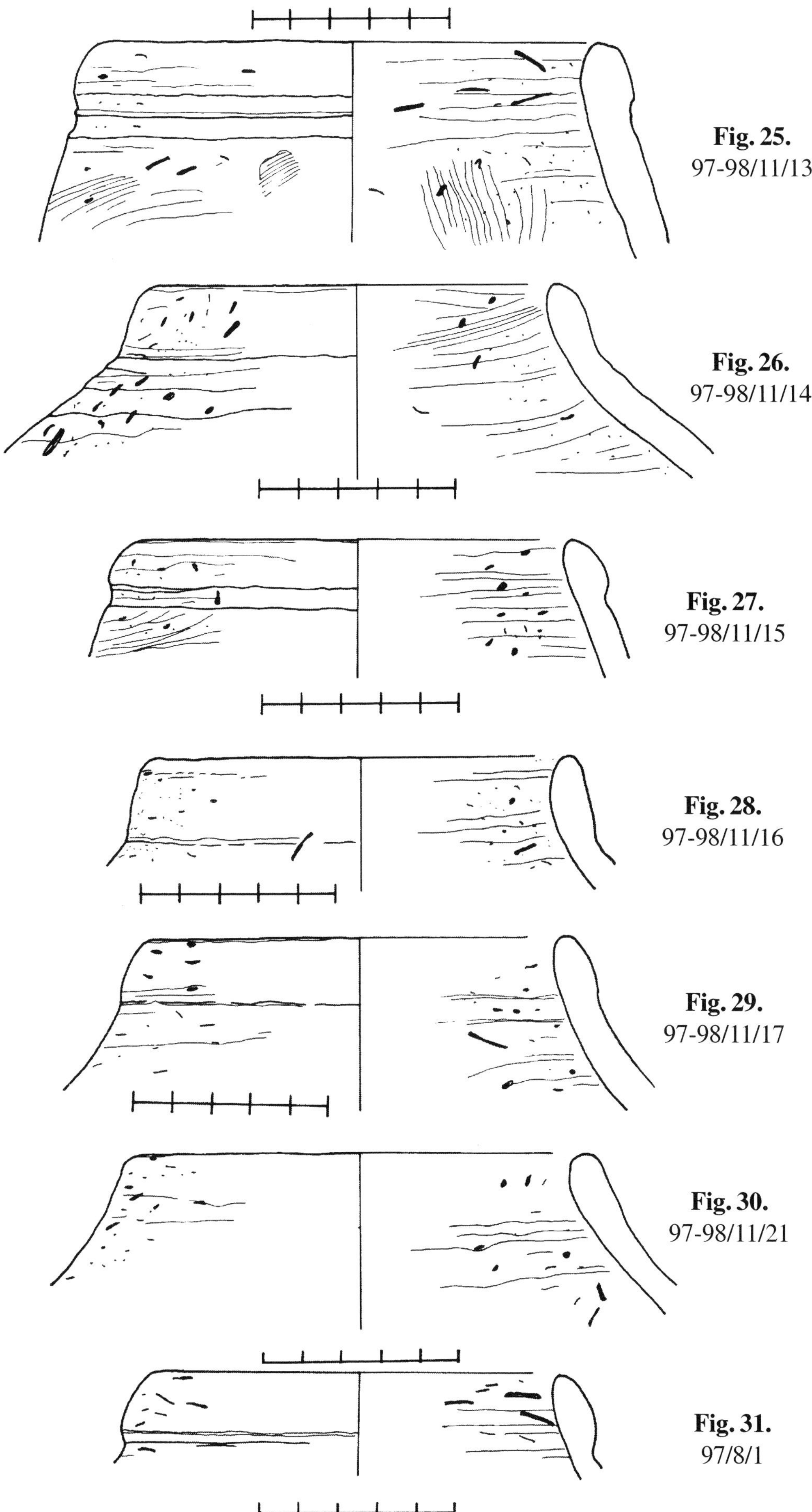

Fig. 25.
97-98/11/13

Fig. 26.
97-98/11/14

Fig. 27.
97-98/11/15

Fig. 28.
97-98/11/16

Fig. 29.
97-98/11/17

Fig. 30.
97-98/11/21

Fig. 31.
97/8/1

PLATE 38

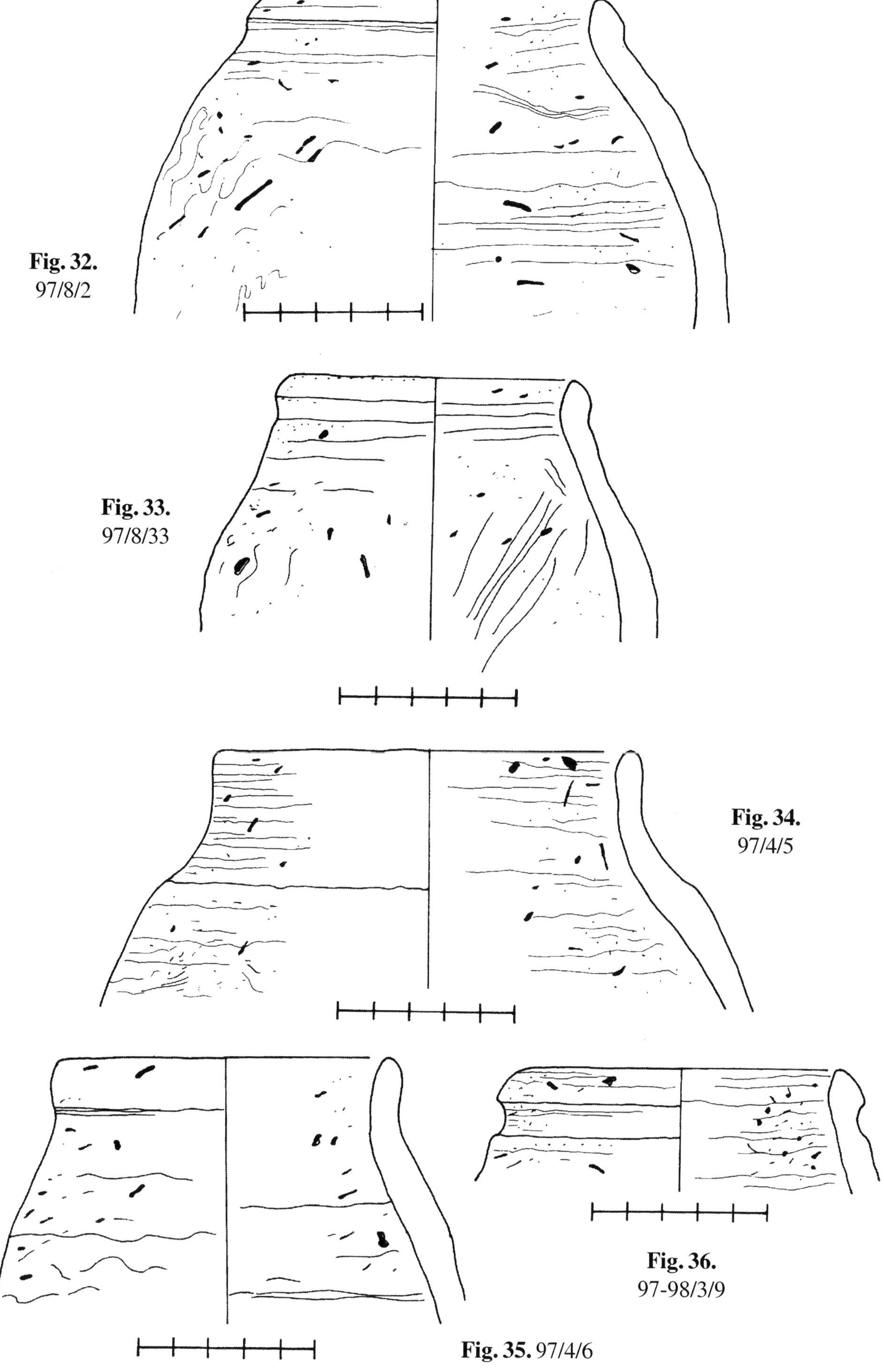

Fig. 32. 97/8/2

Fig. 33. 97/8/33

Fig. 34. 97/4/5

Fig. 36. 97-98/3/9

Fig. 35. 97/4/6

PLATE 39

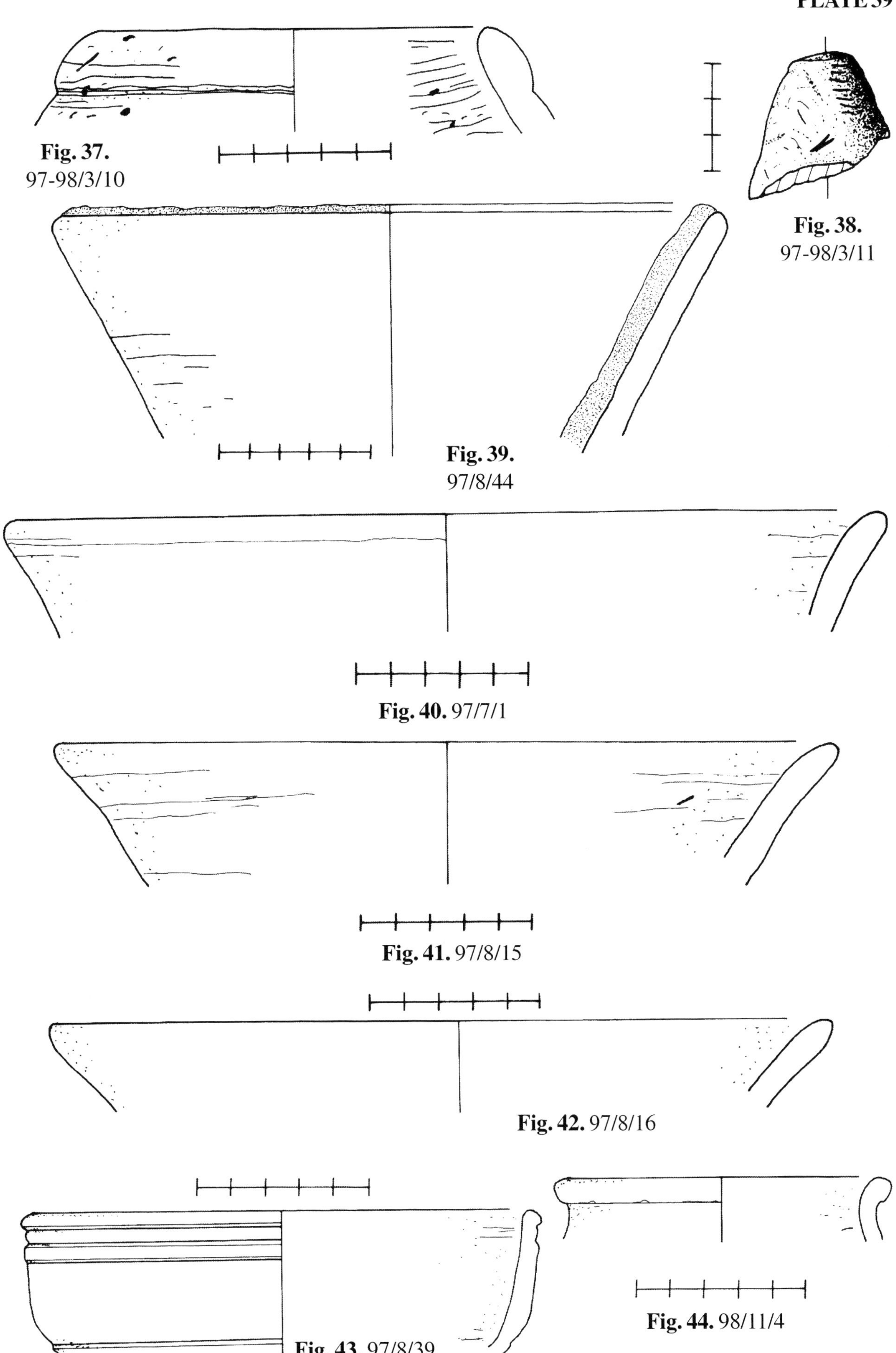

Fig. 37. 97-98/3/10

Fig. 38. 97-98/3/11

Fig. 39. 97/8/44

Fig. 40. 97/7/1

Fig. 41. 97/8/15

Fig. 42. 97/8/16

Fig. 43. 97/8/39

Fig. 44. 98/11/4

PLATE 40

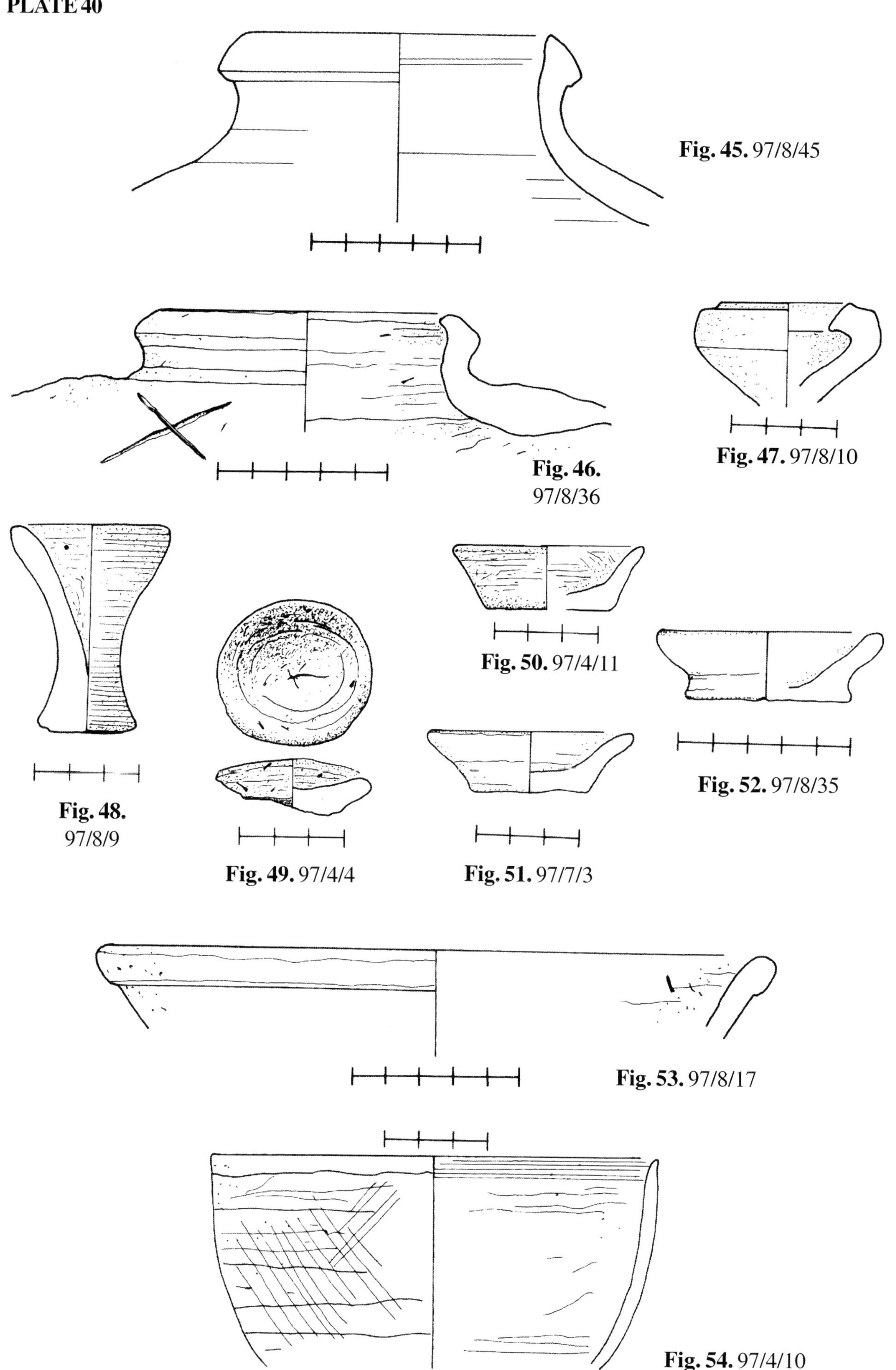

Fig. 45. 97/8/45

Fig. 46. 97/8/36

Fig. 47. 97/8/10

Fig. 48. 97/8/9

Fig. 49. 97/4/4

Fig. 50. 97/4/11

Fig. 51. 97/7/3

Fig. 52. 97/8/35

Fig. 53. 97/8/17

Fig. 54. 97/4/10

PLATE 41

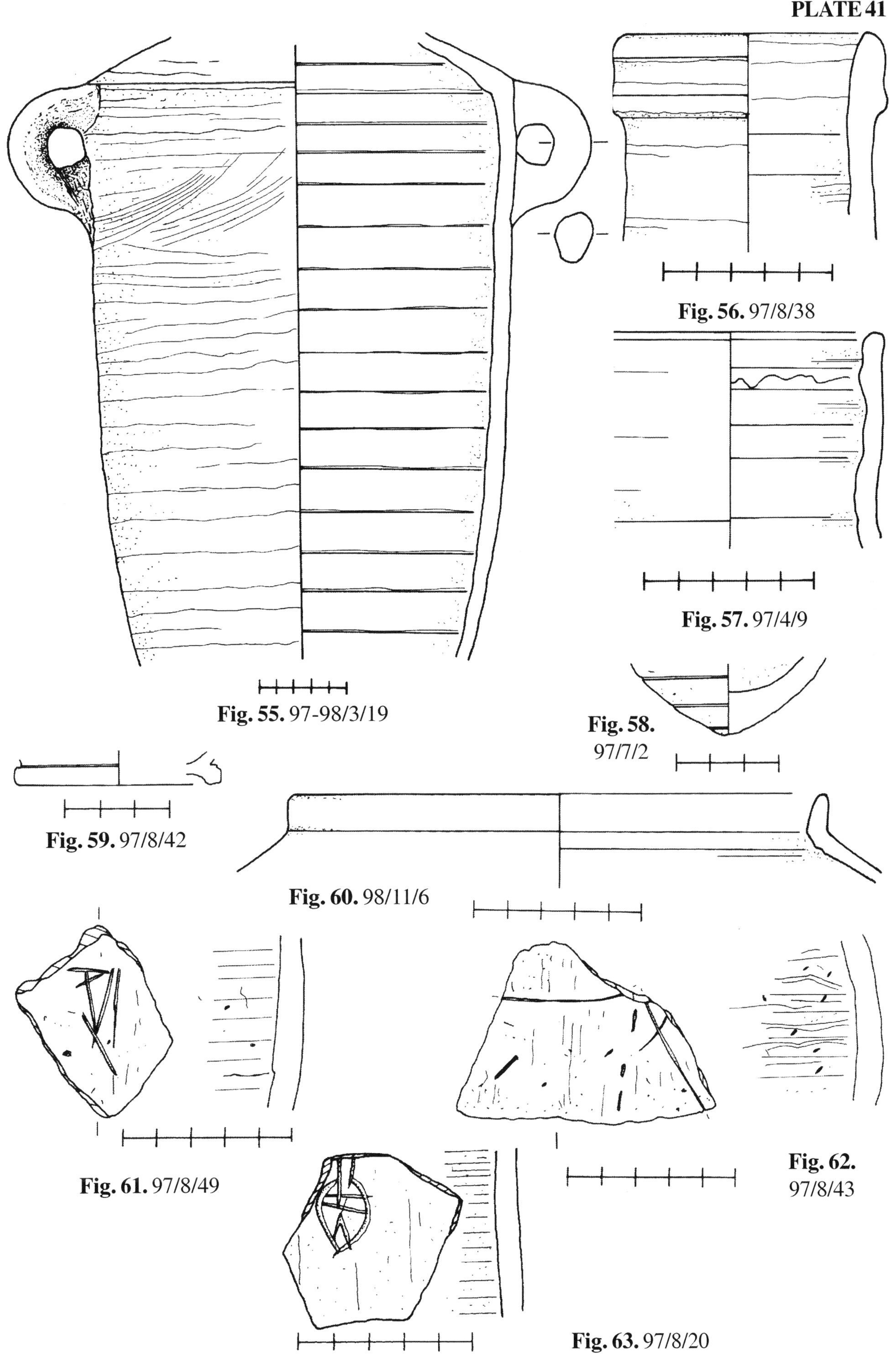

Fig. 55. 97-98/3/19

Fig. 56. 97/8/38

Fig. 57. 97/4/9

Fig. 58. 97/7/2

Fig. 59. 97/8/42

Fig. 60. 98/11/6

Fig. 61. 97/8/49

Fig. 62. 97/8/43

Fig. 63. 97/8/20